ORIENTALISM: EARLY SOURCES

ORIENTALISM: EARLY SOURCES
Edited by Bryan S. Turner

VOLUME I: READINGS IN ORIENTALISM
Edited by Bryan S. Turner

VOLUME II: THE MOHAMMADAN DYNASTIES
Stanley Lane-Poole

VOLUME III: THE CALIPHATE
Sir William Muir

VOLUME IV: THE RELIGIOUS ORDERS OF ISLAM
Edward Sell

VOLUME V: MODERN EGYPT – PART 1
Evelyn Baring (Earl of Cromer)

VOLUME VI: MODERN EGYPT – PART 2
Evelyn Baring (Earl of Cromer)

VOLUME VII: THE ARAB KINGDOM AND ITS FALL
J. Wellhausen

VOLUME VIII: THE MYSTICS OF ISLAM
Reynold A. Nicholson

VOLUME IX: WHITHER ISLAM?
H.A.R. Gibb

VOLUME X: ISLAM AND MODERNISM IN EGYPT
Charles C. Adams

VOLUME XI: HISTORY OF THE ISLAMIC PEOPLES
Carl Brockelmann

VOLUME XII: THE SOCIAL STRUCTURE OF ISLAM
Reuben Levy

ORIENTALISM: EARLY SOURCES

Volume VI

Modern Egypt
Part 2

Evelyn Baring
(Earl of Cromer)

London and New York

First published 1908
by Macmillan and Co.

Reprinted 2000 by Routledge
2 Park Square, Milton Park, Abingdon, Oxfordshire OX14 4RN

Reprinted 2002

Simultaneously published in the USA and Canada
by Routledge
711 Third Avenue, New York, NY 10017

First issued in paperback 2014

Routledge is an imprint of the Taylor and Francis Group, an informa business

Transferred to Digital Printing 2007

All rights reserved. No part of this book may be reprinted or reproduced or utilised in any form or by any electronic, mechanical, or other means, now known or hereafter invented, including photocopying and recording, or in any information storage or retrieval system, without permission in writing from the publishers.

British Library Cataloguing in Publication Data
A catalogue record for this book is available from the British Library

Library of Congress Cataloguing in Publication Data
A catalogue record for this book has been requested

ISBN 978-0-415-20898-7 (set)
ISBN 978-0-415-20906-9 (hbk)
ISBN 978-1-138-00736-9 (pbk)

Publisher's note

The publisher has gone to great lengths to ensure the quality of this reprint but points out that some imperfections in the original book may be apparent.

MODERN EGYPT

BY

THE EARL OF CROMER

In his first interview with the Governor of St. Helena, Napoleon said emphatically: "Egypt is the most important country in the world."

ROSE, *Life of Napoleon*, vol. i. p. 356.

Earum proprie rerum sit historia, quibus rebus gerendis interfuerit is qui narret.

GELLIUS, *Noctes Atticae*, v. 18.

τὰ δ' ἔργα τῶν πραχθέντων ἐν τῷ πολέμῳ οὐκ ἐκ τοῦ παρατυχόντος πυνθανόμενος ἠξίωσα γράφειν, οὐδ' ὡς ἐμοὶ ἐδόκει, ἀλλ' οἷς τε αὐτὸς παρῆν, καὶ παρὰ τῶν ἄλλων ὅσον δυνατὸν ἀκριβείᾳ περὶ ἑκάστου ἐπεξελθών.

THUCYDIDES, i. 22.

IN TWO VOLUMES

VOL. II

MACMILLAN AND CO., LIMITED
ST. MARTIN'S STREET, LONDON
1908

First Edition March 1908. *Reprinted March* 1908

CONTENTS

PART III (*Continued*)

THE SOUDAN

1882–1907

CHAPTER XXVIII

THE FALL OF KHARTOUM

OCTOBER 5, 1884–JANUARY 26, 1885

CHAPTER XXIX

THE EVACUATION OF THE SOUDAN

JANUARY 26, 1885–DECEMBER 30, 1886

CHAPTER XXX

The Débris of the Soudan

CHAPTER XXXI

The Defence of Egypt

1886-1892

CHAPTER XXXII

The Reconquest of Khartoum

October 1895-September 1898

CHAPTER XXXIII

The New Soudan

PART IV

THE EGYPTIAN PUZZLE

CHAPTER XXXIV

The Dwellers in Egypt

CHAPTER XXXV

The Moslems

CHAPTER XXXVI

The Christians

CHAPTER XXXVII

The Europeanised Egyptians

CHAPTER XXXVIII

The Europeans

CHAPTER XXXIX

The Machinery of Government

CHAPTER XL

The British Officials

CHAPTER XLI

The International Administrations

CHAPTER XLII

The Judicial System

CHAPTER XLIII

The Workers of the Machine

PART V

BRITISH POLICY IN EGYPT

CHAPTER XLIV

THE STRUGGLE FOR A POLICY

1882–1883

CHAPTER XLV

THE NORTHBROOK MISSION

SEPTEMBER–NOVEMBER 1884

CHAPTER XLVI

THE WOLFF CONVENTION

AUGUST 1885–OCTOBER 1887

CHAPTER XLVII

THE NEUTRALISATION OF THE SUEZ CANAL

CHAPTER XLVIII

The Anglo-French Agreement of 1904

PART VI

THE REFORMS

CHAPTER XLIX

The Courbash

CHAPTER L

The Corvée

CHAPTER LI

Corruption

CHAPTER LII

European Privilege

CHAPTER LIII

Finance

CHAPTER LIV

Irrigation

CHAPTER LV

The Army

CHAPTER LVI

The Interior

CHAPTER LVII

Sub-Departments of the Interior

CHAPTER LVIII

Justice

CHAPTER LIX

Education

CHAPTER LX

The Soudan

CHAPTER LXI

Conclusion

PART VII

THE FUTURE OF EGYPT

CHAPTER LXII

The Future of Egypt

APPENDIX

PART III (*Continued*)

THE SOUDAN

1882–1907

CHAPTER XXVIII

THE FALL OF KHARTOUM

OCTOBER 5, 1884–JANUARY 26, 1885

Murder of Colonel Stewart—Difficulties of the Expedition—News from General Gordon—Occupation of Jakdul—The battle of Abu Klea—Death of Sir Herbert Stewart—The column reaches the Nile—Two steamers leave for Khartoum—They arrive too late—Events at Khartoum—General Gordon's character—Capitulation of Omdurman—General Gordon's death—Effect on public opinion.

IT is not within the scope of this work to write a detailed history of the military operations which took place in the Soudan. Those operations have been recorded by others who are more competent than myself to deal with military matters. I propose, therefore, as in the case of the Egyptian campaign of 1882, merely to give a brief summary of the chief events connected with the Nile Campaign of 1884-85.

Scarcely had the campaign commenced, when news arrived that Colonel Stewart had been killed. On September 10, he left Khartoum in a steamer accompanied by Mr. Power, M. Herbin, the French Consul, and about forty others. Colonel Stewart had been instructed by General Gordon to inform the various authorities concerned of the true nature of the situation at Khartoum. Berber and Abu Hamed were passed in safety, and it was thought that the main difficulties of the voyage had been overcome, when, on the 18th, the steamer struck on a rock near the village of Hebbah, some sixty miles below Abu Hamed. The boat was hopelessly disabled. Colonel Stewart and his companions landed, and were subsequently induced to lay aside their arms and enter a house in the village, where they were treacherously murdered by Suleiman Wad Gamr, the Sheikh of the Monasir tribe. It is singular that Colonel Stewart, who must have known the treacherous character of the Bedouins, should have fallen into the trap which was laid for him. The explanation has probably been afforded by General Gordon, who said that Colonel Stewart "was not a bit suspicious."[1]

I have frequently in the course of this narrative alluded to Colonel Stewart's high character, judgment, and ability. I can only repeat that by his premature death the Queen and the British nation lost a most capable public servant. A more gallant fellow never lived.

The Nile expedition, Colonel Colville says,[2] "was a campaign less against man than against time. Had British soldiers and Egyptian camels been able to subsist on sand and occasional water, or had the desert produced beef and biscuit, the army might, in spite of its late start, have reached Khartoum in November." The difficulties of supply and transport were, in fact, very great.

[1] *Journal*, p. 281. The whole of this passage is worth quoting, as it shows what a singularly accurate forecast General Gordon made of the manner in which Colonel Stewart had been murdered, before he had learnt any of the details. "I feel somehow," General Gordon wrote on November 5, "convinced they were captured by treachery—the Arabs pretending to be friendly — and surprising them at night. I will own that, without reason (apparently, for the chorus was that the *trip was safe*), I have never been comfortable since they left. Stewart was a man who did not chew the cud, he never thought of danger in perspective; he was not a bit suspicious (while I am made up of it). I can see in imagination the whole scene, the Sheikh inviting them to land, saying, 'Thank God, the Mahdi is a liar,'—bringing in wood —men going on shore and dispersed. The *Abbas* with her steam down, then a rush of wild Arabs, and all is over!"

[2] *History of the Soudan Campaign*, p. 61.

But British energy and perseverance overcame them. By the end of December, Lord Wolseley was ready to move from Korti across the desert to Metemmeh. News had been received that supplies were running short at Khartoum, and it was clear that, if General Gordon was to be saved, not a day would have to be lost in establishing communications with him. It was resolved to divide the British force into two portions. One division, under Sir Herbert Stewart, was to take the desert route. The other, under General Earle, was to follow the course of the Nile with a view ultimately to the capture of Berber, which General Gordon had warned Lord Wolseley "not to leave in his rear."

On December 30, the day on which Sir Herbert Stewart left Korti, a messenger arrived with a piece of paper the size of a postage stamp, on which was written, "Khartoum all right. 14.12.84. C. G. Gordon." This was in General Gordon's handwriting, and his seal was affixed to the back of the document. The letter was, however, accompanied by a verbal message from General Gordon which showed the straits to which he was reduced. "Our troops," he said, "at Khartoum are suffering from lack of provisions. The food we still have is little, some grain and biscuit. We want you to come quickly. . . . In Khartoum there is no butter, no dates, little meat. All food is very dear."

The force which left Korti at 3 P.M. on December 30, under the command of Sir Herbert Stewart, consisted of about 1100 British officers and men, and 2200 camels. It reached the wells of Jakdul, ninety-eight miles distant, early on the morning of January 2. A garrison of 422 men was left there with instructions to rig up pumps and otherwise improve the water-supply. On the evening of the 2nd, Sir Herbert Stewart left with the remainder of the force, and reached Korti at noon on the 5th.

On the 8th, he again started from Korti with the main body of the desert column, consisting of about 1600 effective British troops, some 300 camp-followers, and about 2400 camels and horses. His orders were to advance and occupy Metemmeh, to leave a strong detachment there, and then to return to Jakdul. Sir Charles Wilson accompanied the column, and, after the occupation of Metemmeh, was to proceed to Khartoum at once with a small detachment of infantry on board the steamers which, it was known, were in the neighbourhood. The column reached Jakdul early on the morning of the 12th. After halting for a day, the march was resumed. On the night of the 16th, the force bivouacked about three and a half miles from the wells of Abu Klea, which were occupied in considerable force by the Dervishes.

On the following morning (the 17th), the force advanced in square to attack the enemy. A desperate engagement ensued. The Dervishes charged the square with the utmost gallantry, and succeeded in penetrating a gap which had been temporarily caused in its rear face. The camels, Colonel Colville says, "which up to this time had been a source of weakness to the square, now became a source of strength. The spearmen by weight of numbers forced back the rear face of the square on to the camels; these formed a living traverse that broke the rush, and gave time for the right face and front face to take advantage of finding themselves on higher ground, and to fire over the heads of those engaged in a hand-to-hand struggle on to the mass of the enemy behind. A desperate conflict ensued in the centre of the square, but the slaughter caused by the musketry from the rising ground caused the rearward Arabs to waver and then to fall back. Within the square, the din of battle was such that no words of command could be heard, and each man was obliged to act on the impulse of the moment. Officers and men alike fought well in this short hand-to-hand encounter, and many acts of heroism were performed. . . . Before five minutes had elapsed, the little band of less than 1500 British soldiers had, by sheer pluck and muscle, killed the last of the fanatics who had penetrated into their midst."

The victory was complete, but it had been dearly bought. Eighteen officers and 150 non-commissioned officers and men were killed and wounded. The enemy's loss was heavy; 1100 bodies were counted in the immediate proximity of the square, and the number of wounded is said to have been very great. On the night of the 17th, the troops bivouacked at the Abu Klea wells. The baggage animals did not arrive till early on the morning of the 18th. The result was that the troops passed the night without food, coats, or blankets.

Sir Herbert Stewart then determined to make a night march to Metemmeh, about twenty-three miles distant. At 4 P.M. on the 18th, the column left Abu Klea. The night was dark. Many of the men had been without sleep for two nights. The camels were exhausted. The route lay for a considerable distance through thick bush. Halts were numerous. At last, after a toilsome march of some sixteen hours, the Nile appeared in sight. It was, however, apparent that the river could not be reached without further fighting. Whilst preparations were being made for an advance, the Dervishes kept up a hot fire from the long grass in which they were concealed. It was at this moment that the gallant Stewart received his death-wound. Colonel Burnaby, who it had been intended by Lord Wolseley should succeed Sir Herbert Stewart in the event of the latter's death, had been killed at Abu Klea. The chief command devolved on Sir Charles Wilson.

At 3 P.M. on the 19th, the force advanced in square, and after a sharp engagement, in which an attack of the Dervishes was successfully repulsed, occupied a position on the Nile a short distance north of Metemmeh. The British loss on this day was 9 officers and 102 non-commissioned officers and men killed and wounded.

On the following morning (the 20th), the force moved to Gubat. At 10 A.M. on the 21st, four steamers, which had been sent by General Gordon, arrived from Khartoum. They brought his Journal and several letters, in one of which, dated December 14, he said that he expected a catastrophe in the town after ten days' time. The latest news was written on a small scrap of paper. It was to the following effect: "Khartoum is all right. Could hold out for years. C. G. Gordon. 29.12.84." It was known at the time that General Gordon wrote this so that, in the event of his letter falling into the hands of the Dervishes, they would be deceived. In reality, he was in the greatest straits. Obviously, the next thing to do was to send the steamers back to Khartoum with some soldiers on board of them. It was not, however, until the morning of the 24th that two steamers, the *Bordein* and the *Telahawiyeh*, left. The interval between the 21st and the 24th was occupied in reconnaissances both up and down the river, and in making arrangements for the proper protection of the force at Gubat.[1]

Both the steamers carried small detachments of British soldiers, as well as larger detachments of Soudanese troops. Sir Charles Wilson embarked

[1] The delay at Gubat has formed the subject of much discussion. The conclusion at which I have arrived, after a careful examination of all the facts, is that if the steamers had left Gubat on the afternoon of the 21st, they would probably have arrived at Khartoum in time to save the town.

on board the ***Bordein.*** All went well until, at 6 P.M. on the 25th, the ***Bordein*** struck on a rock in the Sixth Cataract, the navigation of which is intricate. This caused a delay of twenty-four hours. On the night of the 26th, the steamers were only three miles nearer Khartoum than they had been on the previous evening. An early start was made on the 27th. The dangerous gorge of Shabluka was passed without difficulty. The steamers continued their voyage under a musketry fire from the banks, and in the evening stopped near the small village of Tamaniat. During the afternoon, a man on the bank called out that Khartoum had fallen and that General Gordon had been killed, but he was not believed by those on board. The steamers started early on the 28th, hoping to reach Khartoum by the evening. They advanced under a heavy fire of musketry and artillery until they came within sight of the Government House at Khartoum. An eager search was made through glasses to see whether the Egyptian flag was still flying. No sign of it could be discovered. More than this, as the steamers advanced it was seen that Government House and the buildings near it had been wrecked. The Khartoum side of the White Nile was in the possession of the enemy. It was clear that the indomitable defender of Khartoum had at last succumbed. The expedition had arrived too late. Sir Charles Wilson ordered the steamers to be put about and to run down stream. On the return journey, both the steamers were wrecked, but those on board were rescued from the perilous position, in which they were at one time placed, by a party sent out in the steamer *Safieh* under Lord Charles Beresford. On the afternoon of February 4, Sir Charles Wilson and his companions rejoined the main body of the British troops, which were encamped at Gubat.

It is now time to go back to the events which were passing in Khartoum.

In the course of this narrative, I have alluded to General Gordon's numerous inconsistencies. I have pointed out errors of judgment with which he may justly be charged. I have dwelt on defects of character which unsuited him for the conduct of political affairs. But, when all this has been said, how grandly the character of the man comes out in the final scene of the Soudan tragedy. History has recorded few incidents more calculated to strike the imagination than that presented by this brave man, who, strong in the faith which sustained him, stood undismayed amidst dangers which might well have appalled the stoutest heart. Hordes of savage fanatics surged around him. Shot and shell poured into the town which he was defending against fearful odds. Starvation stared him in the face. "The soldiers had to eat dogs, donkeys, skins of animals, gum and palm fibre, and famine prevailed. The soldiers stood on the fortifications like pieces of wood. The civilians were even worse off. Many died of hunger, and corpses filled the streets—no one had even the energy to bury them."[1] Treachery and internal dissension threatened him from within, whilst a waste of burning African desert separated him from the outward help which his countrymen, albeit tardily, were straining every nerve to afford. "All the anxiety he had undergone had gradually turned his hair to silvery white."[2] "Yet," said an eye-witness, "in spite of all this danger by which he was surrounded, Gordon Pasha had no fear." "Go," he said, "tell all the people in Khartoum that Gordon fears nothing, for God has created him without fear."[3] Nor was this an idle boast.

[1] Account given by Bordeini Bey, *Mahdiism, etc.*, p. 166.

[2] *Mahdiism, etc.*, p. 169.

[3] *Ibid.* p. 164.

General Gordon did not know what the word fear meant. Death had no terrors for him. "I would," he wrote to his sister, "that all could look on death as a cheerful friend, who takes us from a world of trial to our true home."[1] Many a man before General Gordon has laid down his life at the call of duty. Many a man too has striven to regard death as a glad relief from pain, sorrow, and suffering. But no soldier about to lead a forlorn hope, no Christian martyr tied to the stake or thrown to the wild beasts of Ancient Rome, ever faced death with more unconcern than General Gordon. His faith was sublime. Strong in that faith, he could meet the savage who plunged a spear into his breast with a "gesture of scorn,"[2] and with the sure and certain hope of immortality which had been promised to him by the Master in whose footsteps he had endeavoured to follow.

From a military point of view, the defence of Khartoum was a splendid feat of arms. When Ismail Pasha tried to use General Gordon as a pawn on his financial and political chessboard, kindly laughter was provoked from all who knew the facts or who knew the man. General Gordon was too rash and impulsive for the conduct of political affairs in this work-a-day world. But as the military defender of a beleaguered city, he was in his element. The fighting instinct, which was strong within him, had full scope for action. His example and precept, his bravery and resource, encouraged the faint-hearted and enabled him, even with the poor material of which he disposed, to keep a formidable enemy at bay for ten long months. His personal influence was felt by all the inhabitants of the town, who regarded him as their sole refuge in distress, their only bulwark against disaster.

[1] *Letters, etc.*, p. xii. [2] *Mahdiism, etc.*, p. 171.

To return to the narrative. After the defeat of El Eilafun on September 1, the position at Khartoum became well-nigh desperate. All the tribes in the neighbourhood submitted to the Mahdi and hurried to Khartoum to take part in the siege. "They fired projectiles from the guns, rockets, and firearms of all descriptions, which fell on the town from all sides. From time to time, the troops made sorties out of the city to drive them off, but almost each time their efforts proved fruitless, and they had to return to the garrison, for the projectiles of the rebels were numerous." On January 5, 1885, Omdurman capitulated. "Khartoum then fell into a dangerous state. The rebels surrounded it from all sides, and cut off all supplies. . . . The soldiers suffered terribly from want of food; some of them deserted and joined the rebels. Gordon Pasha used to say every day, 'They [the English] must come to-morrow,' but they never came, and we began to think that they must have been defeated after all. . . . We all became heart-broken, and concluded that no army was coming to relieve Khartoum." The townspeople began to talk of capitulation. General Gordon appealed to them, on January 25, to make a determined stand for another twenty-four hours, by which time he thought that the English relief would arrive. "What more can I say?" were his words to Bordeini Bey. "The people will no longer believe me. I have told them over and over again that help would be here, but it has never come, and now they must see I tell them lies. If this, my last promise, fails, I can do nothing more. Go and collect all the people you can on the lines and make a good stand. Now leave me to smoke these cigarettes."

The end was very near. Early on the morning of January 26, by which time Sir Charles Wilson's steamers had reached the foot of the

Sixth Cataract, the Dervishes made a general attack on the lines and met with but a feeble resistance from the half-starved and disheartened soldiers. Farag Pasha, the commandant, who was suspected of treachery, escaped to the Mahdist camp, and met his death a short time afterwards at the hands of an Arab with whom he had a blood feud. The Palace was soon reached. General Gordon stood in front of the entrance to his office. He had on a white uniform. His sword was girt around him, but he did not draw it. He carried a revolver in his right hand, but he disdained to use it. The final scene, in which the civilised Christian faced barbarous and triumphant fanaticism, is thus described by Bordeini Bey, and it would be difficult, whether in tales of fact or of fiction, to find a more pathetic, or, it may be added, a more dramatic passage: "Taha Shahin was the first to encounter Gordon beside the door of the Divan, apparently waiting for the Arabs and standing with a calm and dignified manner, his left hand resting on the hilt of his sword. Shahin, dashing forward with the curse, '*Malaoun, el-yom yomak*' (O cursed one, your time is come!), plunged his spear into his body.[1] Gordon, it is said, made a gesture of scorn with his right hand and turned his back, when he received another spear-wound, which caused him to fall forward, and was most likely his mortal wound. The other three men closely following Shahin then rushed in, and cutting at the prostrate body with their swords, must have killed him in a few seconds. His death occurred just before sunrise. He made no resistance, and did not fire a shot from his revolver. From all I know, I am convinced that he never intended

[1] From information subsequently obtained, it would appear that General Gordon received his death-blow, not from Taha Shahin, as stated above, but from Sheikh Mohammed Nebawi, who was eventually killed at the battle of Omdurman.

to surrender. I should say that he must have intended to use his revolver only if he saw it was the intention of the Arabs to take him prisoner alive; but he saw such crowds rushing on him with swords and spears, and there being no important Emirs with them, he must have known that they did not intend to spare him, and that was most likely what he wanted; besides, if he had fired, it could only have delayed his death a few moments, the wild fanatical Arabs would never have been checked by a few shots from a revolver. Gordon Pasha's head was immediately cut off and sent to the Mahdi at Omdurman, while his body was dragged downstairs and left exposed for a time in the garden, where many came to plunge their spears into it."[1]

Foul creatures were not wanting to kick the dead lion. Bordeini Bey goes on to say: "I saw Gordon Pasha's head exposed in Omdurman. It was fixed between the branches of a tree, and all who passed by threw stones at it. The first to throw a stone was Youssuf Mansour, late Mamour of Police at El Obeid, whom Gordon Pasha had dismissed for misconduct, and who afterwards commanded the Mahdi's artillery."

Thus General Gordon died. Well do I remember the blank feeling of grief and disappointment with which I received the news of his death, and even now, at this distance of time, I cannot pen the record of those last sad days at Khartoum without emotion. If any consolation can be offered to those who strove, but strove in vain, to save him, it is to be found in the fact that it may be said of General Gordon, perhaps more than of any man, that he was *felix opportunitate mortis*.

[1] The best evidence obtainable goes to prove that Bordeini Bey's account of General Gordon's death is substantially correct. It differs, however, in many important particulars from the account given by M. Neufeld in chap. xxv. of *A Prisoner of the Khalifa*.

Could we but choose our time and choose aright,
'Tis best to die, our honour at the height,
When we have done our ancestors no shame,
But served our friends, and well secured our fame.
Then should we wish our happy life to close,
And leave no more for fortune to dispose;
So should we make our death a glad relief
From future shame, from sickness, and from grief.

Dryden's lines may well serve as General Gordon's epitaph. He died in the plenitude of his reputation, and left a name which will be revered so long as the qualities of steadfast faith and indomitable courage have any hold on the feelings of mankind.

Rarely has public opinion in England been so deeply moved as when the news arrived of the fall of Khartoum. The daily movements of the relief expedition had been watched by anxious multitudes of General Gordon's countrymen, yearning for news of one who seemed to embody in his own person the peculiar form of heroism which is perhaps most of all calculated to move the Anglo-Saxon race. When General Gordon's fate was known a wail of sorrow and disappointment was heard throughout the land. The Queen's feelings, as a Sovereign and as a woman of lively sympathies, were touched to the quick. Her Majesty wrote a sympathetic letter to Miss Gordon, deeply lamenting her "dear brother's cruel, though heroic fate." On this, as on other occasions, the Queen's language truly represented the feelings of the nation.[1] Yet the

[1] On March 19, 1885, Sir Henry Ponsonby, the Queen's Private Secretary, wrote to me: "I now quite admit that I did not understand Gordon, that I did not see what you did, the force and reality of his position and requirements. The Government were to blame in not understanding this also, but I think we all here—the people, high and low—should share the responsibility, for we did not grasp the situation as we should have done. The Queen was in a terrible state about the fall of Khartoum, and indeed it had a good deal to do with making her ill. She was just going out when she got the telegram, and sent for

British nation had done its duty. Parliament voted supplies in no grudging spirit to enable an expedition to be sent to General Gordon's relief, and public opinion ratified the vote. The British army also sustained its ancient reputation. Mistakes may have been, and, indeed, were made. But whatever judgment may be pronounced by competent critics in connection with some points of detail, the true reasons for the failure must be sought elsewhere. They are thus stated by Sir Reginald Wingate: "To innumerable enemies, flushed with victory and ardent fanaticism, Gordon exposed a skill and experience in savage warfare which few could equal. Ill-provisioned in a place naturally and artificially weak, Gordon for months preserved an undaunted front. Neither treachery in the besieged nor the stratagems of the besiegers caused the fall of Khartoum. The town fell through starvation, and despair at long neglect. There were no elements of chance in the expedition to relieve General Gordon. It was sanctioned too late. As day by day no English came, so day by day the soldiers' hearts sank deeper and deeper into gloom. As day by day their strength wasted, so that finally gum, their only food, was rejected, so day by day the Nile ebbed back from the ditch it had filled with mud, and from the rampart it had crumbled, and left a broad path for who should dare to enter." [1]

me. She then went out to my cottage, a quarter of a mile off, walked into the room, pale and trembling, and said to my wife, who was terrified at her appearance—'Too late!'"

Throughout the whole of this difficult period, I received the utmost support from the Queen. On March 13, 1885, the following note, written by Her Majesty, was communicated to me by my brother (Mr. Edward Baring, subsequently Lord Revelstoke): "The concluding paragraph of Sir E. Baring's telegram" (I am not quite sure to what particular telegram allusion is here made) "is *admirable.* Let the Queen have a copy. She wishes Mary" (Lady Ponsonby, who was Lady Revelstoke's sister) "would tell Mr. Edward Baring that the Queen has endorsed everything his brother has said."

[1] *Mahdiism, etc.*, p. 156.

In a word, the Nile expedition was sanctioned too late, and the reason why it was sanctioned too late was that Mr. Gladstone would not accept simple evidence of a plain fact, which was patent to much less powerful intellects than his own. Posterity has yet to decide on the services which Mr. Gladstone, during his long and brilliant career, rendered in other directions to the British nation, but it is improbable that the verdict of his contemporaries in respect to his conduct of the affairs of the Soudan will ever be reversed. That verdict has been distinctly unfavourable. "Les fautes de l'homme puissant," said an eminent Frenchman,[1] "sont des malheurs publics." Mr. Gladstone's error of judgment in delaying too long the despatch of the Nile expedition left a stain on the reputation of England which it will be beyond the power of either the impartial historian or the partial apologist to efface.

[1] Senancour.

CHAPTER XXIX

THE EVACUATION OF THE SOUDAN

JANUARY 26, 1885–DECEMBER 30, 1886

Lord Wolseley urges the necessity of an autumn campaign—The Government hesitate—And then agree—Sir Redvers Buller retreats to Korti—Battle of Kirbekan—The movement on Berber arrested—Operations at Suakin—Action at Hashin—And at Tofrik—Suspension of the Suakin operations—The autumn campaign abandoned—Question of holding Dongola—Change of Government in England—Evacuation of Dongola—Death of the Mahdi—Battle of Ginniss—Review of British policy.

WHEN Lord Wolseley heard of the battle of Abu Klea and of Sir Herbert Stewart having been wounded, he decided to send Sir Redvers Buller to take command of the desert column, and to reinforce it by two battalions. Shortly afterwards, news arrived of the fall of Khartoum. General Earle was ordered to arrest the forward movement of the river column on Abu Hamed. Pending the receipt of instructions from London as to the policy which was now to be pursued, a discretionary power was left to Sir Redvers Buller to act according to local circumstances. General Earle accordingly halted at Berti, about midway between Korti and Abu Hamed. Sir Redvers Buller arrived at Gubat on February 11. He found that there were only about twelve days' supplies at Gubat, and another twelve days' supplies at Abu Klea, whilst the camels were in a weak and emaciated condition. News had been received that a Dervish force of about 4000 men and six guns was on its way from Khartoum to Gubat. Sir Redvers Buller, therefore, wisely decided to fall back on Jakdul. The retreat began on February 14. Jakdul was reached on the 26th.

In the meanwhile, the British Government were in a position of great difficulty. The sole object of the expedition had been to bring General Gordon and Colonel Stewart away from Khartoum. This object had not been attained. Obviously, unless the policy of the Government was to undergo a complete change, the most logical course to have pursued would have been to desist from any further interference in the Soudan, to withdraw the British troops to some good strategical position in the valley of the Nile, and there to await the attack of the Mahdist forces. This was what was eventually done, and, judged by the light of after events it can scarcely be doubted that it would have been better if the Government had at once decided to take up a defensive attitude. It can, however, be no matter for surprise that, in the first instance, the Government decided otherwise. British public opinion was greatly excited. Both the nation and the army were smarting under a sense of failure. The soldiers were burning to avenge their comrades, and to show the Dervishes that they were no match for British troops. It was certain that the fall of Khartoum would increase the influence and prestige of the Mahdi; neither was it easy to foresee what might be the effect of his success in Egypt,[1] and amongst Mohammedans in other parts of the world.

[1] Directly the news of the fall of Khartoum reached Cairo on February 6, I telegraphed to Lord Granville as follows: "It is too early to express any opinion worth having as to the effect which the fall of Khartoum will produce in Egypt proper. Moreover, much will no doubt depend on the course which Her Majesty's Government now decide to pursue in the Soudan. But I may say that, so far as I can

General Gordon's fame was then at its zenith. His Journal, which had been received, and was immediately published, gave a clear indication of his views. He strongly advocated a policy of "smashing up" the Mahdi. The weight of Lord Wolseley's authority was thrown into the same scale. He deprecated the adoption of a defensive policy. "It must never be forgotten," he said, "that the question of whether this war shall or shall not go on does not rest with us, unless we are prepared to give up Egypt to the False Prophet. We shall not bring about a quiet state of affairs by adopting a defensive policy. The Mahdi has repeatedly declared it to be his full and settled intention to possess himself of Egypt, and his followers look upon themselves as engaged in a war the object of which is not to rest contented with the capture of Berber, but to drive the infidels into the sea." Lord Wolseley thought that the final struggle with Mahdiism might perhaps be staved off for a few years, but these years, he said, "will be years of trouble and disturbance for Egypt, of burdens and strains to our military resources, and the contest that will come in the end will be no less than that which is in front of us now. This is all we shall gain by a defensive policy." There could, he thought, be little difference of opinion as to the line of action which was "most befitting our national dignity and honour." The Mahdi must be crushed. That, Lord Wolseley thought, was the only policy, "worthy of the English nation."

These views were shared by others on the spot. The Government had, therefore, to face a strong

at present judge, I do not anticipate any disturbance so far as the Egyptian population is concerned. The effect produced upon the Bedouins on the frontier is more difficult to forecast, and it would be as well to be prepared to send at short notice another battalion to Assouan, as proposed some little while ago by Lord Wolseley."

body of local opinion favourable to offensive action. At first, the Ministers hesitated, and they might well do so, for they were asked to embark on a crusade against Mohammedan fanaticism, to adopt an adventurous policy of which no one could foresee the end, and to wage a costly war in a remote country under conditions of exceptional difficulty imposed by the climate, by the scantiness of local supplies, and by the absence of facilities for transport and locomotion. Lord Wolseley had warned them that "the strength and composition of his little army was calculated for the relief, not for the siege and capture of Khartoum, the two operations being entirely different in character and magnitude. . . . Khartoum in the hands of the enemy could not be retaken until the force under his command had been largely augmented in numbers and in artillery."

Lord Wolseley's first instructions, which were issued on February 6, were "to check the advance of the Mahdi in districts now undisturbed." "Whether," it was added, "it will be ultimately necessary to advance on Khartoum or not, cannot now be decided." I was at the same time told to give the Khedive general assurances of support, and to inform Lord Wolseley that it was the desire of the Cabinet "that if the Mahdi should make any proposals he should transmit them immediately to Her Majesty's Government for their consideration." The Mahdi never made any proposals, neither was there at this or any other time the smallest likelihood of his doing so. Lord Wolseley replied that Lord Hartington's telegram gave him "no information as to the policy with reference to the Soudan which Her Majesty's Government meant to pursue." Thus pressed, the Government yielded. On February 9, Lord Hartington telegraphed to Lord Wolseley: "Your military policy is to be based on the necessity, which we recognise on the statement of facts now before us, that the power of the Mahdi at Khartoum must be overthrown."

Unquestionably, it was a mistake to issue these orders. It is easy to see now that both General Gordon and Lord Wolseley credited the Mahdi with an amount of strength for offensive purposes which he was far from possessing. But this was not so clear then as it became later. Lord Wolseley, therefore, thanked Lord Hartington for his "explicit statement of policy," and added: "I am sure it is the correct one, as the Mahdi's power is incompatible with good government in Egypt."

The military arrangements necessary for giving effect to the policy of the Government had then to be settled. An immediate advance on Khartoum was out of the question. Time would be required for the necessary reinforcements to come from England. Moreover, the hot season was approaching. Lord Wolseley, therefore, determined to capture Berber and Abu Hamed by a combined movement of the forces under Sir Redvers Buller and General Earle, and to hold those places during the summer, preparatory to an advance on Khartoum during the ensuing cool season. At the same time, a force was to co-operate from Suakin with a view to keeping open the road to Berber. "The sooner," Lord Wolseley telegraphed to Lord Hartington, "you can now deal with Osman Digna the better."

Sir Redvers Buller was ordered, on February 10, to take Metemmeh "as soon as he felt himself strong enough to do so," and then to combine with General Earle in an attack on Berber. He received these instructions late on the night of the 13th, when he had already partly evacuated Gubat, and had made all the arrangements necessary for leaving it entirely at daylight on the following morning. For reasons which have been already given,[1] Sir Redvers Buller decided to continue the retrograde movement on Abu Klea. The course he adopted met subsequently with the approval of Lord Wolseley.

Orders were issued for the desert column to move on Merowi, but in the meanwhile it had become clear that it would be impossible to undertake operations such as those contemplated by Lord Wolseley. Sir Redvers Buller wrote several letters to Lord Wolseley from Jakdul in which "he not only drew attention to the fact that the transport of the desert column was completely exhausted, but further stated that the boots of the men were thoroughly worn out, and that many of them were almost shoeless." Sir Evelyn Wood, who was also at Jakdul, confirmed the views expressed by Sir Redvers Buller. "I do not think," he wrote on February 20, "that the debilitated state of our transport is realised at Korti." Manifestly, a retreat on Korti was imposed by the circumstances of the situation. Lord Wolseley's original plan, under which a combined movement of the river and desert columns was to be made on Berber, was no longer feasible. The last troops of the desert column arrived at Korti on March 16.

I now turn to the movements of the river column. Lord Wolseley's orders to halt reached General Earle on February 5. On the 8th, General Earle received orders to push on to Abu Hamed. These were supplemented later on the same day by orders to advance on Berber, and to co-operate with Sir Redvers Buller in the capture of that place. Shortly after leaving Berti, the enemy were found in force occupying a ridge called Jebel Kirbekan. On the 10th, they were attacked and driven from the position with heavy loss. The British loss was

[1] *Vide ante*, p. 18.

7 officers and 50 men killed and wounded. It was in this action that, to the great sorrow of all who knew him, General Earle lost his life. After his death, General Brackenbury assumed the command of the river column.

Subsequently to the action at Kirbekan, the forward movement was continued. On February 24, when the column was about thirty miles from Abu Hamed, General Brackenbury received a message from Lord Wolseley informing him of the retreat of the desert column. "I have," Lord Wolseley said, "abandoned all hope of going to Berber before the autumn campaign begins." General Brackenbury was, therefore, ordered to withdraw his force to Merowi. He arrived there on March 5.

It is now time to describe the operations in the vicinity of Suakin. Sir Gerald Graham was appointed to the chief command. His instructions were to make the best arrangements he could for "the destruction of the power of Osman Digna." When this had been done, he was to "arrange for the military occupation of the Hadendowa territory, lying near the Suakin-Berber road." He was further directed to do all in his power to facilitate the construction of the Suakin-Berber railway. A force of 13,000 men was placed at his disposal, consisting of British and British-Indian troops, and also of a battalion of infantry and a battery of artillery, which were lent by the Government of New South Wales.

By the middle of March, the force was ready for action, and Sir Gerald Graham proceeded to carry out the first portion of his instructions, namely, to crush Osman Digna. It was reported that the main body of the Dervishes, in number about 7000, occupied Tamai, whilst smaller bodies held Hashin and Handoub, all places lying within a few miles of Suakin. It was decided, in the first instance, to drive the enemy out of Hashin. This object was effected on March 20 and 21, with the loss of 1 officer and 44 non-commissioned officers and men killed and wounded. The force then returned to Suakin.

The next step was to crush the main Dervish force at Tamai. On March 22, a force under Sir John McNeill left Suakin. Sir John McNeill's orders were to establish an intermediate post between Suakin and Tamai. At 10.30 A.M. the troops halted at a spot named Tofrik, a few miles from Suakin, and proceeded to entrench themselves in a stockade. Whilst many of the men were scattered in the act of cutting brushwood, a sudden attack was made by a body of about 5000 Dervishes. A scene of great confusion ensued. Many of the Dervishes penetrated into the half-formed stockade. After twenty minutes of confused fighting, they were driven back with the loss of 1500 in killed besides many wounded, but the British force suffered severely. Fifteen officers and 278 non-commissioned officers and men were killed, wounded, or missing. The camp-followers suffered severely. Five hundred camels were killed or missing. Shortly after this engagement, Osman Digna withdrew his forces from Tamai, which was occupied by Sir Gerald Graham on April 3.

According to the terms of his original instructions, Sir Gerald Graham should now have turned his attention to opening up the route for the railway. On April 15, however, orders were issued from London to suspend the construction of the railway. Suakin was "to be held for the present, as also any position in the neighbourhood necessary for protection from constant attacks as last year."

Whilst the operations described above were going on, the policy of the British Government had undergone a complete change. In the middle of

February, Lord Wolseley wished to issue a Proclamation to the people of the Soudan to the effect that his mission was "to destroy utterly the power of the Mahdi at Khartoum."[1] The Government agreed to the issue of this Proclamation with a characteristic amendment, which was made at the instigation of Mr. Gladstone. It was stipulated that the word "utterly" should be omitted from the Proclamation. Two months later, the Government had decided to go farther than the omission of the word "utterly" from a Proclamation. The Mahdi was neither to be utterly destroyed nor, indeed, destroyed at all, but was to be left alone for the time being to rule undisturbed over the inhospitable deserts of the Soudan.

Many considerations contributed to bring about this change of policy, or perhaps it should rather be said, to bring about a return to the original policy of the Government, which in a moment of excitement had been too hastily abandoned. Public opinion in England, which had been violently excited when the news of the fall of Khartoum arrived, had somewhat calmed down. It had found its natural and constitutional safety-valve in the shape of an acrimonious debate in Parliament, resulting in a division in which the Government narrowly escaped defeat. The military operations subsequent to the fall of Khartoum had shown that any forward movement in the autumn would be a costly and difficult undertaking. The

[1] This Proclamation, as it was originally drafted, consisted of short, crisp sentences, with somewhat of a Napoleonic ring about them, which, it was supposed, would create a deep impression on the people of the Soudan. I gave it to a talented Egyptian friend of mine, after it had been translated into Arabic, and asked him to give me his opinion upon it. He said that he thoroughly understood what was meant, but that to the Soudanese the Proclamation would be quite incomprehensible. At my request, he prepared a counter project conveying the same ideas in different language. It was an extremely eloquent document, and reminded me, more especially in its vituperative passages, of a chapter in Isaiah.

voices of politicians and diplomatists, which had at first been hushed by the clang of arms, began to be heard. The disadvantages of an offensive, and the advantages of a defensive policy became more and more clear as the matter was calmly considered. Further—and this exercised a very material influence on the views of the Government—affairs on the Indian frontier gave cause for anxiety.[1] It was, therefore, undesirable to engage in a campaign in the Soudan, which would in some degree cripple the military strength of the nation in the event of the services of the army being required elsewhere. The sound good sense of the British nation, which was well represented in the Gladstone Cabinet, reasserted itself, and a policy based upon a sober appreciation of national interests was eventually adopted.[2] On April 21, it was announced in both Houses of Parliament that it was not intended to advance on Khartoum or to undertake any further offensive operations in the Soudan. Lord Wolseley was instructed accordingly.

The question then arose whether the British and Egyptian troops should continue to hold Dongola, or whether they should fall back to some more northerly point along the valley of the Nile.

Lord Wolseley's opinions were expressed immediately after the Government had decided to

[1] The news that General Komaroff had attacked and defeated the Afghans at Penjdeh reached London on April 10.

[2] On April 3, I wrote a private letter to Lord Granville in which, after dwelling on the ambiguity of Mr. Gladstone's statements in the House of Commons, I urged the necessity of facing the facts and of laying down some definite Soudan policy for the future. I concluded in the following words: "The main question which I have propounded in this letter is as follows:—Do the English Government intend to establish a settled form of government at Khartoum or not? My own opinion is that this question should be answered in the negative. Hence, I am of opinion that the military decision to advance to Khartoum should be reversed and that no such advance should take place."

abandon the idea of an autumn campaign against the Mahdi. "If," he telegraphed to Lord Hartington on April 14, "our position is to be exclusively one of defence, I would hold Wadi Halfa and Korosko as outposts, with a strong brigade at Assouan." The next day he added: "Hold on to Dongola province. As long as you do this, you prevent Mahdiism spreading in Egypt, secure allegiance of frontier tribes, and save henceforth trouble, disturbances, and possibly local risings, which a policy of retreat will probably entail, and which will necessitate increased garrisons in Egypt and military occupation of the larger towns."

Sir Redvers Buller, Sir Charles Wilson, and Colonel Kitchener were asked their opinions. They all deprecated a retreat from Dongola, but it was clear that their reason for doing so was that they wished to revert to the policy of advancing on Khartoum. "The Soudan," Sir Redvers Buller said, "will never be quiet till the Mahdi is disposed of." "I still believe," Sir Charles Wilson said, "as always, that the control of the Soudan is necessary to Egypt." "The Mahdi must advance or disappear," Colonel Kitchener said, "and I deprecate leaving him this fresh lease of life and power."

I did not agree in the view that Dongola should be held with the intention of advancing on Khartoum. At the same time, I was fearful of the political effect which might be produced in Egypt if an immediate retreat were carried out. I did not like letting the Dervishes come so far down the Nile valley as Wadi Halfa. I was inclined to adopt a proposal put forward by Sir Charles Wilson, to the effect that Dongola should be held until some black troops could be organised, and that the government should be entrusted to

Abdul-Kader Pasha. "I would earnestly impress," I said, "upon Her Majesty's Government that it would be neither politically wise nor dignified to carry out at once the policy of retreat from Dongola and the immediate neighbourhood." The Government, however, held firmly to their original opinions. On May 8, Lord Hartington telegraphed to Lord Wolseley: "The Government, after considering all reports received, adhere to the decision to adopt the proposal for the defence of the Egyptian frontier at Wadi Halfa and Assouan contained in your telegram of April 14."

Whilst measures were being taken to carry out these instructions, a change of Government took place in England. On June 24, 1885, the Ministry of Lord Salisbury succeeded that of Mr. Gladstone. Lord Wolseley urged the new Government to abandon a defensive and to adopt an offensive policy. "No frontier force," he said, "can keep Mahdiism out of Egypt, and the Mahdi sooner or later must be smashed, or he will smash you. . . . To advance on Khartoum and discredit the Mahdi by a serious defeat on his own ground would certainly finish him." After a short interval, Lord Wolseley was informed that the new Government adhered to the decision which had been taken by their predecessors. The retreat was to be continued.

There can be little doubt that the British Government acted wisely in deciding to retreat from Dongola. The views of the military authorities were based on the presumed political necessity of "smashing the Mahdi" at Khartoum. No such necessity existed in reality. It is possible that the policy, which I recommended, of setting up an Egyptian semi-independent Governor at Dongola might have succeeded, if British troops had been allowed to remain long enough to enable a black force to be organised, but I am glad that the experiment was not tried. Indeed, had I at the time thoroughly appreciated the physical features of the country between Wadi Halfa and Dongola, I do not think I should have made the proposal. In the autumn of 1889, I visited Wadi Halfa and went as far as Sarras, about thirty miles south of that place. I saw enough to convince myself that, as an advanced position, Wadi Halfa is far stronger than Dongola.

On July 5, the British troops evacuated Dongola. In view, however, of the threatening attitude of the Dervishes, the movement northwards took place slowly. The Mahdi died suddenly on June 20, and his death exercised a dispiriting effect on his followers. His place was taken by the Khalifa Abdullah - el - Taashi, who proceeded to carry out his predecessor's intention of invading Egypt. It was not, however, till December 30, 1885, that a mixed British and Egyptian force, under the command of Sir Frederick Stephenson, met the Dervishes at Ginniss, about midway between Wadi Halfa and Dongola. The Dervishes were defeated with a loss of about 800 killed and wounded. The British and Egyptian loss was 41 killed and wounded. This action inflicted a severe blow on the Khalifa, and for the time being allayed all fear of a serious invasion of Egypt by the Dervishes. By April 13, 1886, the British and Egyptian troops were concentrated at Wadi Halfa. Wadi Halfa was then left to the care of the Egyptian troops, and the British force retired to Assouan, which place they reached on May 7.

With the action at Ginniss, purely British intervention in the affairs of the Soudan may be said practically to have ceased for the time being. The moment, therefore, is opportune for reviewing the results attained by British policy during the previous two years. My own belief is that the fundamental principles of that policy were sound, if once the fatal mistake of non-interference prior to the Hicks defeat be condoned. If a veto had been placed on the Hicks expedition, the probability is that the Egyptian Government would never have lost possession of Khartoum.

When once General Hicks's army had been destroyed, the policy of withdrawal was enforced by the circumstances of the situation. The British Ministers wisely set their faces against reconquest by British arms. They obliged the Egyptian Government to look the facts in the face, and in doing so they rendered a great service to the Khedive and to the Egyptian people.

But although the fundamental principles of British policy were, with the reserve stated above, perfectly sound, the execution of the policy was defective. At almost every point, failure was incurred.

The British Government endeavoured to assist the Egyptian Government in effecting the peaceable withdrawal of the garrisons and Egyptian civil population from the Soudan. The withdrawal was for the most part never effected at all. Sir Reginald Wingate estimated[1] that the total garrisons in the Soudan, including General Hicks's army and the force sent under General Baker to Suakin, amounted to about 55,000 men. Of these, about 12,000 were killed. 11,000 eventually returned to Egypt, leaving about 30,000 who remained in the Soudan. This figure is exclusive of civilians, women, and children, the number of whom Sir Reginald Wingate roughly estimated at 5000. These figures speak for themselves.

Again, the Government sent two high officials

[1] *Mahdiism, etc.*

on a special mission to the Soudan. They failed to accomplish the objects of their mission.

A military force was then sent to save the lives of the two British emissaries. It arrived too late. Both General Gordon and Colonel Stewart were killed.

Lastly, at one time the Government intended to deal a decisive blow to the power of the Mahdi. The project was abandoned and, in my opinion, wisely abandoned. Nevertheless, the impression was left on the minds of the Dervishes that a British army had attempted to reconquer the Soudan, and had failed to do so.

Eventually, the Government fell back on its original policy of withdrawal, from which it had temporarily drifted.

The Gordon mission and the Nile expedition were thus mere episodes in Egyptian and Soudanese history. They will be remembered as mistakes accompanied by suffering and sorrow to individuals, and by failure in an undertaking on which the British nation had set its heart. It is melancholy to think of the blood and treasure which were wasted. Few of those who have sacrificed their lives for their country have done so to so little purpose as the gallant soldiers who fell at Abu Klea, Kirbekan, and in the neighbourhood of Suakin. The only practical result of the Nile expedition was to inspire in the minds of the Dervishes a wholesome dread of British soldiers, and to break the force of the Dervish advance when it eventually occurred. It would be an exaggeration to say that this result was of no utility, but it was obtained at a cost altogether incommensurate with its real value. The same result would have been more easily and perhaps more thoroughly obtained by the adoption of a defensive policy from the first.

Looking more closely to the details in the execution of the British policy, the following are the conclusions at which I arrive :—

In the first place, it was a mistake to send any British official to Khartoum. The task he had to perform was well-nigh impossible of execution, and his nomination involved the assumption of responsibilities on the part of the British Government, which it was desirable to avoid.

Secondly, if any one was to be sent, it was a mistake to choose General Gordon. In spite of many noble traits in his character, he was wanting in some of the qualities which were essential to the successful accomplishment of his mission.

Thirdly, when once General Gordon had been sent, he should have been left a free hand so long as he kept within the main lines of the policy which he was authorised to execute. It is, in my opinion, to be regretted that General Gordon was not allowed to employ Zobeir Pasha, but any view held as to the probable results of employing him must be conjectural.

Fourthly, the question of whether an expedition should or should not have been sent from Suakin to Berber in the spring of 1884 depends on the military practicability of the undertaking, a point on which the best military authorities differed in opinion.

Fifthly, a great and inexcusable mistake was made in delaying for so long the despatch of the Gordon relief expedition.

Sixthly, the Government acted wisely, after the fall of Khartoum, in eventually adopting a defensive policy and in ordering a retreat to Wadi Halfa.

Lastly, it may be said that the British Government were extraordinarily unlucky. Whatever amount of foresight be shown, success in doubtful and difficult enterprises, such as the Gordon Mission and the Nile Expedition, must always depend a good deal on adventitious circumstances, which cannot be foreseen, and over which no Government can exercise any control. I am far from saying that in all the matters which are discussed in these pages, the British Government exercised a proper amount of foresight, but it must be admitted that whenever the goddess Fortune could play them a trick, she appeared, with proverbial fickleness, to take a pleasure in doing so. The British Government made at the time a great stir in the world. The result in the end was that no object of any importance was attained.

Gratis anhelans, multa agendo nihil agens.

But the situation was one of inordinate difficulty, and those who have had most experience in the conduct of political affairs, and who know how difficult it is to be right and how easy it is to make mistakes, will be least of all inclined to criticise severely the principal actors on the scene.

CHAPTER XXX

THE DÉBRIS OF THE SOUDAN

The outlying provinces :—1. *Darfour* : Surrender of the province—The Senoussieh sect—The revolt of Abu Gemaizeh. 2. *Bahr-el-Ghazal* : Lupton Bey surrenders—His death. 3. *Equatoria* : Emin Pasha summoned to surrender—He maintains his position—The Stanley expedition. 4. *Sennar* : The garrison surrenders. 5. *Kassala* : The garrison surrenders. 6. *The Abyssinian Frontier Garrisons* : The Hewett treaty—The garrisons of Amadib, Senhit, Galabat, Gera, and Gedaref. 7. *Berbera* : Its political status—It is occupied by British troops. 8. *Harrar* : Withdrawal of the Egyptian garrison—Installation of the Emir Abdullah—King Menelek occupies the province. 9. *Zeyla* : It is occupied by British troops. 10. *Tajourrah* : The French occupy it. 11. *Massowah* : Its political status—Attitude of the British Government—The Italians occupy Massowah.

WHEN the collapse of Egyptian authority in the Soudan took place, the *disjecta membra* of Ismail Pasha's huge African estate fell to those whose interest it was to pick them up, and who had the power to give effect to their wishes. Those portions which were remote from the coast relapsed into barbarism. Those which were more easy of access were pounced upon by various European Powers, who about this time began what was aptly called by the British press "the scramble for Africa." In the present chapter the main facts as regards all this Egyptian débris will be briefly stated.[1]

[1] In the preparation of this chapter I have received great assistance from Sir Reginald Wingate's work *Mahdiism and the Egyptian Soudan.*

1. *Darfour.*

When the Mahdist rebellion broke out, the Governor of this province was Slatin Bey, an Austrian officer in the Egyptian service. His position was one of great difficulty, for from the first his own officers were infected with the spirit of revolt. After the destruction of General Hicks's army, the position in Darfour became hopeless. Slatin Bey was at Dara, the capital of the province, against which a force under the command of one of the Mahdi's lieutenants advanced towards the end of 1883. The town at once surrendered. Slatin Bey, writing to General Gordon, described the capitulation in the following terms: "After the annihilation of Hicks's army, the demoralised troops refused to fight any longer. . . . Officers and men demanded capitulation and I, standing there alone and a European, was compelled to follow the majority and compelled to capitulate. Does your Excellency believe that to me, as an Austrian officer, the surrender was easy? It was one of the hardest days in my life."[1]

The events in Darfour during the next few years turned in some degree upon the influence exerted over that remote country and its neighbourhood by the celebrated Sheikh El Senoussi. I take this opportunity, therefore, to describe briefly the rise of the Senoussieh sect.

There are two main divisions of Moslems, namely, the Sunnites and the Shiites. Almost all the Mohammedan inhabitants of the Ottoman

[1] After remaining captive at Omdurman for many years, Slatin Pasha succeeded in making his escape in March 1895. He was appointed Inspector-General in the Soudan, and in that capacity rendered very valuable services to the Government. He is a gallant and very capable officer. Some derogatory remarks made about him by General Gordon in his Journal are wholly undeserved.

dominions and of Africa are Sunnites. They are divided into four Mezhebs, or principal sects, viz. the Hanafi, the Shafaï, the Maliki, and the Hanbali. These sects differ on points of ritual, and as regards the interpretation of certain portions of the Mohammedan law. The Turks in Egypt belong to the Hanafite sect. Most of the Egyptians belong to the Shafaï, but some few to the Maliki sect. Beneath these four main divisions are a number of Tarikas, or minor sects,[1] which were called into existence at a later period of Islamism than the Mezhebs. They have generally been created, and are still being created, by persons noted for their piety and asceticism, who have, for the most part, recommended some special form of prayer or of ceremonial as being particularly efficacious. Some of the Tarikas have risen to considerable importance. Thus, the Wahabi sect caused at one time great political disturbance by reason both of the number and of the aggressive spirit of the sectarians. The Sheikh El Mirghani also founded a large Tarika in the Eastern Soudan. The Sheikh El Senoussi is the head of one of the most important Tarikas which now exist. It has been estimated that his followers number no fewer than 3,000,000, who are scattered widely over the whole of Northern Africa. They are especially numerous in Wadai. In Egypt, the followers of Senoussi are also fairly numerous.

Mohammed Ben Ali El Senoussi, the founder of the sect, was an Algerian by birth, and though originally a Maliki, did not altogether agree with the recognised leaders of that sect. In one respect his teaching resembled that of Abdul Wahab, that is to say, he only recognised the authority of the Koran and the traditions which are contemporaneous with the Koran, rejecting the teaching of later

[1] The literal translation of the word "Tarika" is a "path."

commentators.[1] In 1853, he established himself in an oasis of the Libyan desert named Jerhboub, near Siwa (Jupiter Ammon). He does not appear at any time to have hazarded a definite statement that his son would be the Mahdi, but he gave several indications during his lifetime that such a contingency was not improbable. For instance, on one occasion the father took off the son's sandals and said to those present: "Be witness that I have served him." It is inferred that he would not have performed this act of servitude if he had not wished it to be believed that his son's religious authority was superior to his own. Further, it is said that the principal supporters of Mohammed Ben Ali's son,[2] who succeeded to the headship of the sect on his father's death, constantly pointed out to others that their leader possessed many of the qualities essential to the true Mahdi. On the other hand, in view of the difficulty, not to say the impossibility of fulfilling the whole of those conditions, it may be confidently predicted that, whenever and wherever a Mahdi is proclaimed, a schism will at once occur. Senoussi was, without doubt, well versed in Mohammedan tradition, and, in spite of the aspirations of a few of his over-zealous and ambitious followers, he must have been aware that his claims to be considered the true Mahdi would not meet with general recognition from the Mohammedan world. He, therefore, wisely resisted the temptation to proclaim himself as the Mahdi. It was, however, natural that he should view with disfavour the pretensions of any rival. Hence, from the outset, Senoussi's influence was exercised in a sense antagonistic to the movement of which Mohammed Ahmed was the leader. His views on

[1] An account of the tenets of the Senoussi sect is given in ch. xii. of Mr. Silva White's book *From Sphinx to Oracle*. Mr. White visited Siwa in 1890. He was unable to go to Jerhboub.

[2] He died in 1902.

this subject carried all the more weight from the fact that his reputation for piety and asceticism was higher than that of Mohammed Ahmed. The latter was also grasping and avaricious, qualities which compared unfavourably with the contempt for worldly riches attributed to Senoussi.[1]

Several years of internal dissension followed on Slatin Bey's surrender. As the cruelty and rapacity of the Dervish rule became more and more evident, the religious fervour, which had been at first excited by Mohammed Ahmed, waned. In 1888, a certain Abu Gemaizeh raised the standard of revolt. His programme was "to overthrow the Mahdi imposture and to re-establish the true religion of the Prophet." Abu Gemaizeh was not a member of the Senoussi order, but he attracted the Senoussiyeh to him by giving out that his movement was favoured by the Sheikh of Jerhboub. At first, he gained some successes. "The whole Soudan," Sir Reginald Wingate wrote, "echoed with the wildest reports; even at Cairo it was believed that the end of Mahdiism was near, and that a new Ruler had arisen, who would at least open the roads to Mecca and would no longer be at war with all the world. Relief seemed near. Every arrival from the Soudan reported the growing success of the anti-Mahdist revolt." One of the weak points in the Mahdist religious programme,

[1] There is, however, a practical as well as a religious side to the Senoussi movement. Mr. Weld Blundell, who visited Siwa in 1894, writes: "From the practical side, the whole movement may be described as a very large, well-organised, slave-owning and slave-dealing corporation, managed by the heads of the Brotherhood, with local branches and establishments grouped round the various Zawyas or convents of the order in all parts of North Africa. Without presuming to apportion the real religious sincerity and the purely material element in the movement, it may be taken for granted that, as in similar religious organisations nearer home, religion and business are happily combined in such a way as to give entire satisfaction to the leaders who get the principal benefit of it at present, and to foster vague hopes among the humbler adherents of some great triumph in the future."

on which Abu Gemaizeh seized, was that the Khalifa had placed obstacles in the way of Mohammedans performing the ordinary Haj, and had proclaimed that a visit to the shrine of Mohammed Ahmed at Omdurman might be substituted for the time-honoured pilgrimage to Mecca. When Senoussi's views were eventually made known, it was discovered that he gave full moral support to Abu Gemaizeh, in so far as the latter opposed the heterodox views put forward by the Khalifa on the subject of the pilgrimage. But beyond this he did not go. He was, he said, "the peaceful pioneer of a religious revival, which revolted against the bloodshed and rapine of the false Mahdi of the Soudan. He had no intention or desire to interfere. Mohammed Ahmed and his successor must work their own salvation or destruction; he was in no way responsible."

Thus the great Sheikh of Jerhboub enunciated a policy of non-intervention in terms which might have done credit to Lord Granville. The result of the attitude taken up by Senoussi was that the influence of Abu Gemaizeh speedily waned. On February 22, 1889, he was attacked by Osman Adam, one of the Khalifa's lieutenants: the Dervishes gained a complete victory. Osman Adam's report of this action, which was unearthed by Sir Reginald Wingate, may be quoted as a characteristic specimen of Mahdist official literature. "The Ansar,"[1] he wrote, "not satisfied with their victory, pursued the retreating enemy till sunset, and after that the cavalry still continued pursuing till almost all were killed. They followed them even as far as the caves and forests, where they tried to conceal themselves, but they were

[1] The "Ansar" (literally "Helpers") was the name given to the first converts to Islam made at Medina after the Hegira. The application by the Mahdi of this name to his followers was calculated to excite the resentment of orthodox Mohammedans.

all killed; even those who transformed themselves into apes, wolves, dogs, and rabbits (for the natives of the western countries can be so transformed) were also killed even to the very last. . . . Allah was with us, and we saw several miracles during the battle. Allah sent down fire, which burnt up the dead bodies of the enemy and also their wounded, showing how violent was His wrath upon them. The brethren also saw some sixteen white flags with green borders waving in the air. They also heard the sound of drums beating in the air, and saw objects like mountains falling upon the enemy. The Prophet also revealed himself to many of the followers previous to the battle. . . . It had been my intention to send the heads of all the chiefs to you, but as they have by this time decayed, and would be heavy for messengers, I must be satisfied with sending you only two heads, viz. the head of the devil's agent, and the head of the son of Sultan Salih. . . . The enemy's devil, Abu Gemaizeh, died from small-pox in his house some days ago, and thus Darfour is left without a head." Father Ohrwalder, who escaped from Omdurman in 1891, reported that "the Abu Gemaizeh revolt depopulated almost the entire district. There were but few men to cultivate, and the country became infested by quantities of elephants, lions, and other wild animals."

Further internal dissensions ensued, with the result that the Khalifa eventually withdrew his forces from Darfour.

2. *Bahr-el-Ghazal.*

"The province of Bahr-el-Ghazal," Sir Reginald Wingate wrote, "may be described as about five times as big as England. It is a district covered with forests and mountains, and seamed with low valleys subject to inundation. . . . The soil is exceptionally fertile and there are cattle in abundance, while the population is estimated at between three and four millions."[1] Gessi Pasha, General Gordon's lieutenant, was the first European Governor of the province. In 1881, he was succeeded by Mr. Frank Lupton, who had served in the British mercantile marine, and who subsequently joined General Gordon in the Soudan.

When, in 1882, the news of the Kordofan rebellion reached the Bahr-el-Ghazal province, many of the most important Sheikhs sent in their allegiance to the Mahdi. Lupton, however, amidst many vicissitudes, held his own. Towards the close of 1883, news arrived of the annihilation of General Hicks's army. This disaster was as decisive of the fate of Bahr-el-Ghazal as it had been of that of Darfour. On April 28, 1884, Lupton wrote to Emin Pasha: "It is all up with me here. Every one has joined the Mahdi, and his army takes charge of the Mudirieh the day after to-morrow. What I have passed through these last few days no one knows. I am perfectly alone." On the following day, Lupton surrendered to Karam-Allah, the commander of the Dervish force. He was invited to embrace the faith of Islam, and to assume the name of Abdullah. Lupton, an eye-witness subsequently reported, "replied to Karam-Allah that he had already adopted the Mohammedan religion, but Karam-Allah was not satisfied and insisted that he should openly adopt the creed, and bade Lupton repeat after him: 'There is no God but God, and Mohammed is the Prophet of God,' and while Lupton was repeating this, the Emirs drew their swords, and when he had finished,

[1] This was probably an overestimate. The population of the Bahr-el-Ghazal province, prior to the Dervish rule, was subsequently estimated at 1,500,000.—See *Egypt,* No. 1 of 1904, p. 79.

shouted in one voice: 'Hold to your faith, you are now one of us (Ansar) as we are of you, we are brothers in the faith.'" Lupton was shortly afterwards confined as a prisoner at Omdurman, where he subsequently died.

Thus it was that, in Sir Reginald Wingate's words, "in this vast province, not a shred of Egyptian authority remained; all had been submerged under the waves of Mahdiism, which now rolled placidly over its broad plains, bearing on their way vast bands of slaves for the greatly enlarged households of Mohammed Ahmed, his Khalifas, and his Emirs."

The subsequent history of the Bahr-el-Ghazal province resembles that of Darfour. Mahdist misrule brought in its train its natural accompaniment of discontent and internal dissensions. Eventually, the Dervishes withdrew. Few, in 1885, would have predicted that thirteen years later the ultimate fate of this remote district would bring the two great Western Powers of Europe to the verge of war.[1] Such, however, was to be the case.

3. *Equatoria.*

To the south and south-east of the Bahr-el-Ghazal province lies that of Equatoria, the creation of Sir Samuel Baker, whose work was subsequently carried on by General Gordon. In 1879, General Gordon named Edward Schnitzler, a native of Prussian Silesia, better known as Emin Pasha, to be Governor of the province. The latter, on assuming office, gave the usual account of Egyptian misrule.

[1] I have purposely omitted any account of what is known as the "Fashoda incident" from this work. I should be most unwilling to do anything which might contribute to revive public interest in an affair which is now, happily for all concerned, well-nigh forgotten.

The word "Fashoda" has been erased from the map. The place is now called by its Shillouk name of Kodok.

"Since 1877," he wrote, "no accounts have been sent in from or kept by this administration. Though the Governors receive monies for the payment of wages, no one has been paid a piastre for years; probably, however, the Governors have bought goods with the funds belonging to the Government and sold them at three times the amount. Slaves figure in these accounts as oxen, asses, etc. The making of false seals and fabricating receipts by their use complete the picture of what has been going on here, and with it all the place is full of prayer-places and Fikis."[1]

By the end of 1882, the whole country to the south of Khartoum, with the exception of the Equatorial province, was in open revolt against Egyptian authority. Towards the end of March 1884, the news of the annihilation of General Hicks's army reached Emin Pasha. Shortly afterwards, he was summoned by Karam-Allah to surrender his province. "Now just think of my position," he wrote somewhat later. "For fourteen months I had had no communication with Khartoum, or news from there. The magazines were quite empty of clothes, soap, coffee, etc. . . . In Lado, there was a rabble of drunkards and gamblers, most of them fellow-countrymen of the rebels, the clerks of my divan. The prospect was not brilliant. . . . Accordingly, I asked my officers here in open council whether they considered it more desirable to submit or to prepare to fight. There could be no doubt what the answer would be; the purport of it was submission."

Emin Pasha did not, however, submit. Karam-Allah's advance was stayed owing to disturbances in his rear. Nevertheless, in the anarchy which prevailed, no effective control could be exercised over the outlying portions of the province. "At

[1] A "Fiki" is a man who expounds the law of Islam.

the end of 1885," Sir Reginald Wingate wrote, "the extent of Emin's province was about 180 miles, a narrow strip from the lake to Lado, and an area of about one-seventh of the original extent of the province previous to the revolt."

In February 1886, Emin Pasha received a letter from Nubar Pasha in which he was informed that the Egyptian Government had decided to abandon the Soudan, that they were unable to afford him any assistance, and that he was authorised to take any steps he might consider advisable to leave the country. At the same time, Emin Pasha heard of the fall of Khartoum and of the death of General Gordon. The difficulties of his position were thus increased. He decided, however, to remain where he was. "The greater part of my men," he wrote, "especially my officers, have no desire to leave this country. . . . I shall remain here and hold together, as long as possible, the remnant of the last ten years."

It is unnecessary to give the detailed history of all that followed. How, by reason of rebellion and mutiny, Emin Pasha's position became daily more difficult; how his situation attracted the attention and sympathy of the civilised world; how an expedition was eventually organised to relieve him; how Stanley and his adventurous companions cut their way through the dense untrodden forests of Central Africa; how, when they at last reached Emin, the latter was unwilling to leave; how his hesitation was eventually overcome; and how he and his companions were with infinite trouble at last brought down to the coast,—these are matters of history, which have been described by others who are better informed than myself on the subject.[1]

The Lado Enclave, as it is now termed, was leased to King Leopold II., as Sovereign of the

[1] *Vide* Stanley's *In Darkest Africa*, 1890.

Independent State of the Congo, by an Agreement signed at Brussels on May 12, 1894. The Congolese occupation caused at one time a good deal of friction between the British Government and King Leopold.[1] Eventually, a further Agreement was signed in London on May 9, 1906. Under this Agreement, the Lado Enclave has to be handed over to the Soudanese Government within six months after the demise of King Leopold.

4. *Sennar.*

Of the fate of the province of Sennar and of its once celebrated capital, little need be said. In the spring of 1885, the town was besieged by the Mahdists. The Egyptian commander, Hassan Sadik, made a gallant defence. On his death, which occurred during a sortie, he was succeeded by Nur Bey, who on several occasions repulsed the attacks of the Dervishes and inflicted great loss on them. Eventually, Abdul-Kerim, the Mahdist commander, "having gathered all the neighbouring tribes, completely cut off communication, and soon the garrison, weakened by continuous fighting, was at the last stage of famine. As a final effort, Nur Bey, on August 18, ordered a sortie to be made by Hassan Bey Osman with 1500 of the troops, but the rebels falling on them at Kassab utterly defeated them, and the remnant, with their leader killed, made their way back to the town. On the following day, Nur Bey, having exhausted all the food in the town, was obliged to capitulate. Of the original garrison of 3000 men, 700 only remained,—strong evidence indeed of the severity of the fighting and of the siege." The province of

[1] The facts are briefly stated in *Egypt*, No. 1 of 1906, pp. 121-123, and *Egypt*, No. 1 of 1907, p. 119.

Sennar remained under Dervish rule till the downfall of the Khalifa's power in 1898.

5. *Kassala.*

Kassala is the most important inland town in the Eastern Soudan. Its population numbers about 13,000. In November 1883, it was besieged by one of Osman Digna's lieutenants. The siege continued with varying fortunes until July 1885. Hopes were from time to time entertained that relief would come from Abyssinia. The garrison was also encouraged to hold out by the presence of British troops at Suakin. But no relief came. By April 13, 1885, all the donkeys in the town had been eaten. A successful sally, made on June 15, in which 1000 oxen and 1000 sheep were captured, enabled the defence to be prolonged. But the relief was only temporary. By July 30, every kind of food, including gum and hides, had been exhausted. The garrison capitulated. They received a promise that their lives would be spared, but the promise was broken. "It was believed," Sir Reginald Wingate wrote, "that the inhabitants had secreted treasure, and this was made the plea for every description of torture, cruelty, and robbery." In 1894, Kassala was occupied by the Italians, but three years later (December 1897) was evacuated. It now forms part of the Anglo-Egyptian Soudan.

6. *The Abyssinian Frontier Garrisons.*

When, in the winter of 1883, the policy of withdrawal from the Soudan was adopted, the British Government decided to send a mission to King John of Abyssinia, with whom they were on friendly terms, in the hope that his aid might be enlisted in facilitating the retreat of the garrisons from the Egyptian posts adjoining the frontier of Abyssinia. Sir William Hewett was accordingly sent to Abyssinia to act on behalf of the British Government. He was accompanied by Mason Bey, an American officer in the Egyptian service, who was well acquainted with the affairs of the Soudan, and who acted on behalf of the Egyptian Government.

The result of this mission was that a Treaty was signed at Adowa on June 3, 1884. The main provisions of this Treaty were that the province of Bogos, which the King had for long coveted, was to be ceded to him, and that in return he was to facilitate the withdrawal of the Egyptian frontier garrisons, and to permit their retreat through Abyssinian territory.

Public attention at this time was so exclusively directed to the events which were passing at Khartoum, that the British Government never got due credit for the successful efforts which were made to save the Egyptian garrisons on the Abyssinian frontier.

On September 12, 1884, the province of Bogos was, in accordance with the terms of the Treaty, handed over to Abyssinia.

During the spring of 1885, the Egyptian garrisons of Amadib and Senhit were brought safely down to Massowah.

One of the most important garrisons was that of Galabat. In August 1884, Colonel Chermside, who was at that time Governor-General of the Red Sea Littoral, despatched Major Saad Rifaat to Abyssinia to assist in the preparations which were being made for the relief of Galabat, which was then besieged by the Dervishes. Leaving Adowa with a considerable force of Abyssinians on January 27, 1885, Major Rifaat shortly afterwards attacked and defeated the enemy, and succeeded in bringing the garrison and population, numbering about 3000 men, women, and children, in safety to Massowah, whence those who wished to return were sent back to Egypt.

The garrison of Gera, which had likewise been besieged for some months, was also extricated by the Abyssinians, the Egyptian soldiers being, moreover, subsequently clothed and fed by King John. About 5000 men, women, and children were brought down to Massowah and despatched to Cairo.

In fact, of the posts on the Abyssinian frontier, the only one of which the garrison fell into the hands of the Dervishes was Gedaref, called also Suk Abu Sin. The commandant of this post, which was garrisoned by about 200 men, capitulated in April 1884, that is to say two months before the Hewett Treaty had been concluded. On the whole, therefore, the results of the Treaty were satisfactory.

7. *Berbera.*

Ismail Pasha was not content with extending Egyptian authority to the sources of the Nile. Pashadom, with its baneful accompaniments of misrule and oppression, stretched its tentacles to the Somali coast and inland to the fertile province of Harrar. When the parent trunk rotted, the first of the branches to fall off was Berbera. It fell at the feet of the Queen of England.

The Egyptian Governor of Berbera was of the ordinary type. Mr. F. L. James, who had travelled much in the Soudan and in Somaliland, wrote to me on April 21, 1884: "On all hands we heard nothing but the most bitter complaints as to the ill-treatment the natives (Somalis) met with at the hands of the Egyptian Governor of Berbera, Abdul Rahman Bey. . . . That he is detested by the people and a very bad Governor is not open to doubt; and after what happened two years ago to myself and party, while travelling in the Soudan, I am surprised at no enormity on the part of an Egyptian Governor."

Sir Richard Burton wrote in 1856: "The occupation of the port of Berbera has been advised for many reasons. In the first place, Berbera is the true key to the Red Sea, the centre of East African traffic, and the only place for shipping upon the western Erythraean shore from Suez to Guardafui. Backed by lands capable of cultivation, and by hills covered with pine and other valuable trees, enjoying a comparatively temperate climate, with a regular, although thin monsoon, this harbour has been coveted by many a foreign conqueror. Circumstances have thrown it, as it were, into our arms, and, if we refuse the chance, another and a rival nation will not be so blind."[1] The Indian authorities had always been alive to the desirability of preventing Berbera from falling into the hands of any European Power.

The political status of the coast eastward of Zeyla was on a different footing from that portion of the coast which extends from Zeyla to the straits of Bab-el-Mandeb. The Sultan exercised rights of sovereignty over the territory between Bab-el-Mandeb and Zeyla, which rights, although never formally recognised by the British Government, had not been disputed. On the other hand, the sovereign rights of the Sultan over the Somali tribes lying between Zeyla and Ras Hafoun had been repeatedly denied by the British Government. In 1877, a Convention was negotiated between Ismail Pasha and the British Government, the main object of which was to recognise the jurisdiction of the Khedive, under the suzerainty of the Sultan, as far eastward as Ras Hafoun. The

[1] Burton, *First Footsteps in East Africa*, p. xxxiv.

fifth article of this Convention stipulated that it was not to come into operation until the Sultan gave a formal assurance to the British Government that no portion of the territory on the Somali coast should be ceded to any foreign Power. In spite of repeated invitations, the Sultan had never given this assurance. The Convention was, therefore, invalid, and the hands of the British Government were free. Lord Granville, accordingly, on being pressed by the India Office to move in the matter, instructed Lord Dufferin on May 29, 1884, to denounce the Convention and to inform the Porte that "with regard to the coast eastward of Zeyla, it was the intention of Her Majesty's Government, on the withdrawal of the Egyptians, to make such arrangements as they might think desirable for the preservation of order and the security of British interests, especially at Berbera, from which Aden drew its chief supplies." This communication drew forth some remonstrances from Constantinople; they were set aside. In October 1884, a British official was charged with the administration of Berbera; a small force of police and sepoys was placed at his disposal. A notification of the establishment of a British Protectorate over this part of the coast was conveyed to the French Government by Lord Lyons on April 23, 1885. Thus Berbera, with the neighbouring port of Bulhar, were peaceably absorbed into the British dominions.

8. *Harrar.*

The fertile province of Harrar lies about 200 miles south-west of Zeyla. Sir Richard Burton visited it in 1856. In his time, the province was governed in a barbarous fashion by Emir Ahmed, one of a family which had for long held dominion over the country. The fertility of Harrar excited the ambition of Ismail Pasha. It was annexed, and in 1874 the reigning Emir was put to death by Raouf Pasha, himself a bad specimen of a bad class. The usual results followed. Major Hunter, who visited Harrar early in 1884, reported: "The Khedive's rule is extremely unpopular, and justly so, for the admitted object of the Governors is to tax the inhabitants to the utmost. No justice is obtainable, peculation is rife, trade is stifled, the soldiery pillage the villages, and the troops are discontented owing to deferred payment and prolonged expatriation. . . . The Governor, Ali Pasha, is a shaky, garrulous old man of Turkish extraction, who has no idea beyond filling the Treasury, presumably for the benefit of the Egyptian Government."

Manifestly, the only wise course to pursue, both in the interests of Harrar and of Egypt, was that the Egyptian Government should abandon a trust which had been so grossly abused. The evacuation of the province was pressed upon the Egyptian Ministers, who, albeit reluctantly, accepted the inevitable logic of facts.

The withdrawal of the garrison, and of others who wished to leave, across 200 miles of country, inhabited by tribes who were far from friendly to the Egyptians, was no easy matter. The duty of executing this task was entrusted to Major Hunter, who was assisted by two other British officers. Radwan Pasha was sent from Cairo to act as Egyptian Commissioner; he co-operated loyally with Major Hunter. The retreat was skilfully conducted. The garrison and followers, to the number of 8359 persons, were marched down to the coast in detachments during the early months of 1885, and embarked for Egypt.

The government of the province was then handed over to Abdullah, a son of the last reigning

Emir. The new Emir did not maintain his position for long. In January 1887, King Menelek of Shoa attacked and took possession of Harrar.

9. *Zeyla.*

It has been already mentioned that the political status of Zeyla was different from that of Berbera. In the latter case, the Sultan could not put forward any valid claim to suzerainty. Zeyla, on the other hand, had formed part of the Ottoman dominions before it came under Egyptian jurisdiction. In 1875, it was farmed by the Sultan to Ismail Pasha, on payment of a tribute of £13,500 a year.

The British Government, through their Ambassador at Constantinople, invited the Porte on May 14, 1884, "to resume direct jurisdiction over the ports on the Egyptian coast of the Red Sea and to occupy them with Turkish troops." On July 17, the Porte was again invited to take "the necessary steps, on the withdrawal of the Egyptian troops, to maintain its authority over Tajourrah and Zeyla." It was, at the same time, stated that the British Government were "anxious to receive the reply of the Porte with as little delay as possible." The Porte treated the matter in its usual dilatory fashion. No definite answer was given. In the meanwhile, there was an imminent risk of disturbances in the neighbourhood of Zeyla. On August 1, 1884, therefore, Lord Dufferin was instructed to "inform the Porte that unless the Turkish Government were prepared to take immediate steps for the occupation of Zeyla, it would be necessary for Her Majesty's Government to send a force there to preserve order." Still the Sultan did not move. Action became necessary on the part of the British Government. On August 24, 1884, Major Hunter telegraphed to me: "Force landed at Zeyla. Somalis impressed. Governor obliging." The obliging Governor was kept in his place for a while, because some discussion ensued as to the future of Zeyla. A difference of opinion existed among the British authorities as to whether it was worth keeping or not. It is now British territory.

The Egyptian tribute was paid to the Porte for some while after the British occupation of Zeyla. Eventually, in connection with certain Custom-house negotiations, an understanding was arrived at between Cairo and Constantinople that the payment of the tribute should cease.

10. *Tajourrah.*

It was not to be supposed that, whilst this scramble for Egyptian territory was going on, the French would remain idle. In 1862, they had taken possession of Obokh, in virtue of a Convention made with some local Sheikhs. The French Government now decided to annex the neighbouring territory of Tajourrah. Early in May 1884, a French ship arrived at Richal, a port near Tajourrah; ten sailors, accompanied by the Vizier of Tajourrah, landed, told the local Sheikhs that the place belonged to them, and that they would return to take possession of it. M. Barrère, the French representative at Cairo, "knew nothing of the matter; he knew Tajourrah was Egyptian territory." Mr. Egerton "thought it possible that there might be some misunderstanding." There was, however, no misunderstanding. The Porte uttered some feeble protests, and tried to excite English jealousy of French extension. The British Government, however, wisely remained indifferent. Since 1884, Tajourrah has been a French possession.

11. *Massowah.*

Suakin and Massowah were placed under Egyptian jurisdiction by an Imperial Firman issued in 1865. The tribute payable by Egypt to the Sultan was, at the same time, raised by £37,500 a year.

The same disorder reigned at Massowah as elsewhere. Colonel Chermside telegraphed from Suakin on January 22, 1885: "I do hope you will take a speedy decision as to the Massowah question, as, without wishing to reflect on the long string of my predecessors, it is hard to carry on at all in the chaos everything is in, police, pensions, establishment of employés, dues, contracts, water-supply, public works, military garrison, everything is in indescribable confusion, costly without efficiency." The Egyptian Government were incapable of evolving order out of this chaos. The only possible course was to let Massowah go the way of the other lost possessions of Egypt. The question then arose as to who should step into possession of the property, which was about to be abandoned.

"L'Italie," a French diplomatist said at the time of the Berlin Congress, "rôde autour du monde pour trouver un endroit quelconque où elle pourra placer son drapeau." The Italian nation has, in fact, ever since its creation, shown a good deal of the restless ambition which often attaches itself to youth. The desire manifested of late years in Italy to establish colonies in distant lands appears to be based to some extent on the plea that other great Powers have founded colonies, and that, therefore, Italy must do the same. The Italians, in all the exuberance of youthful national life, forgot, in 1885, that the monk's cowl does not necessarily make the monk, and rushed into

African colonisation with all the impetuosity which characterises Southern nations.

Some years previously, the Italians had established themselves at Assab Bay, a proceeding which was viewed with a good deal of rather unnecessary ill-humour by the Indian Government of the day. When it became apparent that the neighbouring territory of Massowah was likely to be in the political market, Italian ambition fired up. It was thought necessary to acquire this desirable possession before it could fall into the hands of any rival claimant. The first thing to do was to secure the goodwill of England; Lord Granville was sounded on the subject. On December 22, 1884, he wrote to the British Ambassador at Rome: "I have informed Count Nigra (the Italian Ambassador in London) that Her Majesty's Government were desirous of showing their friendly feeling towards Italy in all ways. The Egyptian Government were unable, I said, to continue their hold on all the African littoral of the Red Sea. Under these circumstances, the ports naturally reverted to Turkey. We had for some time been giving advice to the Porte to retake possession of them. I was glad, I continued, to observe that M. Mancini fully recognised that we had no right and made no pretension to give away that which did not belong to us. If the Italian Government should desire to occupy some of the ports in question, it was a matter between Italy and Turkey; but I was able to inform him that Her Majesty's Government, for their part, had no objection to raise against the Italian occupation of Zulla, Beilul, or Massowah."

When, at a subsequent period, many sober-thinking Italians regretted the occupation of Massowah, it was occasionally alleged that England had instigated the occupation, and that Italy had, in fact, been used as a catspaw in order to get the British Government out of a difficulty. These statements are devoid of foundation. The British Government never proposed to Italy to occupy Massowah. All they did was to adopt a friendly attitude towards Italy, and to abstain from creating difficulties which might have proved obstacles to the attainment of Italian aspirations. The British Government did nothing to thwart the Italians; but beyond this they did not go. Indeed, I remember telling M. de Martino, the Italian Consul-General at Cairo, that my personal opinion was that the Italians were making a mistake in occupying Massowah. He was inclined to share my views, but the matter was not one for him to decide. The Italian Government and the Italian Parliament were naturally presumed to be the best judges of Italian interests. M. Mancini, who was then Minister for Foreign Affairs, warmly espoused the cause of occupation, and he was at the time supported by public opinion in Italy. Dissuasion or opposition on the part of England would have been regarded as an unfriendly act dictated by an unworthy jealousy of Italian extension.

When the Italian Government were assured of the absence of objection on the part of England, they acted with promptitude. Plausible excuses for action were not wanting. Some Italian travellers had been murdered in the neighbourhood of Massowah, and the Italian Government had failed to obtain adequate satisfaction. Early, therefore, in the month of February 1885, a formidable squadron appeared at Massowah and took possession of the place. The Egyptian garrison was shortly afterwards withdrawn.

The Sultan was indignant. For a time, the Foreign Offices of Europe rang with angry but ineffectual protests from the Porte. The Powers who had guaranteed the integrity of the Ottoman Empire were implored to interfere. But no one had any real interest in the matter. The Cabinets of Europe turned their heads the other way, and the diplomatic clamour soon died out. From that time forth, Italy has been in possession of Massowah. Whether it is worth while for the Tuscan and Neapolitan peasant to continue to pay taxes for the maintenance of Italian authority over a territory, which will probably never be of any great value either from a commercial or from any other point of view, is a matter for the Italian nation to decide. Nations are not, however, entirely governed by considerations of material interests. The national honour and dignity are supposed to be at stake, and they will, without doubt, so far carry the day as to prevent Italy from abandoning territory which possibly many Italians now think it was unwise ever to have seized.

Thus it was that the huge unwieldy edifice, which Ismail Pasha had sought to erect, fell with a crash which resounded throughout North-Eastern Africa. The Englishman, the Italian, the Frenchman, the Abyssinian, the Dervish, and the slave-hunter divided the spoils between them. And why did the edifice fall? The destruction of General Hicks's army precipitated the catastrophe. But the real reason why Ismail Pasha's empire fell was that it was eventually overtaken by the fate inevitably attending all political fabrics which are rotten to the core. It fell because it deserved to fall. It may be that the light of Western civilisation will some day be shed over the whole of Africa, but if this consummation is ever to be attained, it must be through other agents than the slave-hunting, corrupt, and tyrannical Pashas, who were employed by the Egyptian Government, and who, themselves but semi-civilised, introduced none of the blessings but some of the curses of civilisation amongst the people who, by a cruel fate, were for a time placed under their control.

CHAPTER XXXI

THE DEFENCE OF EGYPT

1886–1892

The Egyptian army—Negotiations with the Dervishes—Fighting on the frontier—The siege of Suakin—Defeat of Osman Digna—Wad-el-Nejumi—Nejumi advances—The battles of Argin and of Toski—Death of Wad-el-Nejumi—Results of the battle—Situation at Suakin—The reoccupation of Tokar—Defeat of Osman Digna.

ALTHOUGH British military aid to a very limited extent was subsequently on one or two occasions afforded to the Egyptian Government, it may be said that from the date of the battle of Ginniss (December 30, 1885) the defence of Egypt against the Dervishes practically devolved on the Egyptian army. That army was now officered by a well-selected body of Englishmen. Its organisation had been greatly improved. The men were gaining confidence in themselves. A small Egyptian Camel Corps had fought at Kirbekan, and its conduct had obtained General Brackenbury's commendations. A more considerable Egyptian force had taken a creditable part in the battle of Ginniss. Hopes, therefore, began to be entertained that for the future the Egyptian army would of itself suffice to repel any attack which might be made by the Dervishes. The sequel showed that these hopes were destined to be realised.

It has been already shown that a great shrinkage

of Egyptian territory had taken place. The army was no longer called upon to defend remote regions in the centre of Africa. Its task was of a more modest nature. In the first place, it had to prevent the Dervishes from descending the valley of the Nile farther than Wadi Halfa; in the second place, it had to maintain whatever was left of Egyptian authority in the Eastern Soudan. For the time being, this latter task was confined to the defence of the town of Suakin, for Egyptian authority did not extend beyond its walls. For obvious reasons, based on the difficulties of communication, the operations in the valley of the Nile and at Suakin were to a great extent independent of each other.

Before entering upon a description of the military operations which were about to take place, it will be as well to allude briefly to an attempt which was made to negotiate with the Dervishes. A Convention between the British Government and the Porte was signed at Constantinople, on October 24, 1885, in virtue of which two Commissioners, one British and one Turkish, were despatched to Cairo.[1] The second article of the Convention provided that the Ottoman Commissioner was to consult with the Khedive "upon the best means of tranquillising the Soudan by pacific measures." After some delay, it was arranged that Youssuf Pasha Shuhdi should be sent to Wadi Halfa in order to try his hand at negotiation with the Dervishes. He left Cairo for the frontier in May 1886.

It was as well to make an attempt to negotiate, if only to show to those who believed in the possibility of successful negotiations that it was hopeless to attempt to come to any arrangement with the Dervishes. But to all who had any appreciation of the true nature of the Mahdist

[1] This subject is more fully treated in Chapter XLVI.

movement, it was obvious that Youssuf Pasha Shuhdi's mission was foredoomed to failure. It proved, in fact, to be wholly unproductive of results. A year later, the Khalifa addressed letters to the Queen, the Sultan, and the Khedive, which breathed the true spirit of Mahdiism. The letter to the Queen terminated in the following eloquent, if somewhat bombastic peroration: "And thou, if thou wilt not yield to the command of God, and enter among the people of Islam and the followers of the Mahdi—grace be upon him—come thyself and thy armies and fight with the host of God. And if thou wilt not come, then be ready in thy place, for at His pleasure and at the time that He shall will it, the hosts of God will raze thy dwelling and let thee taste of sorrow, because thou hast turned away from the path of the Lord, for therein is sufficiency, and salvation is to him who followeth the Mahdi."

For three years subsequent to the battle of Ginniss, desultory fighting continued in the neighbourhood of Suakin, and in the Nile valley. Notably, a brilliant skirmish took place on April 28, 1887, at Sarras, which resulted in the defeat of the Dervishes with a loss of about 200 men, the Egyptian loss being 51 killed and wounded. It was not, however, until December 1888 that any serious engagement occurred. By that time, the indigenous tribes near Suakin had learnt to appreciate the true character of Dervish rule. They were either openly hostile to Osman Digna, or were only prevented by fear from throwing off their allegiance to the Mahdi. Osman Digna, however, still terrorised the country with tribal levies drawn from a distance. He obtained reinforcements and laid siege to Suakin. It was eventually decided that he should be attacked, and for this purpose more Egyptian troops were despatched from Cairo. In addition to these, owing to pressure brought to bear upon the Government in Parliament, a small British force was sent from Cairo to Suakin, though its presence was quite unnecessary. Sir Francis Grenfell, who had succeeded Sir Evelyn Wood as Commander-in-Chief of the Egyptian army, conducted the operations in person. On December 20, 1888, the Dervishes were attacked and driven from their entrenchments with a loss of 500 men. The British and Egyptian loss was 2 officers and 50 men killed and wounded. The result of this action was to relieve the pressure on Suakin. Osman Digna, however, still maintained his hold over the Eastern Soudan generally. A further result of no slight importance was that the Egyptian troops acquired confidence in themselves and inspired confidence in the minds of the public. Previous to this action, few believed in the Egyptian army. Subsequent to the action, the voice of criticism was to a certain extent silenced. It had been proved that some reliance could be placed on Egyptian troops.

After this engagement, the valley of the Nile became the chief centre of interest.

A period of political hurricane, whether the scene be laid in savage Africa or in civilised Europe, generally brings to the front some individual who appears to embody in his own person the genius of the principles which it is sought to assert. Arábi, though no hero, was a fitting representative of the justifiable, but blind, sullen, and unintelligent discontent which prevailed amongst the Egyptians at the time of the rebellion of which he was the leader. The Mahdist Avatar was of a different type. The true incarnation of Mahdiism was not to be found in Osman Digna, nor even in the Mahdi himself. Both of these men were in some degree strutting on the stage. It may well be doubted whether either of them believed in himself. Enlightened self-interest, more especially in the shape of the acquisition of wealth, lurked behind the grandiloquent periods of their Proclamations, and may be traced in the stage tricks by which it was sought to strengthen the faith of a credulous and fanatical population. When a prophet puts pepper under his finger-nails in order to excite his lachrymal glands[1] a safe indication is given that he has descended from his prophetic pedestal, and that, by his own confession, he may be classed amongst Pythonesses, the manipulators of Delphic oracles and winking virgins.

It was reserved for Wad-el-Nejumi to embody in his own person the true principles of militant Mahdiism. He was at once the Peter the Hermit of the Mahdist crusaders and the Prince Rupert of Dervish chivalry. He believed in Mahdiism, and he believed in himself. When summoned by Sir Francis Grenfell to surrender previous to the battle of Toski, he replied, "We are not afraid of any one; we only fear God!" and, without doubt, he spoke the truth. Brave, resourceful, and pertinacious, Nejumi inspired amongst his followers a confidence which he carried to his grave, and which stood the test of military defeat and death. Few pictures are more touching than that of the host of wild Dervish prisoners mourning with heartfelt sorrow in the palm-grove of Toski over the body of the chieftain who had led them, their companions, their wives and their children, through suffering and privation, to the destruction of their political hopes and to death. Sir Reginald Wingate

[1] "The Greek who came in told the Greek Consul that the Mahdi puts pepper under his finger-nails, and when he receives visitors then he touches his eyes and weeps copiously; that he eats a few grains of dhoora openly, but in the interior of the house he has fine feeding and drinks alcoholic drinks."—Gordon's *Journal*, vol. i. p. 32.

thus describes the character of this picturesque savage: "Nejumi's career closed only at Toski, when his devoted bodyguard sold their lives dearly in defence of his revered corpse. He was a Jaalin, but one in whom the Baggara recognised warlike qualities similar to their own, and with whom it was important to keep on good terms. In early life a Fiki, like the Mahdi, and his devoted friend, stern, hard, ascetic, the thin dark man was the incarnation of a blind sincerity of conviction. He never transgressed the self-appointed strictness with which he ruled his conduct. Withal, a spice of madness entered into his composition. There was no man but trusted his word, and his was the distant enterprise, his the forefront of danger always. Mahdiism was the natural outlet for his wild temper. He was the Khalid of the Prophet's wars. He it was who prepared the stratagem which annihilated Hicks. He it was who crept silently round through the shallow mud beyond the crumbled ramparts of Khartoum."

The defeat at Ginniss checked the advance of the Dervishes, but their leaders were not discouraged. It is probable that the Soudanese population failed to realise the fact that any military reverse had been sustained. The Khalifa vied with Napoleon in the mendacity of his bulletins. Moreover, the main facts, as they must have presented themselves to the minds of his followers, were that a British force had invaded the Soudan, that it had failed to accomplish its object, that the capital of the Soudan had fallen in spite of British endeavours to save it, and that the British army had then retired and had assumed a defensive attitude. It can, therefore, be no matter for surprise that "general rejoicings" took place at Khartoum. The Dervishes, confident in the sacred nature and ultimate success of their cause, were stimulated to fresh exertions. As Lord Wolseley, General Gordon, and others had predicted, it was decided to invade Egypt. "Nejumi," Sir Reginald Wingate says, "burnt his house at Omdurman, and vowed that he would not return until he had conquered Egypt. On his departure, the Khalifa Abdullah assembled the four Khalifas and all the Emirs. They all stretched out their hands in the direction of Cairo, and called out 'Allahu Akbar,' three times. Then the Khalifa Abdullah called out in a loud voice, 'O Ansar! fear not for the fight for the land of Egypt; you will suffer much at the battle of Assouan, after which the whole of Egypt will fall into your hands. O Ansar! you will also suffer much at the battle of Mecca, after which the whole country will be yours.'"

Some time, however, elapsed before any forward movement was made. A revolt against the Khalifa's authority took place in Kordofan; troubles occurred in Darfour, and considerable bodies of men had to be detached for service on the Abyssinian frontier. Moreover, the important tribe of Kababish Arabs, who inhabit the territory west of Dongola, assumed an attitude of hostility to Mahdiism, nor was it till 1887 that they were crushed and their chief, Saleh Bey, killed in a decisive engagement. The Mahdist leaders, therefore, had their hands full for the space of three years. As successive seasons passed and no forward movement was made, it began to be thought that Dervish invasion was a mere bugbear.

At last, however, the long-expected invasion took place. In the summer of 1889, Nejumi advanced up the valley of the Nile with a motley force, consisting in all of over 11,000 souls. He was joined at Sarras by a further body of 1200 fighting men, of whom about 300 were armed with rifles, and some 1000 camp-followers. A short distance south of Wadi Halfa, Nejumi left the river. He decided to turn Wadi Halfa, to move along the west bank parallel to, but at some little distance from the Nile, and then to strike the river again at a point somewhere between Wadi Halfa and Korosko. He hoped and believed that he would be joined by the Nubian population.

This plan was faulty in its conception. It was of a nature to facilitate the conduct of defensive operations. It involved toilsome marches under a burning sun over a trackless desert devoid of water. The difficulty of obtaining supplies was great. Even before leaving the river, many of the horses, camels, and donkeys had been killed and eaten. Constant excursions to the river were necessary in order to obtain water, and the river was occupied by Egyptian troops, who could be moved from point to point with comparative ease by utilising the steamers and barges which were at the disposal of Colonel Wodehouse, the commandant of the frontier. In the language of strategists, the Egyptian army was acting on interior lines. By July 2, Nejumi's force occupied a position in the desert a short distance from Arguin, a village on the river about 3½ miles north of Wadi Halfa. His movements were carefully watched and followed by Colonel Wodehouse with a flying column of about 2000 men. The Dervishes attacked the village and, after a sharp engagement, were repulsed with a loss of about 900 men, amongst whom were several important Emirs. The Egyptian loss consisted of 4 officers and 66 men killed and wounded. This spirited action reflected great credit on Colonel Wodehouse and the force which he commanded. It discouraged the Dervishes, and contributed materially to the final and decisive victory at Toski. Many of

Nejumi's men deserted. Abdul Halim, his principal lieutenant, advised a retreat. It was futile, he thought, "to attempt an invasion of Egypt with insufficient men, no food, and enormous difficulties in obtaining water." Nejumi's indomitable spirit was, however, not to be broken. He made an eloquent appeal to the religious zeal of his followers, who resolved to go on, and if needs be to die with him. Accordingly, the unwieldy column, dogged at every step by the watchful and pertinacious Colonel Wodehouse, moved slowly and laboriously northward. The Dervishes suffered greatly. "Desultory skirmishes," Sir Reginald Wingate wrote, "took place daily, and numbers of camp-followers, women and children, were captured. One and all gave pitiable accounts of the state of affairs in the Arab camp. The numbers of camels, horses, and donkeys were rapidly diminishing, as they constituted almost the sole food. Might was right; so the lion's share, such as it was, fell to the fighting men, while the miserable camp-followers subsisted on powdered date-seeds and the core of the date-palm tree, which, when ground, is said to have certain nutritive properties. But many of these unfortunate people were reduced to a state of starvation and, flocking to the river-bank in numbers, were received by patrolling gun-boats, and brought to the Egyptian camp, where they were fed and cared for, and, if wounded, admitted to hospital."

In the meanwhile, reinforcements, both British and Egyptian, were hurrying up from Cairo. The Egyptians were the first to arrive, and Sir Francis Grenfell, who had assumed the command, seeing a favourable opportunity, struck the decisive blow before the main body of British troops came up.[1]

[1] A small body of British cavalry, however, took part in the battle of Toski.

On August 2, the Egyptian force occupied Toski, a village on the west bank of the Nile, about midway between Wadi Halfa and Korosko. Nejumi camped, on the night of the 2nd, in the desert about five miles from the village. Early on the morning of the 3rd, Sir Francis Grenfell made a reconnaissance in force, and, on approaching the Dervish position, at once recognised that the topographical features of the ground were very favourable to the Egyptian troops.

I visited the battlefield of Toski a few months later. Many of the Dervish dead were still unburied. The empty cartridge cases, which were strewed about, showed clearly the positions which had been occupied by the Egyptian troops. It would be difficult to conceive ground better calculated to give disciplined, well-armed, and well-equipped troops every possible advantage over hordes of courageous but ill-disciplined savages. The soil of the desert, which is here undulating, is composed of hard shingly sand, over which infantry, cavalry, and artillery can move with ease and rapidity. Here and there, a few rocks and boulders, behind which shelter can be obtained, rise up from the plain. Save, however, in these localities, the ground is completely bare. Once driven from the shelter of the rocks, it was clear that the arms of precision, with which the Egyptian soldiers were furnished, would work with deadly effect on the Dervishes. Sir Francis Grenfell, therefore, with the eye of a true tactician, determined to bring on an action at once. Orders were sent to Toski for the remainder of the Egyptian troops to come out. In the meanwhile, the cavalry, under Colonel Kitchener, headed Nejumi, who at first wished to avoid an action, and was endeavouring to slip away to the north. It was evident to Nejumi that he had to accept Sir Francis Grenfell's challenge.

He gave his followers an Arab version of Nelson's order at Trafalgar. "We must all," he said, "stand prepared to meet our Maker to-day."

It is unnecessary to give a detailed account of what followed. It will be sufficient to say that Nejumi's force was routed; 1200 of his followers were killed, and the greater portion of the remainder were taken prisoner, either immediately or during the next three days. Sir Reginald Wingate estimates that the total force with which Nejumi crossed the frontier on July 1, together with the reinforcements he subsequently received, amounted to about 5700 fighting men and 8000 camp-followers. Of these, about 1000 fighting men and 2000 camp-followers returned to their homes. The remainder were either killed, died of disease and starvation, or were taken prisoners. The Egyptian loss at the battle was 165 killed and wounded.

What, however, became of him who is the one interesting figure in Dervish history? What became of the savage chieftain who had looked down on the lines of Wadi Halfa but a few weeks previously and had sworn, in words that bring back Border minstrelsy to the mind of an Englishman, that he would "stable his steed in Wodehouse's chamber"? Nejumi was slightly wounded at an early stage of the fight. One of his relations, who was taken prisoner at Toski, said: "On the capture of the first position, one of the Emirs escaped from the onslaught and rushed breathlessly by, crying to Nejumi that all was over and that he should fly. Instead of listening to this advice, Nejumi mounted his horse and, dashing down to the plain, vainly endeavoured to rally his men." He was again wounded, this time severely, and his horse was shot under him, but he reached the shelter of the hills. He appears then to have been wounded yet a third time. "During the artillery attack on the second position," Sir Reginald Wingate says, "a well-directed shell brought down the largest banner, which was subsequently discovered to be Nejumi's, and it is probable that the shell which broke his flag-pole also wounded Nejumi again." He was carefully tended by his faithful bodyguard, who placed him on a rough camel-litter, and endeavoured to carry him to the rear. The party, "on being observed, was fired on by a troop of cavalry; the camel fell, and most of the men appeared to have been killed; the cavalry then followed up, and called on the remainder to surrender, but as they approached, the Arabs supposed to have been killed, suddenly sprang up, and rushing at them, a hand-to-hand encounter ensued; a number were killed, and the remainder returned once more to their camel. They were again called upon to surrender, but their only response was a second charge, which resulted in all being killed except one, who, mounting a passing horse, succeeded in escaping." It was then found that the camel carried the dead body of Nejumi. "One of his sons, a boy of five years old, was found dead beside the camel, while another baby boy scarcely a year old was brought by his nurse into the camp at Toski on the following day."[1]

There is a rude pathos about the life and death of this savage warrior, which brings to the mind an *ἀνὴρ ἄριστος* of Homeric, or a Beowulf of Anglo-Saxon times.

I have already said that the lives lost at Abu

[1] Of all the sons of earth, few have had their destiny more completely changed by accident than this child. Instead of being brought up to detest Christians amidst savage surroundings in the Soudan, he was handed over to the tender care of the English nursing sisters at the principal hospital at Cairo, by whom he was a good deal spoilt, and who were more devoted and certainly more willing slaves to him than any of those whom his father could have captured in the centre of Africa.

Klea, Kirbekan, and other previous battles in the Soudan were wasted, or as good as wasted. The same cannot be said of those who fell at Toski. In this case, the soldier was the executive arm of a wise policy. He was defending the ground secured to civilisation from the attacks of barbarous fanatics. He fought in a good cause. He deserved to triumph, and his triumph was complete. The victory of Toski brought important political results in its train. It pricked the Mahdist bubble. It showed that the Dervishes, although perhaps still strong for purposes of defence in their own remote and inhospitable deserts, were no longer to be feared as aggressors. It gave confidence to the Egyptian army, to the Egyptian people, and to Europe. It showed that those who had dwelt on the necessity of "smashing up the Mahdi" at Khartoum, had been in error; that, although right in supposing that the Dervishes would invade Egypt, they had overrated the Dervish power of offence; that the Mahdist movement had less cohesion and was less formidable than was originally supposed; and that a small Egyptian force led by British officers, with merely the moral support to be derived from the presence of a British garrison in Egypt, was sufficient to guarantee the integrity of the Khedive's dominions. With the defeat at Toski, the aggressive power of Mahdiism collapsed. Sir Francis Grenfell, and those who fought under him, gave tranquillity to the valley of the Nile, and enabled the work of the civilian reformer to proceed without fear of external aggression. These were great achievements, which deserve the acknowledgments of all who are interested in the welfare of Egypt.

The scene must now be shifted back again to the Eastern Soudan. For more than two years after the defeat of Osman Digna on December 20,

1888, no events of importance took place in the neighbourhood of Suakin. Egyptian authority was limited to the ground enclosed by the fortifications of the town. Any isolated wood-cutter or cultivator who roamed beyond the range of the guns was liable to be killed or captured by the stray Dervishes who infested the environs. The indigenous tribes became daily more hostile to Osman Digna, but they had not the strength nor the power of combination necessary to drive him out of the country.

In the meanwhile, a lengthened controversy took place as to whether it was desirable to prohibit or to permit trade with the interior. Considerable difference of opinion existed amongst the local authorities as to the wisest course to be pursued under the circumstances. On the one hand, the military authorities urged that if grain were allowed to leave the coast, it could not be prevented from reaching the Dervishes, and further, that under the cover of legitimate trade, they would receive munitions of war. Thus, attacks on Egyptian territory would be facilitated. A serious attack on Suakin, which was contemplated in 1890, was, in fact, only prevented by the withdrawal of the permission to trade, which had been previously accorded. On the other hand, it was urged that the Dervishes were few in number, that they tyrannised over the rest of the population, and that it was unjust and impolitic to make the mass of the people suffer for the faults of a few, who, moreover, did not form part of the indigenous tribes of the Eastern Soudan, but were strangers coming from distant parts, whose presence was unwelcome to the natives.

A policy, which was almost prohibitive of trade, as also one which placed no hindrance on trade, were, therefore, supported with an equal degree of conviction by competent authorities. Under these circumstances, the course of action dictated from Cairo was necessarily vacillating. At times, trade was allowed; at other times, it was wholly or in part prohibited. Neither could this be any matter for surprise, for the arguments which the advocates of both policies were able to advance were valid, if considered exclusively on their own merits.

Another question, which grew in importance during the year 1890, was the Slave Trade, to which a stimulus was given by the presence of the Dervishes on the coast. The British cruisers in the Red Sea were powerless to stop the traffic. Arab dhows would lie concealed amongst the numerous creeks along the coast, which, owing to the coral reefs, cannot generally be approached by large ships. The slave caravans would wait a short distance inland. A favourable opportunity would be awaited, the slaves would be brought down to the shore, embarked at sunset, and by the following morning, with a fair wind, the dhow would have well-nigh reached the opposite coast of Arabia.

It was frequently pressed upon me during the year 1889 that the only remedy for this state of things was to reoccupy Tokar, which is the granary of the Eastern Soudan. It was pointed out that, if Osman Digna were once driven out of Tokar, he would be no longer able to obtain supplies, and would perforce be obliged to evacuate the Eastern Soudan. For some while, I hesitated to move. I was reluctant to undertake offensive operations of any kind in the Soudan, and, moreover, I was aware that any proposed advance would be viewed with great dislike in England. At last, however, I came to the conclusion that the reoccupation of Tokar was desirable, and that as a military operation it presented no great difficulty. In the spring of 1890, I submitted these views to the British Government.

Lord Salisbury, who then presided at the Foreign Office, was not on principle averse to the employment of force, but, before sanctioning its employment, he wished to be convinced that the adoption of such a course was both necessary and desirable. He habitually viewed military arguments with suspicion. At a later period, when there was a question of giving up to Turkey some forts garrisoned by Egyptian troops on the coast of Midian, Lord Salisbury wrote to me privately: "I would not be too much impressed by what the soldiers tell you about the strategic importance of these places. It is their way. If they were allowed full scope, they would insist on the importance of garrisoning the moon in order to protect us from Mars."

In the case now under discussion, Lord Salisbury was not convinced of the desirability of departing from a defensive attitude.[1] The matter was, therefore, allowed to drop for a while.

[1] Lord Salisbury's objections to an advance on Tokar were stated to me in a private letter, dated March 28, 1890, in the following terms: "The arguments against taking Tokar appear to me to be that the operation must involve some money, and may involve very much, and that the finances of Egypt, though no longer in an embarrassed condition, are only convalescent, and a very slight imprudence might throw them back into the condition from which they have been so painfully and laboriously drawn. Again, when once you have permitted a military advance, the extent of that military advance scarcely remains within your own discretion. It is always open to the military authorities to discover in the immediate vicinity of the area to which your orders confine them, some danger against which it is absolutely necessary to guard, some strategic position whose invaluable qualities will repay ten times any risk or cost that its occupation may involve. You have no means of arguing against them. They are upon their own territory, and can set down your opposition to civilian ignorance; and so, step by step, the imperious exactions of military necessity will lead you on into the desert. To these considerations I must add that they will appear infinitely magnified to the terrified minds of people here at home. They were so deeply impressed with the disasters of six years ago, and the apparently inexorable necessity which had driven them into situations where those disasters were inevitable, that they shrink instinctively from any proposal to advance into the Egyptian desert. I do not say that this is a sufficient argument to prevent such

In the autumn of 1890, the subject was again brought to my notice. "I am convinced," Sir Francis Grenfell wrote, "that the time has come when, without any strain on the finances of the country, and without any assistance from English troops, the country as far as Tokar could be pacified." I reconsidered the question carefully. The evils resulting from the presence of the Dervishes in the neighbourhood of Suakin were daily becoming more apparent. I was more than ever convinced that, as a military operation, the reoccupation of Tokar presented no great difficulties, and that it would not involve any considerable expenditure of money. More than this, I felt certain that there was no serious risk of being dragged into offensive operations on a large scale in the Soudan. No one was more open to conviction than Lord Salisbury. Knowing this, I pressed him to reconsider the matter. Eventually, on February 7, 1891, Lord Salisbury telegraphed to me that the Government sanctioned the occupation of Tokar.

Reinforcements were now sent to Suakin. On February 13, Colonel Holled Smith, with a force of about 2000 men, occupied Trinkitat without opposition. On the 16th, he advanced in the direction of El Teb. On the 19th, he came in contact with the enemy at a short distance from the town of Tokar. A sharp engagement ensued. "The Dervishes," Colonel Holled Smith reported, "pushed home their attack with their usual intrepidity and fearlessness. The troops, however, stood their ground, and did not yield one inch throughout the line." Finally, the Dervishes were routed with heavy loss. Osman Digna escaped, but most of

an advance, if there is a clear balance of undoubted advantage in its favour; but, in the absence of any such evidence, it must be accepted as a strong presumption."

his leading Emirs were killed. The Egyptian loss was 10 killed, including one English officer, and 48 wounded. Whatever remained of the Dervish force fled in confusion towards Kassala. The defeat of the Dervishes was hailed with genuine satisfaction by the population. The number of persons found at Tokar who had been subjected to mutilation of the most cruel description, bore ample testimony to the barbarity of Dervish rule.

The Tokar expedition was, therefore, a complete success. It accomplished for the Eastern Soudan what Toski did for the valley of the Nile. It cleared the country of Dervishes, and enabled the work of the civilian reformer to commence.[1]

To sum up—the three important military events, which took place, during the years immediately following the evacuation of the Soudan in 1885, were, first, the defeat of the Dervishes before Suakin on December 20, 1888; this relieved the pressure on Suakin, but did not produce any further result of importance. Secondly, the defeat of Nejumi's force at Toski on August 3, 1889; this broke the aggressive power of the Dervishes and tranquillised the Nile valley. Thirdly, the defeat of Osman Digna near Tokar on February 19, 1891; this permitted an Egyptian reoccupation of the province of Tokar, and tranquillised the greater part of the Eastern Soudan. After many years of painful transition, therefore, Egypt, reduced to manageable dimensions, at last acquired a settled frontier, which the Egyptian Government were able to defend with the military and financial resources at their disposal.

If a regenerated Egypt is now springing up, its

[1] On February 13, Lord Salisbury wrote to me: "Up to the time when I write all seems to have gone well with the Tokar expedition; very little notice is taken of it here. We are thinking of nothing except strikes, and of the later cantos of the epic of Kitty O'Shea."

existence is in a great measure due to the fact that, through good and evil report, the policy of withdrawing from the Soudan and adhering to a strictly defensive attitude on the Egyptian frontier was steadily maintained for some years.

CHAPTER XXXII

THE RECONQUEST OF KHARTOUM

October 1895–September 1898

Necessity of reconquering the Soudan—Danger of premature action—The Italian defeat at Adua—It is decided to advance on Dongola—Provision of funds—Sir Herbert Kitchener—Indian expedition to Suakin—Railway construction—Battle of Firket—Capture of Dongola—The Egyptian Government repay the money advanced by the Commissioners of the Debt—The British Government advance £800,000—Question of a further offensive movement—Capture of Abu Hamed and Berber—Reoccupation of Kassala—British troops sent to the Soudan—The battle of the Atbara—The battle of Omdurman—Cost of the campaign—The War Office—The policy of reconquest.

The Soudan had been left derelict, not so much because the cargo was valueless, but rather because no hands were available to effect the salvage. It was, however, certain from the first that the reconquest of some, at all events, of the lost provinces would, sooner or later, have to be undertaken. To those who were well acquainted with all the circumstances, it might, indeed, be clear that England was not responsible for the loss of the Soudan, but the broad fact, which had sunk into the minds of the British public, was this—that during a period when British influence was paramount in Egypt, certain provinces, which had before been open to trade, and which might have been subjected to the influences of civilisation, had been allowed to relapse into barbarism. The national honour was touched. It was thought that the British

Government, even if not originally responsible for the loss of the provinces, would become responsible if no endeavour were made to effect their reconquest. A sense of shame was very generally felt that, under British auspices, Egyptian territory should have undergone such severe shrinkage. The popular sentiment on the subject found expression in the feeling that "Gordon should be avenged."

It was from the first obvious that the partial reconquest of the Soudan was not beyond the military and financial resources of England, but little inclination was for some while shown, either by successive Governments or by public opinion, to employ those resources in order to attain the object in view. The problem, which apparently had to be faced, was how the Egyptian Government, with but little or no British help, could reassert their authority in the Soudan. It was a necessary condition to the solution of this problem that it should not entail any increase to the fiscal burdens of the Egyptian people, and that it should not involve any serious risk that the affairs of Egypt proper, which were beginning to settle down, should relapse into disorder.

During the years which immediately followed the retreat of the troops after the abortive Gordon expedition, the main danger, against which it was necessary to guard, was to prevent the British and Egyptian Governments from being driven into premature action by the small but influential section of public opinion which persistently and strenuously advocated the cause of immediate reconquest. During all this period, therefore, I was careful in all my published reports to lay special stress on the desirability of inaction. Indeed, my personal opinion was that the period of enforced inaction would last longer than was actually the case. If, about the year 1886, I had been asked how long a time would probably elapse before it would be possible for the Egyptian Government to abandon a defensive and to assume an offensive policy in the valley of the Nile, I should have conjecturally fixed the period at about twenty-five years. As a matter of fact, the Egyptian army reoccupied Dongola and Berber about twelve years, and Khartoum thirteen years after their abandonment. The main reason why my forecast proved erroneous was that the conditions of the problem were changed. The Egyptian Government were not left to deal single-handed with the military and financial situation. Valuable assistance, both in men and money, was afforded by England.

Before any thought of reconquest could be entertained, two conditions had to be fulfilled. In the first place, the Egyptian army had to be rendered efficient. In the second place, not only had the solvency of the Egyptian Treasury to be assured, but funds had to be provided for the extraordinary expenditure which the assumption of an offensive policy would certainly involve.

The engagements which took place in 1888-89 in the neighbourhood of Suakin and in the Nile valley, showed that some confidence could be placed in the Egyptian army.

Financial rehabilitation and material progress in every direction proceeded at a far more rapid pace than had been anticipated. By 1895, the reconquest of the Soudan had begun to be generally discussed as an undertaking, which would probably be capable of realisation at no very remote period.

In October 1895, the question was raised in the following form. For some while previous, a scheme for holding up the water of the Nile in a large reservoir had been under consideration. By the autumn of 1895, the discussions on the technical aspects of the proposal were so far advanced as to justify the conclusion that action might before long be taken. It was at the time thought that the Egyptian Treasury could not deal simultaneously with both the reservoir and the Soudan.[1] Unless financial help were to be afforded from England, the wisest plan would be to construct the reservoir, and to postpone *sine die* the question of reoccupying the Soudan. Subsequently, the increase of revenue derived from the construction of the reservoir might, it was thought, provide funds which would enable the Soudan to be reconquered. I, therefore, asked the British Government what was their view on this subject. I was told in reply (November 15, 1895) that there was not any present prospect of the Government consenting to the despatch of a military expedition into the Soudan, and that, therefore, the financial arrangements of the Egyptian Government could be made without reference to the cost of any such expedition.

When I received this communication, I thought that the question of reconquering the Soudan had been definitely postponed for some years to come. I was wrong. I was about to receive another object-lesson on the danger of indulging in political prophecy. The utterances of the Oracle of Dodona depended on the breeze which stirred the branches of the speaking oaks around the temple of Zeus. Those of the London oracle are scarcely less uncertain. They depend on the ephemeral indications of the political barometer. When I propounded the question of whether the construction of the reservoir was to be preferred to Soudan reconquest, a steady breeze of caution was blowing

[1] Eventually, an arrangement was made under which the Nile reservoir at Assouan was constructed simultaneously with the Soudan operations. The financial difficulty was met by postponing payment for the reservoir until it was completed.

amongst the political oaks of London. The oracle pronounced, in no uncertain language, in favour of the reservoir. But a sharp squall was about to come up from an opposite direction, with the result that in the twinkling of an eye the decision was reversed, and the oracle pronounced as decisively in favour of an advance into the Soudan as it had previously, under different barometrical indications, rejected any such idea.

The change was in some degree the outcome of the rapid growth of the Imperialist spirit, which about this time took place in England, but the more immediate cause was the turn which affairs took at Massowah. The Italians were being hard pressed by the Abyssinians. Rumours were afloat that the latter were in league with the Dervishes, who were about to attack Kassala. Early in January 1896, some discussion, which was not productive of any practical result, took place as to whether a demonstration, which might possibly relieve the pressure on the Italian forces, could not advantageously be made either from Wadi Halfa or Suakin. Eventually on March 1, the Italian army under General Baratieri was totally defeated by King Menelek's forces in the neighbourhood of Adua.

This brought matters to a crisis. The Italian Ambassador in London urged that a diversion should be made in Italian interests. On March 12, therefore, it was suddenly decided to reoccupy Dongola. It cannot be doubted that this decision was taken and publicly announced with somewhat excessive haste. The financial and military difficulties, which would have to be encountered, were inadequately considered. But it is not on that account to be inferred that the decision was unwise. The absence of consistency, which is so frequently noticeable in the aims of British policy, is, indeed, a never-ending source of embarrassment to those on whom devolves the duty of carrying that policy into execution. A British Prime Minister appears to be in the position of the steersman of a surf-boat lying outside the mouth of an African river. He has to wait for a high wave to carry him over the bar. In the particular instance in point, it appeared at the time that it would on many grounds have been wiser to have delayed action. The arguments based on the desirability of helping the Italians, and of checking any possible advance on the part of the Dervishes, although of some weight, were not conclusive. On the other hand, the policy of eventual reconquest was sound. It is not always possible in politics to choose beforehand the time and method of action. The opportunity must be seized when it occurs. Whether the British steersman was right or wrong in selecting the Italian wave to float him over the Soudan bar, depended in a great measure on whether the operation was or was not successfully conducted. At the time, I was inclined to think the action premature, but there could be no doubt that, when once it had been decided to act, no effort should be spared to ensure success. It was also very necessary to combat the idea, which at first found some favour in London, that the operations should be limited to a mere demonstration so far as Akasha, a short distance south of Wadi Halfa. It was manifest that the advance should either not be undertaken at all, or else that it should be made with the intention of permanently occupying the country at once as far as Dongola, and eventually at least as far as Khartoum. There was something to be said in favour of delay before embarking on a forward policy. There was nothing whatever to be said in favour of trifling with the question. It was essential to discard absolutely the vacillation of the past in dealing with Soudan matters. The idea of limiting the operations to a demonstration was speedily abandoned.

When once it had been decided to advance, one of the first questions which naturally arose was how funds were to be provided for the expenses of the expedition.

Egypt has throughout the occupation benefited greatly by the tendency which exists in England towards administrative decentralisation. No serious attempt has ever been made to govern Egypt from London. It cannot be doubted that this system is wise. It has enabled us to avoid the numberless errors which generally result from the highly centralised systems generally adopted on the continent of Europe. But even a sound system may have some disadvantages, although of a nature in no serious degree to outweigh its merits. One disadvantage of the British system is that, inasmuch as the details of all Egyptian affairs are managed in Egypt, few, if any, of the officials employed in the London public offices are intimately acquainted with all the intricate windings of the Egyptian financial and administrative labyrinth. This ignorance, although ordinarily beneficent, has at times produced some strange and even embarrassing results. In this particular instance, the authorities sitting in London were aware that Egyptian finance was in a flourishing condition. Moreover, they knew that large sums of money, the savings of past years, had accumulated in the Treasury. They considered that the reconquest of Dongola was an Egyptian interest, and that the Egyptian Treasury might justly be called upon to bear the expenses. The possibility of any charge devolving on the British Treasury had not, in the first instance at all events, been adequately considered. It was held not only that the Egyptian Government ought to pay, but that they would be able to pay. The fact that the key of the Egyptian Treasure-house was in international keeping had been insufficiently appreciated, even if it had not been altogether forgotten. It was impossible to obtain access to the accumulations of past years without the consent of the Commissioners of the Debt.

Application was accordingly made to the Commissioners for a grant of £E.500,000 from the General Reserve Fund, in order to cover the expenses of the Dongola expedition. By a majority of four to two, the Commissioners granted the request. The money was paid into the Egyptian Treasury. The French and Russian Commissioners, who constituted the dissentient minority, instantly commenced an action against the Egyptian Government in the Mixed Tribunal of First Instance at Cairo.

The judgment of the Tribunal was delivered on June 8. The Egyptian Government were directed to repay the money granted by the Commissioners of the Debt. An appeal was at once made to the higher Court sitting at Alexandria, with results which will presently be described.

Simultaneously with the financial question, the composition and command of the force had to be considered.

A British battalion was sent from Cairo to Wadi Halfa, more as an indication that in case of need English help would be forthcoming than for any other reason. Some British officers were temporarily lent to the Egyptian army, but beyond this assistance, it was decided to employ only Egyptian troops in the Nile valley.

The command of the force was left to the Sirdar of the Egyptian army, Sir Herbert Kitchener. A better choice could not have been made. Young, energetic, ardently and exclusively devoted to his profession, and, as the honourable scars on his face testified, experienced in Soudanese warfare, Sir Herbert Kitchener possessed all the qualities necessary to bring the campaign to a successful issue. Like many another military commander, the bonds which united him and his subordinates were those of stern discipline on the one side, and, on the other, the respect due to superior talent and the confidence felt in the resourcefulness of a strong and masterful spirit, rather than the affectionate obedience yielded to the behests of a genial chief. When the campaign was over, there were not wanting critics who whispered that Sir Herbert Kitchener's success had been due as much to good luck as to good management. If, it was said, a number of events had happened, which, as a matter of fact, did not happen, the result might have been different. The same may be said of any military commander and of any campaign. Fortune is proverbially fickle in war. The greatest captain of ancient times spoke of "Fortuna, quae plurimum potest quum in reliquis rebus tum praecipue in bello."[1] The fact, however, is that Sir Herbert Kitchener's main merit was that he left as little as possible to chance. A first-rate military administrator, every detail of the machine, with which he had to work, received adequate attention. Before any decisive movement was made, each portion of the machine was adapted, so far as human foresight could provide, to perform its allotted task.

Sir Herbert Kitchener also possessed another quality which is rare among soldiers, and which was of special value under the circumstances then existing. He did not think that extravagance was the necessary handmaid of efficiency. On the contrary, he was a rigid economist, and, whilst

[1] Caesar, *De Bello Civili*, iii. 68.

making adequate provision for all essential and necessary expenditure, suppressed with a firm hand any tendency towards waste and extravagance.

Although it was intended that, with the exception of one British battalion, only Egyptian troops should be employed in the advance on Dongola, at the same time, in view of the uncertainty prevailing as to the amount of resistance likely to be encountered from the Dervishes, it was thought desirable to relieve the Egyptian army temporarily of the duty of guarding Suakin, and thus enable the Sirdar to concentrate all his available forces in the valley of the Nile. An Indian force of about 2500 fighting men was, therefore, despatched to Suakin. It arrived early in June, and left in the following December.

Although these Indian troops merely performed garrison duties, they rendered services of great value; their presence at Suakin relieved both the British and Egyptian Governments of all anxiety as regarded the affairs of the Eastern Soudan.

In conformity with the plan adopted throughout this narrative, no attempt will be made to give a detailed account of the campaign of 1896. A brief statement of the principal incidents will suffice.

From the first it was manifest that one of the main difficulties was how to transport the food and stores for the army whilst on the march to Dongola. Few of those who have not been directly or indirectly concerned with the operations of war, fully appreciate the fact that at least three-fourths of the time of a military commander on active service are taken up with devising means for keeping his own troops alive. "A starving army," the Duke of Wellington wrote from Portugal, "is actually worse than none at all." When, as in the present case, the march of the army lies through a barren and desolate country, and when, in the absence of roads and wheeled transport, every pound of biscuit and every extra round of ammunition has to be carried on the backs of camels, whose slow uniform pace no eagerness on the part of the commander of the force can mend, it may readily be conceived that the difficulties of supply and transport are greatly increased. River transport could only be used in certain localities, that is to say, where the navigation of the Nile was unimpeded by rapids. The obvious solution of these difficulties was to continue in a southerly direction the railway, which already existed between Wadi Halfa and Sarras, the most distant outpost held by the Egyptian army. Akasha, some fifty miles south of Sarras, was accordingly occupied without resistance on March 20. Work on the railway, which was eventually to terminate at Kerma, a few miles short of Dongola, was at once commenced.[1]

The details of the plan of campaign were, of course, left entirely to the discretion of the Sirdar. I had, however, fully discussed the general scheme of operations with him before he left Cairo. The main point was to bring on an action at an early period of the campaign. Once victorious, even on a small scale, the Egyptian troops would acquire confidence in themselves, and the enemy would be proportionately discouraged. It was desirable not to allow the Dervishes to retreat without fighting, and thus delay any action till Dongola was reached. The smallest check had above all things to be avoided. It would be magnified in the eyes of the world, and although perhaps of slight intrinsic

[1] This line, which was very roughly constructed, has now been abandoned. The produce of the Dongola Province will, in future, be conveyed to Port Soudan partly by water, and partly by a railway which extends from Abu Hamed westwards along the right bank of the Nile as far as Kereima.

importance, would produce a bad moral effect. In war, the moral is to the physical as three to one. Nowhere has the truth of this celebrated Napoleonic maxim been more fully exemplified than in the successive petty campaigns which have been conducted in the Soudan. The Sirdar's generalship had, therefore, to be shown in obliging the Dervishes to fight under conditions as regards topography and relative numbers, which would be favourable to the troops under his command.

The general plan of campaign arranged in Cairo was executed to the letter. By the beginning of June, the railway had been constructed to within a few miles of Akasha. A force of about 3500 Dervishes was known to be at Firket, some sixteen miles south of Akasha. It was determined to surprise this force. The utmost secrecy was preserved. On the night of June 6, two columns, numbering in all about 10,000 men, marched by convergent routes, with the object of meeting in the early morning, and surrounding the Dervish camp before a retreat could be made. An operation, the success of which depends on the opportune concentration of two separate columns at a given time and place, is always difficult of execution. The difficulties are enhanced when the march takes place at night. So skilfully, however, were all the arrangements planned and conducted, that the object which it was sought to attain was fully secured. Early on the morning of June 7, the Dervishes, completely taken by surprise, were attacked and routed with heavy loss both in killed and prisoners. The Egyptian loss was 20 killed and 80 wounded. The cavalry continued the pursuit for some miles beyond the battlefield.

Three laborious months followed the battle of Firket. Cholera broke out in the camp, and, in spite of the energy and self-sacrifice of the medical officers, was not suppressed before many valuable lives had been lost. Storms of unprecedented violence occurred, with the result that large stretches of the railway embankment were washed away and had to be reconstructed. But these and many other obstacles were eventually overcome. The dogged perseverance of the British officers, and the willing obedience of the sturdy black and fellaheen troops, were proof against excessive heat, sandstorms, and other incidents which had to be encountered in this inhospitable region.

The whole force, from General to private, deserved success, and they succeeded. After a sharp conflict at Hafir, on which occasion the gunboats, which had been dragged with much labour up the Cataracts, did excellent service, Dongola was occupied on September 23. The campaign was virtually over. At a cost of 411 lives, of whom 364 died from cholera and other diseases, and of £E.715,000 in money—a figure which bore testimony to the Sirdar's economical administration—the province of Dongola had been reclaimed from barbarism. On September 26, the furthest Egyptian outpost was fixed at Merowi, the ancient capital of the Ethiopian Queens of the Candace dynasty, situated at the foot of the Fourth Cataract.

The financial campaign lasted rather longer than the military. It was not altogether inglorious. The Judges of the Court of Appeal—or at all events the majority of them—could not altogether shake themselves free from the political electricity with which the atmosphere of Egypt was at this time so heavily charged. On December 6, the Court condemned the course adopted by the majority of the Commissioners of the Debt as illegal, and ordered the Egyptian Government to refund the money.

I had anticipated the judgment of the Court,

and was, therefore, prepared to act. Immediately after its delivery, I was authorised to promise the Egyptian Government pecuniary help from England. At that time, the Egyptian Treasury happened to be full. It was desirable to act promptly and thus bar the way to international complications. On December 6, four days after the delivery of the judgment, the total sum due, amounting to £E.515,000, was—somewhat to the dismay of official circles in London—paid to the Commissioners of the Debt. Subsequently, with the consent of Parliament, the British Treasury advanced a sum of £800,000 to the Egyptian Government at $2\frac{3}{4}$ per cent interest.

Such, therefore, are the main political, military, and financial facts connected with the reconquest of Dongola. The episode is one to which both Englishmen and Egyptians may look back with pride and satisfaction.

I conceive that in all civilised countries—and perhaps notably in England—the theory of government is that a question of peace or war is one to be decided by politicians. The functions of the soldier are supposed to be confined, in the first place, to advising on the purely military aspects of the issues involved; and, in the second place, to giving effect to any decisions at which the Government may arrive. It has, however, often been said that the practice in this matter not unfrequently differs from the theory; that the soldier, who is generally prone to advocate vigorous action, is inclined to encroach on the sphere which should properly be reserved for the politician; that the former is often masterful and the latter weak, too easily dazzled by the glitter of arms, or too readily lured onwards by the siren voice of some strategist to acquire an almost endless set of what, in technical language, are called "keys" to some position; and that when this happens, the soldier, who is himself unconsciously influenced by a laudable desire to obtain personal distinction, practically dictates the policy of the nation without taking a sufficiently comprehensive view of national interests. Considerations of this nature have more especially been, from time to time, advanced in connection with the numerous frontier wars which have occurred in India. That they contain a certain element of truth can scarcely be doubted. My own experience in such matters leads me to the conclusion that in most semi-military, semi-political affairs there is generally an early stage when the politician, if he chooses to do so, can exercise complete and effective control over the action of the soldier, but that when once that control has been even slightly relaxed, it cannot be regained until, by the course of subsequent events, some fresh development occurs bringing with it a favourable opportunity for the reassertion of civil and political authority.

Thus, in the case of the Soudan, so long as the frontier remained at Wadi Halfa, the policy of the British and Egyptian Governments was well under control. It was possible to weigh the arguments for and against an advance, and to deliberate upon the ultimate consequences, military, political, and financial, if an advance was undertaken. But when once the first onward step had been made, the period for deliberation, even in respect to matters which were not perhaps fully within the original purview of the two Governments, or at all events of the British Government, was at an end. No one, who had seriously considered the subject, imagined for one moment that any sure halting-place could be found between Wadi Halfa and Khartoum. In the spring of 1896, it was possible to adduce reasons of some weight in favour of postponing the reconquest of the Soudan. In the autumn of the same year, it was not possible to adduce a single valid argument in favour of remaining inactive and delaying the completion of the work, which had been already begun. A certain amount of hesitation was, however, in the first instance, displayed before the inevitable conclusion was accepted that the British Government had committed themselves to a policy, which involved the reconquest of the whole of the Soudan. This hesitation was probably due more to financial timidity, and to the reluctance always felt by British Ministers to decide on anything but the issue of the moment, rather than to any failure to realise the true facts of the situation. It was not till February 5, 1897, that the Chancellor of the Exchequer (Sir Michael Hicks Beach), speaking in the House of Commons, publicly recognised that "Egypt could never be held to be permanently secure so long as a hostile Power was in occupation of the Nile valley up to Khartoum," and that the duty of giving a final blow to the "baleful power of the Khalifa" devolved on England.

Some months before this declaration was made, the British Government were, however, practically and irrevocably committed to an offensive policy. Shortly after the capture of Dongola, the construction of a railway to connect Wadi Halfa and Abu Hamed was commenced.

Thanks to the energy and skill of the young Engineer officers to whom this important work was entrusted, two-thirds of the line were completed by August 1897. The Sirdar then determined to occupy Abu Hamed. A column under General Hunter moved from Merowi up the river. Abu Hamed was occupied,[1] on August 7, after a

[1] The interval which elapsed between the occupation of Abu Hamed and the final advance on Khartoum was a period of much anxiety. Sir Herbert Kitchener's force depended entirely on the desert railway for

sharp combat, in which the Egyptian army lost 27 killed, including two British officers, and 61 wounded. Almost the whole of the Dervish force was either killed or taken prisoner. Evidence was steadily accumulating that the Egyptian soldiers were inspired by a very different spirit from that which prevailed fifteen years previously, when the troops of Arábi fled ignominiously almost at the first cannon shot.

On August 31, Berber, which was evacuated by the Dervishes, was occupied by the Egyptian troops. The construction of the railway from Abu Hamed to Berber was at once taken in hand.

In the meanwhile, the Italians, who but a short time before had been eager to occupy the Kassala district, were clamorous to abandon a possession, which they found expensive and of doubtful utility. On Christmas Day 1897, Kassala was occupied by an Egyptian force commanded by Colonel Parsons.

In the Nile valley, no considerable change took place in the situation for some months after the occupation of Berber. It was clear that, without the aid of British troops, Khartoum could not be retaken, but nothing definite had as yet been decided as to their employment. All hesitation was eventually removed by the force of circumstances. Towards the close of the year 1897,

its supplies. I was rather haunted with the idea that some European adventurer, of the type familiar in India a century and more ago, might turn up at Khartoum and advise the Dervishes to make frequent raids across the Nile below Abu Hamed, with a view to cutting the communication of the Anglo-Egyptian force with Wadi Halfa. This was unquestionably the right military operation to have undertaken; neither, I think, would it have been very difficult of accomplishment. Fortunately, however, the Dervishes were themselves devoid of all military qualities, with the exception of undaunted courage, and did not invite any European assistance. They, therefore, failed to take advantage of the opportunity presented to them. To myself, it was a great relief when the period of suspense was over. I do not think that the somewhat perilous position in which Sir Herbert Kitchener's army was unquestionably placed for some time was at all realised by the public in general.

reports were rife of an intention on the part of the Dervishes to take the offensive. Whatever doubt might exist as to the time when a further onward movement should be undertaken, there could be but one opinion as to the necessity of defending the territory already gained. Retreat was out of the question. The Dervish challenge had to be accepted. I had encouraged the Sirdar to ask for British troops directly he thought their presence necessary. On the first day of the year 1898, he sent me an historic telegram, which virtually sealed the fate of the Soudan. "General Hunter," he said, "reports confirming news of a Dervish advance. I think that British troops should be sent to Abu Hamed, and that reinforcements should be sent to Egypt in case of necessity. The fight for the Soudan would appear to be likely to take place at Berber." Four British battalions were at once sent up the Nile. The Cairo garrison was increased. Manifestly, the curtain had gone up on the last scene in the drama, which commenced with the destruction of General Hicks's army fifteen years previously.

A few days after the first demand for troops had been communicated to me, the Sirdar telegraphed that, when the final advance to Khartoum was made, he would require, in addition to the British troops about to be sent to the Soudan, another infantry brigade of four battalions, a regiment of cavalry and a battery of field artillery. His forecast of the force which would be necessary was wonderfully accurate. The force which eventually advanced on Khartoum some six months later, was precisely identical with that which Sir Herbert Kitchener specified early in January 1898. To have advanced with a smaller force would have been dangerous. A larger force would have been unwieldy, and its employment would have increased the difficulties of transport and supply. Amongst other high military qualities, the Sirdar possessed the knowledge of how to adapt his means to his end.

The threatened Dervish advance rendered necessary the despatch of British troops to the Soudan six months before the rise of the Nile allowed of free navigation. Climate, it was thought at the time, might possibly be the most dangerous enemy which would have to be encountered. Some discussion, therefore, ensued as to whether it would not be possible to send up two British brigades at once, and advance straightway on Khartoum. The idea was, however, speedily abandoned. The difficulties of transport and supply would have been enormous. At least 7000 camels, which it would have been well-nigh impossible to have obtained, would have been required. It was, therefore, decided to stand on the defensive, and to await the favourable season before striking a final blow at the Dervish stronghold at Omdurman.

By the beginning of March, a force consisting of one British and two Egyptian brigades, together with a regiment of Egyptian cavalry, 24 field and horse artillery guns, and 12 Maxims, had been concentrated between Berber and the junction of the Atbara and the Nile, where a strong entrenched camp was formed.

About the middle of February, a Dervish force of about 12,000 men, under the command of the Emir Mahmoud, which had been stationed at Metemmeh, crossed to the right bank of the river. Contradictory reports continued to be received as to the intentions of this force. It was known that dissension existed amongst the Dervish leaders. Eventually, Mahmoud abandoned the idea of moving up the right bank of the river. He struck across the desert, and established himself at Nakheila on the Atbara, some 35 miles from its mouth. On March 20, the Sirdar began to move slowly up the Atbara to meet him.

A pause of some duration then ensued. It was hoped that Mahmoud would attack, but time went on and he showed no disposition to move.

On April 1, the Sirdar telegraphed to me as follows :—

"I am rather perplexed by the situation here. Mahmoud remains stationary and his army is very badly off for supplies, and deserters keep coming in to us, though not in such large numbers as I expected. He is waiting apparently for instructions from the Khalifa before advancing or retiring. It seems to be thought by the deserters that, as a retirement would be an acknowledgment of fear, he will eventually advance. Here we are well off and healthy, with sufficient transport, fresh bread every second day, and fresh meat every day. Yesterday, I discussed the situation with Gatacre and Hunter; the former was inclined to attack Mahmoud's present position, the latter to wait here. We should have great advantage of ground if Mahmoud will advance, but if he retires without our attacking him, the opportunity will have been lost of dealing a blow by which future resistance in the Soudan would probably be considerably affected. I have little doubt of the success of our attack on his present entrenched position, though it would probably entail considerable loss. I have decided not to change present policy for three days, before which something definite will, I hope, be known. I should be glad to learn your views on the subject."

The point which struck me most in this message was that General Hunter doubted the wisdom of attacking. I knew him to be a fighting General. Moreover, he had seen Mahmoud's position. On the previous day (March 31), he had returned from a cavalry reconnaissance, as to the results of which the Sirdar had reported to me: "General Hunter was able to get within 300 yards of the enemy's trenches. Position is a strong one with Zariba (stockade) and in heavy bush; it was so thick that they were unable to get more than a partial view of the encampment. Enemy was lying thick in the trenches, which were in some places in three rows, one behind the other." I thought it not improbable that General Hunter, who well knew the strong and weak points of the Egyptian army, hesitated to attack because he was unwilling to risk what might possibly be a hand-to-hand encounter between the Egyptian soldiers and the Dervishes in the "heavy bush" to which allusion was made in this telegram. Past experience in Soudanese warfare enjoined special caution in respect to this point.

On April 2, therefore, I sent the Sirdar the following message, which represented the joint opinion of Sir Francis Grenfell and myself:—

"The following observations are not to be regarded as instructions. It is for you to form a final opinion on their value, as they are merely remarks on the position as it strikes me at a distance. In case you should think it desirable to act contrary to the view to which I incline, I have no desire to cripple your full liberty of action. I wish to assure you that, whatever you may decide to do, you will receive full support both from myself and, I am sure I may add, from the authorities at home.[1]

"You have the following arguments against an immediate attack:—

[1] I repeated to London the Sirdar's telegram of April 1, and at once received the following reply from Mr. Arthur Balfour, who was in charge of the Foreign Office during the temporary absence of Lord Salisbury:—

"The Sirdar may count on the support of Her Majesty's Government whichever course he decides on adopting. Unless he wishes for a military opinion, we refrain from offering any remarks which would interfere with his absolute discretion."

"(1) The extreme importance of obviating, so far as is possible, any risk of reverse, both on local and general grounds.

"(2) That it is rather imprudent to try your force too high in view of the composition of a portion of it.

"(3) The great importance, as has been shown by all former experience of Soudanese warfare, of choosing ground for an engagement which will be favourable to the action of a disciplined and well-armed force.

"(4) The weight of Hunter's opinion. Though I have the greatest confidence in Gatacre, Hunter has more experience in Soudanese warfare, is better acquainted with the Egyptian army, and has, moreover, seen the present Dervish position. This latter is more especially a consideration of the utmost importance.

"(5) The fact that Mahmoud probably cannot stay for long where he is, and that he will be discredited and his men probably discouraged if he retires without fighting.

"You have on the other side the argument that Mahmoud's force, if he now retires without fighting, will go to strengthen the resistance to be ultimately encountered.

"The weight of this argument, though undoubted, does not appear to me sufficient to counterbalance the arguments on the other side, more especially if it be remembered that your British force will be practically doubled in the autumn, if the decisive moment is delayed till then.

"Patience, therefore, is what I am inclined to advise. I am disposed to think that you had better not attack for the present, but wait your opportunity for action and allow events to develop. The above is fully agreed in by General Grenfell, with whom I have discussed the whole question thoroughly."

Before the Sirdar had received this telegram, he sent me (April 3) the following further message:—

"The same story of privation is told by more deserters who are coming in. There is an increased desertion of blacks resulting from the capture of the women at Shendy, which is now known.

"Generals Hunter and Gatacre and myself now think an attack upon Mahmoud's position advisable. We shall probably make it on the 6th April.

"I will postpone the forward movement if your answer to my last telegram, which I have not yet received, should be against this course."

This was followed by a further telegram sent on the same day (April 3) after receipt of my reply to the first inquiry. "I will," the Sirdar said, "for the present postpone the attack on Mahmoud's position, in view of your opinion as stated in your telegram. So as to get new ground and water, we shall to-morrow move about 2½ miles farther on."

When I knew of the change in General Hunter's opinion, my own hesitation as regards attacking completely disappeared. I was unable to consult Sir Francis Grenfell, who was temporarily absent from Cairo, but I at once telegraphed to the Sirdar:—

"With reference to your telegram of yesterday, our telegrams crossed. Do not be deterred by my first telegram from attacking if, after careful consideration, you think it advisable to do so. It is very difficult to give any valuable opinion from here. In your first telegram the point which struck me most was that Hunter, who has seen the Dervish position, was adverse to an advance. He has now, I understand, come round to the other view. The case is, to my mind, materially altered by this. I must leave the decision to you, only again assuring you of full support whatever you decide."

The next day (April 4) I received the following reply:—

"The confidence which yourself and the Home authorities repose in me is greatly appreciated by me. I propose to advance more slowly and with greater deliberation than was originally my intention, and to make as sure as it is possible to do by careful reconnaissances of the success of an attack. I shall not commit myself to a general attack until the right moment has, in my opinion, arrived. The difficulty is at present to know with any certainty how long the Dervishes can hold out under the privations they are undergoing. I think that by getting nearer to them I shall have a better opportunity of satisfying myself on this point."

It was clear that a decisive engagement was imminent. I awaited the result with confidence.

Early on the morning of April 8 (Good Friday), the attack was delivered. After forty minutes' sharp fighting, Mahmoud was a prisoner, 2000 of his men lay dead in their entrenchments, others had surrendered, whilst a large number of those who escaped subsequently died of wounds or thirst in the thick bush on the left bank of the river. The victory was complete, but it cost many valuable lives. Of the British brigade, 4 officers and 104 non-commissioned officers and men, and of the Egyptian army, 5 British and 16 Egyptian officers, as well as 422 non-commissioned officers and men, were killed and wounded. The brunt of the Egyptian fighting fell on the black troops.

Some faint hopes were at one time entertained that the Dervishes would be so demoralised by the crushing defeat they had experienced on the Atbara, that no further resistance would be offered, and that the capture of Khartoum would be peacefully effected. These hopes were not destined to be realised. Had not the impostor who in cruel and depraved state reigned supreme at Khartoum promised his credulous followers, whose fate was about to excite alike pity and admiration, that, although the infidels would be allowed to advance to within a few miles of the walls of Omdurman, their skulls in countless numbers would eventually whiten the Kereri plain? It soon became clear that, in spite of the recent victory, a further application of the Bismarckian blood-and-iron policy would alone suffice to shake the heroic steadfastness with which these savage Soudanese warriors clung to an execrable cause.

I need not describe in detail the measures which were preliminary to the final effort. It will be sufficient for me to say that the first British brigade —possibly encouraged by achieved success, and buoyed up by the hope of coming excitement— bore the summer heat of the Soudan well. As had been pre-arranged, a second brigade was sent up the Nile in the course of the month of July. By the end of August, the Sirdar had concentrated a force of about 22,000 men some 40 miles south of Khartoum.

As was my custom, I had left Egypt in the middle of July, intending to return before the final blow was struck. On all grounds, it was desirable to expedite matters, but the military movements depended in a great degree on the rapidity of the rise of the Nile, a point in respect to which no very early forecast was possible. Early in August, however, the Sirdar, whose calculations of time were never once at fault, warned me that I ought to be back in Cairo by September 1. I had made all my preparations for departure, but I was unable to depart. The first news that the goal which for so many years I had striven to reach, had at last been attained, was conveyed to me in a telegram which the Queen, with her usual thoughtfulness for others, sent to a remote shooting-lodge in the North of Scotland, where I was watching the last moments of her who inspired me to write this book.

The long-expected battle took place under the walls of Omdurman on September 2. The Dervish leaders showed no tactical skill. They relied solely on the courage and devotion of their followers who, ignorant of the fearful powers of destruction which science has placed in the hands of the European, dashed recklessly against the ranks of the Anglo-Egyptian army, and were swept away in thousands by the deadly fire of the rifles and the Maxims. "The honour of the fight," said a competent eye-witness,[1] "must still go with the men who died. Our men were perfect, but the Dervishes were superb—beyond perfection. It was their largest, best, and bravest army that ever fought against us for Mahdiism, and it died worthily of the huge empire that Mahdiism won and kept so long. Their riflemen, mangled by every kind of death and torment that man can devise, clung round the black flag and the green, emptying their poor rotten, home-made cartridges dauntlessly. Their spearmen charged death at every minute hopelessly. . . . A dusky line got up and stormed forward: it bent, broke up, fell apart, and disappeared. Before the smoke had cleared, another line was bending and storming forward in the same track."

The Dervish loss was, in truth, terrible. Out of an army, whose strength was estimated at from 40,000 to 50,000 men, some 11,000 were killed, and about 16,000 wounded.

[1] Steevens, *With Kitchener to Khartoum*, p. 282. Mr. Steevens was the correspondent of the *Daily Mail*.

On the British side, 9 officers and 122 men, and on the Egyptian side, 5 British and 9 Egyptian officers as well as 241 non-commissioned officers and men, were killed and wounded.

These brave men fell in a good cause. It will be the fault of their countrymen, in obedience to whose orders—*τοῖς κείνων ῥήμασι πειθόμενοι*—they lie in their distant graves, if their blood is shed in vain.

On the afternoon of September 2, the victorious army entered the filthy stronghold of Mahdiism, where, it was said, "the stench was unbearable." Two days later (September 4), the British and Egyptian flags were hoisted with due ceremony on the walls of the ruined Palace of Khartoum, close to the spot where General Gordon fell. The sturdy and reverent Puritan spirit, which still animates Teutonic Christianity and which makes the soldier, at the moment of action, look to the guidance and protection of a Higher Power, found expression in a religious service in honour of the illustrious dead.

The Khalifa escaped. For more than a year, he wandered about the almost inaccessible wilds of Kordofan at the head of a considerable force. At length, he approached near enough to the river to enable a decisive blow to be struck. It was reserved for Sir Reginald Wingate, who succeeded Lord Kitchener as Sirdar of the Egyptian army towards the close of the year 1899, to give the final *coup de grâce* to Mahdiism. By a series of rapid and skilful marches, he surprised the Dervish camp on November 24, 1899. The Khalifa and all his principal Emirs were killed. His whole force surrendered.

The financial success was no less remarkable than the military. The total cost of the campaigns of 1896-98 was £E.2,354,000, of which £E.1,200,000 was spent on railways and telegraphs, and £E.155,000 on gunboats. The "military expenditure," properly so called, only amounted to £E.996,000.

Of the total sum of £E.2,354,000, rather less than £E.800,000 was paid by the British, and the balance of about £E.1,554,000 by the Egyptian Treasury.

In writing this work, I have throughout endeavoured to render it as little autobiographical as possible. If I now depart in some degree from this principle, my reason is that I am unable to enforce the military lesson which, I believe, is to be derived from the Khartoum campaign without touching on my personal position. The conditions under which the campaign was conducted were, in fact, very peculiar. In official circles it was dubbed a "Foreign Office War." For a variety of reasons, to which it is unnecessary to allude in detail, the Sirdar was, from the commencement of the operations, placed exclusively under my orders in all matters. The War Office assumed no responsibility, and issued no orders. A corresponding position was occupied by the Headquarters Staff of the Army of Occupation in Cairo. Sir Francis Grenfell and those serving under him rendered the most willing assistance whenever it was required of them, but beyond that point their functions did not extend. The result was that I found myself in the somewhat singular position of a civilian, who had had some little military training in his youth, but who had had no experience of war,[1] whose proper functions were diplomacy and administration, but who, under the stress of circumstances

[1] I was present for a few weeks, as a spectator, with Grant's army at the siege of Petersburg in 1864, but the experience was too short to be of much value.

in the "Land of Paradox," had to be ultimately responsible for the maintenance, and even to some extent, for the movements, of an army of some 25,000 men in the field.

That good results were obtained under this somewhat anomalous system cannot be doubted. It will not, therefore, be devoid of interest to explain how the system worked in practice, and what were the main reasons which contributed towards the success.

I have no wish to disparage the strategical and tactical ability which was displayed in the conduct of the campaign. It is, however, a fact that no occasion arose for the display of any great skill in these branches of military science. When once the British and Egyptian troops were brought face to face with the enemy, there could—unless the conditions under which they fought were altogether extraordinary—be little doubt of the result. The speedy and successful issue of the campaign depended, in fact, almost entirely upon the methods adopted for overcoming the very exceptional difficulties connected with the supply and transport of the troops. The main quality required to meet these difficulties was a good head for business. By one of those fortunate accidents which have been frequent in the history of Anglo-Saxon enterprise, a man was found equal to the occasion. Lord Kitchener of Khartoum won his well-deserved peerage because he was an excellent man of business; he looked carefully after every important detail, and enforced economy.

My own merits, such as they were, were of a purely negative character. They may be summed up in a single phrase. I abstained from a mischievous activity, and I acted as a check on the interference of others. I had full confidence in the abilities of the commander, whom I had practically myself chosen, and, except when he asked for my assistance, I left him entirely alone. I encouraged him to pay no attention to those vexatious bureaucratic formalities with which, under the slang phrase of "red tape," our military system is somewhat overburthened. I exercised some little control over the demands for stores which were sent to the London War Office, and the mere fact that those demands passed through my hands, and that I declined to forward any request unless, besides being in accordance with existing regulations—a point to which I attached but slight importance—it had been authorised by the Sirdar, probably tended to check wastefulness in that quarter where it was most to be feared. Beyond this I did nothing, and I found—somewhat to my own astonishment—that, with my ordinary very small staff of diplomatic secretaries, the general direction of a war of no inconsiderable dimensions added but little to my ordinary labours.

I do not say that this system would always work as successfully as was the case during the Khartoum campaign. The facts, as I have already said, were peculiar. The commander, on whom everything practically depended, was a man of marked military and administrative ability. Nevertheless, I venture to indulge in the hope that some useful lessons for the future may be derived from the Soudan campaigns of 1896 to 1898. It is in no spirit of conventional eulogy that I say that the British army consists of as fine material as any in the world. Apart from any question of national honour and interests, it positively chills my heart to think that the lives of the gallant young men of whom that army is mainly composed, may be needlessly sacrificed by defective organisation or guidance. This is no place to write a general essay on our military administration, but I cannot refrain from saying that, from what I have seen of the administration of the British War Office, it stood at one time in great need of improvement. It was costly. It was hampered by tradition. It was, to use an expressive French word, terribly "paperassier"; neither, for many years, was sufficient care taken, in every branch of the military service, to put the right man in the right place. In order to reform it, men rather than measures were required. I should add that there is reason to believe that, since the South African War, the administration of the War Office has been greatly improved. It is, however, impossible to speak positively on this point until its efficiency has undergone the crucial test of war.

The elation with which the news of the capture of Khartoum was received in England was in direct proportion to the despondency which chilled the heart of the British nation when, thirteen years previously, it was known that Mahdiism had triumphed and that General Gordon had been killed. Lord Kitchener, on his return to London, was received with an enthusiastic and well-deserved ovation. Indeed, one of the principal arguments in favour of recapturing Khartoum was that the British public had evidently made up its mind that, sooner or later, Khartoum had to be recaptured. It might have been possible to have postponed decisive action. It would probably have been impossible to have altogether prevented it. The national honour was not to be indefinitely baulked of the salve for which it yearned. An argument of this sort, albeit it is based on sentiment, is of intrinsic importance. In the execution of the Imperialist policy, to which England is pledged almost as a necessity of her existence, it is not at all desirable to eliminate entirely those considerations which appeal to the imaginative, to the exclusion of the material side of the national character. Moreover, whatever may be thought of the undesirability of admitting any emotional lines of thought as guides to practical action in politics, it may be regarded as certain that the politician who endeavours to run absolutely counter to the impulse of the national imagination, instead of seeking to guide it, will find that he is attempting an impossible task.

The policy pursued by the British Government in 1896 is, of course, capable of ample justification on other and less sentimental grounds than those to which allusion is made above. The effective control of the waters of the Nile from the Equatorial Lakes to the sea is essential to the existence of Egypt.

Whatever opinion may be entertained of the policy itself, or of whether the moment chosen for its execution was opportune or the reverse, it cannot be doubted that the capture of Khartoum did more than appease those sentiments of national honour which had been stung to the quick by the events of 1885. The cannon which swept away the Dervish hordes at Omdurman proclaimed to the world that on England—or, to be more strictly correct, on Egypt under British guidance—had devolved the solemn and responsible duty of introducing the light of Western civilisation amongst the sorely tried people of the Soudan.

My hope and belief is that that duty will be performed in a manner worthy of the best traditions of the Anglo-Saxon race.

CHAPTER XXXIII

THE NEW SOUDAN

Question of the future political status of the Soudan—Anomalies of the British position—Objections to annexation—And to complete incorporation with Egypt—Intricacy of the problem—The two flags—Speech at Omdurman—The right of conquest—The Agreement of January 19, 1899—Its unusual nature—Its reception by Europe—Advantages of a Free Trade policy.

THE Soudan having been reconquered, the question of the future political status of the country naturally presented itself for solution.

British policy in Egypt since the year 1882 may be said to constitute a prolonged and, so far, only partially successful effort to escape from the punishment due to original sin. The ancient adage that truth is a fellow-citizen of the gods[1] is as valid in politics as in morals. British statesmen were continually harassed by a Nemesis in the shape of the *magna vis veritatis*, which was for ever striving to shatter the rickety political edifice constructed at the time of the occupation on no surer foundations than those of diplomatic opportunism. At every turn of the political wheel, fact clashed with theory. Nevertheless, in the year 1898, of which period I am now writing, Ottoman supremacy in the Soudan, whether in the person of the Sultan or the Khedive, presented a sufficient character of solidity to necessitate its recognition as a practical

[1] Ἀλήθεια θεῶν ὁμόπολις.

fact. It could not be treated as a mere diplomatic wraith. However much it tended at times to evaporate into a phantom, its shape was still sufficiently distinguishable through the political mist to enable the outline of a kingly crown to be clearly traced. Hence, the necessity arose of cloaking the reality of fact with some more or less transparent veil of theory.

The difference between the real and the suppositious was brought prominently into relief immediately after the fall of Khartoum. On no occasion had a greater amount of ingenuity to be exercised in effecting an apparent reconciliation between the facts as they existed and the facts as they were, by a pardonable fiction, supposed to exist. The problem in this instance might at first sight appear to have been almost as insoluble as that of squaring the circle. But, as Lord Salisbury once remarked to me, when one gets to the foot of the hills, it is generally possible to find some pass which will lead across them. I have now to describe the pass which, with some difficulty, was eventually found through the political mountains in the particular instance under discussion. It will be seen that an arrangement was made which elsewhere might perhaps have been considered as too anomalous to stand the wear and tear of daily political existence. In Egypt, it was merely thought that one more paradox had been added to the goodly array of paradoxical creations with which the political institutions of the country already teemed.

The facts were plain enough. Fifteen years previously, Egyptian misgovernment had led to a successful rebellion in the Soudan. British rule had developed the military and financial resources of Egypt to such an extent as to justify the adoption of a policy of reconquest. But England, not Egypt, had in reality reconquered the country.

It is true that the Egyptian Treasury had borne the greater portion of the cost, and that Egyptian troops, officered, however, by Englishmen, had taken a very honourable part in the campaign. But, alike during the period of the preparation and of the execution of the policy, the guiding hand had been that of England. It is absurd to suppose that without British assistance in the form of men, money, and general guidance, the Egyptian Government could have reconquered the Soudan.

From this point of view, therefore, the annexation of the reconquered territories by England would have been partially justifiable. There were, however, some weighty arguments against the adoption of this course.

In the first place, although in the Anglo-Egyptian partnership England was unquestionably the senior partner, at the same time, Egypt had played a very useful and honourable, albeit auxiliary part in the joint undertaking. It would have been very unjust to ignore Egyptian claims in deciding on the future political status of the Soudan.

In the second place, the campaign had throughout been carried on in the name of the Khedive. If, immediately on its conclusion, decisive action had been taken in the name of the British Government acting alone, the adoption of such a course would have involved a brusque and objectionable departure from the policy heretofore pursued.

In the third place—and this consideration would, by itself, have been conclusive—it was not in the interests of Great Britain to add to its responsibilities, which were already world-wide, by assuming the direct government of another huge African territory.

These and other considerations, on which it is unnecessary to dwell, pointed to the conclusion that the Soudan should be regarded as Ottoman territory, and that, therefore, it should be governed, in accordance with the terms of the Imperial Firmans, by the Sultan's feudatory, the Khedive.

A very valid objection existed, however, to the adoption of this course. If the political status of the Soudan were to be assimilated in all respects to that of Egypt, the necessary consequence would be that the administration of the country would be burthened by the introduction of the Capitulations, and, in fact, by all the cumbersome paraphernalia of internationalism, which had done so much to retard Egyptian progress. It was manifestly absurd that British lives should be sacrificed and British treasure expended merely in order to place additional arms in the hands of Powers, some one or other of whom might at some future time become the enemy of England. Moreover, the adoption of this course would have been highly detrimental to Egyptian interests. Egypt, more than England, had suffered from the international incubus.

Hence there arose a dilemma, or, if it is permissible to coin so unusual an expression, a trilemma; for three arguments, which were in some degree mutually destructive, had to be reconciled.

In the first place, it was essential that British influence should in practice be paramount in the Soudan, in order that the Egyptians should not have conferred on them a "bastard freedom" to repeat the misgovernment of the past.

In the second place, British influence could not be exerted under the same ill-defined and anomalous conditions as those which prevailed in Egypt without involving the introduction of the baneful régime of internationalism.

In the third place, annexation by England, which would have cut the international knot, was precluded on grounds of equity and policy.

It was, therefore, necessary to invent some

method by which the Soudan should be, at one and the same time, Egyptian to such an extent as to satisfy equitable and political exigencies, and yet sufficiently British to prevent the administration of the country from being hampered by the international burr which necessarily hung on to the skirts of Egyptian political existence.

It was manifest that these conflicting requirements could not be satisfied without the creation of some hybrid form of government, hitherto unknown to international jurisprudence.

The matter was discussed when I was in London in July 1898. At that time, although all saw clearly enough the objects to be attained, no very definite method for attaining them was suggested. In order, however, to give an outward and visible sign that, in the eyes of the British Government, the political status of the Soudan differed from that of Egypt, Lord Kitchener was instructed, on the capture of Khartoum, to hoist both the British and Egyptian flags side by side.[1] These orders were duly executed. Amidst the clash of arms and the jubilation over the recent victory, this measure attracted but little attention. It was not until five months later, that its importance was generally understood. On January 4, 1899, being then at Omdurman, I made a speech to the assembled Sheikhs. As I intended and anticipated, it attracted much attention. It was, indeed, meant for the public of Egypt and Europe quite as much as for the audience whom I addressed. In the course of this speech I said: "You see that both the British and Egyptian flags are floating over this house.[2] That is an

[1] When Lord Kitchener found himself face to face with Captain Marchand at Fashoda, he very wisely hoisted the Egyptian flag only.

[2] The house, in the courtyard of which I spoke, had but a short time before been inhabited by one of the Khalifa's leading Emirs. At the time of my visit, it was being used as a public office.

indication that for the future you will be governed by the Queen of England and by the Khedive of Egypt." There could be no mistaking the significance of these words, and there was no desire that they should be mistaken. They meant that the Soudan was to be governed by a partnership of two, of which England was the predominant member.

Before making this speech, I had submitted to Lord Salisbury the project of an Agreement between the British and Egyptian Governments regulating the political status of the Soudan. It had been prepared, under my general instructions, by Sir Malcolm McIlwraith, the Judicial Adviser of the Egyptian Government. Shortly after my return to Cairo, I was authorised to sign it. It was accordingly signed by the Egyptian Minister for Foreign Affairs and myself on January 19, 1899. I proceed to give a brief summary of the contents of this document.

The first and most important point was to assert a valid title to the exercise of sovereign rights in the Soudan by the Queen of England, in conjunction with the Khedive. There could be only one sound basis on which that title could rest. This was the right of conquest. A title based on this ground had the merit of being in accordance with the indisputable facts of the situation. It was also in accordance, if not with international law—which can obviously never be codified save in respect to certain special issues—at all events, with international practice, as set forth by competent authorities. It was, therefore, laid down in the preamble of the Agreement that it was desirable "to give effect to the claims which have accrued to Her Britannic Majesty's Government, by right of conquest, to share in the present settlement and future working and development" of the legislative and administrative systems of the Soudan.

This principle having been once accepted, the ground was cleared for further action. The shadowy claims of Turkish suzerainty were practically, though not nominally, swept away by a stroke of the pen. Their disappearance connoted the abrogation of all those privileges which, in other parts of the Ottoman dominions, are vested in European Powers in order to check an abusive exercise of the Sultan's sovereign rights. All that then remained was to settle the practical points at issue in the manner most convenient and most conducive to the interests of the two sole contracting parties, namely, the British and the Egyptian Governments.

The 22nd parallel of latitude was fixed as the northern frontier of the new state; on the other hand, the southern frontier was left undefined. It was provided that both the British and Egyptian flags should be used throughout the Soudan;[1] that the supreme military and civil command should be vested in one officer, termed "the Governor-General of the Soudan," who was to be appointed by a Khedivial Decree on the recommendation of the British Government; that Proclamations by the Governor-General should have the force of law; that the jurisdiction of the Mixed Tribunals should "not extend or be recognised for any purpose whatsoever, in any part of the Soudan"; and that no foreign Consuls should be allowed to reside in the country without the previous consent of the British Government.

When this Agreement was published, it naturally attracted much attention. Diplomatists, who were

[1] In the first instance, the town of Suakin was excepted from this and from some other portions of the Agreement, but this arrangement was found to cause a good deal of practical inconvenience. By a subsequent Agreement, dated July 10, 1899, the status of Suakin was in all respects assimilated to that of the rest of the Soudan.

wedded to conventionalities, were puzzled, and perhaps slightly shocked, at the creation of a political status hitherto unknown to the law of Europe. One of my foreign colleagues pointed out to me that he understood what British territory meant, as also what Ottoman territory meant, but that he could not understand the status of the Soudan, which was neither one nor the other. I replied that the political status of the Soudan was such as was laid down in the Agreement of January 19, 1899, and that I could give no more precise or epigrammatic definition. Again, I was asked what, in the absence of any Consuls, was to happen to Europeans who were married or buried in the Soudan? I could only reply that any European who considered it essential that his marriage or burial should be attested by a Consular representative of his country, would do well to remain in the territory lying north of the 22nd parallel of latitude.

But the splutter of amazement caused by British want of political symmetry soon died out. It is true that the Sultan murmured some few words of ineffectual protest, but no serious opposition was encountered from any quarter.

Why was this? The reasons were threefold.

In the first place, whatever fine-spun arguments might be woven from the loom of diplomatic technicality, the attitude taken up by the British Government was in substance manifestly both just and reasonable.

In the second place, their attitude was firm. It was clear that they intended to carry out their programme. The inevitable consequence ensued. No one was prepared to bell the cat, even if he felt any disposition to do so. A mere platonic protest would have caused irritation, and would have been ineffectual.

In the third place, the Powers of Europe, possibly without meaning it, paid a compliment to British rule. However much the Anglophobe press on the Continent might at times rave, it was perfectly well known that, under the British flag, Europeans—albeit they were the subjects of Powers, some of whom were animated by no very friendly spirit towards England—would be treated with perfect justice. Notably, Article VI. of the Agreement, to which at the time I attached great importance, tended greatly to allay any spirit of opposition which might otherwise have been aroused. It laid down that, in all matters concerning trade with, and residence in the Soudan, "no special privileges would be accorded to the subjects of any one or more Power"; in other words, the German, the Frenchman, the Italian and others were placed on a precisely similar commercial footing to that enjoyed by a subject of the Queen of England. Even the most militant Anglophobe could not fail to be struck by the contrast between this liberal attitude and the exclusive commercial policy adopted by other colonising European Powers. Thus, in laying the foundations of the new Soudan, a Free Trade policy—which I trust will never be dissociated from British Imperialism—formed one of the corner-stones of the political edifice.

After this fashion, the new Soudan was born. It was endowed with sufficient strength to support existence. Nevertheless, it was of necessity to some extent the child of opportunism. Should it eventually die and make place for some more robust, because more real political creation, its authors need not bewail its fate.[1]

[1] At a later period of this work (*vide* Chapter LX.) I shall give a brief account of the results which have so far been obtained under the system whose main features are described in this chapter.

PART IV

THE EGYPTIAN PUZZLE

Quand un peuple a souffert trop longtemps, c'est tout au plus si, dans son abaissement, il a la force de baiser la main qui le sauve.

P. J. STAHL.

This country is a palimpsest, in which the Bible is written over Herodotus, and the Koran over that.

LADY DUFF GORDON'S *Letters from Egypt.*

To watch the immemorial culture of the East, slow-moving with the weight of years, dreamy with centuries of deep meditation, accept and assimilate, as in a moment of time, the science, the machinery, the restless energy and practical activity of the West is a fascinating employment.

KENNETH J. FREEMAN, *The Schools of Hellas.*

CHAPTER XXXIV

THE DWELLERS IN EGYPT

The Englishman's mission — Conditions under which it was undertaken — Population of Egypt — Its mixed character — Hostility to England — Main tenets of Islam — Its failure as a social system — Degradation of women — Immutability of the law — Slavery — Intolerance — Incidents of religious belief and ceremonial — Mental and moral attributes — Seclusion of women — Polygamy — Divorce — Coarseness of literature and conversation — Filial piety — Government — Conservatism — Spirit of the laws — Language — Art — Music — Customs — Obstacles to England's mission.

At the conclusion of Chapter XVIII. of this work, the narrative was brought down to the time when Kinglake's Englishman had planted his foot on the banks of the Nile, and sat in the seats of the faithful. He came not as a conqueror, but in the familiar garb of a saviour of society. The mere assumption of this part, whether by a nation or by an individual, is calculated to arouse some degree of suspicion. The world is apt to think that the saviour is not improbably looking more to his own interests than to the salvation of society, and experience has proved that the suspicion is not unfrequently well founded. Yet assuredly the Englishman could in this case produce a valid title to justify his assumption of the part which had been thrust upon him. His advent was hailed with delight by the lawful rulers of Egypt and by the mass of the Egyptian people. The greater portion of Europe also looked upon his action without disfavour, if not with positive approval.

I say only the greater portion of Europe, for there were two notable exceptions. In the East of Europe, the Turk chafed under the reflection that the precious jewel of political opportunity had been offered to him, and that, like the "bird in the story" of Moore's song, he had "cast the fair gem far away." In the West of Europe, on the other hand, the Frenchman was looking on askance with a gradually awakening sense that he had made a mistake in allowing the Englishman to assume alone the part of the Egyptian saviour, and, when he once woke up to a sense of his error, he manifested his irritation in various ways.

With these two exceptions, which, however, for the moment hardly caused any discordant note to be sounded amidst the universal chorus of approbation, the Englishman was able to feel that none, whether in or out of Egypt, were inclined to gainsay the righteousness of his cause. More than this, one of the first qualifications necessary in order to play the part of a saviour of society is that the saviour should believe in himself and in his mission. This the Englishman did. He was convinced that his mission was to save Egyptian society, and, moreover, that he was able to save it.

How was he to accomplish his mission? Was he, in his energetic, brisk, northern fashion, to show the Egyptians what they had to do, and then to leave them to carry on the work by themselves? This is what he thought to do, but alas! he was soon to find that to fulminate against abuses, which were the growth of centuries, was like firing a cannon-ball into a mountain of mud. By the adoption of any such method, he could only produce a temporary ebullition. If he were to do any good, he must not only show what was to be done, but he must stay where he was and do it himself. Or was he, as some fiery spirits advised, to go to the other extreme? Was he to hoist the British flag over the citadel of Cairo, and sweep Pashadom, Capitulations, Mixed Tribunals, and all the heterogeneous mass of international cobwebs to be found in Egypt into the political waste-paper basket? Prudence, which bade him think of the peace of Europe, and the qualms of his political conscience, which obliged him to be mindful of his plighted word, albeit it had perhaps been too lightly pledged, stopped the way.

Being debarred from the adoption of either extreme course, the Englishman fell back on the procedure, which is endeared to him by habits of thought and national tradition. He adopted a middle course. He compromised. Far be it from his Anglo-Saxon mind to ask for that "situation nette" which is so dear to the logical Frenchman. He would assert his native genius by working a system, which, according to every canon of political thought, was unworkable. He would not annex Egypt, but he would do as much good to the country as if he had annexed it. He would not interfere with the liberty of action of the Khedivial Government, but in practice he would insist on the Khedive and the Egyptian Ministers conforming to his views. He would in theory be one of many Powers exercising equal rights, but in practice he would wield a paramount influence. He would occupy a portion of the Ottoman dominions with British troops, and at the same time he would do nothing to infringe the legitimate rights of the Sultan. He would not break his promise to the Frenchman, but he would wrap it in a napkin to be produced on some more convenient occasion. In a word, he would act with all the practical common sense, the scorn for theory, and the total absence of any fixed plan based on logical reasoning, which are the distinguishing features of his race.

I propose eventually to answer the question of how the Englishman fulfilled the mission which, if it was not conferred on him by Europe, was at all events assumed without protest from Europe. Before, however, grappling with this portion of my task, it will be as well to say something of the conditions of the problem which had to be solved. What manner of men were these Egyptians over whom, by accident rather than by design, the Englishman was called upon to rule without having the appearance of ruling? To what influences were they subject? What were their national characteristics? What part must be assigned to the foreign, that is to say, the European, Asiatic, and non-Egyptian African races resident in Egypt? What political institutions and administrative systems existed when the English stepped upon the Egyptian scene? In a word, what was the chaotic material out of which the Englishman had to evolve something like order?

These are important questions. It is essential that they should be answered before the nature of the work accomplished by England in Egypt can be understood.

Modern Egypt measures about 1000 miles from Alexandria to Wadi Halfa. Its breadth from Port Said to Alexandria is about 200 miles. The apex of the Nile Delta lies a little north of Cairo. Southward from that point, the habitable country narrows rapidly, and is in places confined to a few yards on either bank of the river. This habitable area covers an extent of 33,607 square kilometres, or about 8,000,000 acres.

Who are the inhabitants of these eight millions of acres? Of what was the raw material composed with which the Englishman had to deal?

It might naturally be supposed that, as we are dealing with the country called Egypt, the inhabitants of whom the statesman and the administrator would have almost exclusively to take account would be Egyptians. Any one who is inclined to rush to this conclusion should remember that Egypt, as Lord Milner has stated in his admirable work, is the Land of Paradox. If any one walks down one of the principal streets of London, Paris, or Berlin, nine out of ten of the people with whom he meets bear on their faces evidence, more or less palpable, that they are Englishmen, Frenchmen, or Germans. But let any one who has a general acquaintance with the appearance and physiognomy of the principal Eastern races try if he can give a fair ethnological description of the first ten people he meets in one of the streets of Cairo, that "maze of old ruin and modern café, that dying Mecca and still-born Rue de Rivoli," as it has been aptly termed by Sir William Butler.[1] He will find it no easy matter, and with all his experience he may not improbably make many mistakes.

The first passer-by is manifestly an Egyptian fellah who has come into the city to sell his garden produce. The headgear, dress, and aquiline nose of the second render it easy to recognise a Bedouin who is perhaps come to Cairo to buy ammunition for his flint-lock gun, but who is ill at ease amidst urban surroundings, and will hasten to return to the more congenial air of the desert. The small, thick-lipped man with dreamy eyes, who has a far-away look of one of the bas-reliefs on an ancient Egyptian tomb, but who Champollion and other *savants* tell us is not the lineal descendant of the ancient Egyptians,[2] is presumably a Coptic

[1] *The Campaign of the Cataracts*, p. 95.

[2] Maspero, *Histoire ancienne des peuples de l'Orient*, p. 15. Champollion le Jeune's opinion, quoted by M. Maspero, is as follows: "Les Coptes sont le résultat du mélange confus de toutes les nations qui successivement ont dominé l'Égypt. On a tort de vouloir retrouver chez eux les traits de la vieille race." Mr. S. Lane-Poole, however, says

clerk in some Government office. The face, which peers somewhat loweringly over a heavy moustache from the window of a passing brougham, is probably that of some Turco-Egyptian Pasha. The man with a bold, handsome, cruel face, who swaggers by in long boots and baggy trousers, must surely be a Circassian. The Syrian money-lender, who comes next, will get out of his way, albeit he may be about to sell up the Circassian's property the next day to recover a loan of which the capital and interest, at any ordinary rate, have been already paid twenty times over. The green turban, dignified mien, and slow gait of the seventh passer-by denote some pious Sheikh, perhaps on his way to the famous University of El-Azhar. The eighth must be a Jew, who has just returned from a tour in Asia Minor with a stock of embroideries, which he is about to sell to the winter tourists. The ninth would seem to be some Levantine nondescript, whose ethnological status defies diagnosis; and the tenth, though not easily distinguishable from the latter class, is in reality one of the petty traders of whom Greece is so prolific, and who are to be found dotted all over the Ottoman dominions. Nor is the list yet exhausted. Armenians, Tunisians, Algerians, Soudanese, Maltese, half-breeds of every description, and pure-blooded Europeans pass by in procession, and all go to swell the mass, if not of Egyptians, at all events of dwellers in Egypt.

The compiler of the census of 1897 appears to have felt a difficulty which must surely have weighed still more heavily on those amateur politicians who, like Mr. Wilfrid Blunt, have from time to time advocated a policy of Egypt for the true Egyptians. Who, in fact, is a true Egyptian? The compiler

(*Cairo*, p. 205): "Copts, Gypts, Egyptians, they are, indeed, the true survivors of the people whom Pharaoh ruled, and who built the Pyramids of Giza."

of the census very wisely did not attempt to define the term; he must have been aware that precise definition was impossible. At the same time, the instincts of his craft appear to have rebelled at the idea of lumping the whole population of Egypt, exclusive of Europeans, into one seething statistical mass and calling them Egyptians. So he divided the Egyptians as well as he could into, first, natives; secondly, persons born in other parts of the Ottoman dominions, who, as a matter of fact, are for the most part Syrians and Armenians; thirdly, semi-sedentary Bedouins, that is to say, the hybrid between the fellah and the Bedouin, who has one foot on the cultivated land of the Nile Valley, and the other on the desert; and, fourthly, Nomad Bedouins, who are Bedouins pure and simple.

The census of 1897 [1] informs us, therefore, that at that time there were, in round numbers, 9,621,000 Ottoman subjects dwelling in Egypt, who were divided into the following categories:—

Natives	9,008,000
Persons born, not in Egypt, but in other parts of the Ottoman Empire	40,000
Semi-sedentary Bedouins . .	485,000
Nomad Bedouins . . .	88,000
Total .	9,621,000 [2]

These, with 113,000 Europeans and protected subjects of European Powers, brought the dwellers

[1] I am obliged to use the 1897 figures, as those of the census of 1907 are not yet available. I am, however, informed that the provisional figures work out to a total of about 11,206,000.

[2] According to the census of 1882, the population was 6,814,000. There was, therefore, including Europeans, an increase of 43 per cent in fifteen years. It is, however, generally supposed that the census of 1882, which was conducted with very inadequate machinery, underestimated the population at the time.

in Egypt, male and female, up to a grand total of 9,734,000.

The Englishman, I have said, came to Egypt with the fixed idea that he had a mission to perform, and, with his views about individual justice, equal rights before the law, the greatest happiness of the greatest number, and similar notions, he will not unnaturally interpret his mission in this sense, that he is to benefit the mass of the population. There lie those nine or ten million native Egyptians at the bottom of the social ladder, a poor, ignorant, credulous, but withal not unkindly race, being such as sixty centuries of misgovernment and oppression by various rulers, from Pharaohs to Pashas, have made them. It is for the civilised Englishman to extend to them the hand of fellowship and encouragement, and to raise them, morally and materially, from the abject state in which he finds them. And the Englishman looks towards the scene of other administrative triumphs of world-wide fame, which his progenitors have accomplished. He looks towards India, and he says to himself, with all the confidence of an imperial race,—I can perform this task; I have done it before now; I have poured numberless blessings on the heads of the ryots of Bengal and Madras, who are own cousins to the Egyptian fellaheen; these latter also shall have water for their fields, justice in their law-courts, and immunity from the tyranny under which they have for so long groaned; the reign of Pashadom shall cease.

But the Englishman will find, when he once applies himself to his task, that there is, as it were, a thick mist between him and the Egyptian, composed of religious prejudice, antique and semi-barbarous customs, international rivalry, vested interests, and aspirations of one sort or another, some sordid, others, it may be, not ignoble but incapable of realisation. He will find, in the first place, that those 113,000 Europeans, although constituting only 1·16 per cent of the total population, represent the greater part of the wealth and intelligence, and no small proportion of the rascality and aggressive egotism of the country; further, that whether their views be right or wrong, just or unjust, these 113,000 elect often have the power to enforce their behests, for are they not the salt of the Egyptian earth, the Brahmins of Egypt, and have they not behind them the diplomatists, and it may even be, the soldiers and sailors of every State of Europe? In this respect, the Englishman will find that he has to deal with a problem for the solution of which his Indian experience will avail him but little. In the second place, he will find that a majority of the large landowners and all the most important officials are Turco-Egyptians in various stages of Egyptianisation, who enjoy privileges which are wholly inconsistent with Benthamite principles, notably the privilege of oppressing those 9,000,000 Egyptians whose woes wring the heart of their English would-be benefactor. Obviously, the Englishman is not likely to get much sympathy or support from this quarter. In the third place, he will find a host of minor officials, many of whom are of non-Egyptian origin, and who, for various reasons, are indisposed to co-operate loyally in the improvement of their country at the hand of the just, well-intentioned, but somewhat unsympathetic alien. In fact, the Englishman will soon find that the Egyptian, whom he wishes to mould into something really useful with a view to his becoming eventually autonomous, is merely the rawest of raw material, and that the principal tools, with which he will have to work, and on which the excellence of the finished article must largely depend, may be

British, French, Turkish, Syrian, Armenian, or of half-a-dozen other nationalities, but they will rarely be Egyptian.[1]

This, therefore, is the central feature of the local situation which the English found in existence when they took in hand the solution of the Egyptian question. The Egyptians, properly so called, were numerous, but were, from the political and superior administrative point of view, little more than ciphers. The main difficulties of the English politician and of the English administrator will arise from the fact that the minority, consisting of non-Egyptians or of what, for want of a better term, may in some instances be called semi-Egyptians, were relatively powerful, and not unfrequently, for one reason or another, hostile.

I have said that religious prejudice constituted one of the barriers which were interposed between the Englishman and the Egyptian; for, on the one hand, besides being one of the European family in respect to general civilisation, the Englishman, amidst many deviations from the path, will strive, perhaps to a greater extent than any other member of that family, to attain to a high degree of eminently Christian civilisation; that is to say, although he will in his official capacity discard any attempt to proselytise, he will endeavour to inculcate a distinctly Christian code of morality as the basis for the relations between man and man. He is, indeed, guided in this direction by the lights, which have been handed down to him by his forefathers, and by the Puritan blood which still circulates in his veins.

The Egyptian, on the other hand, holds fast to the faith of Islam, that noble monotheism, belief in which takes to a great extent the place of patriotism

[1] I am, of course, speaking here of the state of things which existed in 1882. Since then, the proportion of Egyptian employés in the Government service has very largely increased.

in Eastern countries,[1] and which serves as a common bond of union to all Moslems from Delhi to Fez, from Stamboul to Zanzibar, as they turn to pray towards the cradle of their creed.[2]

And what are the main tenets of this creed, which has exercised so mighty an influence on the destinies of mankind? They are set forth in the Sacred Book of the Moslems. They have been explained in many languages by learned men of many nations. But their original grandeur and simplicity have never been more eloquently expounded than by those early followers of the Prophet, who threw themselves at the feet of the Christian King of Abyssinia to implore his protection against the persecution of the Koreish Arabs. "O King," they said, "we lived in ignorance, idolatry, and unchastity; the strong oppressed the weak; we spoke untruth; we violated the duties of hospitality. Then a Prophet arose, one whom we knew from our youth, with whose descent and conduct and good faith and truth we are all well acquainted. He told us to worship one God, to speak truth, to keep good faith, to assist our relations, to fulfil the rights of hospitality, and to abstain from all things impure, ungodly, unrighteous. And he ordered us to say prayers, give alms, and to fast. We believed in him; we followed him."[3]

These are the main tenets of the Moslem faith.[4]

[1] Some observers think that association with Europe has to some extent resulted in substituting the bond of nationality for that of religion in Moslem countries. Thus M. Le Chatelier, in a work published in 1888, and entitled *Islam au XIXème Siècle*, says (p. 186): "L'évolution contemporaine de l'Europe a introduit dans celle de l'Islam un facteur commun, le développement de l'esprit de nationalité, qu'elle a d'ailleurs propagé dans le monde entier." Recent events, not only in Egypt but elsewhere, tend rather to confirm M. Le Chatelier's view.

[2] See *Studies in a Mosque*, p. 96.

[3] *Ibid.* p. 48, and Muir's *Life of Mahomet*, p. 89.

[4] Mr. Badger, in his admirable article on Mohammed in the *Dictionary of Christian Biography*, says: "Surah CXII., the shortest chapter of

To the many hundreds of millions who have embraced Islam, and more especially to the poor amongst them, the adoption of these tenets has afforded not only spiritual consolation but material blessings in this world, as well as the hope of immortality in the world to come. It cannot be doubted that a primitive society benefits greatly by the adoption of the faith of Islam.[1] Sir John Seeley, speaking of what he aptly terms "the state-building power of religion," says: "Wherever a barbarous tribe has raised itself at all above the level of barbarism and taken any development, it has done so usually through conversion to Islam."[2]

Unfortunately, the great Arabian reformer of the seventh century was driven by the necessities of his position to do more than found a religion. He endeavoured to found a social system, with results which are thus stated by a close observer of the strong and weak parts of Islamism. "As a religion," Mr. Stanley Lane-Poole says, "Islam is great; it has taught men to worship one God with a pure worship who formerly worshipped many gods impurely. As a social system, it is a complete failure."[3]

The reasons why Islam as a social system has been a complete failure are manifold.

First and foremost, Islam keeps women in a position of marked inferiority.[4] In the second place, Islam, speaking not so much through the Koran as

the Koran, is regarded by Moslems as containing the essence of the whole book: 'Say, God is one; God the eternal; He begetteth not, neither is He begotten; neither is there any one like Him.'"

[1] "L'Islam est un progrès pour le nègre qui l'adopte."—Renan, *Histoire du Peuple d'Israel,* vol. i. p. 60.

[2] *Introduction to Political Science,* p. 63. Miss Kingsley (*West African Studies,* ch. v.) makes some very apposite remarks on the adaptability of Islamism to the present condition of African society.

[3] *Studies in a Mosque,* p. 101.

[4] "The degradation of women in the East is a canker that begins its destructive work early in childhood, and has eaten into the whole system of Islam."—Stanley Lane-Poole, *Islam, a Prelection delivered before the University of Dublin.*

through the traditions which cluster round the Koran, crystallises religion and law into one inseparable and immutable whole, with the result that all elasticity is taken away from the social system. If to this day an Egyptian goes to law over a question of testamentary succession, his case is decided according to the antique principles which were laid down as applicable to the primitive society of the Arabian Peninsula in the seventh century. Only a few years ago (1890), the Grand Mufti of Cairo, who is the authoritative expounder of the law of Islam, explained how bands of robbers should be treated who were found guilty of making armed attacks on a village by night. The condemned criminal might be punished in six different ways. He might have his right hand and left foot cut off and then be decapitated; or he might be mutilated, as before, and then crucified; or he might be mutilated, decapitated, and eventually crucified; or he might be simply decapitated or simply crucified, or decapitated first and crucified afterwards. Full details were given in the Mufti's report of the mode of crucifixion which was to be adopted. The condemned person was to be attached to a cross in a certain manner, after which "il sera percé à la mamelle gauche par une lance, qui devra être remuée dans la blessure jusqu'à ce que la mort ait lieu."[1] These terrible penalties could not, however, for some reason, which at first sight appears incomprehensible,[2] be incurred if a dumb man were one of the band of robbers. In this latter case the *lex talionis* was to be applied. The next-of-kin of any one who might have been murdered could demand a life for a life, or could claim blood-money in lieu of expiation.

[1] The original was, of course, in Arabic, but the French translation, which is quoted above, was published in the Official Journal of the Egyptian Government.

[2] See p. 136, note.

The rigidity of the Sacred Law has been at times slightly tempered by well-meaning and learned Moslems who have tortured their brains in devising sophisms to show that the legal principles and social system of the seventh century can, by some strained and intricate process of reasoning, be consistently and logically made to conform with the civilised practices of the twentieth century.[1] But, as a rule, custom based on the religious law, coupled with exaggerated reverence for the original lawgiver, holds all those who cling to the faith of Islam with a grip of iron from which there is no escape. "During the Middle Ages," it has been truly said,[2] "man lived enveloped in a cowl." The true Moslem of the present day is even more tightly enveloped by the Sheriât.

In the third place, Islam does not, indeed, encourage, but it tolerates slavery. "Mohammed found the custom existing among the Pagan Arabs; he minimised the evil."[3] But he was powerless to

[1] A curious instance of the processes of reasoning sometimes adopted in order to evade the rigidity of the Sacred Law is to be found in the provision, to which allusion is made above, that the barbarous punishments of mutilation and crucifixion cannot be inflicted on a band of brigands if a dumb man forms one of the band. The reason is rather abstruse. It appears that certain classes of offences, such as robbery, adultery, etc., are specially provided for by the Koran, the penalties being generally excessively severe, and, as no mitigation is permissible, those penalties have to be applied in their entirety. Thus, for brigandage the penalty is mutilation, crucifixion, etc., as described by the Mufti. But, in order, in some degree, to leave a loophole for escape from the compulsory infliction of these punishments in all cases, the law doctors discovered that it was only intended that they should be inflicted when all the parties were quite sound and in a state to speak in their own defence. For this reason, the presence of a child, an idiot, or a dumb man enables the Sacred Law to be put aside and a milder kind of punishment inflicted on the whole party under the ordinary law, *i.e.* the will of the Sovereign or of his delegate, the Kadi. If I understand rightly, the Mufti did not mean that the dumb man saved all his associates from punishment, but only that they were thereby transferred from the province of the Divine law to that of their human authorities.

[2] Symonds, *Renaissance in Italy*, p. 14.

[3] Syed Ameer Ali, *Personal Law of the Mohammedans*, p. 38.

abolish it altogether. His followers have forgotten the discouragement, and have very generally made the permission to possess slaves the practical guide for their conduct. This is another fatal blot in Islam.

> *ἥμισυ γάρ τ' ἀρετῆς ἀποαίνυται εὐρύοπα Ζεὺς*
> *ἀνέρος, εὖτ' ἄν μιν κατὰ δούλιον ἦμαρ ἕλῃσιν.*

The Christian, to his shame be it said, has before now been not only a slave-owner, but, which is much worse, a slave-hunter. The Christian religion has, however, never sanctioned slavery.

Lastly, Islam has the reputation of being an intolerant religion, and the reputation is, from some points of view, well deserved, though the bald and sweeping accusation of intolerance requires qualification and explanation. The followers of the Prophet have, indeed, waged war against those whom they considered infidels. They are taught by their religious code that any unbelievers, who may be made prisoners of war, may rightly be enslaved.[1] Moreover, sectarian strife has not been uncommon. Sunni has fought against Shiah. The orthodox Moslem has mercilessly repressed the followers of Abdul Wahab. Further, apostasy from Islam is punishable with death, and it is not many years ago that the sentence used to be carried into effect.[2] On the other hand, the annals of Islam are

[1] The Hidayah, which is regarded by the Sunnis as the standard commentary on the Sheriât, or religious code, says: "The Imam, with respect to captives, has it in his choice to slay them, because the Prophet put captives to death, and also because slaying them terminates wickedness; or, if he chooses, he may make them slaves, because by enslaving them the wickedness of them is remedied, and at the same time the Moslems reap an advantage."

[2] Lane saw a woman stripped, strangled, and thrown into the Nile for apostasy (*Modern Egyptians*, vol. i. p. 136). To the best of my belief, the last person executed for apostasy in virtue of a decision of an Ottoman law-court was an Armenian, who in 1843 adopted the faith of Islam, subsequently repented, and returned to the Christian Church. Lord Stratford, who was then Ambassador at Constantinople, rose in

not stained by the history of an Inquisition.[1] More than this, when he is not moved by any circumstances specially calculated to rouse his religious passions, the Moslem readily extends a half-contemptuous tolerance to the Jew and the Christian.[2] In the villages of Upper Egypt, the Crescent and the Cross, the Mosque and the Monastery, have stood peacefully side by side for many a long year. Nevertheless, the general tendency of Islam is to stimulate intolerance and to engender hatred and contempt not only for polytheists, but also, although in a modified form, for all monotheists who will not repeat the formula which acknowledges that

all his wrath, and, after some sharp diplomatic passages, extracted a declaration from the Porte that for the future no apostate should be put to death. The incident is related in Chapter XVIII. of the *Life of Stratford Canning.* Religious freedom was further assured by Articles X.-XII. of the Khatt-i-Humayoun of February 28, 1856, which was issued after the Crimean War.

I once asked a high Moslem authority in Cairo how he reconciled the fact that an apostate could now no longer be executed with the alleged immutability of the Sacred Law. The casuistry of his reply would have done honour to a Spanish Inquisitor. The Kadi, he said, does not recognise any change in the Law. He would, in the case of an apostate, pronounce sentence of death according to the Law, but it was for the secular authorities to carry out the sentence. If they failed in their duty, the sin of disobeying the Law would lie on their heads. Cases of apostasy are very rare, but during my tenure of office in Egypt, I had to interfere once or twice to protect from maltreatment Moslems who had been converted to Christianity by the American missionaries.

[1] Mr. Pickthall (*Folk-Lore of the Holy Land*, p. xv), speaking of the capture of Jerusalem by the Khalif Omar, says: "Omar's severity towards the Christians was so much below their anticipations that he figures in the popular memory almost as a benefactor of their religion. They were deprived of their church-bells, but kept their churches; and if large numbers of them embraced El Islâm, it was through self-interest (or conviction) and not at the point of the sword, as has been represented. Indeed, the toleration displayed by the Moslems towards the vanquished, though less than we should practise nowadays, is without a parallel in Europe till many centuries later. It was not emulated by the Crusaders, who, rushing to wrest the Holy Sepulchre from the clutch of the 'foul Paynim,' were astonished to find it in the hands of Christians, whom, to cloak their disconcertion, they denounced as heretics."

[2] Upon the toleration accorded to the Jews by Moslems, see Milman's *History of the Jews*, bk. xxiii.

Mohammed was indeed the Prophet of God. Neither can this be any matter for surprise. The faith of Islam admits of no compromise. The Moslem is the antithesis of the pantheistic Hindoo. His faith is essentially exclusive. Its founder launched fiery anathemas against all who would not accept the divinity of his inspiration, and his words fell on fertile ground, for a large number of those who have embraced Islam are semi-savages, and often warlike savages, whose minds are too untrained to receive the idea that an honest difference of opinion is no cause for bitter hatred. More than this, the Moslem has for centuries past been taught that the barbarous principles of the *lex talionis* are sanctioned, and even enjoined by his religion. He is told to revenge himself on his enemies, to strike them that strike him, to claim an eye for an eye, and a tooth for a tooth. Islamism, therefore, unlike Christianity, tends to engender the idea that revenge and hatred, rather than love and charity,[1] should form the basis of the relations between man and man; and it inculcates a special degree of hatred against those who do not accept the Moslem faith. "When ye encounter the unbelievers," says the Koran, "strike off their heads until ye have made a great slaughter among them, and bind them in bonds. . . . O true believers, if ye assist God, by fighting for his religion, he will assist you against your enemies; and will set your feet fast; but as for the infidels, let them perish; and their works God shall render vain. . . . Verily, God will introduce those who believe and do good works into gardens beneath which rivers flow, but the unbelievers indulge themselves in pleasures, and eat as beasts eat; and their abode shall be hell

[1] "Le Christianisme a été intolérant, mais l'intolérance n'est pas un fait essentiellement chrétien. C'est un fait juif."—Renan, *Vie de Jésus*, p. 425.

fire."[1] It is true that when Mohammed denounced unbelievers he was alluding more especially to the pagans who during his lifetime inhabited the Arabian Peninsula, but later commentators and interpreters of the Koran applied his denunciations to Christians and Jews, and it is in this sense that they are now understood by a large number of Mohammedans. Does not the word "Ghazi," which is the highest title attainable by an officer of the Sultan's army, signify "one who fights in the cause of Islam; a hero; a warrior; one who slays an infidel"?[2] Does not every Mollah, when he recites the Khutbeh at the Mosque, invoke Divine wrath on the heads of unbelievers in terms which are sufficiently pronounced at all times, and in which the diapason of invective swells still more loudly when any adventitious circumstances may have tended to fan the flame of fanaticism? Should not every non-Moslem land be considered in strict parlance a Dar-el-Harb, a land of warfare?[3] When principles such as these have been dinned for centuries past into the ears of Moslems, it can be no matter for surprise that a spirit of intolerance has been generated.

The Englishman in Egypt will find that, in the

[1] On the other hand, Surah ii. 257, says: "Let there be no compulsion in religion." The numerous contradictory utterances and inconsistencies of the Koran cannot be reconciled. They are probably due to the fact that Mohammed's teaching was greatly influenced by passing events as well as by the personal episodes of his own career.

[2] Hughes's *Dictionary of Islam*, p. 139.

[3] There is, however, considerable difference of opinion amongst Moslem authorities as to the precise definition of a Dar-el-Harb. The question is one of considerable importance to the rulers of India. It is discussed in Sir William Hunter's work entitled *Indian Musulmans*. The highest Moslem authorities have expressed opinions that India is a Dar-el-Islam, and not a Dar-el-Harb. Hence, it is not incumbent on the Moslems of India to carry on a Jihad against the infidels. The truth is that when, twelve centuries ago, these words came into use, it was never contemplated that sixty millions of Moslems would be living peacefully under the rule of a Christian King or Queen. Hence, some *modus vivendi* had to be found, which would bring the facts of the

practical everyday work of administration, this intolerant spirit, though it may not always find expression in word or deed, is an obstacle to the reformer of which it is difficult to overrate the importance. He will find that he has not, as in India, to deal with a body of Moslems, numerically strong, but whose power of cohesion is enfeebled from their being scattered broadcast amongst a population five times as numerous as themselves, who hold to another and more tolerant creed. He will have to deal with a smaller but more compact body of Moslems, who are more subject to the influences of their spiritual leaders than their co-religionists in India. The Englishman will do his best under these circumstances. He will scrupulously abstain from interference in religious matters. He will be eager to explain that proselytism forms no part of his political programme. He will look the other way when greedy Sheikhs swallow up the endowments left by pious Moslems for charitable purposes. His Western mind may, indeed, revolt at the misappropriation of funds, but he would rather let these things be than incur the charge of tampering with any quasi-religious institution. For similar reasons, he will abstain from laying his reforming hand on the iniquities of the Kadi's courts. The hired perjurer will be allowed full immunity to exercise his profession,[1]

present day into apparent conformity with the doctrines of Islam. The law doctors of Northern India wisely laid down the principle that no Jihad was justifiable unless it was likely to be successful. This view was conformable to the worldly interests both of the rulers of India and of their Moslem subjects, but there is a somewhat secular ring about an utterance of this sort. It commends itself to the politician rather than to the uncompromising divine. Even the exponents of unbending Islam seem, however, prepared at times to admit the principle *qu'il y a des accommodements avec le ciel.*

[1] A number of false witnesses ply, or, at all events, used to ply for hire about the precincts of the Kadi's court at Cairo. They are prepared, on payment, to swear to anything. I have been informed that when the British Government took over the administration of Cyprus

for the Englishman is informed that the criminal cannot be brought to justice without shaking one of the props which hold together the religious edifice founded twelve centuries ago by the Prophet of Arabia. He did not for many years allow a murderer, whose offence was clearly proved, to be hanged because Islam declared—or was supposed by many ill-informed Moslems to declare—that such an act is unlawful unless the murderer confesses his crime, or unless the act is committed in the presence of two witnesses; and he accepted this principle in deference to Moslem sentiment, with the full knowledge that, in accepting it, he was giving a direct encouragement to perjury and the use of torture to extract evidence.[1] In the work of civil juridical reform, he will bear with all the antiquated formalities of the Mehkemeh Sheraieh. He will scrupulously respect all Moslem observances. He will generally, amidst some twinges of his Sabbatarian conscience, observe Friday as a holiday, and perform the work of the Egyptian Government on Sunday.[2] He will put on slippers over his boots when he enters a Mosque. He will pay his respects to Moslem notabilities during the fast of Ramazan and the feast of Bairam. He will, when an officer of the army, take part in

it was found that the profession of false witness had been officially recognised by the Turkish Government. Perjurers took out licenses for the exercise of their profession. A good account of the proceedings of these professional witnesses is given in Senior's *Journal in Turkey and Greece*, p. 80.

It ought in fairness to be added that hired perjurers existed at one time in England. The literature of the Elizabethan period abounds with allusions to "Knights of the Post," as they were then termed.

[1] The law on this subject was eventually changed. After prolonged inquiry, it was ascertained beyond doubt that the view commonly held in Egypt was not in conformity with Moslem law or tradition. In 1897, therefore, a law was passed in virtue of which the special provision as regards the evidence necessary in order to permit of a capital punishment being inflicted in a case of murder was abolished.

[2] Some British officials have declined to work on Sundays, and have made up the hours thus lost by working extra hours on week-days.

Moslem religious ceremonies, fire salutes at religious festivals, and sometimes expose his life under the burning rays of an African sun rather than substitute a Christian helmet for the tarboush, which is the distinctive mark of the Moslem soldier in the Ottoman dominions. And when he has done all these things and many more of a like nature, they will only avail him so far that they may perhaps tend to obviate any active eruption of the volcano of intolerance. They will acquire for him a grudging acknowledgment that he is content to let well alone, and that he does not endeavour to evangelise at the point of the bayonet. He will not be able to inspire any strong feeling of gratitude beyond this limit. The English engineer may give the Egyptian fellah water for his fields, and roads and railways to enable him to bring his produce to market; the English financier may afford him fiscal relief beyond his wildest hopes; the English jurist may prevent his being sent to death or exile for a crime of which he is innocent; the English schoolmaster may open to him the door of Western knowledge and science; in a word, his material comfort may be increased, his intellect may be developed, and his moral being elevated under British auspices, but the Egyptian Moslem, albeit he hates and fears the Turkish Pasha, that he recognises the benefits conferred on him by the Englishman and acknowledges his superior ability, can never forget the fact that the Englishman wears a hat whilst he, himself, wears a tarboush or a turban. Though he accepts the benefits willingly enough, he is always mindful that the hand which bestows them is not that of a co-religionist, and it is this which affects him far more than the thought that the Englishman is not his compatriot. Do what he will, through the combined channels of sympathy and of reason, the Englishman will never be able to break down this barrier, that whereas both he and the Egyptian Moslems are prepared to aver that there is no God but God, the Egyptian is, and the Englishman is not prepared to subscribe to the latter part of the formula, which lays down that Mohammed was the Prophet of God. "Islam is all in all to the fellah; the unbelievers he looks on as a miserable minority; and it is only the unpleasant fact that they cannot be crushed at present that prevents his crushing them, and asserting the supremacy of Islam."[1]

Neither is this the sole barrier which is interposed between the two races. Look, not only to the leading dogma, but to the incidents of Divine worship associated with Islamism as opposed to those of Christianity. Examine the consequences which the degradation of women brings in its train. Consider the mental and moral attributes, the customs, art, architecture,[2] language, dress, and tastes of the dark-skinned Eastern as compared with the fair-skinned Western. It will be found that on every point they are the poles asunder.[3] It would seem, indeed, as if even in the most trivial acts of life some unfelt impulse, for which no special reason can be assigned, drives the Eastern to do the exact opposite to that which the Western would do under similar circumstances.[4]

[1] W. Flinders Petrie, *Ten Years' Digging in Egypt*, p. 180.

[2] Dean Milman says: "The East, having once wrought out its architectural type and model, settled down in unprogressive, uncreative acquiescence, and went on copying that type with servile and almost undeviating uniformity. In the West, within certain limits, with certain principles, and with a fixed aim, there was freedom, progression, invention."—*History of Latin Christianity*, vol. ix. 270.

[3] Sir George Cornewall Lewis (*On the Method of Observation and Reasoning in Politics*, vol. ii. ch. xvi.) has some interesting remarks on this subject.

[4] An Englishman, who was a keen observer of Egyptian manners and customs, told me that, as a test of intelligence, he once asked a fellah to point to his left ear. A European would certainly have taken hold

It will be interesting to dwell on this point at somewhat greater length.

Consider first differences, some of great, some of trifling importance, which hinge on religious belief and ceremonial.

The Christian clings to the hope that, in the spiritual heaven to which he looks forward, he will meet with those with whom he has been associated in this world. This hope is, indeed, one of the most beautiful and consolatory features of his faith. The Moslem's belief in immortality is dissociated from any ideas of this nature. The Houris, who people the Paradise which he hopes to gain, were never inhabitants of this world.

The Christian prays for certain qualities to be granted to him, or for certain specific objects to be accomplished. The Moslem generally utters certain set formulæ of adoration; he rarely prays for specific objects.

The Christian will say his daily prayers in private. The Moslem will say them in public. He has no false shame about bearing public testimony to the fact that, in every act he performs, he is in the hands of God. "God," said an English divine who had made a study of Eastern religions, "is present to Mohammedans in a sense in which He is rarely present to us amidst the hurry and confusion of the West."[1]

The Christian, when he fasts at all, fasts moderately by day and sleeps at night. The Moslem, during his fast, neither eats, nor drinks, nor smokes by day, but indulges without restraint at night.

The Christian religion encourages the fine arts,

of the lobe of his left ear with his left hand. The Egyptian passed his right hand over the top of his head and with that hand grasped the upper part of his left ear.

[1] Dean Stanley's *Lectures on the Eastern Church*, p. 334.

and draws a potent influence from them. The Mohammedan religion is iconoclastic. Painting and sculpture, when they represent any living creature, are condemned. Music is never heard in a Mosque.

The Christian will sometimes be cleanly because he thinks that it conduces to his health and comfort. He puts cleanliness next to godliness, but does not associate the two ideas together. The Moslem will be cleanly after a fashion because his religion enjoins him to be so.

Turn now to the mental and moral attributes of the two races. It will be found that the antitheses are striking.

Sir Alfred Lyall once said to me: "Accuracy is abhorrent to the Oriental mind. Every Anglo-Indian official should always remember that maxim." Want of accuracy, which easily degenerates into untruthfulness,[1] is, in fact, the main characteristic of the Oriental mind.

The European is a close reasoner; his statements of fact are devoid of ambiguity; he is a natural logician, albeit he may not have studied logic; he loves symmetry in all things; he is by nature sceptical and requires proof before he can accept the truth of any proposition; his trained intelligence works like a piece of mechanism. The mind of the Oriental, on the other hand, like his picturesque streets, is eminently wanting in symmetry. His reasoning is of the most slipshod description. Although the ancient Arabs acquired in a somewhat high degree the science of

[1] "Pour nous, races profondément sérieuses, la conviction signifie la sincérité avec soi-même. Mais la sincérité avec soi-même n'a pas beaucoup de sens chez les peuples Orientaux, peu habitués aux délicatesses de l'esprit critique. Bonne foi et imposture sont des mots qui, dans notre conscience rigide, s'opposent comme deux termes inconciliables. En Orient, il y a de l'un à l'autre mille fuites et mille détours. . . La vérité matérielle a très peu de prix pour l'Oriental; il voit tout à travers ses préjugés, ses intérêts, ses passions."—Renan, *Vie de Jésus*, p. 263.

dialectics,[1] their descendants are singularly deficient in the logical faculty. They are often incapable of drawing the most obvious conclusions from any simple premises of which they may admit the truth. Endeavour to elicit a plain statement of facts from an ordinary Egyptian. His explanation will generally be lengthy, and wanting in lucidity. He will probably contradict himself half-a-dozen times before he has finished his story. He will often break down under the mildest process of cross-examination. The Egyptian is also eminently unsceptical. He readily becomes the dupe of the magician and the astrologer. Even highly educated Egyptians are prone to refer the common occurrences of life to the intervention of some supernatural agency. In political matters, as well as in the affairs of everyday life, the Egyptian will, without inquiry, accept as true

[1] It is well known that the Arabs of the eleventh and twelfth centuries exercised a considerable influence on European thought by their teaching of the Aristotelian philosophy. See, *inter alia*, Milman's *History of Latin Christianity*, vol. ix. ciii. Also Symonds' *Renaissance in Italy*, p. 68. Dante (*Inf.* c. iv. 143) speaks of Avicenna and of "Avverroès, che 'l gran commento feo."

Renan (*Averroès et l'Averroisme*, pp. ii. and iii.) makes the following remarks:—"Les Arabes ne firent qu'adopter l'ensemble de l'encyclopédie grecque telle que le monde entier l'avait acceptée vers le VIIème et le VIIIème siècle. . . . La philosophie Arabe offre l'exemple à peu près unique d'une très haute culture supprimée presque instantanément sans laisser de traces, et à peu près oubliée du peuple qui l'a créée. L'Islamisme dévoila en cette circonstance ce qu'il y a d'irrémédiablement étroit dans son génie. Le Christianisme, lui aussi, a été peu favorable au développement de la science positive; il a réussi à l'arrêter en Espagne et à l'entraver beaucoup en Italie, mais il ne l'a pas étouffée, et même les branches les plus élevées de la famille chrétienne ont fini par se réconcilier avec elle. Incapable de se transformer et d'admettre aucun élément de vie civile et profane, l'Islamisme arracha de son sein tout genre de culture rationelle. Cette tendance fatale fut combattue tandis que l'hégémonie de l'Islamisme resta entre les mains des Arabes, race si fine et si spirituelle, ou des Persans, race très portée à la spéculation; mais elle régna sans contrepoids depuis que des barbares (Turcs, Berbers, etc.) prirent la direction de l'Islam. Le monde Musulman entra dès lors dans cette période d'ignorante brutalité, d'où il n'est sorti que pour tomber dans la morne agonie où il se débât sous nos yeux."

Averroès is, of course, a Spanish corruption of Ibn-Rushd.

the most absurd rumours.[1] He will, indeed, do more than this. He will often accept or reject such rumours in the inverse ratio of their probability, for, true to his natural inconsistency and want of rational discrimination, he will occasionally develop a flash of hardy scepticism when he is asked to believe the truth.

Contrast again the talkative European, bursting with superfluous energy, active in mind, inquisitive about everything he sees and hears, chafing under delay, and impatient of suffering, with the grave and silent Eastern, devoid of energy and initiative, stagnant in mind, wanting in curiosity about matters which are new to him, careless of waste of time and patient under suffering.

Or, again, look at the fulsome flattery, which the Oriental will offer to his superior and expect to receive from his inferior, and compare the general approval of such practices with the European frame of mind, which spurns both the flatterer and the person who invites flattery. This contemptible flattery, "the nurse of crime," as it was called by the poet Gay, is, indeed, a thorn in the side of the Englishman in Egypt, for it prevents Khedives and Pashas from hearing the truth from their own countrymen.[2]

[1] "The note of the primitive mind is amazing inaccuracy, coupled with wonderful receptivity."—Lyall, *Asiatic Studies*, Second Series, p. 193.

[2] The extent to which servile flattery may be carried at an Oriental court is well illustrated by the account given by Creasy (*Ottoman Turks*, p. 261) of the relations between Sultan Ibrahim (A.D. 1640-48) and his Grand Viziers. His first Vizier was Kara-Mustapha, an honest and courageous man, who dared to tell the truth to his Sovereign. After a short career, he was dismissed from office and strangled. His successor, Sultanzade Pasha, determined not to err on the side of frankness. Even Ibrahim, who was one of the worst of the degenerate Sultans, could not help noticing his servility. "How is it," he said, "that thou art able always to approve of my actions, whether good or evil?" "My Padishah!" replied the Minister, "thou art Khalif; thou art God's shadow upon earth. Every idea which thy spirit entertains is a revelation from Heaven. Thy orders, even when they appear

Perhaps there is no point as to which the difference between Eastern and Western habits of thought comes out into stronger relief than in the views which are respectively entertained by the Oriental and the European as regards provision for the future in this world. The European, especially if he be a Frenchman, is usually economical, and his economy will not unfrequently degenerate into meanness. He will pause before he gives pledges which, whilst providing for his immediate wants, may embarrass him or even reduce him to penury at no distant date. He will usually make provision for his old age, for the wife, who may, and for the children, who probably will survive him. The Egyptian generally cares for none of these things. He takes little heed for the morrow which will dawn on himself, and none for the days which are in store for those whom he will leave behind him. He is, perhaps, unconsciously influenced by the frame of mind engendered in himself and his progenitors from having lived for centuries under a succession of Governments, which afforded no security to the rights of property.[1] Whether he occupies the palace or the mud hut, he will often pledge his future with scarcely a thought of how his pledges may be redeemed. His life is in the past and in the present. The morrow must take care of the things of itself.

unreasonable, have an innate reasonableness, which thy slave ever reveres, though he may not always understand."

Ibrahim, Creasy adds, "accepted these assurances of infallibility and impeccability; and thenceforth spoke of himself as divinely inspired, in the midst of the most disgraceful scenes of folly, vice, and crime." He was eventually deposed and murdered.

[1] Indications are not wanting that, under the influence of good government, the improvident habits of the Egyptian population are being sensibly modified. I have alluded to this subject several times in successive Annual Reports in connection with the scheme which has been introduced with a view to lending small sums to the fellaheen, and thus liberating them from the grip of the village usurers.

But these same habits of improvidence tend perhaps to develop a quality which is worthy of praise. The Oriental may often be blamed for prodigality, but he rarely incurs the charge of meanness. He is charitable to his neighbours, and the fact may be recorded to his advantage without stopping to inquire whether his charity is due to kindliness of heart, or to the self-interest, which impels him, at the dictates of his religion, to lay up riches in the world to come. Moreover, the Oriental is proverbially hospitable. Indeed, his hospitality often errs on the side of being too lavish.

It may be added, whilst on the subject of kindliness of heart, that the cruelty to animals, which so often shocks visitors to Egypt, is no worse than that which may be witnessed amongst Christian nations in the south of Europe, and is probably, as Lane observed in 1835, not a plant of indigenous growth, but is rather due to association with low-class Europeans. The Moslem religion enjoins kindness to animals. "There is no religion which has taken a higher view in its authoritative documents of animal life. 'There is no beast on earth,' says the Koran, 'nor bird which flieth with wings, but the same is a people like unto you,—unto the Lord shall they return.'"[1]

Passing on to the consideration of another difference between the Oriental and the European, which will prove a perpetual stumbling-block to the Englishman in Egypt, it is to be observed that the ways of the Oriental are tortuous; his love of intrigue is inveterate; centuries of despotic government, during which his race has been exposed to the unbridled violence of capricious and headstrong Governors, have led him to fall back on the natural defence of the weak against the strong. He reposes unlimited faith in his own cunning, and

[1] Bosworth Smith, *Mohammed and Mohammedanism*, p. 255.

to some extent his chosen weapon will stand him in good stead. But its employment will widen the breach between him and his protectors, for fate has willed that the Egyptians should be more especially associated with those members of the European family who, perhaps more than any others, loathe and despise intrigue; who, in their dealings with their fellow-men, are frank and blunt, even at times to brutality; and who, though not difficult to beguile, are apt unexpectedly to turn round and smite those who have beguiled them so hardly as to crush them to the dust. From this point of view, one of the more subtle Latin races, had it occupied the predominant position held by the English in Egypt, would probably have had more sympathy with the weaknesses of Egyptian character than the Anglo-Saxon.

Look, again, to the high powers of organisation displayed by the European, to his constant endeavours to bend circumstances to suit his will, and to his tendency to question the acts of his superiors unless he happens to agree with them, a tendency which is especially marked in Englishmen, and which is only kept in subjection by the trained and intelligent discipline resulting from education. Compare these attributes with the feeble organising powers of the Oriental, with his fatalism which accepts the inevitable, and with his submissiveness to all constituted authority.

And if it be held that powers of organisation are only required amongst the educated classes, look to what, for want of a more appropriate term to express the idea, may be called the general muddle-headedness of the ordinary uneducated Egyptian, of which a few instances may be given.

On more than one occasion, a pointsman in the Egyptian railway service has been known to turn his points when the passing train had been *half* transferred from one line to the other, with the natural result that the train was upset. An Egyptian engine-driver has been known to forget which handle to turn in order to stop his locomotive. On several occasions, railway employés have been killed owing to their having gone to sleep with their heads on the rail, that special position having been adopted in order to ensure their being awakened by the noise of an approaching train. A European would think that, where a road and a paved side-walk existed, it required no great effort of the reasoning faculty to perceive that human beings were intended to pass along the side-walk, and animals along the road. The point is not always so clear to the Egyptian. He will not unfrequently walk in the middle of the road, and will send his donkey along the side-path. Instances of this sort might be multiplied. Compare the habits of thought which can lead to actions of this nature with the promptitude with which the European seizes on an idea when it is presented to him, and acts as occasion may demand.

Then, again, side by side with the European's appreciation of arithmetic, consider that in all matters connected with number or quantity, the ordinary Egyptian goes hopelessly astray. Few uneducated Egyptians know their own age. The usual reply of an Egyptian, if asked the age of some old man, is that he is a hundred years old. What importance, he thinks, can be attached to precision about a matter of this sort, or, indeed, to any scientific or quasi-scientific subject? I once asked a former head of the El-Azhar University whether his professors taught that the sun went round the earth or the earth round the sun. He replied that he was not sure, that one nation thought one way, and another another way,—his natural politeness possibly forbidding him to express to me what he really thought of the infidels Kepler and Copernicus and their doctrines,—that his general impression was that the sun went round the earth, but that he had never paid much attention to the matter, and that the subject was too unimportant to merit serious discussion. Tell an Egyptian cook that he puts too much salt into the soup. He will abstain altogether from the use of salt. Or, on the other hand, tell him that he does not use salt enough; he will throw in a bucketful. He cannot hit the happy mean; moderation in the use of salt, or in anything else, is foreign to his nature; he cannot grasp the idea of quantity. Again, ask an Arab from the Soudan how many men were killed at one of the numerous battles which have taken place in that country. The only thing which is certain is that he will not state the precise truth, or anything near it, except by accident. Neither will he reply that he cannot answer the question addressed to him. He will, without hesitation, blurt out the first conjecture, which flashes across his brain, as a fact coming within his personal knowledge. He may say 100, or he may say 2000. He has a very faint conception of what either figure represents, and he will be prepared to bring the original 100 up to 2000, or the original 2000 down to 100, according to the views which, by the light of subsequent conversation, would appear gratifying to his interrogator.

Again, consider the manners of the Oriental as contrasted with those of the European. We hear a great deal in praise of Oriental courtesy, and the praise is in some respects well deserved. A high-class European will be charmed with the manners of a high-class Oriental, albeit he is aware that the exaggerated compliments common in the East are merely figurative, and cannot be taken to represent the real sentiments of the speaker. But look a little deeper and examine the ground on which these outward forms of courtesy are based. The examination will bring out a somewhat unpleasant feature of the Egyptian character. For one of the main reasons why an Egyptian, if he is in any position of authority, is courteous is that he thinks it his interest to be so. In spite of this outside courtesy to his superiors, he will not unfrequently be harsh and tyrannical to his inferiors, to whose feelings and interests he is often indifferent. There are, however, exceptions. Slaves are more often treated with kindness than severity, although in this case motives of self-interest may perhaps be traced. Amongst the middle and lower classes of Egyptians a spirit of real courtesy, not based on self-interest, is often to be found in their hospitality towards strangers. Moreover, among equals of all classes, the outward forms of courtesy are preserved.

These points have been indicated at some length because the differences between Eastern and Western habits of thought constitute a barrier interposed between the Egyptian and the Englishman almost as great as that resulting from differences of religion, ideas of government, and social customs. Indeed, this difference of mental attributes constitutes perhaps the greatest of all barriers. It prevents the Englishman and the Egyptian from understanding each other. Nevertheless, there is one saving clause, which serves in some respects as a bond of union between the two races. Once explain to an Egyptian what he is to do, and he will assimilate the idea rapidly. He is a good imitator, and will make a faithful, even sometimes a too servile copy of the work of his European teacher. His civilisation may be a veneer, yet he will readily adopt the letter, the catchwords and jargon, if not the spirit of

European administrative systems. His movements will, it is true, be not unfrequently those of an automaton, but a skilfully constructed automaton may do a great deal of useful work. This feature in the Egyptian character is of great importance in connection with the administration of the country. It is a source of strength, and also a source of weakness; for, so long as British supervision is maintained, the Egyptian will readily copy the practices and procedures of his English teachers. No necessity will, therefore, arise for employing any large number of English subordinates. On the other hand, inasmuch as the Egyptian has but little power of initiation, and often does not thoroughly grasp the reasons why his teachers have impelled him in certain directions, a relapse will ensue if English supervision be withdrawn.

Look now to the consequences which result from the degradation of women in Mohammedan countries. In respect to two points, both of which are of vital importance, there is a radical difference between the position of Moslem women and that of their European sisters. In the first place, the face of the Moslem woman is veiled when she appears in public. She lives a life of seclusion. The face of the European woman is exposed to view in public. The only restraints placed on her movements are those dictated by her own sense of propriety. In the second place, the East is polygamous, the West is monogamous.

It cannot be doubted that the seclusion of women exercises a baneful effect on Eastern society. The arguments on this subject are, indeed, so commonplace that it is unnecessary to dwell on them. It will be sufficient to say that seclusion, by confining the sphere of woman's interest to a very limited horizon, cramps the intellect and withers the mental development of one-half of the population in Moslem countries. "An Englishwoman asked an Egyptian lady how she passed her time. 'I sit on this sofa,' she answered, 'and when I am tired, I cross over and sit on that.'"[1] Moreover, inasmuch as women, in their capacities as wives and mothers, exercise a great influence over the characters of their husbands and sons, it is obvious that the seclusion of women must produce a deteriorating effect on the male population, in whose presumed interests the custom was originally established, and is still maintained.

When an Egyptian woman interferes in politics, her interference is almost always mischievous. The information she obtains is necessarily communicated to her through a variety of distorted media. The fact of her seclusion renders it well-nigh impossible for her to hear both sides of a question. The most trumpery gossip will be sufficient to set her suspicions ablaze, and to convince her that some danger, which is often imaginary, hangs over the head of herself or her relatives. Ignorance of any world beyond that of the harem renders it impossible for her to discriminate between truth and falsehood, between what is within the bounds of possibility and what is so manifestly absurd as to be impossible.

I need not dwell on the causes which, in Egypt, as in other Oriental countries, have led to the seclusion of women, nor on the extent to which this practice is due to the prevalence of the Mohammedan religion.[2] From the point of view of the politician and administrator, the consideration of these questions, interesting though they be, is

[1] *Cairo*, p. 140.

[2] "The system of the harem is, in its origin, not Moslem, but simply Oriental. The only reproach that can be made against the Prophet is that, by too definite legislation, he rendered subsequent development and reform impossible."—*Turkey in Europe*, p. 190.

of little more than academic interest. I am not endeavouring in this work to discuss the effects of Islamism upon progress and civilisation in general. My task is of a more humble nature. I am merely attempting to describe the state of things which the English found in existence when they took in hand the rehabilitation of Egypt. Amongst other social difficulties it has, therefore, to be noted that Moslem women in Egypt are secluded, and that their influence, partly by reason of their seclusion, is, in all political and administrative matters, generally bad.

The effects of polygamy are more baneful and far-reaching than those of seclusion. The whole fabric of European society rests upon the preservation of family life. Monogamy fosters family life, polygamy destroys it. The monogamous Christian respects women; the teaching of his religion and the incidents of his religious worship tend to elevate them. He sees in the Virgin Mary an ideal of womanhood, which would be incomprehensible in a Moslem country.[1] The Moslem, on the other hand, despises women; both his religion and the example of his Prophet, the history of whose private life has been handed down to him, tend to lower them in his eyes. Save in exceptional cases, the Christian fulfils the vow which he has made at the altar to cleave to his wedded wife for life. The Moslem, when his passion is sated, can if he likes throw off his wife like an old glove. According to the Sunnis, whose

[1] See Lecky, *History of European Morals*, vol. ii. p. 367. No Moslem could appreciate the beauty of Wordsworth's sonnet on the Virgin:—

> Thy image falls to earth. Yet some, I ween,
> Not unforgiven the suppliant knee might bend
> As to a visible Power, in which did blend
> All that was mixed and reconciled in thee,
> Of Mother's love with maiden purity,
> Of high with low, celestial with terrene.

doctrines are quoted because the Egyptians are Sunnis, "A husband may divorce his wife without any misbehaviour on her part, or without assigning any cause. The divorce of every husband is effective if he be of sound understanding and of mature age."[1] There is, however, a good deal of difference of opinion amongst legal authorities as to the law of divorce.[2] The general principle inculcated by Mohammed on this subject is thus explained in the *Traditions*: "The thing which is lawful, but disliked by God, is divorce."[3] The practice of monogamy has of late years been gaining ground amongst the more enlightened Egyptians. The late and the present Khedive, the late Chérif Pasha, and Riaz Pasha may be cited as monogamous notabilities. The movement in this direction may be attributed to several causes. In the first place, education and association with Europeans may have induced the conviction that it is more respectable, and generally more conducive to domestic happiness, to marry one wife rather than to take advantage of the permission granted by Mohammed to "marry what seems good to you of women, by twos, or threes, or fours, or what your right hand possesses" (Surah iv. 3). In the second place, polygamy is expensive. Lane said, so long ago as 1835, "I believe that not more than one husband among twenty has two wives,"[4] and since Lane's time, the practice of polygamy has certainly diminished. Nevertheless, the movement in favour of monogamy cannot be as yet called general. The first thing an Egyptian of the lower classes will do when he gets a little money is to marry a second wife. A groom in

[1] *Dictionary of Islam*, p. 88.

[2] This question is fully discussed by Syed Ameer Ali in his *Personal Law of the Mohammedans*, chapters xi.-xiii.

[3] *Dictionary of Islam*, p. 87.

[4] *Modern Egyptians*, vol. i. p. 231.

my stables was divorced and re-married eleven times in the course of a year or two. I remember hearing of an old Pasha who complained peevishly that he had to go to the funeral of his first wife, to whom he had been married forty years previously, and whose very existence he had forgotten. The great facility given to divorce necessarily weakens the strength of the family tie. Further, in the West, a wife, whose personal attractions have disappeared under the hand of time, can often, in default of other influences, maintain her hold over her husband's affections through the children which she has borne to him.

> Femina quum senuit, retinet connubia partu,
> Uxorisque decus matris reverentia pensat.

The hold which the discarded or neglected Moslem wife might maintain on grounds such as these is weakened by the presence of younger and more attractive rivals, who have perhaps borne other children to her husband.

Amongst other consequences resulting from polygamy and the customs which cluster round polygamy, it may be noted that, whereas in the West the elevation of women has tended towards the refinement both of literature and of conversation, in the East their degradation has encouraged literary and conversational coarseness. This coarseness has attracted the attention of all who have written on Egyptian manners and customs.[1] It is true that the Moslem may fairly argue that he started 600 years later than the Christian in the race to attain civilisation, and that, apart from the English dramatists of the seventeenth century, the writings of Boccaccio and of Rabelais denote a state of society no more refined than that which at present exists in Egypt; and

[1] Lane's *Modern Egyptians*, vol. i. pp. 260 and 273.

he may use this argument with all the greater reason inasmuch as the class of humour which finds most favour in Egyptian society is very much akin to that which we may now read in the *Decameron*. But, in the first place, it is to be observed that the *Decameron* is a model of refinement as compared with many works in Arabic; and, in the second place, it may be doubted whether, even in the Middle Ages, the general coarseness of European society was ever on a par with that of the modern Egyptians.

There is, however, one feature in connection with family life in the East, where the Oriental contrasts very favourably with the European. "Paradise," the Prophet finely said, "lies under the feet of mothers." Greater outward respect is, in fact, shown to parents, and to old age in general, by Eastern than by Western races. "Thou shalt rise up before the hoary head and honour the face of the old man and fear thy God." Egyptians have from time immemorial acted on this Levitical principle. Herodotus says: "Their (the Egyptian) young men when they meet their elders in the streets, give way to them and step aside; and if an elder man comes in where young men are present, these latter rise from their seats."[1] Young Egyptians generally respect and obey their parents and are well treated by them, unless, indeed, both parents and children occupy very high positions, in which case, the principle laid down by the Prophet Micah rather than that prescribed by Moses forms the basis of the family connection: "A man's enemies are the men of his own house."

Consider also the different standpoints from which the European and the Oriental approach the subject of government.

[1] Book ii. chapter 132.

The point of view of the Eastern is wholly different from that of the Western. I speak, of course, of the true Eastern, free from European alloy; for when once the Eastern, and notably the Egyptian, has been semi-Europeanised, he will often develop with amazing rapidity into a root-and-branch reformer. He will not understand moderation in reform any more than the Egyptian cook, who was recently mentioned, will understand moderation in the use of salt. The true Eastern is a staunch conservative. He would probably look upon an Oriental Lord Eldon as a rash innovator. European affairs appear to him to be in a constant state of flux; his frame of mind is fitly represented by Matthew Arnold's fine lines:—

> The East bowed low before the blast
> In patient deep disdain;
> She let the legions thunder past,
> And plunged in thought again.

The mind of the true Eastern is at once lethargic and suspicious; he does not want to be reformed, and he is convinced that, if the European wishes to reform him, the desire springs from sentiments which bode him no good. Moreover, his conservatism is due to an instinct of self-preservation, and to a dim perception that, if he allows himself to be even slightly reformed, all the things to which he attaches importance will be not merely changed in this or that particular, but will rather be swept off the face of the earth. Perhaps he is not far wrong. Although there are many highly educated gentlemen who profess the Moslem religion, it has yet to be proved that Islam can assimilate civilisation without succumbing in the process. It is, indeed, not improbable that, in its passage through the European crucible, many of the distinctive features of Islam, the good alike with the bad, will be volatilised, and that it will eventually issue forth in a form scarcely capable of recognition. "The Egyptians," Moses said, "whom ye have seen to-day, ye shall see them again no more for ever."[1] The prophecy may be approaching fulfilment in a sense different to that in which it was addressed to the Israelites.

Look, moreover, not only to the spirit of the lawgivers, but to the general principles on which the laws are based. The tendency in all civilised European States is to separate religious from civil laws. In Moslem States, on the other hand, religious and civil laws are inextricably interwoven.

In the West, the law recognises and encourages the use of credit,[2] and protects the creditor. It may be remarked incidentally that, in respect to this point perhaps more than any other, the ignorant and improvident Egyptian suffered when the Code Napoléon, like a Juggernaut's car, passed over his back. On the other hand, the Moslem law condemns usury, and thus discourages the outlay of capital.[3] The lax Egyptian Moslem is obliged to have recourse to all sorts of subterfuges in order to lend money without violating the letter of the law. The presence of the Christian usurer, with whom it is at times possible for the Moslem to form an unnatural alliance based on a community of interest, facilitates subterfuges of this sort.

Again, in the East the theory and practice that the Government is the sole proprietor of the soil survives to a certain extent. In the West, on

[1] Exodus xiv. 13.

[2] It should, however, be remembered that, during the Middle Ages, the Christian Church exerted its influence against usury, with the result that the money-lending business fell into the hands of the Jews.

[3] The Moslem depositors in the Government Savings Banks often decline to accept interest on their deposits.

the other hand, the theory has been well-nigh forgotten, and the practice no longer survives. Save in the least civilised portions of Europe,[1] land is held to be the private property of individuals.

So also as regards criminal laws, the differences are striking. The Moslem code is based upon the principle, long since abandoned in the West, that it is the business of the State to oblige its citizens to be religious and moral. A sentence of death for blasphemy could not, of course, at present be carried out, but a case occurred in Egypt, since the British occupation, of a man who received eighty blows with a courbash, under sentence from the Kadi, for smoking a cigarette in the streets during the Ramazan fast. In general also, Oriental punishments are cruel,[2] whilst European punishments are mild. This fact tends towards brutalising the population and rendering them cruel to each other.

Compare, again, the languages, art, architecture, and music of the Oriental with those of the European. It will be found that on almost every point the practices and the tastes of the one are opposed to those of the other.

Oriental alphabets are intricate. The Turk, the Arab, and the Persian begin to write on the right side of the page; the short vowels are almost always omitted. European alphabets, on the other hand, are simple. The European begins to write on the left-hand side of the page.

Orientals continue to copy from one style of art. European art is various and constantly develops new forms.

Oriental music, which is much the same in all parts of the East, is wanting in harmony and

[1] See Sir Donald Mackenzie Wallace's *Russia*.

[2] Moltke, who wrote in 1836, says (*Briefe, etc., in der Türkei*, p. 36) that he had been a personal witness of the barbarous punishment inflicted in Turkey on unfaithful wives.

monotonous to the ears of most Europeans.[1] European music, on the other hand, generally fails to please Orientals.

Turn, again, to the most ordinary customs and expressions, the dress, etc., of the Oriental as compared with the European. It will be found that, even in the most trivial matters, the Oriental will generally do or say the opposite to what the European would do or say under similar circumstances. Numerous instances in point will readily occur to any one who has even a slight acquaintance with Eastern social life.

The ethnologist, the comparative philologist, and the sociologist would possibly be able to give explanations as regards many of the differences which exist between the East and the West. As I am only a diplomatist and an administrator, whose proper study is also man, but from the point of view of governing him rather than from that of scientific research into how he comes to be what he is, I content myself with noting the fact that somehow or other the Oriental generally acts, speaks, and thinks in a manner exactly opposite to the European. "Tout, chez ce peuple, porte l'empreinte d'un contraste frappant avec les habitudes des nations Européennes. Cette différence est l'ouvrage du climat, des institutions civiles et des préjugés religieux."[2]

Many of the observations contained in this chapter may be considered commonplace. Nothing, indeed, has been stated which will be new to those who have paid attention to Eastern affairs, or who are in any degree familiar with the social life of the East. I have, however, thought it desirable to make a catalogue—and, I may add, a very incom-

[1] There can be no doubt that from the earliest times the Arabs have taken extreme delight in their own music. See Kremer's *Culturgeschichte des Orients*, vol. i. p. 149.

[2] *Description de l'Égypte*, p. 83.

plete catalogue—of the main points as to which Egyptian and European habits of thought and customs diverge, for, although each detail taken by itself may be well known, it may be doubted whether even those Englishmen who have been actively engaged in the work of Egyptian administration have always recognised to the full that, in taking in hand Egyptian reform, they had to deal with a society which was not only in a backward state of civilisation, but which was also, from their point of view, well-nigh incomprehensible. They were brought face to face with a population which, in the eyes of the European, was, morally and politically speaking, walking on its head. Lord Dalling, at one time Ambassador at Constantinople, is credited with saying: "When you wish to know what a Turkish official is likely to do, first consider what it would be his interest to do; next, what any other man would do in similar circumstances; and thirdly, what every one expects him to do. When you have ascertained these, you are so far advanced on your road that you may be perfectly certain he will not adopt any of these courses." Often have I thought that an Egyptian would take a certain view of a question based on my idea of the manner in which he would interpret either his own or Egyptian interests. And often have I found that he interpreted those interests in some strange and fanciful manner, which would never have entered into the head of any European.

All these considerations, however, affected the Englishman but slightly when, in 1882, he undertook the regeneration of Egypt. When it is remembered that, in addition to the difficulties arising from the causes to which allusion is made in this chapter, the country had, for at least a century previous to 1882, been governed under a system which exhibited the extremes of savage cruelty and barbarity;[1] that the impulse towards civilisation first imparted, and not unintelligently imparted by the rough men of genius who founded the Khedivial dynasty, was continued on principles, which may almost be characterised as insane, by the incapable Said, and the spendthrift Ismail; that under their auspices all that was least creditable to European civilisation was attracted to Egypt, on whose carcase swarms of needy adventurers preyed at will; that, as a consequence of these proceedings, the very name of European stank in the nostrils of the Egyptian population; that whatever European ideas had taken root in the country had been imported from France; that the French Government and French public opinion were at the outset bitterly opposed to the action of England in Egypt; that, through the medium of an unscrupulous press, Englishmen were vilified and their actions systematically misrepresented; that, under the pressure of Europe and the European creditors of Egypt, a variety of complicated institutions had been created which were in advance of the requirements and state of civilisation of the country; that the Treasury was well-nigh bankrupt; that the army had been disbanded; that no law-courts worthy of the name existed;

[1] Bruce, writing of his visit to Cairo in 1768, says: "The Government of Cairo is much praised by some. It may perhaps have merit when explained, but I never could understand it, and therefore cannot explain it. But a more brutal, unjust, tyrannical, oppressive, avaricious set of infernal miscreants there is not on earth than are the members of the Government of Cairo" (*Travels to discover the Source of the Nile*, vol. i. p. 26). Volney, who visited Egypt in 1783-5, wrote: "Tout ce que l'on voit, ou que l'on entend, annonce que l'on est dans le pays de l'esclavage et de la tyrannie. On ne parle que de troubles civils, que de misère publique, que d'extorsions d'argent, que de bastonnades et de meurtres. Nulle sûreté pour la vie ou la propriété. On verse le sang d'un homme comme celui d'un bœuf. La justice même le verse sans formalité. L'officier de nuit dans ses rondes, l'officier de jour dans ses tournées, jugent, condamnent et font exécuter en un clin d'œil et sans appel. Des bourreaux les accompagnent, et au premier ordre la tête d'un malheureux tombe dans le sac de cuir, où on la reçoit de peur de souiller la place."—*Voyage en Syrie et en Égypte*, p. 162.

that the Englishman's own countrymen, who, according to their custom, judged mainly by results, expected that at the touch of his administrative wand all abuses would forthwith disappear; that the fellah expected immediate relief from taxation and oppression; that the Levantine contractor expected to dip his itching palm into the till of the British Treasury; that the Englishman's position was undefined, and that he was unable to satisfy all these expectations at once; that, having just quelled a rebellion in Egypt, he was confronted with a still more formidable rebellion in the Soudan; and, lastly, that before he had seriously begun the work of reform, he was constantly pressed by Frenchmen, and by some of his own countrymen, to declare his conviction that the work was accomplished,—when all these points are remembered, the difficulty of the task which England undertook may be appreciated in its true light. But the task was ennobled by its difficulty. It was one worthy of the past history, the might, the resources, and the sterling national qualities of the Anglo-Saxon race. I shall presently endeavour to show how it was accomplished. Before, however, dealing with this portion of my task, the component parts of the population of Egypt require some further analysis.

CHAPTER XXXV

THE MOSLEMS

Classification of the population—The Turco-Egyptians—The Egyptians—The hierarchy—The Grand Mufti—The head of the El-Azhar University—The Grand Kadi—The Sheikh el-Bekri—Mohammed el-Saadat—Abdul-Khalik el-Saadat—Mohammed Abdu—Mohammed Beyram—The Omdehs and Sheikhs—Their submissiveness to the Pashas—Their sympathy with Arábi—Their tyranny over the Fellaheen—Their feelings towards England—The Fellaheen—The Bedouins.

According to the census of 1897, the dwellers in Egypt were at that time 9,734,000 in number. These 9,734,000 souls may be classified in various ways.

In the first place, they may be considered as, on the one side, Ottoman subjects, a category which would include almost every species of semi-Egyptian hybrid, and on the other side, Europeans, a category which would include every nondescript who could, by hook or by crook, get his name registered at some European Consulate. Or, they may be classified as officials and non-officials, a classification, the discussion of which would bring into relief the fact that, when the British occupation commenced, it had not yet been realised by the native officials of Egypt that they were the trustees of the non-official classes ; rather were the latter considered to be the legitimate prey of the former. Or, they may be classified as Moslems and Christians, a distinction which, being converted from terms of religious belief into those of political and social life, would differentiate the ignorant, conservative mass from the more subtle, more superficially intellectual, but, if the true Europeans be excluded, by no means more virile minority. In the following remarks, the last of these three classifications will be adopted.

The Moslems consist, first, of Turks and Turco-Egyptians; secondly, of Egyptians; and thirdly, of Bedouins. A few Moslems resident in Egypt will thus remain unclassified; for instance, there are a few Algerians and Tunisians, who are French, and a few natives of India, who are British subjects. There are also a considerable number of Soudanese, an element which was found of importance when the reorganisation of the Egyptian army was taken in hand. But, for the purposes of the present argument, it will suffice to deal with the Moslems under the three main heads given above.

The Turk was the conqueror of Egypt, and within the memory of persons still living behaved as such. But there are now but few pure Turks left. In the absence of fresh importations from Turkey, a process of Egyptianisation set in. Absence from the headquarters of Ottoman thought and action, and intermarriage with Egyptians, produced their natural results. It is thought that no such thing as a pure Turk of the third generation is to be found within the length and breadth of the land. It is, indeed, a misnomer to speak of Turks in Egypt. By the time the English occupied the country in 1882, all the Turks had blossomed or, as some would say, degenerated into Turco-Egyptians. This is a point which the English politician had to bear carefully in mind, for as each year of the British occupation passed by, the Turco-Egyptian element in Egyptian society became more Egyptian and less Turkish in character and habits of thought. In common with other Moslems, the Turco-Egyptians looked to the Sultan as their Pope. But, on the other hand, they were year by year less inclined to regard him as their King. When, in 1892, the British Government stepped in and prevented a Firman of the Sultan from being promulgated, they rallied in a half-hearted and platonic manner round the Commander of the Faithful. They winced at the spectacle of his humiliation at the hands of a Christian Power. But, even then, the feelings of indignation excited in their breasts were probably no stronger than those which would be felt by an Italian patriot, who was also a devout Catholic, and who saw the Vatican obliged to yield to the Quirinal.

Again, in 1906, when the relations between England and Turkey were strained by the occurrence of what is known as the "Sinai Peninsula" incident, a strong wave of pro-Turkish feeling seemed to sweep over Egypt, but it was a purely fictitious movement, manufactured by the Anglophobe press. It speedily died a natural death.

In truth, religious conviction, backed by racial prejudices and by the sympathy generally entertained amongst Orientals for a theocratic form of government, may for a while wrestle with personal interest and political associations, but the chances are that, if the struggle is continued, religious conviction will get a fall. Pro-Turkish sentiment will, therefore, smoulder and occasionally flicker up sufficiently to show some feeble light, but it will never burst into a blaze. For, in fact, many considerations are constantly dragging the Turco-Egyptian in a direction away from Constantinople. Although he may try to deceive others, he cannot deceive himself. He knows well enough what he would do if he got the upper hand; he would plunder every one he could indiscriminately. He knows that his own brethren, whom his ancestors left behind at Constantinople, are prepared to act on precisely similar principles, and he feels that if they, who are certainly the most powerful of the sons of Islam, were once to step on the scene, his affinity of race would avail him little; he would take rank with the plundered rather than with the plunderers; or, at best, he would have to stand by and see the Egyptians robbed without obtaining any adequate share of the plunder. Rather than submit to this fate, it were perhaps better to take the good things the Englishmen offer to him; it is true that they will not let him spoil the Egyptian, but they will prevent the Constantinopolitan Turk from spoiling him; they give him wealth and security for his life and property; perhaps it will be as well to pause before throwing away these benefits in order to obtain the doubtful advantages of being governed by a number of co-religionists, whose community of religion will in no degree temper their rapacity. Then, again, as time went on, a few Turco-Egyptians were animated by sentiments which, however unpractical, were by no means ignoble. They became identified with Egyptian aspirations, and wished to establish a government free from the interference of either Turk or European. A few also recognised the benefits conferred on the country by the British occupation, and loyally co-operated with the British officials in furthering the cause of reform.

Thus, in 1882, the English found a body of Turco-Egyptians who occupied the principal places under Government; who were the chief landowners in the country; who disliked the English, inasmuch as they knew by intuition that their intervention would save the Egyptians from being plundered; who occasionally cast a glance towards Constantinople, and were willing enough to try and scare the Englishman with the bugbear of the Khalif's spiritual authority; who would have been bitterly disappointed if their political flirtations with the Porte had been taken seriously, and if the Mohammedan Pope, doffing his mitre, had assumed the crown, handled the sword, and commenced to assert his authority in temporal affairs; and who, lastly, in the presence of the alien and the Christian, showed a tendency to amalgamate with the other dwellers on Egyptian soil in the creation of a sort of spurious patriotism. I say spurious patriotism, because the alliance between the semi-Egyptianised Turk and the pure Egyptian is unnatural. The people of Egypt are not really with the representative Turco-Egyptians. The peculiar characteristic of the typical Turco-Egyptian is his catholic capacity for impotent hatred. He hates the Englishman, because the Englishman curbs him. He hates and fears the pure Turk, because the pure Turk is difficult to curb. He despises the Egyptian, whom he regards as his prey, and who, in fact, would be his prey were it not for the English watchdog who keeps him off.

Amongst the many vague ideals incapable of realisation which are floating about in the Egyptian political atmosphere, nothing is more certain than that the ideal of the Turco-Egyptian can never be realised. He can never be restored to the position of trust, which he formerly occupied and abused.

But, with all this, the Turco-Egyptian has some redeeming qualities. The glamour of a dominant race still hovers as an aureole, albeit a very dimmed aureole, round his head. He is certainly not more corrupt than the Egyptian; he is more manly, and the greater the quantity of Turkish blood running in his veins, the more will his manly qualities appear. He is sometimes truthful and outspoken after his own fashion. He has a rude standard of honour. Go where you will in Egypt, if any bit of administrative work requiring a certain amount of energy has been well done by a native official, it will generally be found that the official in question is a Circassian or a Turco-Egyptian, who is probably more Turk than Egyptian. The Turco-Egyptian can, in fact, still to a certain extent command, and that is why, with all his defects, and in spite of the fact that the class to which he belongs is generally Anglophobe — although there are some notable exceptions,—it will often be found that the individual Englishman will get on well with the individual Turk, and better with the Turco-Egyptian than with the pure Egyptian, the Syrian or the Armenian. The northerner and the Oriental meet on the common ground that the Englishman is masterful, and that the Turco-Egyptian, though less masterful than the pure Turk, is more so than the pure Egyptian. The Englishman belongs to an imperial race, and the Turco-Egyptian to a race which but yesterday was imperial. The English, Nubar Pasha once said to me, "are the Turks of the West."

The second category of Egyptian Moslems may be divided into three heads. These are—first, the hierarchy; second, the squirearchy; and third, the fellaheen.

The Ulema—the learned men[1]—of the El-Azhar Mosque constitute a distinct religious corporation, which is divided into grades, and which is officially recognised by the Government. A University is attached to the Mosque. The number of Ulema is limited; in order to qualify for the rank of "Alim," which carries with it the right to wear a pelisse conferred by the Khedive,

[1] "Ulema" is the plural of the Arabic word "Alim," signifying learned, a doctor of laws.

a candidate must have studied at the University, and have passed certain examinations to test his knowledge of the Koran, the Traditions (Hadith), and the Sacred Law of Islam. Many a Moslem may be learned in the ordinary acceptation of the term; he may, for instance be a "Hafiz," who can repeat the whole Koran by heart, or, at all events, is supposed to be able to do so; but unless he has undergone the necessary examination at the El-Azhar University, he is not, technically speaking, considered an "Alim." He may officiate at religious services, but he will not have acquired the right to expound either the tenets of Islam or the Sacred Law at any of the principal Mosques.

The three chief Ulema are the Grand Mufti, the head of the El-Azhar University, and the Grand Kadi. The last named takes what is the equivalent of his degree, not at Cairo, but at Constantinople.

The Grand Mufti is the chief law-doctor of the country. It is his duty to pronounce *ex cathedra* opinions (Fetwas) upon any doubtful points of the Sacred Law, which may be submitted to him. He is a magnate of whose spiritual authority the temporal rulers of the country must take account. Despotic Khedives and even, it is said, Suleiman the Magnificent,[1] have tried to force the hand or override the decisions of the Grand Mufti, and like their Christian prototype who tried to throw off

[1] It is related that Sultan Suleiman the Magnificent asked Sheikh Abu Saoud, who was one of the greatest of the Ottoman Muftis, to issue a Fetwa declaring it lawful to put to death all the inhabitants of conquered European provinces who refused to embrace the faith of Islam. The Grand Mufti would not comply with this request.

Abbas I. is said to have requested the Grand Mufti (Sheikh-el-Abbasi, who died in 1893 at the age of ninety) to issue a Fetwa stating that the power of ratifying a sentence of death lay not, as was then the practice, with the Sultan, but with the Viceroy. The Grand Mufti refused. He was exiled to the Soudan, but, in the face of the strong protests made by many of the leading Mohammedans of Cairo, even despotic Abbas was obliged to yield. The Mufti was recalled.

the spiritual yoke, they have generally been obliged to go to Canossa.[1] The English politician also has to recognise the Mufti's existence. When, indeed, the venerable old man, who at one time occupied the post of Grand Mufti, advocated, as the most natural thing in the world, the crucifixion of criminals,[2] it was scarcely necessary for the Englishman to raise his little finger in order to remind the Egyptian world that, although the onward tramp of civilisation might be heard but faintly within the sacred precincts of the Mosque, he was nevertheless standing outside its walls with his treaties, his newspapers, and if needs be, his soldiers, to assert the validity of anti-crucifixionist principles. But, though in an extreme case such as this the Englishman could impose a veto on some barbarous act, he could not do much more. He could not make the Egyptian horse drink of the waters of civilisation, albeit the most limpid streams of social and juridical reform were turned into the trough before him, if the Mufti condemned the act of drinking as impious. Popes and other ecclesiastical dignitaries have before now shown that they cannot be dragooned into submission. Neither do Muftis fear red-coated soldiers. Moreover, they fear the wrath of the European press even less than they fear redcoats.

The head of the famous El-Azhar University exercises a certain degree of control in temporal matters over those of the Ulema who lecture in the mosques, and must himself be, *par excellence*, an "Alim." The incumbent of this office during the first few years of my residence in Egypt was a worthy old man, with whom I entertained excellent personal relations, although, as has been already

[1] I say "generally" because there have been exceptions to the rule. Thus, in 1637, Amurath IV. put the Grand Mufti to death.—Creasy, *Ottoman Turks*, p. 253.

[2] *Vide ante*, p. 135.

mentioned,[1] our views as to the movements of the planets were not identical.

The Grand Kadi is perhaps the greatest of the Ulema. Up to the present time, he has always been a Turk from Constantinople. He pronounces final judgment on all subjects which come within the domain of personal law, having been bereft of criminal and civil jurisdiction by the progress which is constantly kibing the heel of his decadent system. I well remember the Grand Kadi who was in office when I first went to Cairo. His venerable face, long white beard, small hands, dignified mien, and graceful robes rendered him a striking figure. Such, I can fancy, were the Pharisees who were members of the Jewish Sanhedrim. His manners were perfect, perhaps more so than his judgments. His successor was a younger man with a fine intelligent face. He arrived at Cairo with excellent intentions; he was going to purify his court of false witnesses, and he was delighted when he found that I was able to talk to him in Turkish, albeit very bad Turkish, on the subject. I welcomed an ally, and awaited the result with interest. I had not long to wait. The Kadi soon came to the conclusion that the Egyptians were an uninteresting race. As they appeared to like the corrupt system to which they were accustomed, why should he kick against the pricks in trying to reform it?

These three are, from their official positions, the most important of the class, who, by reason of their acquaintance with theological lore and ancient custom, are termed "learned." It may, however, be interesting to sketch a few other types of their class.

The Sheikh el-Bekri is an "Alim," and a notable one of his class. The first incumbent of the office

[1] *Vide ante*, p. 153.

during my residence in Cairo was a small wizened man with a pock-marked countenance, who, when I paid him my Ramazan visit, used to peer at me through a pair of cunning little eyes, in which fear and hatred of his visitor seemed to be struggling for predominance. I always felt that, when I left his house, he cursed me, my race, and my religion, and I never entertained the least ill-will against him for doing so. When he died, his brother, a much younger man, succeeded him. It soon became apparent that a new Sheikh el-Bekri had arisen. When the spiritual head of a variety of Moslem sects boasted of his acquaintance with Lord Salisbury and Mr. Gladstone; when he quoted Jean Jacques Rousseau to me on the Rights of Man in excellent French; when he indulged in platitudes on the blessings of parliamentary government; and when he asked me to lend him a few books which might enable him to understand the "philosophy of the French Revolution,"—then I asked myself whether I was in a dream. Was this *fin de siècle* Sheikh, this curious compound of Mecca and the Paris Boulevards, the latest development of Islamism? I should add that the combination produced no results of any importance. The new Sheikh soon sank into political insignificance.

I can best describe another "Alim" by relating an anecdote about him. Sheikh Mohammed el-Saadat, as his name signifies, was a Seyyid, a descendant of the Prophet.[1] He was, moreover, wealthy and influential. I happened to hear at one time that he was raving against the English. My experience had taught me that political opinions in Egypt are not unfrequently connected with some personal grievance. I called on the Sheikh, and asked him how he thought matters were going on.

[1] "Saadat" is the plural form of the Arabic word "Seyyid," which means a descendant of the Prophet, an aristocrat, lord, master.

Everything, he said, was very bad. I encouraged him to talk. Then he burst out into a long tirade about the desperate state of the country. Could he, I asked, point out any particular abuse, for it was difficult to deal with generalities? Certainly he could do so; he had no water for a portion of his property, whereas he always got water before the English came into the country. I inquired into the matter. As I had expected, I found that the Sheikh's statement was quite correct. He belonged to the privileged class. Under the old régime, he always got water, although his neighbours often went without it. Since the English engineers had taken the irrigation of the country in hand, they had recognised no privileges. All were treated alike. The Sheikh had to await his turn. Naturally enough, he did not like this levelling process. Fortunately, shortly after my interview with him, the Sheikh's turn came. He, of course, attributed this to the exercise of my influence on his behalf. I heard afterwards that his language at once changed. He spoke in terms of warm commendation of the British administration.

Sheikh Abdul-Khalik el-Saadat, a nephew of the last-named Sheikh, is the head of one of the oldest purely Egyptian families in Egypt. Napoleon made great efforts to ingratiate himself with one of this Sheikh's ancestors, who was at first decorated with the Legion of Honour, and on this treatment proving ineffectual to produce the required results, was bastinadoed. The present Sheikh is a member of the Legislative Council. He is ignorant of public affairs, but, by reason of the respect in which his family is held, exerts, or at all events might exert a certain amount of influence. I used to see a good deal of him at one time, but eventually, for reasons on which I need not dwell, I had to drop his acquaintance.

Sheikh Mohammed Abdu was an "Alim" of a different and, I should add, a very superior type to those of his brethren whom I have so far described. He was one of the leading spirits of the Arábi movement. When I came to Egypt in 1883, he was under a cloud. Good-natured Tewfik, acting under British pressure, pardoned him, and made him a judge.[1] He did his work well and honestly. Sheikh Mohammed Abdu was a man of broad and enlightened views. He admitted the abuses which have sprung up under Oriental Governments. He recognised the necessity of European assistance in the work of reform. But he did not belong to the same category as the Europeanised Egyptian, whom he regarded as a bad copy of the original. He was anti-Khedivial and anti-Pasha, not that he would have objected to a certain degree of Pashadom if he could have found good Pashas, but in his experience he had met but few Pashas who were good. In fact, Sheikh Mohammed Abdu was a somewhat dreamy and unpractical but, nevertheless, genuine Egyptian patriot; it were perhaps well for the cause of Egyptian patriotism if there were more like him. But, regarded from the point of view of possible politicians of the future, there were some weak points in the armour of Mohammed Abdu, and of those who follow his teaching. Mr. Stanley Lane-Poole remarks that an upper-class Moslem must be "a fanatic or a concealed infidel."[2] This dilemma, in a somewhat different form, has presented difficulties to those Christians who look to the letter rather than to the spirit of Christ's teaching. It presents far greater difficulties to strictly orthodox Moslems, who look almost exclusively to the letter rather than to the spirit

[1] Mohammed Abdu was, in 1899, appointed Grand Mufti. He died in 1905.

[2] *Studies in a Mosque*, p. 111.

of their faith. I suspect that my friend Abdu, although he would have resented the appellation being applied to him, was in reality an Agnostic. His associates, although they admitted his ability, were inclined to look askance at him as a "filosouf." Now, in the eyes of the strictly orthodox, one who studies philosophy or, in other words, one who recognises the difference between the seventh and the twentieth centuries, is on the high road to perdition.

The political importance of Mohammed Abdu's life lies in the fact that he may be said to have been the founder of a school of thought in Egypt very similar to that established in India by Syed Ahmed, the creator of the Alighur College. The avowed object of those who belong to this school is to justify the ways of Islam to man, that is to say, to Moslem man. They are the Girondists of the Egyptian national movement. They are too much tainted with a suspicion of heterodoxy to carry far along with them the staunch conservative Moslem. On the other hand, they are often not sufficiently Europeanised to attract the sympathy of the Egyptian mimic of European ways. They are inferior to the strictly orthodox Moslem in respect to their Mohammedanism, and inferior to the ultra-Europeanised Egyptian in respect to their Europeanisation. Their task is, therefore, one of great difficulty. But they deserve all the encouragement and support which can be given to them. They are the natural allies of the European reformer. Egyptian patriots—*sua si bona norint*—will find in the advancement of the followers of Mohammed Abdu the best hope that they may gradually carry out their programme of creating a truly autonomous Egypt.[1]

[1] For many years, I gave to Mohammed Abdu all the encouragement in my power; but it was uphill work, for, besides the strong antagonism which he encountered from conservative Moslems, he was unfortunately

I give yet one further sketch of a typical "Alim." Sheikh Mohammed Beyram, who is now, alas! dead, was one of my best friends in Egypt. He was, moreover, one of the most remarkable types with which I have met in the course of my Eastern experience. He looked like a thorough gentleman. I have rarely seen a more striking figure than that of this grave Oriental, with his high intellectual forehead, refined features, melancholy eyes, dignified mien, exquisite manners, and graceful costume, who would sit with me by the hour[1] and sing a dirge over the decadence of Islam. Moreover, Sheikh Mohammed Beyram not only looked a gentleman; he was one. In no country have I come across a man of more elevated and refined feelings, or one whose

on very bad terms with the Khedive, and was only able to retain his place as Mufti by relying on strong British support.

In my Annual Reports I frequently spoke of him in high terms, and no one regretted his premature death more sincerely than myself. At the same time, I must confess that I experienced a shock in reading some of the revelations in Mr. Wilfrid Blunt's book. Mr. Blunt's views on Egyptian affairs appear to have been mainly based on what he heard from Mohammed Abdu, whom he calls (*Secret History, etc.* p. 7) a "great philosopher and patriot." Notably, I read with surprise and regret (p. 489) the following statement of Mohammed Abdu's: "Sheykh Jemal ed Din proposed to me, Mohammed Abdu, that Ismail should be assassinated some day as he passed in his carriage daily over the Kasr-el-Nil bridge, and I strongly approved, but it was only talk between ourselves, and we lacked a person capable of taking lead in the affair." Without going into the ethics of tyrannicide, it will be sufficient to say that the civilised world generally is disposed to look askance at patriots, and still more at philosophers, who are prepared to further their political aims by resorting to assassination.

[1] One of the obstacles which lie in the path of the European when he wants to arrive at the true opinion of the Oriental is that the European, especially if he be an official, is almost always in a hurry. If, he thinks, the Oriental has anything to say to me, why does he not say it and go away? I am quite prepared to listen most attentively, but my time is valuable and I have a quantity of other business to do; I must, therefore, really ask him to come to the point at once. This frame of mind is quite fatal if one wishes to arrive at the truth. In order to attain this object, the Oriental must be allowed to tell his story and put forward his ideas in his own way; and his own way is generally a lengthy, circuitous, and very involved way. But if any one has the patience to listen, he will sometimes be amply rewarded for his pains.

opinions and actions were less tainted with worldly self-interest, than this Tunisian aristocrat.[1] Few things have given me a more unfavourable impression of native Egyptian society than that the fine qualities of this really eminent man—whose appearance and character were alike remarkable, whose private life was irreproachable, whose religious faith was founded on a rock, whose patriotism was enlightened, and whose public aims were noble—should have been scarcely recognised by the herd of Pashas, place-hunters, and greedy Sheikhs, who were not worthy to unloose the latchet of his shoe. When he went down to his grave, none but a few knew that a star, which under happier auspices might perhaps have been of some magnitude, had fallen from the political firmament of Egypt, or perhaps, it would be more correct to say, of Islam. Pope's fine lines well describe my honoured friend:—

> Statesman, yet friend to truth! of soul sincere,
> In action faithful, and in honour clear!
> Who broke no promise, served no private end,
> Who gained no title, and who lost no friend.

Mohammed Beyram was a devout Moslem. His faith was far more earnest than that of Mohammed Abdu, and men of a similar type. The subject which mainly interested him was how to bring Islam and its ways into harmony with modern society; in other words, how to square the circle; and in discussing the sundry and manifold branches of this question with him, any tendency to disparage the Mohammedan religion at once disappeared. From the point of view of the moralist, criticism

[1] Mohammed Beyram belonged to the Beylical family of Tunis, and, on his mother's side, was descended from the Moorish kings of Spain. His ancestors held the highest offices in Tunis without intermission for 300 years.

cannot be directed against the fundamental principles of the faith, but only against the abuses which have sprung up and which now obscure its primitive simplicity. Mohammed Beyram, regarded, not as a practical politician, but as a believer in the faith of Islam, was, in fact, a type of the best class of Moslem, a type which is, unfortunately, of rare occurrence. He looked sadly out over a world which appeared to him to have gone mad; he saw all that was noble in the faith which he revered stifled by parasitic growths; he noted that Islam was tottering to its fall by reason of internal decay; he did not so much fear the advance of needy disreputable Europe, for he knew that, though the Moslem might be robbed and cheated, there was still a hope for Islam so long as its moral code and the material benefits it conferred were only contrasted with the practice and principles of adventurers who were the dregs of European civilisation; but he knew that the tap of the northern drum, which had been heard in the streets of Cairo and might ere long be heard in those of Stamboul, brought more than the dragoon and the rifleman in its wake; his instinct taught him that the institutions, which his forefathers had cherished, must in time crumble to the dust when they were brought face to face with the lofty principles which were inscribed on the Englishman's banner. He was not blind to these things and, albeit he still clung tenaciously to the skirts of the Prophet of Arabia, he cried out in the agony of his spirit: "Where shall wisdom be found? and where is the place of understanding?" And the answer he gave to himself was that which was delivered by the patriarch Job when the world was young: "The fear of the Lord, that is wisdom: and to depart from evil, that is understanding." On that common ground, the Moslem of the Mohammed Beyram type could meet the Christian, and discuss matters of common interest without stirring the fires of religious strife. But when the discussion took place, how melancholy was the result! The Moslem and the Christian would agree as to the nature of the fungus which was stifling all that was at one time healthy in the original growth; they would appreciate in like fashion the history of its extension; but, whilst the sympathetic Christian would point out with courteous but inexorable logic that any particular remedy proposed would be either inefficacious or would destroy not only the fungus but at the same time the parent tree, the Moslem, too honest not to be convinced, however much the conviction might cost him pain, could only utter a bitter wail over the doom of the creed which he loved, and over that of the baneful system to which his creed has given birth. We may sympathise, and, for my own part, I do very heartily sympathise, with the Mohammed Beyrams of Islam, but let no practical politician think that they have a plan capable of resuscitating a body, which is not, indeed, dead, and which may yet linger on for centuries, but which is nevertheless politically and socially moribund, and whose gradual decay cannot be arrested by any modern palliatives however skilfully they may be applied.

I have dwelt on the characters of these few individuals, not in order to disparage some, or in order to deliver a panegyric on others, but because each of those who have been depicted may to some extent be regarded as one type of the hierarchical class. It must not, however, be supposed that the Ulema are the only members of the hierarchy. A crowd of Imams (preachers), inferior Kadis, and others may be considered as affiliated to the Ulema. These are all so many agents scattered over the face of the country who keep alive religious sentiment and hierarchical influence. The special point to be noted for the purpose of the present argument is that the attitude of the whole of the hierarchy, from the highest "Alim" to the smallest teacher in a "Kuttab,"[1] has generally been more or less hostile to the work of the British reformer in Egypt. This was, indeed, inevitable. The hostility of the hierarchy is, however, based on somewhat different grounds from that of the Pashas. In respect to one point, indeed, the sentiments of the two classes coincide. Both are inspired by an instinct of self-preservation. At the time when the British occupation took place, both were in the enjoyment of privileges which they had abused, and the continuance of which they thought was threatened. Both had a pecuniary interest in resisting reform. Whilst the Pasha feared lest the fellaheen, whom he had for so long plundered, should, under the aegis of England, escape from his grasp, the "Alim," on the other hand, was somewhat nervous lest the Englishman, in spite of his protestations that he would not interfere in religious matters, might some day begin to ask unpleasant questions about the appropriation of funds belonging to religious endowments and such like matters; and the "Alim" would resent this, for although there are some honourable exceptions, he is but too often so profoundly self-deceived that he considers it an essential portion of the relations between man and his Maker that a few privileged persons should be allowed to appropriate to their own use funds which were intended to be applied to the maintenance of Mosques, the feeding of the poor, or other charitable objects. But, in addition to this cause of suspicion, based on self-interest, there is this further point to be borne in mind that, as guardians of the citadel of

[1] The school attached to a Mosque, where the Koran is taught.

Islam, the hierarchy naturally represent the *ne plus ultra* of conservatism. Hence, the representatives of the Mohammedan religion mistrusted the English reformer even before he began to reform, both by reason of his creed, and because they could not help suspecting him of some sinister intentions in the direction of shaking the foundations of their ancient faith. In spite of the Englishman's care and tenderness in dealing with them, their religion, and their vested interests, some of them will mistrust him all the more, the more he succeeds in introducing reforms for which they have no sympathy. They will continually expect that their turn is coming next.

Turning from the hierarchy to the squirearchy, it will be found that, as we descend the social ladder, we enter strata where the prejudice entertained against the alien and the Christian is more or less mitigated by recognition of the material benefits conferred by the reformer. The squirearchy consists, for the most part of Omdehs (village mayors) and Sheikhs of villages. These are generally landed proprietors on a small scale. They occupy a position midway between the Pasha and the fellah. Many of them are sturdy, honest yeomen who are well deserving of respect. Others are inclined to cringe before the Pashas and to bully the fellaheen. I should add that these latter tendencies, which were especially marked in the pre-reforming days, are rapidly disappearing.

As to the submissiveness of the village Sheikhs, the following picture drawn by a careful observer of Egyptian social life was, at one time, by no means exaggerated. The scene is the court of a Mudirieh. The Pasha is presiding. "Gradually the court becomes more and more crowded with brown-skinned and brown-mantled country people. The village mayors and village patriarchs (Sheikhs) are summoned into the divan. With a deep obeisance, they go through the usual form of lifting dust from the smooth marble floor and pressing it to their lips as a mark of respect. . . . A Decree is read, and the people are required to signify their assent to it, and bind themselves to obey it. 'Right willingly,' answer the honourable village mayors with one voice, 'as your Excellency commands; we are thy slaves and the slaves of our Sovereign; nothing but good comes from thee; thy opinion is our opinion.' 'Then seal the document,' says the Governor; and the heads of the communes, one after the other, give their brass seal to the scribe, who smears it with ink, and fills the sheet with their important names. When the Sheikh has sealed, the villager does so likewise, although he has only a glimmering of what it is that he has pledged himself to."[1]

When the English took Egyptian affairs in hand, the submissiveness of the Sheikhs to the Pashas had been somewhat tempered by recent events, for the backbone of the Arábist party, in so far as that party represented a national movement and not a military mutiny, was to be found amongst this class. The greater part of the yeomanry of the country were sympathisers with Arábi; he was of their kith and kin; they looked to him to deliver them from the usurer and the Pasha. Arábi ruled for a moment. During that short period,

Chaos umpire sat,
And by decision more embroiled the fray
By which he reigned.

Though, at the time of the Arábi revolt, the Sheikh class suffered from the general disorder, though even the short experience which they gained of the manner in which Arábist principles were put in

[1] Klunzinger, *Upper Egypt*, p. 73.

practice led the most intelligent amongst the Sheikhs to doubt whether it was wise to hand themselves and their cause over to a mutinous army, nevertheless, when order was restored, they fell back on the recollection that Arábi to some extent represented the ascendency of Sheikhdom in substitution for that of Pashadom. They never forgot that, had not England thrown her weighty sword into the scale, the Turco-Egyptian Pasha and his satellites would have been swept into the sea, and that the Sheikh class would have thus been left to plunder the fellaheen alone, instead of being obliged to content itself with whatever escaped from the rapacity of the Pashas. To all outward appearance, the ancient submissiveness to Pashadom returned after Tel-el-Kebir. When the Pasha gave the order, the village Sheikh, with smiles on his lips and curses in his heart, would pay considerable sums of money, which the Pasha, after levying a contribution for his personal use, would devote to fireworks in honour of a ruler for whom the Sheikh in reality felt but little sympathy. When, in 1893, the relations between the British Government and Abbas II. were somewhat strained, the Sheikh, always acting under orders, would form part of a deputation to congratulate the ruler of his country on his courage and patriotism.[1] But for all that, his submissiveness was the old submissiveness with a difference. He was anxious to have it whispered behind the scenes to the diplomatic representative of England that, though he was constrained to all this lip-service, in reality he meant nothing by it; that he was in deadly fear; and that his one hope was that England would stand firm and save him from being again cast into the jaws of Pashadom.

[1] I give in an Appendix to this chapter one amongst many letters from the Sheikh class, which was shown to me at this time. It shows a capacity for trimming which is characteristic.

Moreover, when Moukhtar Pasha, the representative of the Khalif, came to Egypt, very mixed feelings were excited in the minds of the village Sheikhs, who let the British Consul-General know that, in spite of the spiritual connection, they did not want to be brought into any closer connection with their Khalif or his agents; on the contrary, that they preferred to receive water for their fields at the hands of the English engineer. Moreover, as time went on, the minds of the squirearchy underwent some change. In spite of all outward and visible signs of submissiveness, they are now no longer mere Egyptian clay in the hands of the Turkish potter, as in the pre-reforming days. Years of British rule have taught them that they too have their rights, and it may be that they would not remain so passive as of yore if those rights were infringed.

I have said that when the English came to Egypt, many of the village Omdehs and Sheikhs, though they cringed before the Pashas, revenged themselves by bullying the fellaheen. The latter part of this statement merits some further development.

The village is the administrative unit in Egypt. The Omdehs and Sheikhs are the corner-stone on which the edifice of provincial society rests. They have certain duties to perform. They are considered responsible for public security. If, in past times, a crime was committed in the neighbourhood of the village, and if the criminal was not forthcoming, the imperious rulers of the country had some rude methods for ensuring his arrest. The usual practice was to make the Sheikhs suffer vicarious punishment,[1] until the criminal was

[1] Sir Donald Mackenzie Wallace (*Egypt and the Egyptian Question*, p. 261) tells a characteristic story, which was related to him by an old fellah, of how Mehemet Ali paid a visit to his village and ordered the

produced. This generally had the desired effect. The head of the village was responsible for the assessment and, to a certain extent, for the collection of the taxes. He furnished gangs for the corvée. He was answerable for obtaining recruits for the army. The exercise of these functions supplied him with opportunities for illicit gain; for, provided the taxes were paid, the corvée gangs forthcoming, and a sufficient number of youths delivered annually to feed the vultures of the Soudan, no questions were asked. The village Sheikhs were practically uncontrolled. They naturally abused the privileges of their position, and developed into petty tyrants.

The village Sheikh, like the Pasha and the "Alim," felt an instinct of self-preservation alive within him at the approach of the English reformer. He foresaw that his privileged position would be shaken. Neither did his prophetic instinct err. For, before the Englishman had been long at work, the corvée was abolished; the assessment and collection of the taxes, as well as the recruiting for the army, were taken out of the hands of the village authorities. So far, indeed, did the zeal of the English reformer go, that the Sheikh began to mutter *Nolo episcopari*. The position of the head of a village became no longer lucrative. The Sheikh class began to doubt whether, under these circumstances, it was worth while to assume responsibilities from which little or no compensating advantage was to be derived. The Englishman, on the other hand, found that not the least

Sheikhs to produce two robbers, who were supposed to be hiding in the neighbourhood. The Sheikhs stated that they were unable to do so. "In the twinkling of an eye, all six Sheikhs were lying on the ground, face downwards, receiving the bastinado from a dozen of His Highness' stalwart attendants." Before the bastinadoing process had proceeded far, one of the Sheikhs said that he knew where the criminals were. Two men were accordingly produced, and at once hanged.

difficult part of his administrative task was to preserve what was good and useful in the village system, whilst purging it of all that was bad.

It may, therefore, be said that in the pre-reforming days, the tyranny of the Sheikhs over the fellaheen was only one degree less oppressive than that of the Pashas. In some respects, indeed, the oppression of the former was more burdensome and more irksome than that of the latter; for the Sheikh was always present in the village, whilst the Pasha was distant, and only swooped down occasionally to plunder and to flog. There are a number of Arabic proverbs which owe their origin to the sentiments entertained by the fellaheen as regards the Pasha and the Sheikh respectively. For instance, "Let the lion eat me at a mouthful rather than the mosquito piecemeal." Another is, "The tyranny of the cat is better than the justice of the mouse."

The feelings of the Sheikh class towards the English were, therefore, divided. On the one hand, they were willing to rely on English aid for protection against the tyranny of the Pashas; on the other hand, they resented the interference which curbed the exercise of their own time-honoured tyranny over the fellaheen. As time went on, and the benefits of the British occupation became year by year more apparent, the former of these two sentiments probably predominated over the latter; but any praise which the Sheikh class might perhaps otherwise have accorded to English efforts on behalf of the Egyptian population, was tempered by the idea that the Englishman was, after all, only carrying out the original programme of Arábi. A few of the most observant did, indeed, recognise that in Arábi's hands the programme would not have been executed with so much skill and intelligence. On the other hand, no inconsiderable number regretted that Arábi was not allowed to have his way, not only because he was their compatriot and co-religionist, but also because they thought, and perhaps with some degree of reason, that whilst Arábi would have executed that portion of the English programme which involved placing a restraint upon the Turco-Egyptian Pasha, he would have been more careful of their interests in that he would have allowed the tyranny of the Sheikh to continue unchecked.[1]

I now turn to that class of Egyptian society which, if not the most interesting, is certainly more deserving of sympathy than any other. It is unnecessary to describe at any length the character and condition of the blue-shirted Egyptian fellah. Every Nile tourist knows what he is like. Any handbook of Egypt can tell all that the practical politician need know of his past history. Every writer on Egyptian affairs has touched, in a greater or less degree, on the sufferings which he has undergone at the hands of a long succession of despotic rulers. From time immemorial, his main end in life has been to find some means for evading the extortionate demands of the tax-gatherer. "The Romans," Mommsen says, "assure us that the Egyptians were proud of the scourge-marks received for perpetrating frauds in taxation."[2] As it was in the days of Augustus, so was it in the days of Ismail. "It is a point of honour," Mr. McCoan wrote in 1877, "to bear any amount of 'stick,' if, by so doing, the impost or any part of it can be evaded. The fellah, indeed, who will

[1] These remarks were written some few years ago. I leave them unaltered, as they were at one time quite correct. But they are so to a less extent now. The recollection of the events of 1882 is rapidly dying out. Other influences have taken the place of the Arábi myth. Further, whatever defects may still exist generally amongst the Sheikh class, I have little doubt that their moral and intellectual standard is now considerably higher than was the case in 1882.

[2] *The Provinces of the Roman Empire*, vol. ii. p. 258.

not do so is despised by even his own wife as a poltroon, and if, after only a dozen or score of blows, he disgorges the coin which endurance of fifty might perhaps have saved, the conjugal estimate of his spirit is generally shared by his fellows."[1] Next to evading taxation, the fellah above all things wishes to evade military service. His favourite method of attaining this object was, at one time, not to cut off a finger, as was done by the poltroons[2] of the Roman army, but to sacrifice an eye.

In dealing with the fellah, the English politician had mainly two points to bear in mind. The first point was that the immense majority of the population of Egypt are fellaheen. The fellaheen, therefore, deserve consideration on account of their numbers. This fact would at first sight appear sufficiently obvious, but it was at one time frequently forgotten by Pashas and others.

The second point was that, as the fellah, at the time of the British occupation, possessed no privileges, unless the liability to be indiscriminately robbed and flogged can be called a privilege, there would be no difficulty in dealing with him on the ground that the reformer was laying a rash hand on his vested rights. As he stood on the lowest rung of the social ladder, there was no one below him over whom he could tyrannise.

The main problem which the Englishman had to solve was this: How to confer on the fellah the privilege of no longer being robbed and flogged, without shattering the edifice, which, rotten as it was, had still kept Egyptian society together for centuries past. In dealing with this problem, one thing was certain. The fellah had everything to

[1] *Egypt as it is*, p. 26.

[2] The derivation usually given for the word "poltroon"—*pollice truncus*—is, however, more than doubtful. See Skeat's *Etymological Dictionary*.

gain and nothing to lose by the work of the English reformer. There cannot, in fact, be a shadow of doubt that the fellah has gained enormously owing to the efforts made on his behalf by the Englishman. He has gained far more than any other class of society, because in his case there is absolutely no disadvantage to throw into the scale against the immense benefits which he has received.

Does the Egyptian fellah appreciate the benefits which have been conferred on him? Does he entertain any feelings of gratitude towards his benefactor? These are questions which are interesting in themselves, and, moreover, are not altogether devoid of political importance.

After a fashion, the fellah appreciates very highly the benefits which have been conferred on him. Ignorant though he be, he is wise enough to know that he is now far better off than he was prior to the British occupation. He would shudder at any notion that the old régime was to be re-established. Moreover, in a vague sort of way he probably recognises that these benefits have been conferred upon him by the Anglo-Saxon race. But he is singularly wanting in the logical faculty. He is incapable of establishing clearly in his mind that, for the time being at all events, good administration and the exercise of a paramount influence by England are inseparably linked together. It has been the misfortune of the English in Egypt that the classes who, under their political programme, most benefited by British rule, were those who were least of all able to make their voices heard. The fellaheen are, politically speaking, ciphers. They are too apathetic, too ignorant, and too little accustomed to take the initiative, to give utterance in any politically audible form to their opinions even when they have any. Moreover, in the event of a premature withdrawal of the British garrison, they would probably not form any definite opinion as to the results of the measure until positive proof had been afforded to them that a fatal mistake had been made. Then it is possible that, having tasted the fruits of good administration and being emboldened by the freedom conferred on them by the Englishman, they might turn round and rend the Pashas.

As to whether the fellaheen are grateful or the reverse, it is to be observed that gratitude is not, generally speaking, a national virtue. Moreover, many of those who have mixed in native society in Egypt consider that ingratitude is one of the predominant features of the Egyptian character.[1] However this may be, the ordinary fellah is kindly and jovial. If he were left to himself he would certainly not entertain any unfriendly feelings towards the Englishman, in spite of the difference of race or creed; indeed, although he might not be effusively grateful, it may be doubted whether on his own initiative he would ever do anything to render himself open to the charge of ingratitude. Unfortunately, he is emotional, ignorant, and credulous. He is easily led away by lying agitators and intriguers. Under the influence of ephemeral passion, his sense of gratitude for past favours would disappear like chaff before the wind. At such a moment, the same man, who was but yesterday blessing the English engineer for watering his fields, might to-morrow, should the occasion arise, brain his benefactor with a "nabout"[2] in a fit of savage passion. It should be added that, immediately afterwards, he would probably be very sorry for what he has done.

My reason tells me that this is so. Yet I hate

[1] "The natives of Egypt in general, in common with the Arabs of other countries, are (according to our system of morals) justly chargeable with a fault, which is regarded by us as one of great magnitude; it is want of gratitude."—Lane, *Modern Egyptians*, vol. i. p. 366.

[2] A "nabout" is a staff, which is sometimes loaded with lead.

to believe it. A diplomatist, and especially a diplomatist in Egypt, sees a good deal of the ignoble side of life. Constant dealings with corrupt Pashas, scheming adventurers, and other hostile elements, who think that all is fair in business or politics, are apt to shake one's faith in the goodness of human nature. More than this, the question of whether the fellaheen of Egypt are happy or unhappy, grateful or ungrateful, though a matter of some interest to themselves and of somewhat more than philanthropic interest to others, is, after all, only one of the factors which must contribute to guide the action of the British diplomatist. He has to think, or at all events the Government whom he is serving has to think of the interests of the farmers of Yorkshire, the fishermen of Yarmouth, the artisans of Sheffield, and their brother taxpayers, who are his own countrymen, and he has to ask himself, what is it to these whether or not the Egyptian fellaheen are flayed alive by greedy Pashas and tyrannical Sheikhs? All this I know. *Mais pour être diplomate, on n'est pas moins homme.* Even a matter-of-fact official may be allowed to cherish what is perhaps an illusion. He may be pardoned, especially if he has lived much in the inconsistent East, if he nourishes a trace of inconsistency in the recesses of his heart, if he struggles against being reasoned out of a noble hope. Often during the long period when my countrymen and myself were engaged in what at one time seemed the hopeless task of evolving order out of the Egyptian chaos, have I repeated to myself those fine lines of the Latin poet which Pitt quoted when he dealt the first blow to the infamous traffic in slaves:

Nosque ubi primus equis Oriens afflavit anhelis,
Illic sera rubens accendit lumina Vesper.[1]

[1] Stanhope's *Life of Pitt*, p. 146. The quotation is from the first *Georgic*, 250-251.

Was the prophecy of the English statesman, I asked myself, about to be fulfilled? Is it destined that, under the guiding hand of England, the rays of true civilisation shall at last pierce into the oldest and most interesting corner of the dark African continent, and lighten with their sunshine even the mud hut of the Egyptian fellah? Is the Englishman to show, by precept and example, that usury and drunkenness are not the only handmaids of Christian education? Pray Heaven it may be so! When Sir Robert Peel committed that great and wise act of political apostasy for which his name will ever live in English history, he said that although he had suffered much in separating himself from his former political friends, he still hoped that he would "leave a name sometimes remembered with expressions of goodwill in those places which are the abode of men whose lot it is to labour and to earn their daily bread by the sweat of their brow." I may perhaps be permitted to paraphrase this memorable passage. In spite of the ignorance and alleged ingratitude of the Egyptians, I still dare to cherish a hope that the present and future generations of fellaheen, who certainly earn and will continue to earn their daily bread by the sweat of their brow, will remember with some feeling akin to gratitude that it was the Anglo-Saxon race who first delivered them from the thraldom of their oppressors, who taught them that they too had the right to be treated like human beings, who conferred upon them the material blessings which follow in the train of true Western civilisation, and who opened out to them the path which leads to moral progress and elevation of thought. The time, it may be hoped, is past when Egypt[1] and the

[1] Hoary Memphis boasts her tombs alone,
The mournful types of mighty power decayed.
SHENSTONE, *Elegy XIV.*

Egyptians could be cited as one of the most striking contrasts the world has ever known between past grandeur and modern decadence.

In any case, whether the Egyptian fellah be capable or incapable of gratitude, there can be no doubt that it was the hand of England which first raised him from the abject moral and material condition in which he had for centuries wallowed. If, now that he is beginning to emerge from his slough of despond, I thought that he would be permitted to relapse into his former state, and that the work on which, in common with many of my countrymen, I have spent the best years of my life would be undone, then would I say *τότε μοι χάνοι εὐρεῖα χθών*. I hasten to add that I not merely hope, but strongly believe that no such disappointment of my political hopes is, in the smallest degree, probable.

The last category of Moslem dwellers in Egypt of whom it is necessary to speak is the Bedouins, semi-sedentary and nomad. Of these, but little need be said. A number of proverbs are current in Egypt indicative of the dislike entertained by the dwellers in the valley of the Nile to those in the desert. Of these, the best known is, "Better the tyranny of the Turk than the justice of the Bedouins." The Bedouins are, in fact, supposed to be very cruel and unjust. Another proverb is in the form of a narrative: "The Bedouin told my wife that there was no water in the well. She at once went hastily to the well with four buckets." This is in allusion to the alleged selfishness and untruthfulness of the Bedouins.[1]

On the other hand, the Bedouins despise the fellaheen, whom they consider an unmanly race. The Bedouins occasionally complain that in the

[1] Burckhardt (*Arabic Proverbs*, p. 123) gives another: "Entertain the Bedouin, he will steal thy clothes."

matter of military service, from which they are exempted, the Egyptian Government wish to "reduce them to fellaheen." It is wise policy to keep them contented and to encourage them to settle on the cultivated lands. Otherwise, they are apt to turn into marauders and to cause disturbances of various sorts. Their ancient privileges have, therefore, for the most part, been preserved to them. This treatment has proved effective. The figures of the census of 1897 compared with those of 1882 show that, since the British occupation, there has been a strong tendency on the part of the Bedouins to abandon their nomadic habits, and to settle in the villages bordering on the desert. Broadly speaking, the Bedouins, for the purposes of the present narrative and argument, may be considered a *quantité négligeable.* They did not exercise any considerable influence on the course of British policy in Egypt.

APPENDIX

Translation of a Letter from a Sheikh of Keneh to a Sheikh of the Mosque of Seyyidna-Hussein at Cairo.

February 2, 1894.

During these days, the talk has been great among the people, and tongues have wearied as to the difference which had sprung up, so they said, between our Lord the Khedive and Baring. There were those who said: "The English have many soldiers, and must prevail." Others said, and among these many of the Ulema: "HE has said (Grace be on Him!) how often hath a small force overcome a great one by the aid of the Almighty, be His name exalted!"

Then it was reported in our districts: "Behold the Infidel is overcome, and Baring has fled in haste to his own country. The days of Abbas shall be like those of his forefathers; the people and the Pashas shall be bread for him to eat; the foreigner will be his servant."

So we took counsel, and thought to send a mission from Keneh to say: "Good news! Effendina has returned to his fit place!" For the poet has said: "The wise man gives honey to the bear in the day of his fatness, but the fool smites him on the head with a pole."

Then, while we still pondered, came a message from Cairo that Baring and his English walked in the city like leopards among dogs, and that Abbas had withdrawn into his castle and sat scowling, for the Government of Baring had said: "Be meat that we may devour you!" So we were hushed, and resolved to say nothing of any deputation. And, of a truth, I think that it is not easy, and will be less so in time to come, to send deputations of good tidings to our Lord the Khedive.

Now, I had myself thought that the end could only be thus, for I have seen the English and I know them. But aloud I said: "The blessing of God on the deputation, and the aid of His mighty arm! for are we not all Moslems and brethren? (God increase the might of Islam!)"

But, O my friend! I beg you to keep this letter very secret, for the poet has said: "Ill is his lot in the court whom the Kadi has heard to whisper, 'There is justice amongst the unbelievers.'"[1]

[1] A change has been made in the last paragraph without altering the general sense. The original was too coarse to be reproduced.

CHAPTER XXXVI

THE CHRISTIANS

The COPTS—The conservatism of their religion—Their character—Their attitude towards the English—The reform movement—The SYRIANS—Their position—Their unpopularity—Their attitude towards the English—The ARMENIANS—Their subserviency to the Turks—Nubar Pasha—His son Boghos—Yacoub Pasha Artin—Tigrane Pasha—The Egyptians should not be weighed in European scales.

THE Egyptian native Christians may be divided into three categories, viz. (1) the Copts; (2) the Syrians; and (3) the Armenians. Of these, the most important in point of numbers are the Copts. The census of 1897 showed that there were at that time 608,000 Copts in Egypt. Of these, some few are Catholics and some Protestants, but by far the greater number belong to what is termed the Orthodox Church.

Beyond mentioning that the Orthodox Copts are Monophysites, and that they separated from the main body of the Christian Church subsequent to the Council of Chalcedon in A.D. 451, it is needless to dwell on the special tenets of the Coptic creed. One point in connection with the religion of the Copts should, however, be mentioned, inasmuch as it is intimately connected with an understanding of the general characteristics of the Coptic community. The Christianity of the Copt has been as conservative as the Islamism of the Moslem. "The Eastern Church," Dean Stanley says, "was, like the East, stationary and immutable; the Western, like the West, progressive and flexible. . . . The theology of the East has undergone no systematising process. The doctrines remain in the same rigid yet undefined state as that in which they were left by Constantine and Justinian." If a religious belief cannot adapt itself to the requirements which are constantly cropping up as the world grows older, one of two things will probably happen. Either society advances and the religious belief is stranded and eventually forgotten, or the creed holds society in its grip and bars the way to advancement. It is the proud boast of the Christian religion, and more especially of the Protestant variety of that religion, that it is not obliged to choose between either of these alternatives. It possesses sufficient elasticity to adapt itself to modern requirements.

It is true that the Coptic Christian has remained stagnant, but there is this notable difference between the stagnation of the Moslem and that of the Copt. The Moslem stands in everything on the ancient ways because he is a Moslem, because the customs which are interwoven with his religion, forbid him to change. "Swathed in the bands of the Koran, the Moslem faith, unlike the Christian, is powerless to adapt itself to varying time and place, keep pace with the march of humanity, direct and purify the social life, or elevate mankind."[1] The Copt, on the other hand, has remained immutable, or nearly so, not because he is a Copt, but because he is an Oriental, and because his religion, which admits of progress, has been surrounded by associations antagonistic to progress. In the case of the Copt, it is not necessary, as in that of the Moslem, to strike off any religious shackles before he can proceed along the path of political and social advancement. The reformer in temporal

[1] Sir William Muir, *The Caliphate*, p. 594.

matters does not at every turn find himself face to face with the priest, who in the name of religion or religious custom bars the way to progress. From the point of view of principle, the difference is immense. From the point of view of practice, the difference has so far been slight. In spite of his religion which, as the history of the world has shown, admits of progress, the Copt has been arrested by barriers very similar to those which have applied in the case of the Moslem. It is, indeed, natural that such should have been the case. The minority must of necessity submit to the influence of the majority. In India, the Moslems have to a certain extent become Brahminised. In spite of the unbending tenets of their creed, custom and association have been too strong for them. The Hindoos, being in a majority of five to one, have copied nothing from the Moslems. The Moslems, on the other hand, have insensibly assimilated certain Hindoo ideas, notably the idea of caste. The Indian Moslem will not eat with the Christian, although there is nothing in his religious code which forbids him to do so, and although his brother-Moslem, who is not exposed to Hindoo association, does so willingly. The same principle has applied in the case of the Egyptian Copts. The Moslem has in no way become Christianised. The Copt, on the other hand, has, without knowing it, assimilated himself to the Moslem. "The modern Copt has become from head to foot, in manners, language, and spirit, a Moslem, however unwilling he may be to recognise the fact."[1] Coptic women are almost as secluded as Moslems. Coptic children are generally circumcised. The marriage customs and funeral ceremonies of the Copts are very similar to those of Moslems.

Much has been written about the general

[1] *Upper Egypt, etc.*, p. 89.

characteristics of the Copts. All generalisations about the attributes of a nation or of a class are apt to be imperfect, and must necessarily do injustice to exceptional individuals. The Copts have somewhat specially suffered from hasty generalisation. Until of recent years, when by reason of the British occupation a flood of light has been thrown on everything connected with Egypt, most Englishmen who paid any attention to the national characteristics of the "Modern Egyptians" took their ideas from the classic work, which has immortalised the name of Lane. Now Lane was a strong Mohammedan sympathiser. He knew but little about the Copts. All the information he supplies about them appears to have been based on the testimony of one "respectable Copt" whose acquaintance he happened to make,[1] and who certainly gave a most unfavourable account of his co-religionists. "One of the most remarkable traits," Lane says, "in the character of the Copts is their bigotry. They bear a bitter hatred to all other Christians, even exceeding that with which the Moslems regard the unbelievers in El-Islam. . . . They are, generally speaking, of a sullen temper, extremely avaricious, and abominable dissemblers; cringing or domineering according to circumstances. The respectable Copt, to whom I have already acknowledged myself chiefly indebted for the notions which I have obtained respecting the customs of his nation, gives me a most unfavourable account of their character. He avows them to be generally ignorant, deceitful, faithless, and abandoned to the pursuit of worldly gain, and to indulgence in sensual pleasures."[2]

[1] "I had the good fortune to become acquainted with a character of which I had doubted the existence, a Copt of a liberal as well as an intelligent mind; and to his kindness I am indebted for the knowledge of most of the facts related in the following brief memoir."—*Modern Egyptians*, vol. ii. p. 273.

[2] *Modern Egyptians*, vol. ii. p. 295.

This judgment appears to err greatly on the side of severity. Even if it be admitted that the unpleasing qualities, which Lane indicates, are sometimes to be found amongst the Copts, it is to be observed that the Copts have no monopoly of those qualities. Bigotry, ignorance, dissimulation, deceit, faithlessness, the pursuit of worldly gain, and indulgence in sensual pleasures, may, to a certain extent, be Egyptian, but it can scarcely be held that they are especially Coptic attributes. They are to be found in an equal degree amongst Egyptian Moslems.

Sir John Bowring, who next to Lane is probably the best of the less recent authorities on Egyptian national characteristics, passes a more kindly judgment on the Copts. Although, he says, the Turks have always considered the Copts as "the pariahs of the Egyptian people, yet they are an amiable, pacific, and intelligent race, whose worst vices have grown out of their seeking shelter from wrong and robbery."

Lane appears to me to be prejudiced in this matter. His statement is, to say the least, much too highly coloured as regards the present race of Egyptians, whether Moslems or Copts. Bowring, on the other hand, hardly states the whole case. My own experience leads me to the following conclusions: first, that, owing to circumstances unconnected with the difference of religion, the Egyptian Copt has developed certain moral attributes which also belong to the Egyptian Moslem; secondly, that, owing to circumstances which are accidentally connected with, but which are not the consequences of his religion, the Copt has developed certain intellectual qualities, in which, mainly from want of exercise, the Egyptian Moslem seems to be deficient; thirdly, that for all purposes of broad generalisation, the only difference between the Copt and the Moslem is that the former is an Egyptian who worships in a Christian church, whilst the latter is an Egyptian who worships in a Mohammedan mosque.

The question now under discussion is one of great interest, for it involves nothing less than this—has the Christian religion, taken by itself and apart from all other influences, been able in the course of centuries to develop moral qualities in the Coptic community superior to those generally attributable to the non-Christian community by which the Copts have been surrounded?

I am reluctantly constrained to answer this question in the negative.[1] It is, so far as I am aware, impossible to indicate any moral quality in respect to which the Copt, with his 1500 years of Christianity behind him, is notably superior to the Moslem. The moral code by which the relations between man and man are regulated is, in the case of the Copt, no more elevated than in the case of the Moslem. In spite of his religion and his monogamous habits, the Copt has developed no high ideal of womanhood. More than this, in respect to one important point the Moslem occupies a more elevated moral position than the Copt. The former, when untainted by European association, is distinguished for his sobriety—a moral quality which is noticeable to a less extent amongst the Copts.[2] It is, of course, true that the defects of Coptic character are not attributable to their religion. It is also true that

[1] It is, however, to be remembered, looking to the past history of the Copts, that they deserve great credit for the steadfastness with which they have adhered to their faith in the face of persecution. As to the persecution see, *inter alia*, Makrizi's *History* (Malan's translation), p. 88. In Dr. Butler's admirable work, *The Arab Conquest of Egypt*, a full account is given of the persecution to which the Copts were at one time subject.

[2] "Intoxication is a frequent vice amongst the Copts."—Bowring's *Report*, p. 8. See also *Cairo*, p. 206.

the Copt has been exposed to the influence of a somewhat debased form of Christianity; that that influence has been exerted under specially unfavourable conditions; and that the defects in the Coptic character are, more often than not, "the vices of servitude."[1] Nevertheless, to those who believe in the moralising and civilising influence of the Christian religion, it is disappointing to find that, in differentiating the Egyptian Copt from his compatriots who are Moslems, it is not possible to indicate any one special virtue, and to say that, in spite of every adventitious disadvantage, the Christian religion has fostered and developed that virtue, and has thus given a certain moral superiority to the Christian over the Moslem. Such, however, appears to be the case. I fear it must be admitted that so far the Copt has stood before the world as a Christian who, by reason of adverse circumstances, has been unable to profit to any great extent by his Christianity.

Turning from moral attributes to mental qualities, it cannot be said that, in any of the higher branches of intellectual life, the Copts have shown any superiority over the Moslems. But, under the stress of circumstances, they have developed certain mediocre aptitudes. As compared with the unbending Moslem, they have shown a greater degree of flexibility in adapting themselves to a few of the elementary requirements of civilisation. They have seized on those crumbs from the Moslem table which the Moslem was too proud, too careless, or too unintelligent to appropriate to himself. They made themselves useful, indeed almost indispensable to their oppressors, and the aptitudes which they thus acquired during the period of oppression, ought to have stood them

[1] *Cairo*, p. 208.

in good stead when the flood-tide of European civilisation set in. For the European will recognise that the Copt possesses in some degree that accurate habit of thought which is wanting in the Moslem, and which is the god at whose altar the logical European is an unceasing devotee. He will accord a lukewarm welcome to the Copt, not on account of his religion, but because the Copt can add and subtract, because he knows his multiplication table, because he can measure the length and breadth of a plot of ground without making any gross error in the measurement, and because, although his system of accounts is archaic, at the same time it is better to be in possession of a bad system of accounts than, like the Egyptian Moslem, to have scarcely any system at all. "The Copts," Bowring said, "are the surveyors, the scribes, the arithmeticians, the measurers, the clerks, in a word, the learned men of the land. They are to the counting-house and the pen what the fellah is to the field and the plough."

What, however, was the attitude of the Copts towards the English reformer?

The question is of some interest and importance, for although the Englishman, strong in the righteousness of his cause, was confident of the ultimate result, at the same time, looking to all the obstacles in his path, to the inertia of the mass of the population whom he wished to befriend, and to the activity of various hostile elements of Egyptian society, who would assuredly never cease from harrying him, he would have been glad to welcome the most humble allies. And where would the Englishman more probably find allies than amongst a body of persons who were bound to him by a general community of religion, who had suffered from the oppression of the Moslem and notably from that of the Moslem Pasha, and who possessed various humble aptitudes, which it would be in the interest of the Englishman to turn to account, and in that of the Copt to display to the best advantage in the presence of the Englishman? The premises of this argument were seemingly correct; the inference was plausible; but, as we are dealing with the illogical East, we need not be surprised to find that it was erroneous. For, in fact, the Copt was, in the first instance at all events, animated by no very friendly feelings towards the English reformer.

The principles of strict impartiality on which the Englishman proceeded were foreign to the nature of the Copt. When the British occupation took place, certain hopes began to dawn in his mind. I, said the Copt to himself, am a Christian; if I had the power to do so, I would favour Christians at the expense of Moslems; the English are Christians; therefore—and it was here that the Copt was guilty of a sad *ignoratio elenchi*—as the English have the power, they will assuredly favour Christians at the expense of Moslems. When the Copt found that this process of reasoning was fallacious, and that the conduct of the Englishman was guided by motives which he had left out of account, and which he could not understand, he was disappointed, and his disappointment deepened into resentment. He thought that the Englishman's justice to the Moslem involved injustice to himself, for he was apt, perhaps unconsciously, to hold that injustice and absence of favouritism to Copts were well-nigh synonymous terms.

The Copt, moreover, had another cause of complaint against the English reformer. Not only was he disappointed that no special favours were accorded to him, but he saw with dismay that, under British auspices, he was in danger of being supplanted by his rival, the Syrian Christian.

When the English took Egyptian affairs in hand, the accountants in the employment of the Egyptian Government were almost exclusively Copts. Their system of accounts was archaic. Moreover, it was well-nigh incomprehensible to any but themselves. All tendencies in the direction of reform were resisted, partly from conservatism, and partly from instincts of self-preservation, for it was clear that if the system were simplified to such an extent as to be comprehensible to the uninitiated, the monopoly, which the Copts had heretofore enjoyed, would be endangered. Finding that he could not untie the knot, the Englishman, with characteristic energy, cut it. The Coptic system of accounts had manifestly to be abolished, and as the Copts either could not or would not assist in the work of abolition, they had to give way to other agents. In the early days of the English occupation a good many Syrians, therefore, took the places of Copts. The reform was necessary, but it naturally caused much dissatisfaction amongst the Coptic community.

The English, therefore, found that the Copts were, during the early days of the occupation, generally unfriendly, but they did not show their unfriendliness in any very overt form, for there is one quality in which the Copt excelled. He was an accomplished trimmer. He wished to pose both as Anglophobe and as an Anglophile according to the requirements of his audience, and according to the part which for the moment appeared to be most in harmony with his personal interests. His remarkable powers of intrigue, which were developed in the days of Moslem oppression, here came to his assistance. I should add that, as the occupation was prolonged, the benefits derived from the British administration of Egypt were gradually more and more recognised by the Copts.

They began to understand that they had to rely mainly on their own efforts, and those efforts were often crowned with success. Many of the Copts now in the Government service are very capable men. A Copt of marked ability (Boutros Pasha Ghali) has occupied for a long time, and with great credit to himself, the post of Minister of Foreign Affairs.

Before leaving this branch of the subject, it should be mentioned that for many years past a large number of Copts have been educated in the excellent schools established throughout Egypt by the American missionaries. Many of the younger generation speak English, and show a tendency to develop moral and intellectual qualities greatly superior to those of their fathers, to whom the description given above mainly applies. This process of education has produced its natural result. The young Copts see that, unless they wish to be left behind in the race of life, they must bestir themselves. Once having eaten of the tree of knowledge, they begin to recognise the decrepitude of their antique hierarchical and educational systems, and they are stimulated in the acquirement of this knowledge by the fact that the Syrian, by reason of his superior intellectual attainments, is taking away the birthright of the Copts. The young Copt, starting with Christianity developed by Western education in his favour, has sufficient versatility to draw from this fact the conclusion at which the slow-thinking Moslem, weighted by his leaden creed, arrives more tardily. If I am to outstrip the Syrian, the young Copt says, it is of no use simply cursing him; I must abandon my ancient ways, and strive to be his equal. So a movement has been developed, the object of which is to apply Coptic religious endowments to useful purposes; to question the necessity of devoting funds, drawn from the general body of the community, exclusively to the maintenance of a number of priestly sinecures; to establish seminaries, where those who wish to enter holy orders may learn something more than how to mumble a few set formulæ expressed in an archaic language, which has been dead for the last two centuries;[1] to devote any surplus funds to secular education; and, generally, to instil life into a body which has been stagnant since its earliest creation. The movement naturally meets with resistance from the hierarchy. At first, it appeared as if this resistance would be at once overcome. The crisis happened to take place at the moment when Abbas II. succeeded to Tewfik I. An enlightened Prime Minister (Mustapha Pasha Fehmi), acting in general conformity with English ideas, favoured the views of the Coptic reformers. The Coptic Patriarch, who was the incarnation of the most stolid form of conservatism, was sent to one of those desert monasteries, where in the early days of Christianity the misguided anchorites of Egypt tortured their bodies in the belief that they were doing God service. But a turn in the political wheel brought about a different order of things. Riaz Pasha, who was a conservative Moslem, succeeded to power. Moslem opinion was adverse to the cause of the Coptic reformers. This opposition was based on two grounds. In the first place, the staid Moslem was shocked at rebellion against legitimate hierarchical authority, neither did he care to inquire whether that authority was wisely or unwisely

[1] M. Cogordan, at one time French Consul-General in Egypt, whose premature death was deplored by all who were privileged to know him, wrote: "Le Père Vansleb a vu à Assiout, en 1672, un vieillard qu'on lui présentait comme le dernier Égyptien parlant le Copte. Mais il est probable que bien d'autres le parlèrent après celui-ci; la petite ville de Nagadeh passe pour être celle où cet idiome se conserva le plus tard, jusqu'à la fin du XVIIIe siècle probablement."—*Relation du Voyage fait au Couvent de Saint Antoine*, p. 116.

exercised. In the second place, the Moslem, conscious of his own defects, was alarmed at the appearance of a new rival in the shape of a Coptic progressionist. These influences being in the ascendant, the Patriarch was recalled from his eremitic retreat. The British diplomatist, who alone could have prevented this consummation, stood aside. However much he might sympathise with the cause of Coptic reform, his worldly knowledge told him that he would act unwisely in thrusting himself into the midst of a quarrel between the temporal and spiritual authorities of a creed which was not his own. For the time being, therefore, the anti-reformers triumphed. But the triumph is assuredly but temporary. Time is on the side of the reformers; they must eventually gain the day in spite of Patriarchal opposition. The reformers themselves are not without the faults which belong to political youth and inexperience. Their self-esteem is somewhat inflated. Nevertheless, we may wish them well. "The Copts," Bowring said, "will probably occupy no small part of the field in the future history of Egypt." Until recently, there appeared but little prospect of this prophecy being fulfilled; but this latter-day movement of the young Copts affords ground for hope. If it be continued, the Coptic community may in time develop attributes which will generate and foster self-respect. When they have done this, they will deserve and will obtain the respect of others. They will be carried on by the stream of social and political progress, instead of being engulfed or remaining stranded on the shore.

Turning from the Copts to the Syrians, it is to be observed that there are a certain number of Moslem Syrians resident in Egypt, but, from a political point of view, the Christian Syrians are far more important than the Moslems. In the following remarks, therefore, attention will be confined to the Christians.

It is not possible to state how many Syrian Christians there are in Egypt. Without doubt, the Syrians constitute a very small community as compared with the Copts. They derive their importance, however, not from their numbers, but from the positions which they occupy. Considerable numbers of upper and upper-middle class Syrians are Government employés. In almost every village in Egypt, a usurer is to be found who, if he is not a Greek, is generally a Syrian. There are numerous Jews in Egypt; nevertheless, it is correct to say that the Syrians occupy to a great extent in Egypt the positions held by the Jews in many countries of Europe. Thus, on the one hand, the Syrians encounter the jealousy of those Moslems and Copts who are aspirants for public employment. On the other hand, they are regarded by the mass of the population with those feelings of dislike which improvident debtors usually entertain towards creditors who hold them in their grip. The Syrian moneylender has the reputation of being singularly grasping and merciless. Moreover, his exactions have been facilitated by the onward march of civilisation in Egypt, for the Code Napoléon, which was suddenly applied without sufficient modification to the regulation of the monetary transactions of the country, affords little protection to the poor and ignorant debtor, whilst it is capable of becoming a terrible engine for legalised oppression in the hands of a grasping creditor.

It is only of recent years that the Syrians have acquired their present position in Egypt. Lane and Bowring scarcely allude to them. When, however, Ismail Pasha began to Europeanise the

Egyptian administrative services, it was natural that a demand should arise for intelligent employés, who could speak both Arabic and French, in which latter language most of the European work of the country was conducted, and who, from their training and habits of thought, possessed some aptitude for assimilating European administrative procedures. It was at the time hopeless to expect much assistance from the ordinary unassimilative Moslem who, as the movement swept by him, merely looked up for a moment with a scowl from the Koran, and then relapsed into a state of political torpor. The Copt was a little more helpful, but he also had developed no high degree of versatility, and, moreover, was rarely acquainted with any foreign language. When the demand for employés was first felt, the supply of Europeanised Egyptians was insufficient, and further, the Europeanised Egyptian was often a less useful agent than his social and political kinsman, the Syrian. The Syrian's opportunity, therefore, came, and he profited by it. He possessed all the qualifications required. Arabic was his mother tongue. He was generally familiar with French, having been educated at some French college in Syria. He was versatile, pushing, and ambitious. His confidence in his own capacity was as boundless as that of the esurient Greek of the Roman satirist. He possessed in no small degree the talent, which was particularly useful in a cosmopolitan society, of being all things to all men. He found, therefore, little difficulty in jostling himself into some position of authority, and once there, being animated by strong feelings of race affinity, he opened the door to others amongst his countrymen, and took little heed of the charges of nepotism which were brought against him.

When the English took Egyptian affairs in

hand, circumstances again favoured the Syrian. For the Englishman, himself generally ignorant of Arabic and only semi-conversant with French, looked over the Egyptian administrative chaos, and said to himself: Where am I to find subordinates who will assist me? The Moslem is for the time being, useless; the Copt is little better. I am debarred by political and financial reasons from employing Europeans. Under these circumstances, the Syrian was a godsend.

It is probable that the employment of Syrians did at one time more towards rendering the British régime unpopular amongst certain classes in Egypt than anything else. For the more intelligent Moslem, when he gradually woke up to what was going on around him, said to himself: The Englishman I understand; I recognise his good qualities; he brings to bear on his work, not only knowledge, but energy superior to my own; I do not like him, but I am aware that he means well by me, and I see that he confers certain material benefits on me, which I am very willing to accept; but what of this Syrian? Am I not as good as he? If native agents be required, why should not my kinsman be employed rather than this alien, who possesses neither the advantages of the European nor those of the true Egyptian? Accordingly, the Moslem, followed at no great distance by the Copt, poured forth all the vials of his wrath on the Syrian. Even Tewfik Pasha, whose views were habitually temperate, warmed to fever-heat when he spoke of the Syrians, whilst the same subject roused Riaz Pasha's more sturdy Islamism to the boiling-point of vituperation. In 1890, Riaz Pasha proposed to issue an edict, which virtually prohibited all Syrians from entering the Egyptian service. Then the British diplomatist had to step forward and to point out in a cold-blooded, accurate, European fashion that, so long as red-coated soldiers were walking about the streets of Cairo, no absolute proscription on the ground of race or creed could be tolerated; moreover, that, from the point of view of equity and common sense, a distinction should be drawn between those Syrians whose families resided in Syria, and who had merely come to Egypt to make their fortunes, and those who, though of Syrian origin, had been born and bred in Egypt, and who were, therefore, to all intents and purposes, Egyptians. The result was a compromise. Syrians who had lived for fifteen years in Egypt were admitted to the public service on the same terms as Egyptians.

The Mohammedan sentiment on this subject is very natural. The Egyptian Moslems are, in fact, now in the transitionary phase through which their co-religionists in India have already passed. When, after the events of 1857, all the paraphernalia of European administrative systems were introduced into India, the more subtle and assimilative Hindoo everywhere got the better of the slow-moving Moslem. In course of time, however, the latter woke up to the fact that there was need for self-exertion; and accordingly, if all accounts be true, he is now running neck and neck with the Hindoo, having possibly cast aside some of the obstructive customs which hang on to the skirts of his creed before he could attain the goal. The Egyptian Moslem must of necessity undergo the same process. He will find that protective laws against Syrian and Coptic encroachments will be of little avail, but, if he braces himself to the work, he may yet beat the Syrian with the latter's own weapons. He must, however, bestir himself, or he will be outstripped in the race. It is difficult to predict what will become of the Mohammedan religion if the Moslem wins. It will possibly suffer slightly in the excitement of the contest.

The Syrian, equally with the Copt, has to a certain extent developed "the vices of servitude." He has been obliged to bend before Moslem oppression or European intellectual superiority, and the process of adapting himself to Moslem caprice, or of imitating European procedures and habits of thought, is not calculated to develop the manly qualities. Nevertheless, whether from a moral, social, or intellectual point of view, the Syrian stands on a distinctly high level. He is rarely corrupt. There are many gradations of Syrian society. A high-class Syrian is an accomplished gentleman, whose manners and general behaviour admit of his being treated on a footing of perfect social equality by high-class Europeans. His intellectual level is also unquestionably high. He can do more than copy the European. He can understand why the European does what he does, and he is able to discuss with acuteness whether what is done is wisely or unwisely done. He is not by any means wanting in the logical faculty. It would, in a word, be wholly incorrect to say that he merely apes civilisation. It may be said with truth that he really is civilised. In this respect, he is probably superior, not only to the Copt, but also to the Europeanised Egyptian, who is but too often a mere mimic.

There is yet one further point to be considered as regards the Syrians. What was the attitude of the Syrian towards the British reformer? This question was at one time a never-ending source of difficulty to the Syrian himself, for he was torn with conflicting emotions. His French education had predisposed him to look askance at everything English. The Englishman's direct, common-sense mode of procedure, and his scorn for formalities, were foreign to the subtle, formalistic mind of the Syrian, whose tendencies were ultra-bureaucratic. These considerations, coupled with a certain amount of resentment at insular haughtiness, led the Syrian to dislike the Englishman. On the other hand, was it not possible that in the long run it would pay better to show English rather than French proclivities? Amidst the doubts which hung over the future of Egypt, it was difficult to give any positive answer to this question. Under the circumstances, the best thing the Syrian could do was to be Anglophile or Francophile according to the requirements of the moment. He would even, under the pressure of self-interest, occasionally emit sparks, which to the uninitiated might appear to emanate from the forge of Egyptian patriotism. But in reality his heart, or perhaps it should rather be said his head, was attracted by the theoretical perfection of French administrative systems. He had no sympathy with the English or with English methods, though he rendered lip-service to the Englishman and gladly accepted anything which the Englishman had to give him. This view held good more especially at the commencement of the British occupation, for, as time went on, the Anglophobia of the Syrians was, to say the least, greatly diminished in intensity.

Lastly, something should be said of the Armenians. The Armenian community in Egypt is small. It consists for the most part of shopkeepers. The political importance of the Armenians, however, is derived from the fact that, almost ever since the dynasty of Mehemet Ali was founded, a few Armenians of distinction have occupied high positions under the Egyptian Government. The Copts have, for the most part, never occupied any but subordinate posts in the Egyptian administration. The Syrians, in spite of their ability, have so far never been able to push beyond places of secondary, though considerable, importance. Armenians, on the other hand, have attained the highest administrative ranks, and have at times exercised a decisive influence on the conduct of public affairs in Egypt.

The number of upper-class Armenians in Egypt is insufficient to justify my attempting any broad generalisation of Armenian characteristics based on personal observation. But I may say that those few Armenians with whom I have been brought in contact appear to me to constitute, with the Syrians, the intellectual cream of the near East.

There is one point about the Armenians which is worthy of note. Observe a middle-class Armenian enter the room of a Turkish Pasha. On arriving at the door, he will make several profound obeisances. The Pasha, without rising from his seat, will, with contemptuous condescension, motion to him to sit down, but the Armenian will not do so at once; he will cross his hands in front of his body, cast his eyes on the ground, sidle along the wall or shuffle gradually forward without ever lifting his feet from the floor; at last, he will sink slowly down on the edge of a chair or divan, join his knees in front of him, cross his hands on his breast, and in this attitude of profound humility will wait until the lordly Pasha thinks fit to address a few words to him. A highly educated or highly placed Armenian will not, indeed, go through all this pantomime. Moreover, the younger Armenians are less deferential to the Turks than their fathers. But no Armenian, in the presence of a Turkish Pasha, can ever forget that he is a Christian raya and that the Turk is his oppressor; neither can this be any matter for surprise, for the oppression of the Turk has, indeed, in the case of the Armenians, been extreme.

The most distinguished of the present generation of Armenians in Egypt was unquestionably Nubar Pasha, to whose character and aptitudes incidental allusion has already been made, and of whom it will become necessary to speak more fully at a later period of this narrative.

Nubar Pasha's son, Boghos Pasha Nubar, is a man of marked ability. He at one time occupied, with great credit to himself, the post of Egyptian member of the Railway Administration, and, since his retirement from the service, has taken a most useful and intelligent interest in public affairs.

Yacoub Pasha Artin is a highly cultivated gentleman, who has done excellent work in the cause of educational reform.

But perhaps one of the most typical Armenians in Egypt was Nubar Pasha's son-in-law, Tigrane Pasha, who for a long time occupied the post of Under-Secretary for Foreign Affairs, and who subsequently became Foreign Minister.[1] He was a highly educated gentleman of polished manners. He spoke French perfectly; in fact, French was the language in which he was most at home. He spoke English well. He knew no Arabic, and but little Turkish. Without being, from a political point of view, a Gallophile, his habits of thought were cast in a French mould. Most of the young Egyptians of the early days of the occupation, although by no means always sympathisers with the aims and policy of the French Government, were saturated with ideas which had their origin in French education, in association with Frenchmen, and in the fact that they were more conversant with French than any other European literature.

[1] Tigrane Pasha, to the great regret of all who knew him, died in 1904. Although I often disagreed with him, I preserve the most pleasant recollection of our long and intimate personal relations.

One of the peculiarities of the Anglo-Saxon race is that when they take possession or semi-possession of a country, which does not belong to them, they are apt in one respect to forget the position which they occupy towards the inhabitants. They are conscious of their own good intentions; they earnestly desire to govern the people of the country well and justly; they cannot understand how any one can question the excellence of their motives; and they look with much dislike and suspicion, which is not at all unnatural, on all who place obstacles in the way of their praiseworthy designs being executed. Thus, forgetful of the fact that they are not dealing with the inhabitants of Kent or Norfolk, the English speedily apply the term "loyal" to those who co-operate with them, and the term "disloyal" to those who display hostility or merely lukewarm friendship.

From this point of view, Tigrane Pasha was far from being "loyal," neither can any moral blame be imputed to him for the degree of disloyalty which he at times displayed. He was not an Anglophobe in the ordinary sense of the term, but he disagreed with the broad lines of British policy in Egypt. Personal ambition may have had something to do with this mental attitude. It is possible that the class to which Tigrane Pasha belonged,—unless, indeed, as is not improbable, it was swept away at the first breath of discontent from the *alumni* of the El-Azhar University,—would occupy positions of greater importance in the world of Egyptian politics if British influence were diminished than those to which they can attain whilst that influence remains paramount. It may be, also, that, in order to remove the taint of being a Christian and an alien ignorant of the vernacular language, Tigrane Pasha was obliged to display a somewhat more ardent degree of patriotism in the cause of his adopted country than would have been necessary had he been, in fact as well as in name, a real hall-marked Egyptian struggling for the cause of Egypt. But it is doubtful whether Tigrane Pasha was consciously influenced by either of these considerations. It is more probable that he honestly thought that the Egyptians, that is to say, the Europeanised Egyptians, of whom for all practical purposes he may be said to have been one, were capable of governing Egypt without any considerable degree of British assistance, and certainly without the presence of a British garrison in the country.[1] In holding this opinion he was certainly wrong, but the fact that he did entertain an opinion of this sort, though it may have afforded ground for criticising his reasoning powers, afforded no ground whatever for moral reprobation. Tigrane Pasha was, in fact, a perfectly honourable and straightforward gentleman, with somewhat doctrinaire views, whose standard of public and private morality was in no way inferior to that of men of honour in any European country.

It is, however, from the intellectual and not from the moral point of view that the study of Tigrane Pasha's character was mainly of interest. It is here that his national—that is to say, Armenian, not Egyptian—characteristics came out in strong relief. Tigrane Pasha's mind may be characterised as having been Franco-Byzantine, that is to say, the foundation was Byzantine, whilst the superstructure was French. He was, intellectually speaking, the direct descendant of those Orientals who, in the

[1] There is some reason for believing that Tigrane Pasha's political views were a good deal modified before his death. During the last few years of his life, he was not in office, and, moreover, suffered from very bad health. The consequence was that, to my great regret, I saw less of him than at previous periods. I cannot, therefore, speak with confidence on this point.

early days of Christianity, engaged in endless disputes over barren and almost incomprehensible points of theology. He would have revelled in the subtleties submitted to the decision of the Council of Nice, but he would probably never have come to any definite conclusion as to whether Arius or Athanasius was in the right. He was very intelligent, particularly about matters of detail, and quick-witted, but was often incapable of grasping the true point at issue. When any plain, practical question had to be decided, he would sometimes rush off into an *a priori* discussion of some principle, which was only remotely connected with the matter in hand. On the other hand, when some broad question of principle was at stake, Tigrane Pasha would split hairs over a minor issue, which was almost incomprehensible, or which was at all events devoid of importance to the non-Byzantine mind. In political affairs, he had but little idea of proportion. He endeavoured to understand European, and especially British politics,—a rock on which many Orientals have split,—and as the result of his studies, he was generally able to give the most plausible reasons for arriving at conclusions, which were usually erroneous. To make use of a French expression, *Il prenait des vessies pour des lanternes.* His minor premiss appeared to him to be of such importance, that he was apt to forget the existence of his major premiss. His mind refused to accept a simple inference from simple facts, which were patent to all the world. The very simplicity of the conclusion was of itself enough to make him reject it, for he had an elective affinity for everything that was intricate. He was a prey to intellectual over-subtlety—*Graecorum ille morbus*, as it was termed by Seneca.

Tigrane Pasha was the *âme damnée* of a succession

of Egyptian Ministries. He always proffered advice, which he honestly considered was in the best interests of Egypt; yet on most occasions of importance, the result of following his advice was to produce an effect the opposite of that which he had intended. His main desire for many years was to diminish the power of the English in Egypt, and he became instrumental in augmenting their power. From time to time, he laboriously constructed a diplomatic house of cards, which he thought must produce the required result. When one house of cards was overturned by a movement of the Englishman's little finger, he was not dismayed. He did not see that the way to get rid of the Englishman was, not to oppose him, but to co-operate with him. Untaught by experience, he set to work to construct some other flimsy fabric, which also disappeared at the first tiny blast of the British diplomatic horn. The motives, which led Tigrane Pasha into a number of honest but very palpable errors, are worthy of respect. Those errors were due to the Franco-Byzantine frame of mind, which is hypercritical, and which is, moreover, unwilling to adopt a severe process of inductive reasoning. In politics, it is essential to ascertain the facts correctly before coming to any conclusion. This Tigrane Pasha was apt to forget. His sympathies drove him to a certain conclusion; he was wont to accept that conclusion, and to let the facts, on which the conclusion ought to have been based, take care of themselves.

With one exception, to which allusion will presently be made, the various elements which make up native Egyptian society have thus been described. Some of the judgments which have been passed may appear harsh. They have, however, been written with an object, which will now be explained.

At the period of history of which this narrative treats, it happened that Egypt had to be Europeanised. The English were the main agents in this process of Europeanisation. It is true that the English reformers attempted in some measure to Egyptianise themselves. They were possessed of little social, but of much political and administrative elasticity, which enabled them to adapt themselves and their procedures to strange circumstances more readily than would have been the case with some other members of the European family. At the same time, the Egyptian had to meet the Englishman more than half-way. European civilisation, though not absolutely a bed of Procrustes, is not very elastic. Broadly speaking, in spite of every effort, the bed could not be made to fit the Egyptian; the Egyptian had to adapt himself to lying on the bed. Viewed in this light, it is more important to know what the Egyptian is from the point of view of the educated European, than it is to inquire what Europeans, whether educated or the reverse, are from the point of view of the Egyptian. I have, therefore, endeavoured to depict the Egyptians of different classes of society as they appear in the eyes of an educated European. I have attempted to show how little suited the Egyptian is to lie on the bed which, as an incident of modern progress, has been prepared for him. I have wished to bring into relief how his religion, his history, his moral and intellectual attributes, and his social customs contribute to establish a gulf between him and his European guides. But I have no wish whatever to blame the individual Egyptian, be he Moslem or Christian, for being that which I find him to be. An Englishman who had been long resident in

China, once said: "It is the misfortune of the Chinese Government and people to be weighed in a balance, which they have never accepted, and to have their shortcomings, so ascertained, made the basis of reclamations of varying degrees of gravity."[1] This observation holds as good about Egypt as it does about China. I am aware that in the remarks made in this and the two preceding chapters, the Egyptian has been weighed in a balance which he has never accepted, and in which, moreover, it is somewhat unjust to weigh him; for, from whatever point of view we look at the Egyptian, we should never forget that he is what the accidents of his history, climate, religion, and geographical position have made him. It is useless and, indeed, hurtful to hide his defects, or to disguise from ourselves the fact that the reception of true European civilisation by a population such as that which is described above must be the work of generations. But there is no occasion to point the finger of pharisaical scorn at the Egyptians, whilst any feeling of self-congratulation that we are not as these less fortunate political publicans should surely be checked by the reflection that some, at least, of the defects in the Egyptian character are due to association with European civilisation in a debased form. Rather let us, in Christian charity, make every possible allowance for the moral and intellectual shortcomings of the Egyptians, and do whatever can be done to rectify them.

[1] Mr. Alexander Michie, *China and Christianity*, p. 1, 1892.

CHAPTER XXXVII

THE EUROPEANISED EGYPTIANS

The Europeanised Egyptians are generally Agnostics—Effects of Europeanising the East—Gallicised Egyptians—Attractions of French civilisation—Unsuitability of the French system to form the Egyptian character—The official classes generally hostile to England.

A MOMENT'S reflection will show how it is that, in the peculiar political phase through which Egypt is now passing, the Europeanised Egyptian occupies a position of somewhat special importance. If the country were still governed on the lines of the old Oriental despotisms, a small number of educated Egyptians might perhaps be employed in subordinate positions, but they would be mere adjuncts; they would not truly represent the spirit of the Government. If, on the other hand, the Government and society of Egypt were farther advanced on the road to civilisation, the Europeanised Egyptian would probably be something different from what he actually is; he would have become in spirit, though not necessarily in sentiment, less Egyptian and more thoroughly European. But inasmuch as Egyptian society is in a state of flux, the natural result has been to produce a class of individuals many of whom are, at the same time, demoslemised Moslems and invertebrate Europeans.

In dealing with the question of introducing European civilisation into Egypt, it should never be forgotten that Islam cannot be reformed; that is to say, reformed Islam is Islam no longer; it is something else; we cannot as yet tell what it will eventually be. "Christian nations," Sir William Muir says, "may advance in civilisation, freedom, and morality, in philosophy, science, and the arts, but Islam stands still. And thus stationary, so far as the lessons of history avail, it will remain."[1] But little assistance in the work of reform can, therefore, be expected from the steady orthodox Moslems, who cling with unswerving fidelity to their ancient faith, and whose dislike to European civilisation often increases as that civilisation advances. The Syrians and Armenians are foreigners. The Copts, besides being Christians, are—or, at all events, in 1882, were—but little better educated than the ordinary Moslems. Having regard, therefore, to the disqualifications of his competitors, the Europeanised Egyptian naturally becomes, if not the only possible, at all events the principal agent for administering the country, except in so far as it is administered by Europeans.

Nominally, the Europeanised Egyptian is in the majority of cases a Moslem. In reality, he is generally an Agnostic. The gulf between him and the "Alim" of the El-Azhar University is as great as between the "Alim" and the European. Indeed, it may be doubted whether the gulf is not in reality greater in the former than in the latter case. For a thoughtful European will not only look with interest at the "Alim" as the representative of an ancient faith, which contains much that is highly deserving of respect; he will, if the "Alim" is a worthy specimen of his class, sympathise with him because he is religious, albeit his religion is not that of Christ. The Europeanised Egyptian, on the other hand, will often look on the "Alim"

[1] *The Caliphate*, p. 597.

with all the pride of an intellectual *parvenu*. From the pedestal of his empirical knowledge, he will regard the "Alim" as a social derelict, who has to be tolerated, and even occasionally, for political purposes, to be utilised, but who need not be respected.

The truth is that, in passing through the European educational mill, the young Egyptian Moslem loses his Islamism, or, at all events, he loses the best part of it. He cuts himself adrift from the sheet-anchor of his creed. He no longer believes that he is always in the presence of his Creator, to whom he will some day have to render an account of his actions. He may still, however, take advantage of the least worthy portions of his nominal religion, those portions, namely, which, in so far as they tolerate a lax moral code, adapt themselves to his tastes and to his convenience in the affairs of this world. Moreover, in losing his Islamism, the educated Egyptian very rarely makes any approach towards Christianity. There are practically no cases of Christian converts amongst the educated classes. More than this, although the Europeanised Egyptian is no true Moslem, he is often as intolerant, and sometimes even more intolerant of Christianity than the old orthodox Moslem, who has received no European education. He frequently hates Christians with a bitter hatred, and he does so partly because many of the Christians with whom he has been brought in contact deserve to be hated, and partly because the Christian, in his capacity of being a European, is a rival who occupies positions, which the Europeanised Egyptian thinks he should himself occupy.

It is doubtful whether the price which is being paid, or which, at all events, may have to be paid for introducing European civilisation into these backward Eastern societies is always recognised so fully as it should be. The material benefits derived from Europeanisation are unquestionably great, but as regards the ultimate effect on public and private morality the future is altogether uncertain.[1] European civilisation destroys one religion without substituting another in its place. It remains to be seen whether the code of Christian morality, on which European civilisation is based, can be dissociated from the teaching of the Christian religion. This question can only be answered by generations which are now unborn. For the present, there is little to guide us in any forecast as to what the ultimate result will be.

It may, however, be noted that there is an essential difference between the de-moslemised Moslem and the free-thinker in Europe. The latter is surrounded by an atmosphere of Christianity: he will often, sometimes with a pang of envy, admire trustfulness and faith, in which qualities his reasoning faculties forbid him to share; if he is a politician, he will, or at all events he should recognise the utilitarian side of Christianity; he will, more often than not, reject the idea that there is no alternative presented to him but that of being either an atheist or a full believer in the Christianity of the schools; the fact that he is a free-thinker does not cut him off from association and co-operation with his friends, who may not share his disbelief or his doubts; his reason, his associations, and his hereditary qualities alike impel him to assert, no less strongly than the orthodox Christian, that the code of Christian morality must

[1] The whole of this question has been admirably treated, from the Hindoo point of view, in the second series of Sir Alfred Lyall's brilliant *Asiatic Studies*. Every European who occupies a high position in the East should study Sir Alfred Lyall's works. They display a profound knowledge of Eastern habits of thought, and a remarkable grasp of the difficulties underlying the treatment of Eastern problems.

form the basis to regulate the relations between man and man in modern society. That morality has, indeed, taken such deep root in Europe that if, as would appear probable, the hold which revealed religion and theological dogma has on mankind is destined to be gradually relaxed, no moral cataclysm is to be anticipated.

Far different is the case of the Egyptian free-thinker. He finds himself launched on a troubled sea without any rudder and without any pilot. Neither his past history nor his present associations impose any effective moral restraint upon him. He finds that, amongst many of his own countrymen, the cause of religion is often identified with opposition to the most reasonable reforms, and in trampling indignantly on the particular religion which can lead to such results, he is disposed to cast aside religion altogether. Having cut himself loose from his creed, no barrier, save that of cynical self-interest, serves to keep him within the limits of the moral code which is in some degree imposed on the European, whose system he is endeavouring to copy. The society in which he moves does not seriously condemn untruthfulness and deceit. The social stigma with which vice of various kinds is visited is too feeble to exercise much practical effect. As he leaves the creed of his forefathers, he casts no lingering look behind. He not only leaves it, but he spurns it. He rushes blindfold into the arms of European civilisation, unmindful of the fact that what is visible to the eye constitutes merely the outward signs of that civilisation, whilst the deep-seated ballast of Christian morality, which regulates the occasionally eccentric movements of the vessel, is hidden beneath the surface, and is difficult of acquisition by the pseudo-European imitator of the European system. He calls Heaven to witness that he has cast aside all prejudices based on religion, and that he despises the teachings of his forefathers. See, he says to the European, I have my railways, my schools, my newspapers, my law-courts, and all the other things which, as I can plainly see, go to make up your boasted civilisation; in what, then, am I inferior to you? Alas! the de-moslemised Moslem, although he is wholly unaware of the defect, is inferior in one respect wherein his inferiority cannot be removed by a stroke of the pen, for the civilised European, as we understand him, though he may not be an orthodox Christian, is in spite of himself to a great extent the outcome of Christianity, and would not be what he is had he not 1900 years of Christianity behind him. "No hostility to Christian doctrine can justify indifference to the truth, that the world owes to Christianity the matured idea of Progress, and the one serious attempt to realise it."[1]

It is at present useless to speculate on the ultimate product of the forces which are now being brought into play in the Moslem world.[2] That any great accession of strength will accrue to Christianity is improbable. A revival of Islam, that is to say, the Islam of the Koran and the *Traditions*, is nothing but the dream of poetic natures whose imaginations are carried away by the attractions which hover round some incidents of this faith. Yet, as has been often observed, history records no instance of a nation being without a religion. "Man everywhere shows

[1] Liddon, *University Sermons*, 1873, p. 33.

[2] M. Leroy-Beaulieu makes the following remarks as regards the dissolvent effect exercised by Western civilisation on Judaism: "Qu'est ce qui a conservé le juif à travers les siècles et l'a empêché de disparaître au milieu des nations? C'est sa religion. Or, ces rites protecteurs, cette cuirasse ou cette carapace d'observances qui l'a defendu durant deux mille ans, et que rien ne pourrait transpercer, notre esprit occidental l'a entamée. . . . Si le judaisme, débilité, venait à se décomposer et à se dissoudre, qu'adviendrait-il du juif? Formé et saufgardé par sa religion, le juif ne risque-t-il point de s'évanouir avec le judaisme?"—*Israel chez les Nations*, p. 77.

invincible religious tendencies."[1] It is conceivable that, as time goes on, the Moslems will develop a religion, possibly a pure Deism, which will not be altogether the Islamism of the past and of the present, and which will cast aside much of the teaching of Mohammed, but which will establish a moral code sufficient to hold society together by bonds other than those of unalloyed self-interest. The Europeanised Egyptian, as we now see him, is the first, not the last, word of reformed Moslem society. It is possible that, in course of time, some higher moral and intellectual ideal will be developed. In the meanwhile, let the European politician bear this in mind, that in the process of his well-intentioned and very necessary reforms he will do well to abstain, on utilitarian grounds, from any measure which is calculated to undermine the Moslem faith more than the strict requirements of the case demand. The missionary, the philanthropist, the social reformer, and others of the same sort, should have a fair field. Their intentions are excellent, although at times their judgment may be defective. They will, if under some control, probably do much good on a small scale. They may even, being carried away by the enthusiasm which pays no heed to worldly prudence, effect reforms more important than those of the administrator and politician, who will follow cautiously in their track, and perhaps reap the results of their labours. Nevertheless, let those who have to guide the machine of state beware how they wittingly shake the whole moral fabric of Eastern society. It is dangerous work, politically, socially, and morally, to trifle with the religious belief of a whole nation.

The first point, therefore, to be borne in mind in dealing with the Europeanised Egyptian is that

[1] Boyd Carpenter, *The Permanent Elements of Religion*, p. 77.

he is generally an Agnostic. The second point is that the term Europeanised, when applied to the Egyptian educated in Europe, though not a misnomer, is lacking in precision. For the majority of Europeanised Egyptians at the commencement of the British occupation, and for some years subsequent to that event, were, in truth, Gallicised Egyptians.

When Mehemet Ali took some tentative steps towards introducing European civilisation into Egypt, he naturally turned to France for assistance. He was haunted with the idea that England would one day take possession of Egypt.[1] An increase of French influence in Egypt would, he thought, constitute some barrier against British aggression. A number of young Egyptians were, therefore, sent to France to be educated, and several schools were established in Egypt at the heads of which French professors were placed. Thus, the first impress of civilisation given to Egypt was through the medium of the French language, which, it may be added, has during the latter part of the last century been supplanting Italian as a common language for the use of divers nationalities throughout the Levant. The French thus obtained a start which they have never lost. The Government and the people of France, being gifted with more political foresight of a certain kind, and being more capable of grasping a general idea than the English, saw their advantage, and followed it up. They were aware that, if the youth of Egypt learnt the French language, they would, as a necessary consequence, be saturated with French habits of thought, and they hoped that sympathy with France and

[1] *Vide ante*, vol. i. p. 16, note. Sir Charles Murray, in his *Short Memoir* (p. 5), says that Mehemet Ali's sympathy for the French was in some degree due to the kindness shown to him when a child by a French resident at Cawala, named Lion.

French political aims would ensue. For half a century prior to the British occupation, therefore, during which time the British Government were wholly inactive in respect to Egyptian education, no effort was spared to propagate a knowledge of French in Egypt. The agents for the accomplishment of this object have been mainly Catholic priests. The great apostle of anti-clericalism in France, M. Gambetta, was careful to explain that his anti-clerical ideas were only intended for home consumption; they were not meant for export. The French Republic claims to be the defender of the Catholic Church in the East, and is very sensitive if its right to do so is in any way questioned. A Republican Government and their agents, be they never so anti-clerical at home, are fully alive to the advantages of taking clericalism by the hand abroad as a useful instrument to further their political aims.

Apart, however, from any consequences resulting from the action taken either by Mehemet Ali or by the French Government, it is to be observed that French civilisation possesses a special degree of attraction, not only to the Asiatic, but also to the European races of the Levant. This point is one of considerable importance, for amongst the obstacles, which have stood in the way of the British reformer in Egypt, none is more noteworthy than that both Europeanised Egyptians and Levantines are impregnated with French rather than with English habits of thought.

The reasons why French civilisation presents a special degree of attraction to Asiatics and Levantines are plain. It is, as a matter of fact, more attractive than the civilisations of England and Germany, and, moreover, it is more easy of imitation. Compare the undemonstrative, shy Englishman, with his social exclusiveness and insular habits, with the vivacious and cosmopolitan Frenchman, who does not know what the word shyness means, and who in ten minutes is apparently on terms of intimate friendship with any casual acquaintance he may chance to make. The semi-educated Oriental does not recognise that the former has, at all events, the merit of sincerity, whilst the latter is often merely acting a part.[1] He looks coldly on the Englishman, and rushes into the arms of the Frenchman.

Look, again, to the relative intellectual attractions which the two Western races present. The Englishman is a follower of Bacon without knowing it. Inductive philosophy has become part of his nature. He instinctively rejects *a priori* reasoning. He will laboriously collect a number of facts before arriving at any conclusion, and, when he has collected his facts, he will limit his conclusion to the precise point which is proved. Compare this frame of mind with that of the quick-witted Frenchman, who, on the most slender basis of fact, will advance some sweeping generalisation with an assurance untempered by any shadow of doubt as to its correctness. Can it be any matter for surprise that the Egyptian, with his light intellectual ballast, fails to see that some fallacy often lies at the bottom of the Frenchman's reasoning, or that he prefers the rather superficial brilliancy of the Frenchman to the plodding, unattractive industry of the Englishman or the German? Look, again, at the theoretical perfection of French administrative systems, at their elaborate detail, and at the

[1] Shortly after the Franco-German War, in defending the French against General Blumenthal, I said, "You must admit, General, that the French are good actors." The sturdy old Gallophobe replied, "It is the only thing they can do. They are always acting." I do not at all agree with the first part of the distinguished General's view. The French can do a great many things besides act well.

provision which is apparently made to meet every possible contingency which may arise. Compare these features with the Englishman's practical systems, which lay down rules as to a few main points, and leave a mass of detail to individual discretion. The half-educated Egyptian naturally prefers the Frenchman's system, for it is to all outward appearance more perfect and more easy of application. He fails, moreover, to see that the Englishman desires to elaborate a system which will suit the facts with which he has to deal, whereas the main objection to applying French administrative procedures to Egypt is that the facts have but too often to conform to the ready-made system. From whatever point of view the subject be regarded, the same contrast will be found. On the one side, is a damsel possessing attractive, albeit somewhat artificial charms; on the other side, is a sober, elderly matron of perhaps somewhat greater moral worth, but of less pleasing outward appearance. The Egyptian, in the heyday of his political and intellectual youth, naturally smiled on the attractive damsel, and turned his back on the excellent but somewhat ill-favoured matron.

In some respects it is, for his own sake, greatly to be regretted that he did so. What the Egyptian most of all requires is, not so much that his mind should be trained, as that his character should be formed. It is certain that a very high tone of morality pervades those admirable educational institutions which spring, Pallas-like, from the fertile brain of the Vatican, and most of which, in Egypt, are under French control. It is also certain that those who base their opinion of French character and morals on the light French literature of the day are wholly in error. I believe that in no country are the domestic virtues more generally cherished than in France. It has, however, to be remembered[1] that the Oriental has a remarkable capacity for assimilating to himself the worst and rejecting the best parts of any European civilisation with which he may be brought in contact. It is not from the best, but rather from the least admirable traits in the French character that those young Egyptians who have been brought under French influences, have generally drawn their moral inspirations.

It is not to be supposed that the educated Egyptian fails to note the defects of his European monitors, be they French or English. He often sees those defects clearly enough, and the result not unfrequently is that, even though he may himself become partially Europeanised, he will despise European civilisation. In what respect, he says to himself, are we Egyptians morally inferior to our teachers? We may be deceitful, untruthful, and unchaste, but we are not one whit worse than those whom we are told to regard as the ultimate product of European civilisation.[2] The result is that the Europeanised Egyptian often returns to Egypt in order to become, both by precept and example, an apostle of anti-European ideas. The conservatism of older Moslems, who regard him as a living warning that they should beware of European civilisation,

[1] *Vide ante*, vol. i. p. 59.

[2] The moral superiority of English over French training is recognised by the Egyptians themselves, and has at times been recognised by cultivated Frenchmen. Senior (*Conversations, etc.*, vol. i. p. 213) relates the following conversation: "*Hekekyan.*—It is remarkable that all the Egyptians and Asiatics whom Mehemet Ali sent to England for education came back, like myself and young Stephan, Anglomaniacs; while all whom he sent to France returned disgusted with Europe. . . . *Clot* (the founder of the Egyptian School of Medicine).—I have made the same remark. . . . Our students see only bad company in Paris, and are disgusted with it. In London they get, if not into the fashionable world, at least into a respectable world, infinitely superior in morals, knowledge, and intelligence to anything in the East."

becomes stereotyped on observing his behaviour and on hearing his language; whilst he himself, in spite of his partial Europeanisation, will, with an inconsistency which would be strange were we not dealing with the "Land of Paradox," hate the Europeans quite as much as the less educated sections of his own countrymen.

The question of the effect of European, and notably French education on the rising generation of Egyptians has to be considered from another point of view. The tendency of every Egyptian official is to shirk responsibility. He thinks less of what should be done than of acting in such a manner that no personal blame can be attached to himself. This habit of thought makes the Egyptian official instinctively shrink from the British system of administration, for under that system much is left to the discretion of the individual, who is, therefore, obliged to think for himself. He flies for refuge to the French system, and there he finds administrative procedures prescribed which exactly suit his character and habits of thought. He finds that provision is apparently made for everything, to the most minute detail, in a series of elaborate codes. Entrenched behind these codes, the Europeanised Egyptian is, to his joy, relieved in a great degree from the necessity of thinking for himself. Some emergency may, indeed, occur which requires prompt action and the exercise of common sense. The Europeanised Egyptian, however, but too often does not recognise emergencies, and he spurns common sense. He refers to some article in his regulations, and maintains that he cannot depart from the provisions of that article by one hair's-breadth. The result may be disastrous, but he is indifferent as to the result; for, having conformed strictly to his orders, he cannot be blamed by his superiors. The

Egyptian official was always predisposed to be an automaton.[1] Once Europeanised—more especially if he be Gallicised—his automatic rigidity becomes more wooden than it was before.

It can scarcely be doubted that, from this point of view, French training has done little to rectify the defects of the Egyptian national character. In everything, it has tended to stereotype the Egyptian predisposition to look to the letter which killeth, and neglect the spirit which giveth life.

Scores of cases could be mentioned illustrative of the tendency to which allusion is here made. One or two instances will, however, suffice.

A case occurred of a stationmaster declining to send a fire-engine by a train which was about to start, in order to help in putting down a serious fire. He pointed with inexorable logic to the regulations, which did not permit of trucks being attached to that particular train. No exception was to be found in the code, with which he had been furnished, to meet the case of a burning town to which a fire-engine had to be despatched. Again, at one time it was the practice, if an accident occurred in the streets, not to transport the individual who had been injured at once to the hospital, but to leave him lying on the ground, whatever might be his condition, until the proper official had arrived to make a "Procès-verbal" of the facts connected with the accident. On one occasion, a doctor was sent to examine into the condition

[1] It has been conclusively shown by Taine and others that many ot the administrative methods generally practised on the continent of Europe are not, as is very commonly supposed, the result of the French Revolution, but that they existed—often under a different form—in pre-Revolutionary days. Similarly, the idea, which is somewhat prevalent, that the extreme formalism which characterises Egyptian official life is the result of contact with Europe, though it may be partially correct, does not convey the whole truth. Mr. St. John (*Egypt and Mohammed Ali*, vol. ii. p. 419) gives a remarkable instance of the extreme formalism with which Egyptian official work was conducted in his time.

of a stationmaster, supposed to be insane. On entering the room, he was attacked and nearly strangled by the madman. He was able, after a sharp struggle, to call on two orderlies, who had been present all the time, to seize the man. They saluted and did so. On being asked why they had not interfered sooner, they replied that they had received no orders to that effect. Without doubt, they considered that the struggle on the floor, which they had witnessed, was part of some strange European process, with which they were unfamiliar, for dealing with insane stationmasters.[1]

I may mention that a subordinate Egyptian official, notably a policeman, regards the preparation of a "Procès-verbal" as a proceeding of peculiar sanctity. It matters little what the document contains. Provided he can get a "Procès-verbal" prepared in due form, the Egyptian official considers that he is free from responsibility, and he is, therefore, happy. Otherwise, he feels that a certain amount of personal responsibility weighs upon him, and he is miserable. This plethora of "Procès-verbaux" has done a good deal to nip in the bud any feeble tendencies towards individualism which might otherwise have been developed.

In a word, the French bureaucratic and legal systems, although there is much to be said in their favour when they are carried into execution by a highly civilised and intelligent race such as the French, are little adapted to the formation of either competent officials or useful citizens in a country such as Egypt.

Such, therefore, is the Europeanised Egyptian. His intellectual qualities have, of late years,

[1] These cases have already been cited in my Report for the year 1903 (*Egypt*, No. 1, of 1904, p. 78). An endless number of similar illustrations of the tendency to which allusion is made above, might be given.

certainly been developed. His moral attributes have generally been little, if at all, improved by contact with Europe. The old orthodox Moslem is bound hand and foot by ancient custom based on his religion. The Europeanised Egyptian is often bound almost as fast by a set of rigid formulæ, which he mistakes for the substance, whereas they are in reality but some fortuitous incidents of European civilisation.

Although the description given above holds generally good as regards the class now under discussion, it is to be noted that there are exceptions, and, moreover, that the exceptions are year by year becoming more numerous. Some of the younger generation of Egyptians are turning into excellent officials, especially those employed under the Department of Justice. In view of the character of the modern Egyptian, it is obviously more easy to develop a certain amount of judicial capacity than it is to train good executive officers. The judge merely has to interpret his code. The executive official must of necessity rely to a greater extent on his individual resource and judgment.

One point remains to be considered. What was the attitude of the Europeanised Egyptian towards the British reformer? After what has been already said, it is needless to dilate on this subject. Envy, dislike of British administrative systems, ignorance of the English language,[1] resentment at the stand-off manners and at the airs of conscious superiority which the Englishman, somewhat unwisely, is prone to give himself, and want of appreciation of the better side of the English character, all drove the Europeanised Egyptian in one direction. With a few exceptions, the whole

[1] This fertile source of misunderstanding is, it may be hoped, rapidly disappearing. The number of young Egyptians who understand English is steadily increasing, as also the number of British officials who speak Arabic.

class was, at the commencement of the British occupation, Anglophobe.

It may be doubted whether of late years this Anglophobia has diminished. Indeed, indications are not wanting that, mainly by reason of the misrepresentations of the vernacular press, it has somewhat increased in intensity. It is the duty of the British officials in the service of the Egyptian Government to use their utmost endeavours to mitigate feelings of this description by sympathetic treatment, and by abstaining from passing too harsh a judgment on whatever defects they may find to exist amongst the rising generation of Egyptians. Those defects are the natural outcome of the peculiar political conditions under which the country is governed, and of the unhealthy influences to which the young Egyptians are often exposed.

CHAPTER XXXVIII

THE EUROPEANS

Number of Europeans—The Levantines—Their characteristics—The Greeks—Their commercial enterprise—The English—The Army of Occupation—Anglo-Egyptian officials—Feelings entertained by other Europeans towards the English—Summary of the classes friendly and hostile to England.

According to the census of 1897, there were at that time about 113,000 Europeans resident in Egypt.[1] These 113,000 persons were divided as follows:

Greeks	38,000
Italians	24,000
French	14,000
Austrians	7,000
English (including Maltese and other British subjects, as well as the Army of Occupation)	20,000
Other nationalities	10,000
Total	113,000

The classification by nationalities, though important in many respects, is misleading to this extent, that when it is said that there are 24,000 Italians, 14,000 Frenchmen, 7000 Austrians, and so on in Egypt, it is not to be supposed that there are that number of Italians, Frenchmen, or Austrians in the country possessing the special national

[1] There can be no doubt that since the census of 1897 was taken, the number of Europeans in Egypt has largely increased. I have already stated (*vide ante*, p. 129, note) that the detailed figures of the census taken in 1907 are not yet available.

characteristics, which are generally held to belong to the inhabitants of Italy, France, or Austria. Apart from the fact that there are a large number of protected subjects, who are often Orientals, it is to be observed that in many cases the Frenchman resident in Egypt is only technically a Frenchman, the Italian may in reality be only half an Italian in so far as his national characteristics are concerned, the Austrian is often merely a subject of the Emperor of Austria for purposes of Consular protection and nothing more. For, in truth, many individuals of these and of other nationalities are, above all things, Levantines, and the Levantines, though not a separate nation, possess characteristics of their own which may almost be termed national.

Every one who has lived in the Eastern part of the Mediterranean knows what is meant by a Levantine, though a precise definition of this term is difficult, if not impossible. The Levantine can, of course, be described as a European resident in the Levant, generally in the Ottoman dominions situated in the Levant. This definition is, however, not satisfactory, for some Europeans may be born and bred in the East and pass all their lives in the Levant, without losing the special characteristics of their country of origin, or acquiring in any considerable degree those of the Levantine. In the case of others, a short residence in the Levant will suffice to produce typical Levantine characteristics. Others, again, already approached so nearly to Levantines in their country of origin, that they may almost be said to have been Levantines before they emigrated to the Levant. In fact, inasmuch as the Levantines are more or less Orientalised Europeans,[1] just as Egyptian Moslems educated in

[1] The process of manufacturing Levantines is at least as old as the Crusades. Thus, Mr. Stanley Lane-Poole says (*Saladin*, p. 28): "The early Crusaders, after thirty years' residence in Syria, had become very much assimilated in character and habits to the people whom they had

France are Gallicised Egyptians, they necessarily present every gradation of character, from the European with no trace of the Oriental about him, to the European who is so thoroughly orientalised as scarcely to have preserved any distinctive European characteristics. A considerable number of Levantines lie midway between these two extremes. Starting sometimes with national characteristics which bear some resemblance to those of Easterns, they develop those characteristics to a still greater degree by residence in the East. They become semi-orientalised Europeans. If compared with the northern races of Europe, the predominance of the Oriental portion of their characters will come out in strong relief. If, on the other hand, they are compared with the southern European races, any process of differentiation will bring out their distinctive Oriental characteristics in a less striking manner. The majority of Levantines are recruited from the southern races of Europe, and, in respect to these more especially, their technical nationality is, from the point of view of the present argument, of slight importance. The particular Consulate at which the Levantine is inscribed is a mere accident. He is, above all things, a Levantine, though he dislikes to be designated by that appellation; for, partly because he is aware that the Levantines do not generally bear a high character, partly because he dislikes to merge his national individuality in a cosmopolitan expression, and partly because he is sensible of the material benefits which he derives from his foreign nationality, the Levantine will often develop a specially ardent degree of patriotism for the country which affords him Consular protection.

partly conquered, among whom they lived, and whose daughters they did not disdain to marry; they were growing into Levantines; they were known as *Pullani* or Creoles."

Germans and Englishmen, however long they may reside in the Levant, rarely become typical Levantines. Starting with strongly marked national characteristics, they generally preserve those characteristics more or less intact. As a class, they do not differ materially from their fellow-countrymen of the same social standing in Germany or England.

The case of the Italians, of whom there are a large number in Egypt, is different. Many of the skilled artisans in Egypt, the bricklayers, masons, carpenters, etc., are Italians. They are, as a rule, a steady, industrious race, whose presence is very useful to the Egyptians, as it enables the latter to learn various crafts requiring skill in their application. As a body, these Italians do not differ from their countrymen of the same social position in Italy. On the other hand, there are some middle-class Italians, who, with their families, have been long resident in Egypt, and who may, as a class, be considered representative Levantines. The transition from being Italian to being Levantine is, in these cases, more easy than in the case of the Englishman or the German.

Much the same may be said of the Austrians, who do not generally come from Austria proper, but from the neighbourhood of Trieste. Many of these are Jews. Their language is generally not German but Italian.

The French occupy a peculiar position. The French colony contains every gradation of type, from the most Gallic Gaul to the ultra-Levantinised Levantine. In respect to the latter class, however, the question arises of whether the Frenchman has become Levantinised, or whether the counter-process has not taken place; whether it is not that the Levantine has become Gallicised. The fact is that both processes are constantly in operation.

Next, what are the main characteristics of the Levantines? There are, of course, many Levantines—merchants, professional men, shopkeepers, and others—who are highly respectable members of society, and who carry on their business upon the same principles as they would adopt were they living at Trieste, Genoa, or Marseilles. But these are not representatives of the class, which is conjured up in the mind of the Egyptian Minister or his British adviser, when the word Levantine is mentioned. It is the misfortune of the Levantines that they suffer in reputation by reason of qualities which are displayed by only a small minority of their class. It cannot, in fact, be doubted that amongst this minority are to be found individuals who are tainted with a remarkable degree of moral obliquity. These are the Levantines who regard the Egyptians, from prince to peasant, as their prey. In days now happily past, they brought all their intellectual acuteness, which is of no mean order, to bear on the work of depredation. Whatever national defects they may have possessed in their country of origin, appear to have been enhanced when, on arrival in Egypt, they had to deal with a people who were ignorant, credulous, and improvident, and, therefore, easily despoiled; who, by reason of their own low moral standard, seemed, to a perverted mind, in some degree to justify reciprocity of low morals in dealing with them; and who, being weak and defenceless, invited spoliation at the hands of the unprincipled adventurer armed with all the strength which he drew from intellectual superiority, diplomatic support, and intimate acquaintance with all the forms and back-alleys of the Civil Code. This is the class which has to a certain extent made European civilisation stink in the nostrils of the Egyptians. The Levantines of this description have done a small amount of good by introducing European capital on a limited scale into the country. They have done a vast amount of harm by associating the name of European in the minds of the Egyptians with a total absence of scruple in the pursuit of gain. The upper-class Levantine naturally used to consider the upper-class Egyptian as his prey. The lower-class Levantine tricked the fellaheen.

The Greeks are so numerous that they deserve consideration by themselves. In 1897, there were 38,000 Greeks in Egypt. The question of who is and who is not a subject of the King of the Hellenes is a never-ending cause of dispute between the Ottoman and Greek Governments. Under what conditions of birth and residence are the Greeks, who were born and bred outside Greece and who have only casually lived in that country, to be considered Greek subjects? It is needless to dwell on the details of this wearisome question. It will be sufficient to say that, in spite of the resistance of the Egyptian authorities, most Greek-speaking Greeks generally manage to produce sufficient evidence to enable them to claim the privileges attaching to Greek nationality.

In Alexandria, which may almost be said to be a Greek town, a great many influential and highly respectable Greeks are to be found. Their presence in Egypt is an unmixed benefit to the country.[1] More than this, many of the small

[1] I wish to insist very strongly on this point. None have suffered more than the Greeks from the practice, which is but too common, of condemning a whole class or community because the conduct of certain individuals belonging to it is worthy of condemnation. I have the best reasons for knowing that none regret more than the very numerous high-class Greeks established in Egypt the fact that their national reputation should at times be tarnished by the behaviour of some individuals belonging to their nation. In spite of the blemishes recorded in these pages, it may be said with truth that the Greeks in Egypt have, as of old, carried high the torch of civilisation in their adopted country.

Greek traders are fully deserving of respect. Still the fact remains that a portion of the Greek colony in Egypt consists of low-class Greeks exercising the professions of usurer, drink-seller, etc. The Greek of this class has an extraordinary talent for retail trade. He will risk his life in the pursuit of petty gain. It is not only that a Greek usurer or a *bakal* (general dealer) is established in almost every village in Egypt; the Greek pushes his way into the most remote parts of the Soudan and of Abyssinia. Wherever, in fact, there is the smallest prospect of buying in a cheap and selling in a dear market, there will the petty Greek trader be found. In 1889, I visited Sarras, some thirty miles south of Wadi Halfa. It was at that time the farthest outpost of the Egyptian army, and is situated in the midst of a howling wilderness. The post had only been established for a few days. Nevertheless, there I found a Greek already selling sardines, biscuits, etc., to a very limited number of customers, out of a hole in a rock in which he had set up a temporary shop.

We may, therefore, give the low-class Greek credit for his enterprising commercial spirit. Nevertheless, his presence in Egypt is often hurtful. Whatever healthy moral and political influences remain untouched after the Turco-Egyptian Pasha, the tyrannical Sheikh, and the fanatical "Alim" have done their worst, these the low-class Greek seeks to destroy. He tempts the Egyptian peasant to borrow at some exorbitant rate of interest, and then, by a sharp turn of the legal screw, reduces him from the position of an allodial proprietor to that of a serf. He undermines that moral quality of which the Moslem, when untainted by European association, has in some degree a speciality. That quality is sobriety. Under Greek action and influence, the Egyptian villagers are taking to drink. Mr. Gladstone, in a speech which has become historical, once said that it would be a good thing if the Turks were turned "bag and baggage" out of Europe.[1] This may or may not be the case. But there can be no doubt that a counter-proposition of a somewhat similar nature holds good. It would be an excellent thing for Turkey and its dependencies if some of the low-class Greeks, who inhabit the Ottoman dominions, could be turned bag and baggage out of Turkey.

Before passing on to a consideration of the sentiments entertained by the Europeans resident in Egypt towards the English reformer, it will be as well to say something of the English themselves.

The English in Egypt may be divided into three categories, viz. (1) the non-official residents; (2) the army of occupation; (3) the officials in the Egyptian service.

The permanent British colony in Egypt is small. It consists mainly of a few merchants who reside at Alexandria, and who employ a small number of subordinate English agents to watch over their business in the provinces. The greater part of the export trade is in the hands of British firms. The Alexandrian Englishman, like most of his countrymen, is somewhat exclusive. He mixes little in foreign society. The general standard of probity in business matters amongst

[1] Mr. Gladstone was guilty of an unconscious plagiarism. Few people probably know that the expression, as applied to the Turks, originated with Lord Stratford de Redcliffe, whose opinions have passed down to posterity as representing the *ne plus ultra* of Turcophilism. Such, however, is the case. Writing to Mr. Canning on September 29, 1821, Lord Stratford said: "As a matter of humanity, I wish with all my soul that the Greeks were put in possession of their whole patrimony, and that the Sultan was driven, bag and baggage, into the heart of Asia" (*The Life of Stratford Canning*, vol. i. p. 307). Canon MacColl says (*Fortnightly Review*, June 1898): "What Mr. Gladstone proposed was that the Turkish administration should 'all, bag and baggage, clear out'—not 'from Europe, but from the provinces which they had desolated and profaned.'" The difference does not appear very material.

the English in Egypt is high. The English are, for the most part, eminently fair and reasonable. They never give any trouble. They have the great merit of attending exclusively to their own affairs. During the many years that I was Consul-General in Egypt, I do not remember an instance in which I was asked by an Englishman resident in Egypt to support any manifestly unfair or preposterous claim. The Englishman knows his rights; he knows that if they are infringed he has his legal remedy, and that it is unnecessary to apply for the support of his Consul-General. I doubt whether the representative of any other Power in Egypt could say the same.

Passing to a different stratum, there are a certain number of Englishmen in Egypt, who are employed in various unofficial capacities, and who are generally vigorous, honest, straightforward specimens of humanity, but who in exceptional cases sometimes make the British race unpopular by their bad manners and self-assertion. Their conduct is in this respect highly reprehensible. Nevertheless, taken as a whole, the English dwellers in Egypt are a sturdy, self-respecting, and, therefore, respected race, who do credit to their country of origin, and whose presence is useful to their country of adoption.

Little need be said of the army of occupation. The discipline and good conduct of the British army in all its ranks are recognised by the most bitter Anglophobes. The worst that can be said of the soldiers is that some of them disgrace themselves by getting drunk off the vile liquor supplied to them in the bazaars. From the political point of view, the main characteristic of the British officer is his exclusiveness. In whatever clime he may serve, he carries his insular habits and national pastimes with him. In Egypt, he rarely mixes in any society which is not English, and he abstains from doing so, partly because of his ignorance of any language but his own, and partly because his social habits differ from those of the cosmopolitan society of the Egyptian towns. What does the Frenchman or Italian care for horse-races, polo, cricket, golf, and all the other quasi-national institutions, which the British officer establishes wherever he goes, whether his residence be in the frigid or the torrid zone? This exclusiveness has its advantages and also its disadvantages. If a French army had been in Egypt, the officers would have fraternised with the European residents. They would have been seen sitting outside every café. The result would have been, on the one hand, the creation of greater social sympathy between the army and certain classes of the urban population, and, on the other hand, the occurrence of more frequent quarrels. The British officer does not attract the sympathy, but he avoids the quarrels. He is respected. On the other hand, he does not excite any lively sentiment of sympathy or friendship. On the whole, it may be said that, from the point of view of the politician, the advantages predominate over the disadvantages. The British officers obey orders; they neither know, nor care to know anything about local politics; they rarely cause any trouble; they behave for the most part like English gentlemen. Under all the circumstances of the case, these are ideal qualities. They are qualities which were appreciated by the most astute of Egyptian statesmen, Nubar Pasha.

I was once talking to a Levantine in a Cairo street when a young British officer rode by. My friend stopped in the middle of his conversation and said: "Che bella razza! Come sono forti e *puliti*!" That was what most struck him—that the British officers were physically strong, and, moreover, that they were washed. I was struck with the expression. I fancy it represents the opinions of a good many Southerners.

At a later period of this narrative, the positions held by the British officials in the Egyptian service will be more fully treated. For the present all that need be said is that, being for the most part better linguists, they are generally less exclusive than the officers of the army of occupation. At the same time, the society in which they move is mainly English.

The next point to consider is the attitude of the Europeans resident in Egypt towards the English, and more particularly towards the small band of Englishmen who were instrumental in carrying out the work of Egyptian reform.

Enough has been already said to show that there is little social sympathy between the English, and any class of Europeans in Egypt. The best amongst the Europeans respect the British officials; they admire their good qualities—their honesty, their energy, and above all their tenacity. But few like them. Moreover, few understand them. To the European resident in Egypt the British officials were, in the first instance at all events, somewhat of an enigma. Being generally accustomed to Continental official procedure, they could not understand a member of a bureaucracy who rather despised forms and had no bureaucratic tendencies, and who, moreover, did his work in an unobtrusive way without any unnecessary fuss. But as the occupation was prolonged, and the effects of British predominance became year by year more apparent, the ways of the British official became better understood.

The usurer, the drink-seller, and others of the same species, naturally looked askance at the Englishman and his reforms from the very first. Though these classes recognised that the presence of a British army in Egypt afforded security to their lives and properties, and though they were aware that, in the event of an ebullition of Moslem fanaticism, they would be the first to suffer, still they would not readily forgive the Englishman for standing between them and their prey; they could not forget that, had British influence not been predominant, the rate of interest would have been quadrupled; they, therefore, at one time looked back regretfully to those halcyon days before the British occupation, when they were able to plunder the Egyptian Government at will, and when they and the Egyptian Government agreed together to plunder the Egyptians.

The political sympathies of the various nationalities count also for a good deal in the formation of European public opinion as regards the action of the British officials in Egypt. On these, I need not dwell. Inasmuch as they depend on the occurrence of political events outside Egypt, they naturally varied greatly during the period of my tenure of office.

In this, and in the four preceding chapters, an attempt has been made to describe the principal elements of Egyptian society with special reference to the attitude which each section assumed towards the English reformer, more especially in the early days of the occupation. It is now possible to marshal the opposing forces and to distinguish between friends and foes. Some were avowedly hostile. Some vacillated between lukewarm friendship and covert hostility. Others, constituting a large numerical majority, were friendly, but dared not give expression to their friendship, and were, moreover, powerless to help the cause of their benefactors. Lastly, a small minority were friendly and had the courage of their opinions, but the occasion for asserting them was generally wanting.

The Turco-Egyptian Pashas, the Moslem hierarchy, the Europeanised Egyptians, and the French were, in the first instance, for various reasons hostile.

The squirearchy, the Copts, the Syrians, and the Levantines hovered between friendship and hostility, being torn by conflicting sentiments and driven hither and thither by every passing breeze of self-interest.

The mass of the population, that is to say, the fellaheen, were certainly from the very first friendly, but they were politically speechless, and, moreover, were so credulous and ignorant that, had they attempted to make their voices heard, they would just as likely as not have fallen into the hands of frothy demagogues or unprincipled newspaper editors, who would have made them say the opposite of what they really thought.

A small body of respectable and intelligent Europeans were friendly, but their friendship was platonic. They took little part in local politics, and were, for the most part, mere spectators of what was passing on the political stage.

It will be seen that the hostile, quasi-hostile and apathetic forces, though less numerous, were more powerful than those who were friendly. On the one side, stood the stolid conservatism of the East, religious prejudice, ignorance, international jealousy, and a number of powerful vested interests, some of an ignoble type. On the other side, stood the force derived from an honest endeavour to secure the well-being of a whole population, which had been trodden under foot for centuries.

The battle seemed in some respects unequal. Yet the Englishman took heart of grace. He proceeded with caution and he won the day.

He felt from the first that he was fighting in a good cause. He had the goodwill of intelligent and impartial Europe. He had a military force behind him to prevent any premature upset of the whole machine. He was able to employ agents of experience trained in all the intricacies of Oriental government. Ten years after the battle of Tel-el-Kebir a competent observer was able to write: "Even our superb administration of India is hardly a brighter jewel in our imperial crown than the marvellous regeneration of Egypt."[1] More than this. As the occupation continued, a great change came over the opinions of various sections of Egyptian society. The benefits conferred by the exercise of British influence were, indeed, so palpable that they could not be denied. Amongst both European and Egyptian society, all but a very small class ranged themselves, either actively or passively, on the side of England.[2] Notably, both Italian and Greek sympathy was on many occasions displayed in a very remarkable degree. The representatives of the various Christian communities resident in Egypt seized every possible opportunity for expressing their friendliness to England. With a few exceptions, even the Moslems acquiesced in the policy of reform.

The open or covert hostility of various sections of society in Egypt has not been the only, neither, indeed, has it been the principal difficulty which has beset the path of the English reformer. Under

[1] *Cairo*, p. 243.

[2] I wrote these remarks in 1903, and, in spite of any appearances to the contrary, my conviction is that they still (1907) hold good. During the last three or four years, a strong and very legitimate desire to take a greater part than heretofore in the administration of the country has made itself felt among intelligent Egyptians, but my belief is that the number of those who would really wish the reforming work of England in Egypt to be brought prematurely to a close still comprise a "very small," and, I may add, a wholly unrepresentative, class.

the combined influences of rival diplomatists, bondholders, foreign jurists, and others, who have from time to time borne a part in Egyptian affairs, a variety of fantastic institutions grew up, many of which were originally devised to check misgovernment, but which, under altered circumstances, have, as a matter of fact, acted as powerful obstacles to reform. An endeavour will now be made to guide the reader through some of the intricate windings of this administrative labyrinth.

CHAPTER XXXIX

THE MACHINERY OF GOVERNMENT

Nature of the machinery—Parts of the machine—1. THE SULTAN—The Firman of 1892—The Sinai Peninsula—2. THE KHEDIVE—Rescript of August 28, 1878—Constitutionalism of Tewfik Pasha—3. THE MINISTERS—The Departments—Position of an Egyptian Minister—4. THE ORGANIC LAW of May 1, 1883—The Provincial Councils—The Legislative Council—The Legislative Assembly.

IF any one unacquainted with mechanics enters a factory where a quantity of steam machinery is at work, he is for a moment deafened with the noise, and his first impression will not improbably be one of surprise that any delicate bit of workmanship can result from the apparent confusion which he sees before him. Gradually, however, he comes to understand that the rate at which each wheel turns is regulated to a nicety, that the piston of the steam-engine cannot give a stroke by one hair's-breadth shorter or longer than that which it is intended to give, that the strength with which the hammer is made to descend is capable of the most perfect adjustment, that safety-valves and a variety of other checks and counterchecks exist which are sufficient guarantees against accident, and that, generally, each portion of the machinery is adapted to perform a certain specified bit of work and is under such perfect control that it cannot interfere with the functions of any other portion. He will then no longer be surprised that, with a little care in oiling the different parts of the machinery, a highly finished piece of workmanship is eventually produced.

If, on the other hand, he finds on examination that the confusion is even worse than at first sight appeared, that the movement of each wheel is eccentric in the highest degree, that the piston is liable at any moment to stop working, that there is no adequate machinery for adjusting the strength of the stroke to be given by the hammer, that safety-valves and other guarantees against accident are wanting, that the work to be performed by each separate portion is uncertain and variable, that some portions are of the latest and most improved patterns whilst others are old, rusty, and obsolete, that a strong centrifugal force is constantly at work impelling the different parts of the machinery to fly out of their own orbits, and that a mistake on the part of the engineer in not removing any small particle of grit betimes, or not applying the right amount of oil at the right moment, may bring about a collapse of the whole fabric,—he will then no longer look for the production of any highly finished article. Indeed, he will be surprised that the mechanical chaos before him is capable of producing any article at all.

The Egyptian administrative system bears to the administration of any highly civilised European State much the same relation as the second factory described above bears to the first. In Europe, we know what a despotism means, and we know what constitutional government means. The words absolute monarchy, limited monarchy, republic, parliamentary government, federal council, and others of a like nature, when applied to the government of any country, will readily convey to an educated European a general idea of how the government of the particular country in question is conducted. But the political dictionary may be ransacked in vain for any terse description of the Government of Egypt.

In the first place, that Government is, in reality, not a Government at all. Nubar Pasha frequently said: "Ce n'est pas un Gouvernement; c'est une administration." This is quite true. The Khedive is deprived by the Egyptian constitutional charter of all rights of external sovereignty, neither does he possess to the full those rights of internal sovereignty which are inherent in the rulers of all independent, and even of some semi-independent states.

In the second place, the manner in which the legislative power is exercised in the Ottoman dominions, of which Egypt forms a part, is unique. We readily understand what a Ukase issued by the Czar of Russia means. An intelligent foreigner will at once seize on what is meant when it is said that the King of the United Kingdom of Great Britain and Ireland has given his assent to a Bill which has passed through both Houses of Parliament. But the Khedive's power is dissimilar to that of either a despotic or a constitutional ruler. He cannot, on his own authority, issue any Decree the provisions of which will be binding on all the inhabitants of Egypt. Legislation has to be conducted by diplomacy. The President of the United States and the King of Sweden have to give their consent before the provisions of any new law can be applied to the subjects of the Emperor of Austria or the King of the Belgians, for in legislation by diplomacy unanimity amongst the diplomatic legislators is required; otherwise no legislation can take place. The system, as Lord Salisbury once wrote to me, "is like the *liberum veto* of the Polish Diet, without the resource of cutting off the dissentient's head."

In the third place, the executive power is so disseminated as to render it impossible to say where it resides. In certain matters, the Khedive and his Ministers are practically vested with despotic power. In others, their hands are tied to a greater extent than those of the Governors of the most democratic States. Moreover, it often happens that, although the text of the document which confers some special power may be clear, it will be found, on closer inspection, that some international or other ligament exists, which is apparently so flimsy as to be only visible to the eye of a trained diplomatist, but which is in reality of so tough a texture as to place an effectual obstacle in the way of the practical exercise of the power.

In the fourth place, the judicial system is a tangle of conflicting jurisdictions. The law is at times applied by a body of foreign judges who, being free from the restraints of any legislature, are practically a law unto themselves. At times, again, the law is administered by Egyptian judges. Each Consul judges his own countrymen for criminal offences according to the laws of his own country, whilst close by the Kadi is endeavouring to settle some dispute over a will according to the rusty principles laid down thirteen centuries ago by Mohammed.

The complicated machinery, whose general nature is described above, will now be explained in detail. It will be as well, in the first instance, to enumerate the parts of the machine. They are as follows :—

1. The Sultan. 2. The Khedive. 3. The Ministers. 4. The Legislative Council and Assembly. 5. The superior European officials, mostly British, who are attached in various capacities to the different Ministries.

The above constitute the Turkish, Egyptian, and

Anglo-Egyptian, as opposed to the International portions of the administration. The International, or, as they are usually called, the Mixed Administrations were created in virtue of arrangements made, from time to time, between the Egyptian Government and the Powers. Neither their functions nor their constitution can be changed without the assent of the Powers. In 1882, when the British occupation commenced, they were as follows:—1. The Commission of the Public Debt. 2. The Railway Board, under which was also placed the administration of the Telegraph Department and of the Port of Alexandria. 3. The Daira Administration. 4. The Domains Administration.

Lastly, justice is administered by the following law-courts:—1. The Mixed Tribunals. 2. The Native Tribunals. 3. The Consular Courts. 4. The Mehkemeh Sheraieh.

1. *The Sultan.*

The relations between the Sultan and the Khedive are laid down in a variety of Firmans dating from 1841 to 1892. Of these, the most recent is naturally the most important. It was issued to Abbas II. on March 27, 1892. Save in respect to one point, to which allusion will presently be made, this Firman does not differ from that of August 7, 1879, granted to Tewfik Pasha.

The main provision of the Firman of 1892 is that under certain restrictions, the civil and financial administration of Egypt is confided to the Khedive Abbas II. and his male descendants taken in order of primogeniture. The restrictions are as follows:—

In the first place, it is laid down that all Egyptians are Ottoman subjects. The taxes are to be levied in the name of the Sultan. There can, therefore, conformably with the Firman, be no such thing as a separate Egyptian State, or a separate Egyptian nationality.

In the second place, it is taken for granted that the Khedive has no right to make political Treaties with foreign states. Conventions dealing with commercial affairs, or with those which relate solely to matters of purely internal administration, may, however, be made. Mr. James Scott, the lecturer at the Khedivial School of Law, says: "In regard to the right of the Egyptian Government to make International Conventions, it would appear that it has power to make Conventions in reference to every question except the cession of territory, or the making of peace or war."[1] As a natural result of this political relationship, the Khedive has no right to appoint a diplomatic representative to any European court. Further, as a general rule, when the European Powers meet in conclave, Egypt is represented by the Ottoman delegate. Separate Egyptian representation has, however, been allowed at Conferences assembled to deal with special subjects, in which Egypt is interested. It is not easy to lay down any very precise rule on this subject. Thus, when, in 1884, a Conference was assembled in London to consider the financial affairs of Egypt, the Egyptian Government were denied any separate representation. Musurus Pasha, the Turkish Ambassador in London, sat, and often slept at the Council table,[2] whilst the Egyptian delegates,

[1] *The Law affecting Foreigners in Egypt, as the Result of the Capitulations*, p. 145.

[2] I cannot refrain from relating a somewhat amusing incident which happened at this Conference. At that time, all the Powers, except perhaps Italy, were acting in concert against England. England was defending Egyptian interests. Count Münster proposed that the quarantine question, in which Germany at that moment took much interest, should be discussed. Lord Granville pointed out that, if once the Conference went beyond the limits for which it had been assembled, there was no reason why every description of Eastern question should not be brought within its cognisance. Thus, an undesirably wide

Tigrane Pasha and Blum Pasha, occupied a side table, and were not allowed to take any direct part in the discussions. On the other hand, at the Conference, which met at Venice in 1892 to discuss quarantine affairs, the Egyptian Government were accorded the right of separate representation to this extent, that the Egyptian delegates could speak but could not vote. A further step in advance was made at the Sanitary Conference held at Paris in 1904. The Egyptian delegates were accorded the right of voting in Committee, but not at the plenary sittings of the Commission.

In the third place, the Khedive cannot abandon to a third party any of the territorial rights of the Sultan. In respect of this matter, theory and fact came into collision when the Italians occupied Massowah.

In the fourth place, traditional Turkish jealousy of Egypt is shown by the provision that the Egyptian army cannot, under ordinary circumstances, exceed 18,000 men. If, however, Turkey is at war, the Egyptian army may be called upon to fight in the cause of the Sultan, in which case it may be increased according to the requirements of the moment. Following on the same order of

field would be opened up for discussion. The French and Russian representatives pointed out that no danger of this sort was to be feared, for that no one wished to raise any other question save that of quarantine. The question was put to the vote, which proceeded on what may be termed strictly party lines, until it came to the turn of Musurus Pasha. A true emblem of the country which he represented, Musurus Pasha was fast asleep, and had heard nothing of the discussion which led to the vote. He was awakened, and was informed that he had to vote on the question of whether quarantine matters should or should not be brought before the Conference. He was at the time acting in general concert with the anti-English party, but, as he had not been told beforehand what he had to do, he gave utterance to a perfectly independent opinion. "Parfaitement," he said, "je suis de cet avis ; mais alors j'ai beaucoup d'autres questions que je voudrais porter à la connaissance de la Conférence." Lord Granville had found an unconscious and involuntary ally. He carried his point. Quarantine affairs were not discussed.

ideas, it is provided that the Khedive cannot construct any ironclads (*bâtiments blindés*) without the authority of the Sultan. The Turkish flag is to be the Egyptian flag. The distinctive marks of military rank are to be identic in the two armies. The Khedive may grant the rank of Colonel to military, and that of Sanieh (second-class Bey) to civil officials, but he may not confer any higher titles.

In the fifth place, the coinage of Egypt is to be issued in the name of the Sultan.

In return for concessions made at various times by the Sultans, Ismail Pasha undertook to pay a Tribute of £682,000 a year to the Porte.[1] The original sum paid in 1841 by Mehemet Ali was £377,000, but under the combined influence of ambitious Khedives and of impecunious Sultans, the figure was nearly doubled at subsequent periods.

It has been already stated that, save in respect to one point, the Firman of 1892 was a reproduction of that of 1879. It will be as well to allude briefly to the exception.

The Firman of 1879 laid down that the Khedivate of Egypt was to be "tel qu'il se trouve formé par ses anciennes limites et en comprenant les territoires qui y ont été annexés." When the Firman of 1892 was in course of preparation, the British Ambassador at Constantinople was assured that it was identic with that of 1879. There was, however, reason to believe that this statement was incorrect. The Porte had always been sensitive as regards European interference in or near the Hedjaz. Indeed, the law allowing foreigners to acquire real property in the Ottoman dominions forbids any European to settle in the Hedjaz.

[1] Practically the whole of the Tribute is mortgaged to the Ottoman bondholders.

More than this, the Sultan's suspicions had been aroused by two recent incidents. One was that Turkish misgovernment had produced a revolt in the province of the Yemen, which was, without a shadow of foundation, attributed to British intrigue. The second was that a well-intentioned German enthusiast, named Friedmann, of Jewish origin, was, at the moment when the Firman was under discussion, endeavouring to establish a settlement of some couple of dozen Jews, who had been expelled from Russia, on the eastern shore of the Gulf of Akaba. This was suspicious. Moukhtar Pasha pointed out that the Jews had always been waiting for a Messiah to reconquer Jerusalem, and that, without doubt, they would think he had now appeared in the person of Mr. Friedmann. It was not difficult to convince Moukhtar Pasha that Mr. Friedmann was devoid of any such pretensions.[1] But the suspicions of the Sultan were not so easily calmed. The result was that the Firman laid down the Egyptian frontier as drawn from Suez to El-Arish. The Peninsula of Sinai, which had been administered by the Khedives of Egypt for the last forty years, would thus have reverted to Turkey. It was undesirable to bring Turkish soldiers down to the banks of the Suez Canal. When, therefore, the Firman arrived, the British Government interposed and placed a veto on its promulgation. After a short delay, the Grand Vizier telegraphed to the Khedive accepting a proposal, which had been offered to the Sultan some weeks previously, but which His Imperial Majesty had then refused to entertain.[2] Under

[1] Mr. Friedmann may be known to some Englishmen as the author of a history of Anne Boleyn.

[2] The settlement of this question was in a great measure due to the skill with which the negotiations at Constantinople were conducted by the late Sir Edmund Fane, who was at the time in charge of the Embassy.

this arrangement, the frontier of Egypt was drawn from El-Arish to the head of the Gulf of Akaba. The incident was thus for the time being terminated, and the Firman was promulgated with all customary pomp. Occasion was taken to lay down again the principle that "no alteration could be made in the Firmans regulating the relations between the Sublime Porte and Egypt without the consent of Her Britannic Majesty's Government."

In 1905, another and more determined effort was made by the Sultan to occupy the Sinai Peninsula, but after a brief, and somewhat stormy negotiation, the arrangement made in 1892 was confirmed. Shortly afterwards, the Turco-Egyptian frontier was delimited by a Joint Commission.

Such, therefore, are the official relations between the Sultan and the Khedive. From the observations which have been made in the course of this narrative, it will have been gathered that the constant endeavour of the Sultan has been to encroach on the rights of the Khedive. On the other hand, the sentiments of the ruling classes in Egypt towards the Sultan may be described as a compound of fear, religious sympathy, and political dislike. Which of these sentiments is predominant depends on the fleeting circumstances of the moment.

2. *The Khedive.*

It was explained in the first part of this work how an unwilling recognition of the principle of ministerial responsibility was wrung from Ismail Pasha. Ismail's Rescript of August 28, 1878,[1] was, indeed, violated almost immediately after its issue. Nevertheless, it forms to this day the Magna Charta of Egypt.

Naturally enough, more depends on the spirit

[1] *Vide ante*, vol. i. p. 62.

in which the Rescript is applied than on the terms of the document itself. By a fortunate accident, Ismail Pasha was succeeded by a Khedive who had a natural turn for constitutionalism. Tewfik Pasha acted up to the spirit of his father's declarations. He asserted his legitimate prerogatives, but he governed "through and with his Council of Ministers." The terms of the Rescript are, however, sufficiently elastic to enable all the most objectionable abuses of personal government to be re-established without any apparent violation of the letter of Ismail Pasha's declaration. So long as the British occupation lasts, a solid guarantee exists that any tendency towards the re-establishment of a bad form of personal government will be checked before disastrous consequences ensue.

3. *The Ministers.*

The Egyptian administrative machine is divided into seven Departments, over each of which a Minister presides. These are Foreign Affairs, Finance, Justice, War, Public Works, Education, and the Interior.

The Post Office, the Customs, and the Lighthouses are under the Financial Department. The Sanitary Department and the Prisons are attached to the Interior. The Wakfs (religious endowments) are administered by a Director-General, who in practice takes his orders direct from the Khedive.

The proceedings of the Council are conducted partly in Arabic and partly in French, the latter language being employed to suit the convenience of those European officials who have a right to be present at the meetings of Council, and of Egyptian Ministers[1] who are not acquainted with the Arabic language.

[1] *E.g.* Nubar and Tigrane Pashas.

The position of an Egyptian Minister is difficult and delicate. There are usually in his Department one or more high European officials, who are subordinate to him. The ideal state of things would be if the Minister showed no jealousy of his subordinate, worked cordially with him, followed his advice when it was sound, and stated his objections intelligently when he thought it was questionable; and if, on the other hand, the European official was careful never to be aggressive, or to press unduly for the adoption of his views in doubtful cases. It has not always been easy to find Egyptian Ministers who will carry out the first, or Europeans who will carry out the second part of this programme. Nevertheless, the system has on the whole worked smoothly. More especially of late years, the relations between the Egyptian Ministers and their British coadjutors have been most cordial and friendly.

4. *The Organic Law of May* 1, 1883.

Briefly stated, the provisions of the Organic Law of May 1, 1883, which was framed under Lord Dufferin's auspices, are as follows:—

A Provincial Council, composed of from eight to three members, according to the size of the province, is established in each Moudirieh. The Moudir is the President. The functions of these Councils are to deal with local matters, such as the alignment of roads and canals, the establishment of markets, etc. The total number of Provincial Councillors is seventy. When we are liberal in Egypt, we do not content ourselves with half-measures. The members of the Council are elected by universal suffrage.

The Legislative Council is composed of thirty members. Of these, fourteen, including the

President, are named by the Egyptian Government. Of the remainder, fourteen are elected by the Provincial Councils from amongst their own members, one is elected by the town of Cairo, and one by Alexandria and some other less important towns. No Law or Decree "portant règlement d'administration publique" can be promulgated without its having been previously submitted to the Council. The Government are not obliged to adopt the views of the Council, but, in the event of their not doing so, the reasons for the rejection must be communicated to the Council. "L'exposition de ces motifs ne peut donner lieu à aucune discussion." The Budget has to be submitted to the Council, who may "émettre des avis et des vœux sur chaque chapitre du Budget." The Government are, however, not obliged to conform to any views which may be expressed by the Council in connection with the Budget, nor may the latter discuss any financial charge incumbent on the Egyptian Treasury, which results from an international arrangement. The Egyptian Ministers may take part in the discussions of the Council, or may cause themselves to be represented by any high functionaries of their respective Departments.

The Legislative Assembly consists of eighty-two members, viz.: The six Ministers, the thirty members of the Legislative Council, and forty-six delegates who are elected by the population. Certain qualifications are necessary in order to become a candidate for election to the Assembly. The candidate must be not less than thirty years old, he must be able to read and write, and he must pay direct taxes to the amount of not less than £E.30 a year. No new direct tax can be imposed without the approval of the Assembly. The Assembly must also be consulted about any public loans, about the construction of canals and railways, and about the classification of lands in connection with the payment of the land-tax. The Assembly may also spontaneously express its views on all economic, administrative, and financial questions. As in the case of the Legislative Council, the Government are not under any obligation to adopt the opinions of the Assembly in such matters, but the reasons for not adopting them must be stated. The Assembly must meet at least once in two years. The public are not admitted to the sittings either of the Council or of the Assembly.

In the last Report I wrote before leaving Egypt[1] I expressed myself favourably to the proposal that reporters should be admitted to the sittings of the Council. If this proposal encounters opposition, it will come, not from any European authority, but from the members of the Council themselves. I have reason to believe that, amongst these, a good deal of difference of opinion exists as to the desirability of effecting this reform.

Besides these institutions, the Organic Law of May 1, 1883, provided for the establishment of a Council of State (Conseil d'État) whose organisation and functions were to be explained in a subsequent Decree. This institution was borrowed from France. Its alleged object was to prepare draft laws for submission to the legislature. When I arrived in Egypt, in September 1883, I found that the formation of the Council of State was a burning question. It very soon became apparent that, under cover of this institution, international government was to be introduced into every branch of the Egyptian administration. The discussion went on for several months until, on January 19, 1884, I informed Lord Granville that the Council of State would be a useless and expensive body. Nubar Pasha was of the same opinion. Egypt

[1] *Egypt*, No. 1 of 1907, p. 29.

was thus mercifully saved from this particular form of international plague.

Such, therefore, are the constitution and functions of the Egyptian Houses of Parliament. Lord Dufferin's law was conceived in a liberal and statesmanlike spirit. The leading idea was to give the Egyptian people an opportunity of making their voices heard, but at the same time not to bind the executive Government by parliamentary fetters, which would have been out of place in a country whose political education was so little advanced as that of Egypt.

The question of the extension of representative institutions in Egypt has recently formed the subject of much public discussion. I do not propose to deal with this question at any length. The main object of this work, which will, I fear, extend to greater length than I originally intended, is to narrate the history of the past, rather than to discuss questions which now occupy the attention of the public, and of the responsible Egyptian authorities. Moreover, my views on this particular issue have already been fully and publicly expressed.[1] My remarks will, therefore, be very brief.

In the first place, I wish to say that Lord Dufferin was under no delusion as to the time which would elapse, and as to the difficulties which would have to be encountered before free institutions could take root in the somewhat uncongenial soil of Egypt. All he hoped to do was "to erect some sort of barrier, however feeble, against the intolerable tyranny of the Turks." He hoped that, "under British superintendence," the legislative bodies which he created "might be fostered, and educated into fairly useful institutions, proving a

[1] *Vide, inter alia, Egypt,* No. 1 of 1906, pp. 11-13; *Egypt,* No. 1 of 1907, pp. 3-8, 26-32, and 56; and *Egypt,* No. 3 of 1907.

convenient channel through which the European element in the Government might obtain an insight into the inner mind and the less obvious wants of the native population."[1] There cannot be a shadow of doubt that, far from considering that progress had been objectionably slow, Lord Dufferin was not merely gratified, but also somewhat astonished at the extent to which, up to the time of his death, the services of the institutions, of which he was the creator, had been utilised.

Next, I have to observe that, if anything is to be done in the direction of a further development of the institutions created in 1883, by far the wisest course will be to begin at the bottom of the legislative ladder. "It is certain," Lord Dufferin very truly said in his Report, "that local self-government is the fittest preparation and most convenient stepping-stone for anything approaching to a constitutional régime." During the last twenty-four years, a good deal more has been done in the way of developing local self-government than many of those who write on Egyptian affairs seem to be aware of.[2]

In many of the most important provincial towns, Mixed Municipalities—that is to say, municipal bodies of which some of the members are European and others are Egyptian—have been established. The difficulty of extending the system lies in the fact that whilst, on the one hand, no very great or rapid progress can be made unless the Municipal Commissioners are invested with certain powers of local taxation, on the other hand, no local taxes can be imposed on Europeans without the consent of the Powers. Hence, until the régime of the

[1] These passages are quoted from a letter addressed to me by Lord Dufferin. It is given in Sir Alfred Lyall's *Life of the Marquis of Dufferin*, vol. ii. p. 260.

[2] This branch of the subject is more fully treated in my Report for the year 1906. See *Egypt*, No. 1 of 1907, pp. 29-32.

Capitulations is modified, it will not be possible to create Mixed Municipalities in any towns unless the whole of the population are willing to submit to a system of voluntary taxation.

In a large number of other towns, Local Commissions have been appointed who administer the funds placed at their disposal by the Egyptian Government.

It is, I think, in the direction of increasing the numbers and extending the powers of the Municipalities and Local Commissions that the principal development of local self-government is, in the near future, to be anticipated. Care, however, will have to be taken in dealing with this matter. One of the greatest errors into which Europeans employed in the East are liable to fall is to imagine that Orientals are as much impressed as they are themselves with the necessity of speedily providing roads, drains, lighting, and all the other paraphernalia of civilisation. The present race of Egyptians are, indeed, willing enough to profit by all these things, if they are provided for them from the proceeds of general taxation, but the crucial question is whether they are themselves willing to pay additional taxes in order to attain these objects. They have not, up to the present time, shown much disposition to do so. It will be wise, therefore, not to force the pace. It should always be remembered that what the mass of the population in a backward Eastern country care for above almost all things is that taxation should be light,

As regards the Provincial Councils, a detail which slipped into the Organic Law of 1883—very possibly without its effect being fully realised—has done a good deal to impair their utility. It was laid down that no Provincial Council could meet without being convoked by the Moudir, and that the latter could not convoke the Council without the issue of a Khedivial Decree, laying down both the time and duration of the meeting. The practical result of this arrangement has been that the Councils have never met more than once a year. The time has certainly come when the whole of this question may usefully be considered. One of the last proposals I made before leaving Egypt[1] was that the Provincial Councils should be reorganised, their powers somewhat increased, and that steps should be taken to carry out more fully what was unquestionably Lord Dufferin's intention, viz. that the Councils should be real working bodies, acting as advisers to the Moudir. Sir Eldon Gorst has this matter in hand, and will, I do not doubt, with the help of the British and Egyptian officials, be able to devise a scheme suitable to the requirements and present condition of the country.

The question of whether the powers and constitution of the Legislative Council may advantageously be changed is one of far greater difficulty. As I have already said, I do not propose to discuss it at length. I will, therefore, only say that whilst I am not prepared to maintain that some cautious steps in this direction might not before long be prudently taken, I am very strongly of opinion that any attempt to confer full parliamentary powers on the Council would, for a long time to come, be the extreme of folly and would be highly detrimental to the true interests of the Egyptians themselves. The facts that many of the members of the Council are men of unquestionable honesty and intelligence, and that some are personal friends of my own, cannot blind me to the fact that, as a whole, the Council,—as would, indeed, be the case with any similar body which could, under present circumstances, be constituted in Egypt,—possesses two great defects.

[1] See *Egypt,* No. 1 of 1907, pp. 29-32.

The first is one which they share with representative bodies in some other countries. It is that, acting under public pressure, they are too apt to propose important changes in the fiscal system, and, at the same time, to advocate large additional expenditure on public objects, without sufficient consideration of the financial results which would ensue were effect given to their proposals. It should never be forgotten that any extension of representative institutions, which was obtained at the risk of again plunging Egypt into all the financial embarrassment from which the country has been so hardly and so recently rescued, would be far too dearly bought.

The second defect, which in the eyes of any one acquainted with the past history of modern Egypt is extremely pardonable, is that the most enlightened members of the Council have not, as yet, acquired all those qualities necessary to give them the moral courage to assert their true opinions fearlessly. Notably, many of them are terrorised by the local press. To the European mind, it may seem a contradiction in terms to say that freedom of speech is checked by the freedom of the press. But in the Land of Paradox all things are possible. I have no doubt whatever that a large number—probably a majority — of the members of the Legislative Council would welcome the enactment of a rigorous press law as a measure calculated to free them from the moral shackles which now hamper their liberty of speech and action.

Of all the institutions created by Lord Dufferin, the Legislative Assembly has, in practice, turned out to be the least useful and efficient. It was, and still is, too much in advance of the requirements and political education of the country. No real harm would be done if it were simply abolished, and, indeed, the cause of representative government would, I believe, benefit if simultaneously with its abolition, the Legislative Council were re-organised, and its powers somewhat increased. Without doubt, however, the adoption of this course would be regarded by many—erroneously, in my opinion—as a retrograde measure. It may, therefore, be politically desirable not to entertain the idea. In that case, I hold that, for the time being, the Legislative Assembly should be left alone. I deprecate any attempt to enlarge its powers, and I think it would be extremely difficult to amend its constitution.

The purely Egyptian portion of the machinery of government has now been described. This part of the machinery would, however, never get into motion were it not impelled by some strong motive power. That motive power is furnished by the British officials in the service of the Egyptian Government. The special functions of these officials will be described in the next chapter.

CHAPTER XL

THE BRITISH OFFICIALS

Qualifications required of an Anglo-Egyptian official—Positions of the civil and military officials—The French in Tunis—The Financial Adviser—Sir Edgar Vincent—The Judicial Adviser—History of his appointment—Sir Raymond West—Justice under Egyptian management—Sir John Scott—The Public Works Department—Sir Colin Scott-Moncrieff—Sir William Garstin—The Financial Secretary — Blum Pasha — Lord Milner—Sir Eldon Gorst — Sub-Departments of Finance—The Interior—Public Instruction—European and Egyptian officials.

It is related that a lady once asked Madame de Staël to recommend a tutor for her boy. She described the sort of man she wished to find. He was to be a gentleman with perfect manners and a thorough knowledge of the world; it was essential that he should be a classical scholar and an accomplished linguist; he was to exercise supreme authority over his pupil, and at the same time he was to show such a degree of tact that his authority was to be unfelt; in fact, he was to possess almost every moral attribute and intellectual faculty which it is possible to depict, and, lastly, he was to place all these qualities at the service of Madame de Staël's friend for a very low salary. The witty Frenchwoman listened with attention to her friend's list of indispensable qualifications and eventually replied: "Ma chère, je comprends parfaitement bien le caractère de l'homme qu'il vous faut, mais je dois vous dire que si je le trouve, je l'épouse."

This story is applicable to the qualifications demanded of an ideal Anglo-Egyptian official.

The Anglo-Egyptian official must possess some technical knowledge, such as that of the engineer, the accountant, or the lawyer; otherwise, he will be unable to deal with the affairs of the Department to which he is attached. At the outset of his career, he is usually placed at a great disadvantage. He must often explain his ideas in a foreign language, French, with which he has probably only a limited acquaintance. Unless he is to run the risk of falling into the hands of some subordinate, often of doubtful trustworthiness, it is, at all events in respect to many official posts, essential that he should acquire some knowledge of a very difficult Oriental language, Arabic. These, however, are all faculties to which it is possible to apply some fairly accurate test. The Anglo-Egyptian official must be possessed of other qualities, which it is more difficult to gauge with precision, but which are in reality of even greater importance than those to which allusion is made above. He must be a man of high character. He must have sufficient elasticity of mind to be able to apply, under circumstances which are strange to him, the knowledge which he has acquired elsewhere. He must be possessed of a sound judgment in order to enable him to distinguish between abuses, which should be at once reformed, and those which it will be wise to tolerate, at all events for a time. He must be versatile, and quick to adapt any local feature of the administration to suit his own reforming purposes. He must be well-mannered and conciliatory, and yet not allow his conciliation to degenerate into weakness. He must be firm, and yet not allow his firmness to harden into dictation. He must efface himself as much as possible. In fact, besides his special technical knowledge, he must possess all the qualities which we look for in a trained diplomatist, a good administrator, and an experienced man of the world.

It is not easy in any country to produce a number of officials, who have undergone a departmental training, and who at the same time possess all these qualities. It is especially difficult, when they are found, to attract them to Egypt on salaries of £2000 a year and less. The efficient working of the administrative machine depends, however, mainly on choosing the right man for the right place. What often happens when any place has to be filled is this,—on the one hand, are a number of candidates who wish to occupy the post, but who do not possess the qualifications necessary to fill it with advantage to the public interests; on the other hand, are a very small number of persons, who possess the necessary qualifications, but who, for one reason or another, are reluctant to accept the appointment. Under these circumstances, it is a matter for congratulation that administrative successes have been the rule, whilst the failures have been the exceptions.

Looking to the anomalous positions occupied by the Anglo-Egyptian officials, it is, indeed, greatly to their credit that, as a body, they should have succeeded in performing the several tasks allotted to them. Without doubt, they have had diplomatic support behind them. Moreover, and this is perhaps more important than the support itself, it has been felt by all concerned that the possibility of stronger support than that which was actually afforded lay in the background. Nevertheless, the British officials in Egypt have had to rely mainly on their individual judgment and force of character. The British Consul-General can occasionally give advice. He may, when speaking to the British official, temper the zeal of the latter for reform, or, when talking to the Egyptian Minister, advocate the views of the reformer. But he cannot step seriously upon the scene unless there is some knot to be untied which is worthy of a serious effort. He cannot at every moment interfere in matters of departmental detail. The work done by the Anglo-Egyptian official is, therefore, mainly the outcome of his own resource and of his own versatility. If he is adroit, he can make the fact that the soldiers of his nation are in occupation of the country felt without flaunting their presence in any brusque fashion before the eyes of his Egyptian superior. As a matter of fact, the most successful Anglo-Egyptian officials have been those who have relied most on their own powers of persuasion, and have rarely applied for diplomatic support.

In describing more particularly the position of the Anglo-Egyptian officials, a distinction must be drawn between civilians and soldiers. The British officers of the Egyptian army have had to contend against considerable difficulties, but, as compared with their civilian colleagues, they have from one important point of view been at an advantage. There is a reality about the position of the soldier which does not exist in the case of the civilian. The Egyptian Commander-in-Chief, or, to call him by his Egyptian title, the Sirdar, not only commands the army. It is recognised by the Egyptian Government and by the public that he commands it. There is thus no flagrant contradiction between his real and his nominal position. Most of the superior officers of the army, whether departmental or regimental, are British. The Sirdar is, therefore, master of the situation. He can decide on what orders to give, and he can rely on his orders being obeyed, not only in the letter but in the spirit. He is not obliged to trim his sails to every passing political breeze.

Far other is the position of the Anglo-Egyptian civilian. Some of the most important civil functionaries possess no executive functions. They can only advise. No special system exists to enforce the acceptance of their advice. All that can be said is that, in the event of their advice being systematically rejected, the British Government will be displeased, and that they will probably find some adequate means for making their displeasure felt. Further, of those Anglo-Egyptian civil officials who possess executive power, few can be certain that their power is effective; they cannot rely confidently on their subordinates, who are rarely British, to carry out the letter, and still less the spirit of their instructions. The Anglo-Egyptian official is also driven by the necessities of his position into being an opportunist. The least part of his difficulties lies in deciding what should be done. That is usually easy. When once he clearly sees before him the action which ought to be taken, he has to decide the more difficult questions of when to act and how to conduct himself in order to get others to act with him. And, in deciding on these latter points, he often has to take into consideration matters which at first sight appear to be not even remotely connected with the immediate subject under discussion. Every Anglo-Egyptian civil official, therefore, has not only to be guided by the general impulse given by British diplomacy to Egyptian affairs, but he also has to do a good deal of diplomatic work on his own account.

Comparisons have been occasionally instituted between the position of the English in Egypt and that of the French in Tunis. In 1890, a report on Tunisian affairs was prepared by M. Ribot. A glance at this report is sufficient to show that, for all practical purposes, the French Government have annexed Tunis. Scarcely a semblance of native authority remains. The French officials have a free hand in dealing with the administration of the country. The French Resident-General presides at the Council of Ministers and directs the Ministry of Foreign Affairs. No law is valid which has not been countersigned by him. The Ministry of War is in the hands of the General in command of the French army of occupation. All the important offices of the State are held by Frenchmen. A French Secretary-General receives all the letters addressed to the Tunisian Government and prepares the answers. "Ainsi," it is said, "aucune affaire ne peut échapper à sa surveillance, et dans toutes, il peut donner ses conseils et faire prévaloir la pensée du Protectorat." By the side of each of the "Câïds," who answer to the Egyptian Moudirs, is placed a French Controller who, amongst other functions, has the Police under his command.

M. Ribot concluded his account of the system of administration in the following terms: "Il fallait ensuite qu'aucun détail dans l'application de ces décisions ne pût nous échapper. Aucun document n'entre dans les bureaux de l'Administration centrale ou n'en sort, aucune lettre n'est présentée à la signature du Premier Ministre, aucune correspondance n'est envoyée aux destinataires sans passer par l'intermédiaire du Secrétaire général et être soumis à son examen. Tout ce qui arrive aux Câïds ou émane d'eux est de la même manière soumis à l'examen des Contrôleurs civils. Rien ne peut donc se faire dans la Régence qui ne soit approuvé par nous." This is sufficiently explicit. In point of fact, Tunis is just as much a part of France as the Department of the Seine. A qualified Tunisian has explained the position of the Bey of Tunis in the following terms: "Les attributions du Bey de Tunis se réduisent seulement à la nomination de quelques employés subalternes et même ces nominations sont soumises à l'approbation du Ministre Résident de France, ou de son premier secrétaire, qui est en même temps Secrétaire-Général du Gouvernement Tunisien."

More than this, the attitude of the other Powers, and notably of England, towards the French administration of Tunis has been persistently friendly. The British Government speedily abandoned the Capitulations at the instance of France, an example which was followed by Italy and other Powers.[1]

It is, therefore, clear that no analogy exists between the conditions under which France took in hand the Tunisian problem and those which obtained, and still obtain, in respect to the Anglo-Egyptian administration of Egypt.

The most important British official in Egypt is the Financial Adviser. After the Arábi revolt, the question of how to place the financial administration of Egypt under European control had to be reconsidered. It was decided to appoint a British official with the title of Financial Adviser. He was to have no executive functions, but he was to be present at the meetings of the Council of Ministers. No attempt has ever been made to define his duties in any very precise manner. Broadly speaking, however, it may be said that, as his official title implies, he has to advise on all important financial matters, without unduly encroaching on the prerogatives of the Finance Minister. Outside his special duties, his position is also of importance. As he is present at all the meetings of the Council, he has the best opportunities for knowing what is going on in Egyptian

[1] The friendly attitude of England and Germany towards France in Tunis has been recognised in a work entitled *La Politique Française en Tunisie* (p. 374), which, though published anonymously, was, it is well known, written by a member of the French diplomatic corps.

ministerial circles. He can often guide the Ministers on matters which are unconnected with finance. He can keep the British Consul-General well informed. Being an Egyptian official, he can often give advice on his own behalf in a form which is more palatable than if it were tendered with all the weight of the British diplomatic representative speaking on behalf of his Government.

Sir Auckland Colvin was the first Financial Adviser. In the autumn of 1883, he was succeeded by Sir Edgar Vincent. At the time, some doubts were expressed as to whether Sir Edgar Vincent was not too young for the post. These doubts were soon removed. A more fortunate selection could not have been made. Sir Edgar Vincent possessed in a high degree the quality specially necessary for the performance of his duties. He was eminently resourceful; he never despaired during the blackest period of the Egyptian financial chaos. He was sanguine of ultimate success, and as at every turn new and unexpected difficulties had to be encountered, he was always ready with some ingenious device to stave off the evil day of bankruptcy, and thus to gain breathing time during which the financial ship would, at all events, have a chance of righting herself. He stayed long enough to see that his labours had not been in vain. The rehabilitation of Egyptian finance is in a large degree the work of Sir Edgar Vincent. After his departure in October 1889, he was succeeded by Sir Elwin Palmer, who again was succeeded in 1898 by Mr. (afterwards Sir Eldon) Gorst. In 1904, Sir Eldon Gorst's place was taken by Sir Vincent Corbett. On the latter's resignation in 1907, he was succeeded by Mr. Harvey.

I now turn to the Judicial Department. When I arrived in Egypt, in September 1883, I found that Native Tribunals, based on a French model, were about to be established, and that Sir Benson Maxwell had been appointed to the post of Procureur-Général. He did not remain long. Mr. (afterwards Sir) Raymond West, an Indian judge of distinction, was named to succeed him. He was a man of great learning and capacity. No one could be better qualified to devise a sound judicial system for Egypt. For several months, he studied his subject, and then produced a voluminous report. It contained many valuable suggestions, some of which were, after a considerable lapse of time, carried into execution. Nubar Pasha, who was at the time in office, did not, however, concur in Mr. West's views. The result was that the latter returned to India.

This happened in 1885, that is to say, at the most involved period of Egyptian history since the British occupation. It was necessary to throw overboard a certain amount of cargo in order to lighten the political ship. Nubar Pasha enjoyed a reputation as a judicial reformer. There was much to be said in favour of leaving the Department of Justice in Egyptian hands. It was resolved, therefore, not to press for any British successor to Mr. West, but to see what the Egyptians could do in the way of judicial reform if left to themselves.

The experiment had a fair trial, and proved a complete failure. For the next five years, constant complaints were made as regards the administration of justice, but it was desirable to give public opinion time to mature before taking any definite action in the matter. In the meanwhile, Nubar Pasha, fearful of English interference, named a Belgian, M. Le Grelle, to be Procureur-Général.[1] M. Le Grelle brought to light the

[1] M. Le Grelle resigned his appointment in 1895, and was succeeded by an Egyptian. In 1897, an Englishman (Mr. Corbet) was appointed to the place.

existence of some serious abuses. Notably, he discovered that for several years past the ordinary Tribunals had not been dealing with the most important cases of crime which occurred in the country. They had been practically superseded by certain "Commissions of Brigandage," which were in reality Courts-Martial sitting under the presidency of the Moudirs. Under the auspices of these Commissions, every species of abomination had been committed. Witnesses had been tortured. Some 700 or 800 people had been condemned to imprisonment, and a certain number had been hung. In many cases, the evidence was wholly insufficient to justify a conviction; it cannot be doubted that a good many innocent persons were punished. After a good deal of rather acrimonious discussion, the Commissions of Brigandage were abolished. The evidence in the most doubtful cases was re-examined; some of the prisoners were released, either at once or subsequently.[1]

[1] Mr. Morice, an English official attached to the Department of Justice, who was subsequently deputed to inquire into the cases of these prisoners, reported as follows:—"I may here state that in the 126 cases examined, I have never once come across any witnesses for the defence; it would, therefore, seem to have been generally decided that this was not of any importance; individuals once arrested and brought before the Commission seem to have had very little chance of regaining their liberty. I was so struck by the total absence of any defence being set up by the accused, apart from a denial of the charge, that I closely questioned those men in whose cases, after a careful examination of the documents, I had formed a conviction that they had been most unjustly sentenced, and I was invariably informed that although they, at the time of their trial, stated that they could produce witnesses to prove their innocence, their demands were never listened to, but they were informed that one thief's word was as good as another's, and that witnesses produced would be treated as accomplices, etc. Indeed, it was sufficient for one man, whose guilt was fully established, either by recognition on the part of the victim of the assault or robbery, or by the finding of stolen property in his possession, to accuse another, for this latter to be sentenced to a very severe term of imprisonment. I have been told the most pitiful stories by convicts I have interrogated concerning the horrible treatment they received when in prison, a treatment which, it is needless to say, invariably ended in a confession being obtained. One has only to examine the preliminary inquiries in order to be convinced of this."

This episode is very Egyptian, and is illustrative of the extent to which an Egyptian Minister often cares more for theory than for practice. An elaborate system of justice existed in appearance. In reality, the system was inoperative. Persons accused of crime were condemned to death or to lifelong imprisonment at the will of some ignorant and tyrannical Moudir.

With the suppression of the Commissions of Brigandage, crime of a serious nature increased. This had been anticipated. It became daily more and more clear that no Egyptian Minister was capable of coping with the situation. The Egyptian Government, therefore, reluctantly consented to appoint an Englishman to the post of Judicial Adviser. It was not easy to find a competent man, for few English lawyers have made a study of the French legal system. A fortunate selection was, however, made in the person of Mr. (afterwards Sir John) Scott. His appointment created a flutter in the Egyptian political dovecot. Riaz Pasha shortly afterwards resigned, and his resignation was in some measure due to his dislike to Sir John Scott's nomination. The establishment of a sound judicial system in Egypt may be said to date from the time of Sir John Scott's assumption of the office of Judicial Adviser. In 1898, Sir John Scott resigned his place to take up an appointment in London. He was succeeded by Sir Malcolm McIlwraith.

Previous to the British occupation, the Public Works Department had been mainly in French hands. In 1883, it was resolved to appoint a British Under-Secretary to this Department, and to bring a staff of British officials from India to superintend the improvements in the canalisation of the country. Sir Colin Scott-Moncrieff was named Under-Secretary. The selection was a most happy one. Apart from his very remarkable technical attainments, Sir Colin Scott-Moncrieff was a man of the highest character. The most prejudiced Pasha respected qualities which were so dissimilar to any which he himself possessed. The most venomous journalist paused before he threw his political vitriol over a character so transparently honest. No Englishman employed in the Egyptian service during the early days of the occupation did more to make the name of England respected than Sir Colin Scott-Moncrieff, who, by the way, is not an Englishman, but one of that race which so frequently succeeds in foreign parts by virtue of its sterling good qualities. Sir Colin Scott-Moncrieff comes from well north of the Tweed.

In 1892, Sir Colin Scott-Moncrieff found a very worthy successor in the person of Sir William Garstin, under whose intelligent auspices very large sums of money were, to the great advantage of the country, spent on public works of various descriptions. It would be difficult to exaggerate the debt of gratitude which the people of Egypt owe to Sir William Garstin.

The Financial Secretary also occupies a post of great importance. He is an executive officer. He performs the duties of the Financial Adviser when the latter is absent. During the early days of the occupation this post was held by Blum Pasha, a very intelligent Austrian, who had the rare merit of having served the Egyptian Government during the lax and corrupt rule of Ismail Pasha without the most censorious critic being able to whisper a word against his honesty. He was a most capable official and worked cordially with the English. On his retirement in 1889, he was succeeded by Mr. (now Lord) Milner, the well-known author of *England in Egypt*. Of Lord Milner all that need be said in this place is that he is one of the most able Englishmen who have served the Egyptian Government. Not only was he versed in all the technicalities of his own Department, but he had a wide grasp of the larger aspects of Egyptian affairs. On his being named, in 1892, to an appointment in England, he was succeeded by Sir Eldon Gorst, who belonged to the diplomatic service. Sir Eldon Gorst had occupied his leisure time in acquiring a knowledge of Arabic. Being endowed with a singular degree of tact and intelligence, he generally managed to get all he wanted done without applying for diplomatic support. Since 1894, when Sir Eldon Gorst was appointed Adviser to the Ministry of the Interior, the post of Financial Secretary has changed hands more than once, but it has always been held by a very carefully selected British official.

There are three sub-departments attached to the Ministry of Finance. These are the Customs, the Lighthouses, and the Post Office. The first two of these are under superior British supervision. The Post Office was reorganised by an English Director-General, who was eventually succeeded by an extremely competent Syrian, Saba Pasha, under whose direction various postal reforms of great importance and utility have been introduced.

Until 1894, the Police was commanded by an English Inspector-General who had a small staff of British officers under him. In the autumn of 1894, a change of system was effected. The post of Inspector-General was abolished and an Adviser (Sir Eldon Gorst) was appointed to the Ministry of the Interior. In 1898, Mr. Machell was appointed to succeed Sir Eldon Gorst. The duties attached to the post of Adviser underwent, at the same time, some modifications of no great importance. The head of the Sanitary Department is English, as is also the Director-General of Prisons.

The supreme direction of the Educational Department has always been in Egyptian hands, but, in 1906, an English Adviser (Mr. Dunlop) was appointed to this Department. A considerable number of Europeans are employed as schoolmasters.[1]

Allusion has so far only been made to the highest appointments. It will, however, be as well to speak briefly of the total number of Englishmen employed in Egypt. The subject is one of importance, for it has at times given rise to much exaggeration, and, moreover, the employment of Europeans is naturally viewed with jealousy by those Egyptians who are aspirants for official positions.

It is generally recognised that European assistance, to a certain extent, is necessary to carry on the work of government in Egypt. Differences of opinion, however, arise when any attempt is made to lay down with any degree of precision the extent to which recourse should be had to European agency. Weighty arguments may be advanced on both sides. On the one hand, it is frequently urged that the efficiency of the service suffers by reason of the inadequacy of the European staff; that the welfare of the mass of the population must be placed before all other considerations; that the vast majority of voiceless Egyptians prefer good administration to national government; and that, therefore, for the present, and probably for a long time to come, the employment of a large number of Europeans is absolutely necessary. On the other hand, it is stated that the Egyptians prefer

[1] The numbers were, in 1896, Egyptians, 631; Europeans, 92, and, in 1906, Egyptians, 794; Europeans, 160.

a defective system of government administered by their own countrymen to a relatively perfect system administered by aliens; that it is in the highest degree impolitic to push on education and at the same time to close the door of high Government employment to the educated classes; that the Egyptians can never learn to govern themselves unless they are allowed to make the attempt; that any causes which tend towards maladministration will be temporary and will gradually disappear as a result of the experience which will be gained; and that, therefore, the number of Europeans in the service of the Government should not merely be reduced to the lowest limit compatible with efficiency, but that that limit should be exceeded, and that temporary inefficiency, even in a somewhat marked degree, should be tolerated in order to attain the desired end.

There is not much to be gained by dwelling at length on the abstract principles enunciated above. The subject under discussion is eminently one as to which, for all purposes of practical politics, a compromise has to be effected between the extremes of the conflicting principles invoked on either side. What is quite clear is, that if Western civilisation is to be introduced into Egypt, it can only be done by Europeans, or by Egyptians who have imbibed the spirit of that civilisation, and have acquired the knowledge necessary in order to apply Western methods of government. The extent to which Europeans, or Egyptians who have received a European training, should respectively be employed, depends mainly on the supply which is available of the latter class. The main difficulty of dealing with the question is that, for the present, the demand for qualified Egyptians of this class is greatly in excess of the supply.

The general policy which has been pursued since

the British occupation of the country took place, in 1882, has been to limit the number of Europeans in the employment of the Government as much as possible, to employ Egyptians in the very great majority of the subordinate and in a large number of the superior administrative posts, and gradually to prepare the ground for increasing the number of Egyptians in high employment. This policy is thoroughly understood by all the leading British officials in Egypt. Some, possibly, have been more successful than others in training their Egyptian subordinates. Some, again, may be inclined to insist on a rather excessive standard of efficiency on the part of the Egyptian before they will readily acquiesce in foregoing the appointment of a European. But the higher British officials in Egypt have never shown any tendency to question the wisdom of the policy, or the least reluctance to give effect to it when once they were convinced that a qualified Egyptian could be found to take any post which might happen to be vacant.

This matter is frequently discussed on the assumption that a number of places under Government are now occupied by Europeans for which competent Egyptians could, without difficulty, be found. I will not go so far as to say that this assumption is absolutely unfounded, but it certainly gives a very incorrect view of the facts of the situation. I do not doubt that there are a few cases as to which it may be said that, if the European occupant of some post vacated his place, a competent Egyptian might at once be found to replace him. But, in the very large majority of cases, the reason why the European holds the post is that to which I have already alluded, namely, that the supply of competent Egyptians is not nearly equal to the demand.

To any one who will calmly and impartially

consider the recent history and the present situation in Egypt, the state of things which I have described above can be no matter for surprise. Rather would it be astonishing if the difficulties to which I have alluded had not occurred.

European agency is required in Egypt for two reasons: in the first place, to supply the technical knowledge, which, until very recently, the Egyptians have had no opportunity of acquiring; in the second place, to remedy those defects in the Egyptian character which have been developed by a long course of misgovernment.

In so far as numbers are concerned, the first is by far the more contributory cause. The rapidity with which the material prosperity of Egypt has advanced during the last fifteen or twenty years is probably without a parallel in history. The suddenness of the movement has proved by no means an unmixed blessing to the country. I will not dwell on the moral aspect of this question beyond saying that it is a commonplace of economics to hold that a great and sudden accretion of wealth, without any corresponding increase of knowledge as to how the newly acquired wealth should be used, is a very doubtful benefit, whether to an individual or a nation.

From the point of view of the question immediately under discussion, it cannot be doubted that this sudden leap from poverty to affluence greatly increased the difficulties of executing the policy of employing Egyptian rather than European agency in administrative work. For, when once the full tide of prosperity set in, demands arose on all sides for the employment of agents possessing technical knowledge of all sorts. European lawyers were required to deal with the numerous legal questions which arose, and in which a knowledge of Europeans and their laws was indispensable.

Hydraulic engineers were required to deal with irrigation questions; medical men, to look after the hospitals and the sanitary condition of the country; veterinary surgeons, to arrest the cattle plague; trained surveyors, to map the fields; mechanical engineers and mechanics, to perform a great variety of work—and so on. All these demands fell suddenly on a country almost wholly unprepared to meet them. Neither, although the difficulties which have subsequently arisen were in some degree foreseen, were the British advisers of the Egyptian Government able, during the early years of the occupation, to do much towards providing for them. For at least six years, all that could be done was to struggle against bankruptcy, to throw off the incubus of the Soudan, and by scraping together funds in order to improve the system of irrigation, to lay the foundations of the prosperity which the country now enjoys.

I shall, at a later period of this work, deal more fully with the question of education. Here I will only say that, for some years, educational progress was, owing to the financial difficulties against which the Government had to contend, necessarily slow. Recently it has been more rapid, and I now take a somewhat sanguine view of the possibility of gradually substituting Egyptian for European agency in those offices where the necessity for employing Europeans is at present based on the want of technical knowledge on the part of the Egyptians. But any attempt to hurry can only lead to disappointment, and, eventually, in all probability, to a reaction which will be to the detriment of Egyptian interests.

I have said that, besides those Europeans who are employed on the ground that their technical knowledge is indispensable, the services of others are necessary to act as some corrective to the defects of the Egyptian character. The number of those who may be classed in this category is comparatively small. On the other hand, they often occupy positions of greater importance than those who are employed merely by reason of their technical skill. The substitution of Egyptian for European agency must necessarily take even more time in these cases than in those where the transfer depends on the acquisition of technical knowledge by the Egyptians. National character is a plant of slow growth. Such instruction as can be afforded in schools and colleges only constitutes one of the elements which contribute to its modification and development. All that can be said is that no effort should be spared to foster the growth of all those moral and intellectual qualities which, collectively, tend to the formation of character. I may add that amongst the defects which, for purposes of administration, appear most of all to require rectification, are, the fear of assuming individual responsibility; the absence of adequate capacity to exercise with firmness, intelligence, and consideration for others, such functions as are usually vested in responsible agents; and the tendency, so common amongst Egyptians, of running to extremes both in thought and action.

Before leaving this branch of the subject, it may be as well that I should give some figures showing the extent to which Europeans are now employed in the Egyptian service.[1]

The following table shows the composition of the Egyptian Civil Service at the close of the years 1896 and 1906 respectively:—

[1] A more detailed analysis of these figures was given in my Report for the year 1906, *Egypt*, No. 1 of 1907, pp. 33-44. The remarks made above are quoted almost textually from this Report.

Year.	Egyptians.	Europeans.	Total.
1896	8444	690	9134
1906	12,027	1252	13,279

In the course of the decade, therefore, the total number of officials increased by 4145. Of these, 3583 were Egyptians, and 562 were Europeans. I should mention that, out of the total increase of 562 Europeans, no less than 303 belonged to the Railway Administration, over which, until quite recently, the Egyptian Government have been able to exercise little or no control. Further, it is to be remembered that not only the convenience, but also, to a great extent, the lives of the travelling public depend on efficient railway administration. Hence, there is in this case relatively little scope for the application of the general and semi-political arguments involved in the issues now under discussion.

These figures bear eloquent testimony to the fact that the number of Europeans appointed to the Egyptian public service has been strictly controlled. It may be that in some few cases additional Europeans will be required, but these will be more than counterbalanced by the increase of Egyptians in other Departments. In view of the rapid strides being made in education—more especially in technical education—there now appears for the first time to be a prospect of carrying out more fully than heretofore what has always been the real policy of the British Government in Egypt. The execution of that policy was retarded by financial difficulties which, since the Anglo-French Agreement was signed, have been to a great extent removed.

One observation may be added before leaving this branch of the subject. It is that in countries such as India and Egypt the best policy to pursue is to employ a small body of well-selected and well-paid Europeans. Everything depends on finding the right man for the right place. If he can be found, it is worth while to pay him well. It is a mistake to employ second or third-rate Europeans on low salaries. They often do more harm than good. Public opinion generally condemns high salaries, but on this particular point the European administrator in the East will do well to follow his own judgment and not to be unduly influenced by outside criticism. It is worth while to pay something extra in order to secure the services of a really competent and thoroughly trustworthy official.

CHAPTER XLI

THE INTERNATIONAL ADMINISTRATIONS

Internationalism—1. THE COMMISSION OF THE PUBLIC DEBT—Functions of the Commission—The Egyptian Accounts—The Reserve Fund —Uselessness of the Commission—2. THE RAILWAY ADMINISTRATION—3. THE DAIRA SANIEH—4. THE DOMAINS ADMINISTRATION.

COSMOPOLITANISM, as opposed to exclusive patriotism, has ever been the dream of theorists and the butt of practical statesmen. Probably, few lines of any British poet have been more frequently quoted—especially of late years—than those in which Canning ridiculed the "friend of every country but his own." Of recent years, although there has been no diminution but rather a recrudescence of international rivalry, a tendency towards the international treatment both of European and of extra-European questions has become manifest, not only amongst theorists, but amongst practical statesmen. This tendency is the natural outcome of the circumstances which obtained in the latter part of the nineteenth century. There appears little prospect that the Utopia of the early free-traders will be realised. Trade, with its handmaids, the railway and the telegraph, does not so far appear to have bound nations together in any closer bonds of amity than existed in the days of slow locomotion and communication. On the other hand, the European body politic has become more sensitive than heretofore. National interests tend towards cosmopolitanism, however much national sentiments and aspirations may tend towards exclusive patriotism. The whole world is quickly informed of any incident which may occur in any part of the globe. Not only in the cabinet of every Minister, but in the office of every newspaper editor the questions to which its occurrence instantly give rise are, how does this circumstance affect the affairs of my country? What course should be taken in order to safeguard our interests? It is more difficult than heretofore to segregate a quarrel between any two States. In a certain sense Europeans, in spite of themselves, have become members of a single family, though not always of a happy family. They are all oppressed by one common dread, and that is that some accident may precipitate a general war, of which not the wisest can foretell the final issue. If any minor State shows a tendency to light the match which may lead to a general conflagration, the voice of international rivalry is to some extent hushed in presence of the danger, and the diplomatic fire-engine is turned on from every capital in Europe in order to quench the flame before it can spread. A certain power of acting together has thus been developed amongst the nations and Governments of Europe, and it cannot be doubted that the world has benefited by the change. In all the larger affairs of state, internationalism constitutes a guarantee for peace. It in some measure obliges particular interests to yield for the general good of the European community.

Internationalism has, however, done more than group together certain States and ensure common or quasi-common action on occasions of supreme importance. Semi-civilised countries, in which the rulers are sometimes only possessed of incomplete sovereign rights, open up a wide field for the development of internationalism. In such countries, some European Powers have interests which they wish to safeguard without arousing the jealousy of their rivals by too open an assertion of strength, whilst others are led to claim a seat at the international table in order to assert their political existence and to remind the world that their interests, albeit they are of relatively slight importance, cannot be altogether neglected. Cases sometimes arise which involve prolonged supervision and control in the interests of the European Powers, but which do not justify exclusive action on the part of any one of them, or which, if they justify it, are of a nature not to allow of exclusive action without a risk of discord in respect to the particular nation by whom it is to be exercised. What can be more natural in cases of this kind than for the Powers to say—we are agreed as to all that is essential; certain points of detail remain to be settled locally; let us each appoint an expert who will represent our interests and see that they get fair play, but who at the same time will have no very marked political bias, and who will treat the technical questions which come under his consideration on their own merits? Nothing could in appearance be more equitable or more calculated to obviate the risk of serious friction.

But alas! however much exclusiveness may in appearance be expelled by the cosmopolitan pitchfork, it but too often comes back again to its natural resting-place. The experiment of administrative internationalism has probably been tried in the No Man's Land of which this history treats to a greater extent than in any other country. The result cannot be said to be encouraging to those who believe in the efficacy of international action in administrative matters. What has been proved is that international institutions possess admirable negative qualities. They are formidable checks to all action, and the reason why they are so is that, when any action is proposed, objections of one sort or another generally occur to some member of the international body. Any action often involves a presumed advantage accorded to some rival nation, and it is a principle of internationalism, which is scornfully rejected in theory and but too often recognised as a guide for practical action, that it is better to do nothing, even though evil may ensue, than to allow good to be done at the expense of furthering the interests, or of exalting the reputation of an international rival. For all purposes of action, therefore, administrative internationalism may be said to tend towards the creation of administrative impotence.

1. *Commission of the Public Debt.*

The Commission of the Public Debt originally consisted of four members, an Englishman, a Frenchman, an Austrian, and an Italian. In 1885, a German and a Russian Commissioner were added, thus bringing the total number of Commissioners up to six. Until 1904, the functions of the Commission were briefly as follows.

The officials responsible for the collection of the revenues pledged to the service of the Debt were under an obligation to pay all monies collected by them into the hands of the Commissioners, and to furnish them with the information necessary in order to enable an effective financial control to be exercised. The Commissioners had a right to name and dismiss their own employés. No loan could be contracted without their consent. Lastly, and this was a provision of the highest importance, the Commissioners, in their capacity of legal representatives of the bondholders, were empowered to sue the Egyptian Government in the Mixed Courts in the event of any infringement of the Law of Liquidation taking place.

It will be seen that the powers thus conferred on the Commissioners were extensive. Nevertheless, those portions of the Law of Liquidation to which allusion has so far been made, did not in practice give rise to much difficulty subsequent to the British occupation. They were provisions intended to guard against an act of bankruptcy, and inasmuch as the result of the British occupation was to place the Egyptian Treasury in a state of assured solvency, any preventive action on the part of the Commission of the Debt became unnecessary when once the first few years of acute crisis were passed.

Other functions were, however, vested in the Commissioners, which were of greater practical importance.

The Law of Liquidation, coupled with the Decree of July 27, 1885, which was promulgated on the occasion of the issue of an Egyptian Loan of £9,000,000 guaranteed by the Powers of Europe, laid down a method for balancing the accounts of the Egyptian Treasury at the end of each year which was a triumph of financial cumbersomeness and ineptitude. At the time of the London Conference, the French, who were supported by some other Continental Powers, were politically hostile to England, and, moreover, looked almost exclusively to the interests of the bondholders. The British Treasury officials could see but one point, namely, that the Government of Egypt were embarrassed by having spent too much money in the past; therefore, it was held, a stringent control should be exercised to prevent extravagant expenditure in the future. The argument was sound, but it was forgotten at the time that the expenditure was being incurred under conditions wholly different from those which had obtained in the past. A wise foresight would have given greater latitude to the British advisers of the Egyptian Government than could have been prudently accorded to Ismail Pasha. It was, however, impossible to obtain a hearing for arguments of this nature. The Egyptian Government did, indeed, manage to obtain a sum of £1,000,000 to spend on Irrigation, but beyond this it was found impossible to shake the mistrust of the French and the preconceived ideas of the British Treasury officials. The latter aided in establishing a system which proved subsequently to be a fertile source of embarrassment to their own countrymen in Egypt.

It had been laid down by the Decrees of 1876 that certain revenues should be pledged to the service of the Debt, whilst other revenues should be left at the disposal of the Egyptian Government to provide for their administrative expenditure. When the Guaranteed Loan of 1885 was contracted, the distribution of what, in Gallicised English, are called the "affected" and the "non-affected" revenues, had to be reconsidered. Care was taken to increase the relative amount of the former, so that the bondholders should not run any risk, with the result that the amount of the latter was relatively diminished. The administrative expenditure was fixed at a certain figure, the only concession, which was with difficulty obtained, being that the working expenses of the Railway administration should not be unalterable, but should be taken at 45 per cent[1] of the gross receipts. If the non-

[1] In 1902, after prolonged negotiations, this figure was increased to a maximum of 55 per cent.

affected revenues did not yield the sum at which the administrative expenditure was fixed, the deficit had to be made good from the affected revenues. The surplus on the whole account consisted of the money remaining in the hands of the Commissioners of the Debt from the affected revenues after the deficit in the non-affected revenues, if any, had been made good. This surplus was divided into two portions. One portion remained in the hands of the Commissioners; the other was paid to the Egyptian Government. The result was that, if the Government wished to spend £10 in excess of the administrative limit prescribed by international agreement, revenue to the extent of £20 had to be collected in order to meet the expenditure. As the country progressed, legitimate demands for fresh expenditure arose, but under the system devised in 1885, the anomaly was presented that the Government had to pay double for everything in the nature of an improvement involving fresh expenditure; that the administration was starved; that money was plentiful; but that no one benefited in any adequate degree from its abundance.

It would be tedious to describe in detail the involved calculation which had to be made before the true surplus at the disposal of the Egyptian Treasury could be ascertained. It will be sufficient to quote the figures of one year as an example of the results obtained under the system.

In 1892, the revenue of the Egyptian Government amounted to £E.10,364,000, and the expenditure to £E.9,595,000. It would naturally be supposed by any one unacquainted with the intricacies of Egyptian finance that a surplus remained at the disposal of the Government amounting to the difference between these two sums, namely,

£E.769,000. Any such conclusion would have been altogether erroneous.

After winding through the financial labyrinth, which was constructed by the Powers, and which is a typical instance of the results of international administration, it was found that the real surplus in the hands of the Egyptian Treasury was only £E.179,000, a difference of no less than £E.590,000. Appearances in Egypt are deceptive.

It was originally intended that any surplus remaining in the hands of the Commissioners should be applied to the extinction of debt. For the first few years of the British occupation, this matter was not of much practical importance, as no surplus was available. But when financial affairs became more settled, Sir Edgar Vincent's inventive mind gave birth to a scheme under which the surplus at the end of each year was to be allowed to accumulate in a Reserve Fund. Extinction of debt was not to begin until the Reserve Fund amounted to £E.2,000,000. Thus, the Treasury would, it was hoped, eventually have a large sum of money in hand to guard against any unforeseen contingencies which might occur.

The idea was excellent. It obtained the assent of the Powers, and was embodied in a Decree dated July 12, 1888. Article 3 of this Decree described how the money belonging to the Reserve Fund might be spent. *Inter alia*, it was to be applied to "extraordinary expenditure undertaken with the previous assent of the Commission of the Debt." This was a provision of great importance, for as the Reserve Fund increased, it was found possible to turn the money over, and, by making advances to the Government, to allow various works of public utility to be constructed. As, however, it rested with the Commission to decide whether any advance should be made, it is obvious that, under the Decree of 1888, the powers vested in the Commissioners were notably increased.[1]

Such, therefore, were the attributes of the Commission of the Public Debt. During Ismail Pasha's time, this institution, though its organisation was in many respects defective, played an important and useful part in Egyptian affairs. Subsequent to the British occupation, the inutility of the Commission became, year by year, more apparent. It cost the Treasury some £E.40,000 a year. All the necessary work of a National Debt Office could have been done by one official and a small staff of clerks.

In blaming the institution, however, it would be unjust to cast indiscriminate blame on the individuals concerned. Some of the Commissioners have been intelligent and capable men who have performed their duties in a reasonable spirit of impartiality. Indeed, the Egyptian authorities have always preferred dealing with the Commission of the Debt to dealing with the Powers. The Commissioners, being on the spot, are exposed to local influences, and possess a certain amount of local knowledge. They are, therefore, more likely to judge financial matters on their own merits than those who, sitting at a distance, look at Egyptian affairs from a wholly political point of view. It is, however, none the less true that whatever reforms have been accomplished with the co-operation of the Caisse could have been equally well and probably better accomplished had the Caisse not existed. The only purpose which this institution eventually served was to act as an obstacle to progress, and occasionally as an agency for the manifestation of hostility

[1] The question of how this Decree should be interpreted gave rise to a lawsuit when, in 1896, a majority of the Commissioners of the Debt made a grant of £E.500,000 to meet the expenses of the Dongola campaign.—*Vide* p. 85 *et seq.*

towards England. It often happens that an institution survives after the circumstances to which it owes its origin have passed away. The result is that the institution becomes hurtful, although the individuals associated with it may be deserving of respect. This is what took place with regard to the Commission of the Public Debt.

In 1904, as a result of negotiations with the Powers, the functions of the Commission of the Debt underwent a radical change. Without going into any elaborate detail, it may be said that the Commissioners are now merely receivers on the part of the bondholders. They cannot in any way interfere with administrative affairs.

In 1912, the Egyptian Government will be free to convert the whole of the Debt. If the conversion takes place, the Commission of the Debt will presumably disappear altogether.

2. *Railway Administration.*

Under the Decree of November 18, 1876, a Board was constituted to administer the Railways, the Telegraphs, and the Port of Alexandria. It originally consisted of two Englishmen, of whom one was President, a Frenchman, and two Egyptians. Subsequently, the number of English and of Egyptian members was reduced to one of each nationality.

The English and French members were named on the proposal of their respective Governments. The Board made appointments to all subordinate places in the administration. The superior officials were nominated by the Khedive on the proposal of the Board. Changes of tariff were made by the Board with the sanction of the Egyptian Government.

Two very competent Englishmen, Colonel Marindin and Mr. (now Lord) Farrer, were employed in 1887 to report on the Egyptian Railways. This is the judgment which they passed on the system of administration :—

"The administration of the Egyptian Railways, as at present constituted, differs considerably from any with which we are acquainted. The control is vested in three members whose functions are undefined as regards the different branches of the working of the railway. We understand that there is no one individual who is separately responsible for the management of the railways. It is obvious that the result of this divided responsibility has been especially injurious to the working of a commercial business such as railways must necessarily be, and we are of opinion that it is absolutely essential for the satisfactory working of the Egyptian Railways, and for the maintenance of discipline upon them, that the management of them, as a whole, together with the control of heads of Departments, should be vested in one person with a position analogous to that of the Managing Director or General Manager of Railways in other countries."

Obviously, the management should have been vested in one person, but internationalism abhors the one-man system as much as nature abhors a vacuum. The sheet-anchor of internationalism is, indeed, that several men should be set to do the work of one.

It was, however, said of Richelieu, by one of his enemies, "il est capable de tout, même du bien." So also it may be noted that international administration, although it can never yield fruits at all comparable with those which may be obtained under more rational administrative systems, may at times be forced into some degree of action, and will then produce results which the casual observer may think are due to the excellence of the system, whereas they are in reality for the most part obtained by the occurrence of adventitious circumstances in spite of the system. Administrative internationalism, like Richelieu, is occasionally capable, if not of absolute good, at all events of assuming a fictitious appearance of goodness.

Thus, the Egyptian Railways benefited by the increase of prosperity and by the general reforming impulse which was imparted to the Egyptian administrative machine by the predominance of British influence in the country. They would have benefited still more had the British reformers been from the first allowed a free hand in dealing with their administration.

In 1904, as a consequence of the arrangements with the Powers, to which allusion has already been made, the Egyptian Government acquired full right to deal with the Railway Administration in any way they might think fit.

Few, save those behind the scenes, have probably recognised fully that the Anglo-French Agreement was only signed just in time to prevent a complete breakdown of the Railway Administration. Such, however, is unquestionably the case. If means had not been found to spend a large amount of capital on developments and improvements, the railways of Egypt would have been wholly unable to cope with the growing requirements of the country.

Towards the close of 1905, Sir Charles Scotter visited Egypt and made a full report on the condition of the Egyptian Railways.[1] His suggestions are now being carried out. The Railway Administration is being thoroughly reorganised. Capital

[1] See *Egypt*, No. 1 of 1906, pp. 110-113.

expenditure to the extent of £3,000,000 has been sanctioned, of which £1,635,000 was expended before the close of 1906. It is probable that an additional grant of £1,000,000 will be eventually required. Thus, it may be hoped that before long the Egyptian Railway Administration will be in thoroughly good order.

Looking back to one of my earliest Reports[1] I notice that in 1890, the Egyptian Railways carried 4,700,000 passengers and 1,683,000 tons of goods. In 1906, they carried no less than 22,550,000 passengers and 20,036,000 tons of goods. These figures serve as a striking illustration of the immense improvement in the material condition of the country which has taken place during the last few years. They also afford an ample justification for the large reductions which have been made in the rates.[2]

In addition to the State Railways, a network of 1145 kilometres of Agricultural Railways, which are owned by private companies, exists in Egypt. These railways are largely used. In 1906, they carried 6,924,000 passengers and 929,000 tons of goods.

3. *Daira Sanieh.*

The Daira properties formed part of the huge estates which Ismail Pasha contrived, generally by illicit and arbitrary methods, to accumulate in his own hands. They originally extended over an area of more than half a million of acres. When Ismail got into financial difficulties, he borrowed

[1] *Egypt,* No. 1 of 1892, p. 20.

[2] I may remark that the same lesson is to be learnt from an examination of the statistics of the Post Office and Telegraph Departments, in both of which the rates have been largely reduced. In 1885, only 12,500,000 letters and 83,000 parcels passed through the Post Office. In 1905, the figures were: letters, 50,700,000; parcels, 250,000. In 1906, no less than 1,925,000 telegrams, of which 1,248,000 were in Arabic, passed over the lines, as compared to about 311,000 in 1890.

£9,500,000 on the security of these properties. They were administered by a Board of Directors, consisting of an Egyptian Director-General, and two Controllers, one British and one French. The Director-General was the executive officer, but the Controllers had ample powers of supervision and inspection. They alone were the legal representatives of the bondholders.

Until the year 1891, the Daira expenditure was always in excess of the revenue. On several occasions the deficits exceeded £200,000. With the exception of the year 1895, when there was a deficit amounting to £102,000, the accounts of every year subsequent to 1890 showed a surplus. In the two years 1904-5, the revenue exceeded the expenditure by no less than £817,000.

In 1898, an arrangement was made under which the Daira estates were sold to a company, who again resold them in lots. The sales are now complete. Most of the purchasers were Egyptians. The Government share in the profits of the liquidation amounted to about £3,280,000.

4. *The Domains Administration.*

The properties, known by the name of the Domains, comprise the estates ceded, under pressure, by Ismail Pasha in 1878.[1] On the security of these estates, a loan of £8,500,000 was negotiated with Messrs. Rothschild. It was, at the same time, arranged that the Domains should be administered by a Commission consisting of an Englishman, a Frenchman, and an Egyptian.

Up to the year 1899, the revenue yielded by the estates was invariably less than the expenditure. In one year (1885) the deficit amounted to no less than £275,000. From 1900 onwards, a

[1] *Vide ante*, vol. i. p. 63.

surplus, varying from £26,000 to £150,000, was always realised.

By gradual sales[1] the extent of the Domains properties, which originally consisted of nearly 426,000 acres of land, was reduced by the close of 1906 to about 147,000 acres. Simultaneously, the outstanding capital of the loan was reduced from £8,500,000 to about £1,316,000.[2] It cannot be doubted that the whole of this loan will be paid off before long, and that, when this is done, some very valuable lands will remain at the disposal of the Government.[3]

With the sale of the Daira and Domains lands, almost the last traces of the injury which Ismail Pasha inflicted on his country, by accumulating 1,000,000 acres of the best land in Egypt in the hands of himself and his family, will disappear.

Some comprehension of these institutions is necessary in order to understand the extent to which the freedom of action of the British officials in Egypt was at one time crippled. A brief examination of that curious mosaic termed the Judicial System of Egypt will tend to bring into still stronger relief the anomalous position occupied by the Anglo-Egyptian reformer. In the case of those institutions of which I have so far treated, the shackles have now been, for the most part, struck off. In the case of those with which I am about to deal, they still remain and bar the way to reform.

[1] The great majority of the purchasers have been Egyptians. The land was, for the most part, sold in small lots.

[2] On November 30, 1907, the outstanding capital of this loan amounted to only £1,050,940.

[3] If the present price of land is maintained, the value of the estates which will remain over after the complete liquidation of the loan will probably be about £5,000,000.

CHAPTER XLII

THE JUDICIAL SYSTEM

The Mixed Courts—Nubar Pasha's objects in creating them—Attributes and composition of the Mixed Courts—Defects in the institution—The Consular Courts—The Native Tribunals and the Kadi's Courts—Summary of jurisdictions in Egypt.

IN creating the International Tribunals, or, as they are more frequently called, the Mixed Courts, Nubar Pasha had two objects in view. In the first place, he was struck with the fact that, inasmuch as the European adventurers who flocked to Egypt during the reigns of Said and of Ismail had no legal means for obtaining a redress of any real or imaginary grievances, they fell back, in case of need, on diplomatic support, with results that were not unfrequently disastrous to the Egyptian Treasury. Nubar Pasha, therefore, conceived the statesmanlike project of creating law-courts, which should command the confidence of Europe, and which should be empowered to try civil suits between Europeans, on the one hand, and Egyptians or the Egyptian Government, on the other hand. In the second place, although in dealing with Ismail Pasha this aspect of the case was kept in the background, Nubar Pasha wished to erect a legal barrier between the population of Egypt and the capricious despotism of the Khedive. His original intention was to place all the inhabitants of Egypt, whether Europeans or Egyptians, under the jurisdiction of the Mixed Courts. This part of the project, however, fell to the ground owing to the strong opposition which it encountered at Constantinople, and perhaps it was as well that it did so, for the complete realisation of Nubar Pasha's idea would have entailed the internationalisation of the whole judicial system of the country.

Nubar Pasha's first object was, however, attained. From 1875 onwards, any European who has had a claim either against an Egyptian or against the Egyptian Government, has no longer been under the necessity of seeking diplomatic support. He has been referred both by the Egyptian Government and by the diplomatic agent of his country to a properly constituted law-court in which it was competent for him to make good his claim, if it was a just one. From every point of view, the result has been beneficial. The claimant, with the Egyptian code before him, has been able to form a fair idea of what he might expect from the law-courts. The Egyptian Government have, on the one hand, been obliged to acknowledge their legal and contractual obligations; on the other hand, they have been relieved from capricious diplomatic pressure on behalf of individuals, and they have not unfrequently invoked the law with success in order to be saved from the exorbitant demands of contractors and others. The diplomatic agent has been relieved from the unpleasant obligation of supporting claims, which were often of doubtful validity from a technical, and of more than doubtful morality from an equitable point of view.

By the irony of fate, the institution to which Ismail Pasha was induced to assent, probably with only a half knowledge of what it meant, was the instrument which dealt him his political deathblow. When the law-courts, to whose creation the Powers of Europe had been parties, condemned him to pay certain sums of money, and when he found himself unable to pay them, the cup of his iniquity overflowed, and Europe—legally outraged, and politically timorous of what the future might bring forth—spoke out and said, "You must pay or go." Ismail Pasha could not pay. After a few ineffectual struggles, he went.

It is unnecessary to describe at length the attributes and composition of the Mixed Courts. It will be sufficient to say that a Court of Appeal sits at Alexandria, and that three Courts of First Instance exist, one at Cairo, one at Alexandria, and one at Mansourah. Egyptian judges sit on all these Courts, but most of the real work is done by Europeans. The European judges of the Court of Appeal are for the most part chosen from amongst the subjects of the Great Powers. All the Powers, without distinction, are represented on the Courts of First Instance. The choice of judges rests nominally with the Egyptian Government. In reality, the judges have until quite recently been nominated by their respective Governments. The jurisdiction of the Mixed Courts extends over all civil cases between Europeans and Egyptians, whether the European appears as plaintiff or defendant; also, over civil cases between Europeans of different nationalities.

The principal defect of the Mixed Courts is that the judges are not merely interpreters of the law; they are also to a great extent makers of it. They are not under the effective control of any legislature. If, as is both natural and occasionally almost unavoidable, they attempt, by a somewhat strained interpretation of their charter, to usurp functions which do not belong to them, there is no one to restrain them. In order that any new law should be recognised by the Mixed Courts, it must receive the assent of all the

Powers, and experience has shown that it is generally impossible, and always difficult and tedious, to ensure the required unanimity. Legislation by diplomacy is probably the worst and most cumbersome form of legislation in the world. Under these circumstances, it is easy to understand that the judges of the Mixed Courts are practically a law unto themselves.

When the Indian code was framed, some of the most acute intellects of the time devoted themselves to a lengthy examination of the subject with a view to deciding what provisions of European law and procedure, whether British or Roman, could be adapted to the circumstances and requirements of India. The result was the production of an admirable code, which was essentially Indian. No such care was taken in Egypt. The Egyptian code was originally little more than a textual copy of the French code, and, moreover, it was applied by judges who, although in some instances men of ability, were necessarily ignorant of Egyptian manners and customs. The result was that great hardship was at times inflicted, more especially in respect to the application of the laws regulating the relations between debtor and creditor. The ignorant Egyptian debtor found himself, before he was aware of it, gripped in the iron hand of the law, which was mercilessly applied by his Levantine creditor. Eventually, some modifications were made, but even now the law and procedure are too European for the country.

The Mixed Courts only exercise criminal jurisdiction over Europeans in a certain number of specified cases, most of which are of rare occurrence. For the most part, any European resident in Egypt who is accused of crime is tried by his Consul according to the laws of his own country.

The Native Tribunals instituted under Lord

Dufferin's auspices exercise civil and criminal jurisdiction over Ottoman subjects, save in respect to matters relating to personal status, which are decided by the Kadi according to the system of ecclesiastical jurisprudence embodied in the Sacred Law of Islam. The working of these Tribunals will be discussed at a later period of this work.

To sum up, if an Egyptian and a European wish some civil cause of dispute between them to be decided, they go to the Mixed Courts. If an European commits a criminal offence against an Egyptian, he is tried by his Consul, with an appeal possibly to Aix, Ancona, Odessa, or elsewhere, according to the nationality of the accused. If an Egyptian brings a civil suit against another Egyptian, or if he commits any criminal offence whether against a European or another Egyptian, he comes under the jurisdiction of the Native Tribunals, which administer the French code, modified in some respects to suit Egypt. If an Egyptian wishes to prove a will or to dispute a succession, he has to go to the Kadi, who will decide according to the Sheriat.

Enough has now been said to give an idea of the main features of the judicial labyrinth which time and international rivalry have built up in Egypt.

CHAPTER XLIII

THE WORKERS OF THE MACHINE

Importance of persons rather than of systems—The British Consul-General—Tewfik Pasha—The Prime Ministers—Chérif Pasha—Nubar Pasha—Riaz Pasha—Mustapha Pasha Fehmi.

An endeavour has been made in the four preceding chapters to give some idea of the machinery of Government in Egypt in so far as the different parts of the machine can be described by reference to documents setting forth the official functions which are assigned to the various individuals and corporations who collectively make or, at one time, made up the governing body. This description is, however, incomplete; indeed, in some respects it is almost misleading; for allusion has so far only been made to those portions of the State machinery whose functions can be described with some degree of precision. There are, however, other portions of that machinery whose functions are incapable of exact definition, but whose existence is none the less real. Whether, in fact, the whole machine works well or ill depends in no small degree upon the action of those parts of the machinery which, to a superficial observer, might appear unnecessary, if not detrimental to its efficient working. In the Egyptian body politic, the unseen is often more important than the seen. Notably, of late years a vague but preponderant power has been vested in the hands of the British Consul-General. The defects in this system of government are obvious. Its only justification is that, under the existing condition of affairs in Egypt, it is impossible to substitute anything better in its place.

I proceed to give a sketch of the duties of the British Consul-General, but inasmuch as during the greater portion of the period of which this history treats, I occupied the post of Consul-General, I must, for obvious reasons, leave it to others to appreciate the manner in which those duties were performed.

Looking to the general condition of Egyptian society; to the unscrupulous methods by which it was customary to advance personal aims; to the untruthfulness, corruption, and intrigue with which Egyptian society was honeycombed; and finally, to the fact that whatever pseudo-civilisation existed in Egypt was often tainted by reason of its having drawn its inspirations from those portions of the European social system which are least worthy of imitation,—it always appeared to me that the first and most important duty of the British representative in Egypt was, by example and precept, to set up a high standard of morality, both in his public and private life, and thus endeavour to raise the standard of those around him. If I have in any way succeeded in this endeavour; if I have helped to purge Egyptian administration of corruption; if it is gradually dawning on the Egyptian mind that honesty is not only the most honourable but also the most paying policy, and that lying and intrigue curse the liar and intriguer as well as his victim,—I owe the success, in so far as public matters are concerned, to the co-operation of a body of high-minded British officials who have persistently held up to all with whom they have been brought in contact a standard of probity heretofore unknown in Egypt, and, in so far as social life is concerned, I owed it, until cruel death intervened to sever the tie which bound us together, mainly to the gentle yet commanding influence of her who first instigated me to write this book.

The duty of a diplomatic agent in a foreign country is to carry out to the best of his ability the policy of the Government which he serves. My main difficulty in Egypt was that the British Government never had any definite policy which was capable of execution; they were, indeed, at one time constantly striving to square the circle, that is to say, they were endeavouring to carry out two policies which were irreconcilable, namely, the policy of reform, and the counter-policy of evacuation. The British Government are not to be blamed on this account. The circumstances were of a nature to preclude the possibility of adopting a clear-cut line of action, which would have enabled the means to be on all occasions logically adapted to the end.

I never received any general instructions for my guidance during the time I held the post of British Consul-General in Egypt, and I never asked for any such instructions, for I knew that it was useless for me to do so. My course of action was decided according to the merits of each case with which I had to deal. Sometimes I spurred the unwilling Egyptian along the path of reform. At other times, I curbed the impatience of the British reformer. Sometimes I had to explain to the old-world Mohammedan, the Mohammedan of the Sheriât, the elementary differences between the principles of government in vogue in the seventh and in the nineteenth centuries. At other times, I had to explain to the young Gallicised Egyptian that the principles of an ultra-Republican Government were not applicable in their entirety to the existing phase of Egyptian society, and that, when we speak of the rights of man, some distinction has necessarily to be made in practice between a European spouting nonsense through the medium of a fifth-rate newspaper in his own country, and man in the person of a ragged Egyptian fellah, possessed of a sole garment, and who is unable to read a newspaper in any language whatsoever. I had to support the reformer sufficiently to prevent him from being discouraged, and sufficiently also to enable him to carry into execution all that was essential in his reforming policy. I had to check the reformer when he wished to push his reforms so far as to shake the whole political fabric[1] in his endeavour to overcome the tiresome and, to his eyes, often trumpery obstacles in his path, and thus lay bare to the world that measures which were dictated in the true interests of Egypt were opposed by many who had, by accident or by the political cant of the day, been elevated to the position of being the putative representatives of Egyptian public opinion. I had to support the supremacy of the Sultan and, at the same time, to oppose any practical Turkish interference in the administration, which necessarily connoted a relapse into barbarism. I had at one time to do nothing inconsistent with a speedy return to Egyptian self-government, or, at all events, a return to government by the hybrid coterie of Cairo, which flaunts before the world as the personification of Egyptian autonomy; whilst, at the same time, I was well aware that, for a long time to come, European guidance will be essential if the administration is to be conducted on sound principles. I had at times to

[1] Sir John Seeley (*Growth of British Policy*, ii. p. 323), speaking of William III., says: "The main reason why his work has proved so strangely durable is that it was never excessive. He had a wise parsimony in action. . . . The masterpieces of the statesman's art are for the most part not acts, but abstinences from action." A somewhat similar view was frequently advanced by Burke.

retire into my diplomatic shell, and to pose as one amongst many representatives of foreign Powers. At other times, I had to step forward as the representative of the Sovereign whose soldiers held Egypt in their grip. At one time, I had to defend Egypt against European aggression, and, not unfrequently, I had in the early days of the occupation to defend the British position against foreign attack. I had to keep in touch with the well-intentioned, generally reasonable, but occasionally ill-informed public opinion of England, when I knew that the praise or blame of the British Parliament and press was a very faulty standard by which to judge the wisdom or unwisdom of my acts. I had to maintain British authority and, at the same time, to hide as much as possible the fact that I was maintaining it. I had a military force at my disposal, which I could not use save in the face of some grave emergency. I had to work through British agents over whom I possessed no control, save that based on personal authority and moral suasion. I had to avoid any step which might involve the creation of European difficulties by reason of local troubles. I had to keep the Egyptian question simmering, and to avoid any action which might tend to force on its premature consideration, and I had to do this at one time when all, and at another time when some of the most important Powers were more or less opposed to British policy. Lastly, the most heterogeneous petty questions were continually coming before me. If a young British officer was cheated at cards, I had to get him out of his difficulties. If a slave girl wanted to marry, I had to bring moral pressure on her master or mistress to give their consent. If a Jewish sect wished for official recognition from the Egyptian Government, I was expected to obtain it, and to explain to an Egyptian Minister all I knew of the difference between Ashkenazian and Sephardic practices. If the inhabitants of some remote village in Upper Egypt were discontented with their Sheikh, they appealed to me. I have had to write telegrams and despatches about the most miscellaneous subjects—about the dismissal of the Khedive's English coachman, about preserving the lives of Irish informers from the Clan-na-Gael conspirators, and about the tenets of the Abyssinian Church in respect to the Procession of the Holy Ghost. I have been asked to interfere in order to get a German missionary, who had been guilty of embezzlement, out of prison; in order to get a place for the French and Italian Catholics to bury their dead; in order to get a dead Mohammedan of great sanctity exhumed; in order to prevent a female member of the Khedivial family from striking her husband over the mouth with a slipper; and in order to arrange a marriage between two other members of the same family whom hard-hearted relatives kept apart. I have had to take one English maniac in my own carriage to a Lunatic Asylum; I have caused another to be turned out of the English church; and I have been informed that a third and remarkably muscular madman was on his way to my house, girt with a towel round his loins, and bearing a poker in his hands with the intention of using that implement on my head. I have been asked by an Egyptian fellah to find out the whereabouts of his wife who had eloped; and by a German professor to send him at once six live electric shad-fish, from the Nile. To sum up the situation in a few words, I had not, indeed, to govern Egypt, but to assist in the government of the country without the appearance of doing so and without any legitimate authority over the agents with whom I had to deal.

Under these somewhat bewildering circumstances, the only general principles which I was able to lay down for my own guidance were, first, to settle all purely local matters on the spot, with as little reference as possible to London; secondly, to refer for instructions in respect to any matter which was calculated either to raise diplomatic questions outside the local sphere of interest, or to attract serious attention in Parliament. On the whole, I think it may be said that this system worked as well as could, under the very peculiar circumstances of the situation, have been expected. A middle course was steered between the extremes of centralisation and decentralisation.

It is clear that the working of a nondescript Government, such as that which has existed in Egypt since 1882, must depend mainly on the personal characteristics of the individuals who are at the head of affairs. The principal person who figured on the Egyptian stage during the first nine years of the British occupation was the late Khedive, Tewfik Pasha.

The best friends of Tewfik Pasha would probably not contend that he was a great man or an ideal Khedive. There was, in fact, no real greatness about him. He was a monogamist, and thus set a good example to his countrymen. He was an indulgent and well-intentioned father who endeavoured to educate his children well. He acquired a reputation for devotion, whilst he was devoid of any tinge of the intolerance with which devout Islamism is sometimes tainted. His piety kept him in touch with his Moslem subjects, and thus constituted a political factor of some importance. Judged by the standard of his surroundings, he was loyal and straightforward. Like most of his countrymen, he would shirk responsibility, and would endeavour to throw as much as he could on the shoulders of others. He would complain of the number of Europeans in the Egyptian service, and when any European asked him for a place, he would reply that personally he would be delighted to grant the request, but that some British authority prevented him from following the benevolent dictates of his heart. He was apathetic, and wanting in initiative, but, when forced to take a decision, would not unfrequently show a good deal of dignified common sense and shrewdness. He was kind-hearted, and even at times displayed some signs of gratitude for services rendered to him, a quality which is rare in an Oriental ruler. Warned by the example of his father, he shunned extravagance to the extent, indeed, of being occasionally accused of avarice, but he sometimes performed acts of real generosity. There was little of the typical Oriental despot in Tewfik Pasha's character. He professed a deep, and, without doubt, genuine dislike to all arbitrary, oppressive, or cruel acts. He was never personally responsible for the commission of any such act, although it may well be that from apathy and negligence he allowed injustice to be occasionally perpetrated in his name. He was not highly educated. He rarely, if ever, read a book, but he studied the newspapers; he conversed with all sorts and conditions of men; he was fairly quick in mastering any facts which were explained to him, and in picking up the thread of an argument. From the point of view of intellectual acuteness, he was probably rather above the average of his countrymen. He obtained, not by study but by practical experience in dealing with men and things, a fair education of a nature which is useful to a man occupying a high public position. Like most of his countrymen, he would yield a ready assent to any high-sounding general principle. In practice, he would often fail to see that some action, which it was proposed to take, was at variance with the principle to which he had assented; nevertheless, when the dissonance between the particular act and the principle was brought home to him, he would generally, by some process of reasoning, which would be unfamiliar, if not incomprehensible, to the clear-cut European mind, arrive at the conclusion that the commission of the act was reprehensible. His conduct during the events of 1882 showed that he was not wanting in courage. On the whole, it may be said that, if Tewfik Pasha's virtues were mediocre, his faults were of a venial character. If he excited none of the admiration due to moral greatness or to high intellectual qualities, neither did he excite reprobation by sinking below the moral and intellectual standard of his surroundings. He was morally and intellectually respectable, and, considered as a man rather than as a ruler of men, he met with the qualified commendation which is usually meted out to respectability. His character and conduct were not of a nature to excite enthusiasm on his behalf. On the other hand, they rarely formed the subject of severe condemnation. In the majority of cases which attracted public attention, the faint praise, which is scarcely distinguishable from an implication of blame, was accorded to him. He probably deserved more praise than he ever obtained. He honestly wished to do his duty. He was really interested in the welfare of his subjects, but he was bewildered by the involved nature of his position, and did not see clearly how his duty could best be performed. For this he may be pardoned, more especially when it is remembered that he had no experience of the world outside Egypt. Tewfik Pasha never visited Europe.

If he was not a great man, neither was he an

ideal Khedive. If he had been a man of exceptionally firm will, high character, and acute intellect, he would have put himself at the head of the policy of reform in Egypt; he would have asserted his own authority; he would have shown no jealousy of the Englishmen who were employed in his service; he would have co-operated actively with them in the cause of reform, and he would have forced the Egyptians in his service to yield a similar loyal co-operation. Tewfik Pasha did not possess the strength of character to adopt a bold policy of this sort, and perhaps it would have been Utopian to expect that he should have done so.

Although, however, Tewfik Pasha was not an ideal Khedive, nevertheless, looking to all the circumstances of the time, and to the characteristics of Oriental rulers generally, it may be said that he possessed, in a somewhat exceptional degree, many qualities which singularly fitted him to occupy the post he held during the time he held it. Under the régime of a fanatical Moslem, or of a man of arbitrary temperament and despotic tendencies, or of a feeble voluptuary indifferent to everything which did not minister to his own pleasures—all types which are common in the history of Oriental countries—the difficulties in the way of launching Egypt on the path of progress would have been greatly increased. Tewfik Pasha possessed the negative virtue that he answered to none of these descriptions, and, under the circumstances, this was a virtue of incalculable value. But he possessed more than negative virtues. He could lay claim to some good qualities of a positive character. If he did not take any active part in initiating reforms, he was content that others should do so for him. If he could not lead the reformers, he had no objection to following their lead. If he did not afford any very active assistance to the small band of Englishmen who were laying the foundations of a prosperous future for Egypt, neither did he interfere actively to place obstacles in their path; indeed, he often used his influence to remove obstacles. His position was one of great difficulty. On the one hand, it was dangerous to oppose the English, and, moreover, he was sufficiently intelligent to see that it was contrary to his own interests and to those of his country to do so. On the other hand, if he threw himself into the arms of the English, he was sure to lose popularity amongst certain influential sections of his own countrymen. The natural result was that Tewfik Pasha developed a considerable talent for trimming. The circumstances of the time were, indeed, such that he could scarcely with prudence adopt any other line of policy; and, as a trimmer, he played his part remarkably well. He afforded an admirable link between the Englishman and the Egyptian, and he often performed useful work in moderating the views of either side. In the performance of this task, he naturally came in for a good deal of criticism from both quarters. He might often have said:

In moderation placing all my glory,
While Tories call me Whig, and Whigs a Tory.

Moreover, Tewfik Pasha possessed another very valuable quality. He knew his country and his countrymen well. It was not in vain that Arábi had marched with horse, foot, and artillery into the square of Abdin Palace, and had imposed his will on his reluctant Sovereign. It was not in vain that he had listened to the inflated rubbish talked by would-be patriots about free institutions, which were uncongenial to the soil of Egypt. He had laid these matters to heart. He knew the ignorance and credulity of the mass of the population. He recognised the danger of fanning the smouldering embers of Moslem fanaticism. He appreciated the difficulties of his position, and he knew that if he did not lean on the strong arm of England, many of those who knelt at his feet would be ready, should the occasion arise and should they see their own profit in doing so, to turn on him and rend him. He was deeply impressed with the fact that he owed his position to British interference. He recognised his weakness, and he knew that, should he ever incur the serious displeasure of England, that two-handed engine at the door, in the shape of the British fleet and the British army, stood ready to strike once and strike no more. Thus, though he would coquette with those who urged him to oppose the English, he never allowed himself to be pushed too far in this direction. I once had to remind him that Ismail Pasha was on the shores of the Bosphorus, and that his return to Cairo was not altogether outside the verge of practical politics, upon which Tewfik Pasha made the significant remark: "Un Ministre on peut toujours changer, mais le Khédive—c'est autre chose." A change of Ministry shortly afterwards occurred, for Tewfik Pasha was wise enough never to identify himself fully with the policy of any Minister. He knew that a change of Ministry was an admirable political safety-valve, and when he felt his own position in any danger, he very wisely did not hesitate to send a ministerial scapegoat into the wilderness.

I bear Tewfik's name in kindly and respectful remembrance, for though I daresay he winced under the pressure, which I occasionally brought to bear on him, my relations with him were very pleasant and friendly, neither did they in any way redound to his discredit. The idea, which under the influence of the Anglophobe party took some root in Egypt, to the effect that he was a mere tool in my hands, is wholly untrue and most unjust to his memory. I used to discuss matters with him. When any difference of opinion occurred, I yielded to him quite as often—indeed, I think more often—than he yielded to me. We generally came to some equitable compromise between our conflicting views.

When he died, he was just beginning to reap the fruits of the reforming policy. He had become popular by reason of the reforms, although, as a matter of fact, he had not taken any leading part in effecting them. He acquiesced in them of his own free will, but sometimes with an unwilling mind,—ἑκὼν ἀέκοντί γε θυμῷ. His death was a great loss to Egypt. Whatever may have been his faults, he deserves a somewhat prominent niche in the Valhalla of Oriental potentates. Posterity will be unjust if they forget that it was during the reign of Tewfik Pasha that Egypt was first started on the road to prosperity, and that he took not, indeed, the most leading part in the rehabilitation of his country, but still a part of which his descendants may well be proud; for, without his abstention from opposition, and without his support, albeit it was at times rather lukewarm, the efforts of the British reformer would have been far less productive of result than has actually been the case. Had he been a man of stronger character and more marked individuality, it is possible that his country would have progressed less rapidly. He should be remembered as the Khedive who allowed Egypt to be reformed in spite of the Egyptians.

The leading personage in the Egyptian political world is the Khedive. The Prime Minister, however, also occupies a position of great importance. After the bombardment of Alexandria in

1882, Chérif Pasha was named to this office. In January 1884, he was succeeded by Nubar Pasha, who remained in office till June 1888. On Nubar Pasha's fall, Riaz Pasha became Prime Minister. His Ministry lasted till May 1891. His successor was Mustapha Pasha Fehmi. On January 7, 1892, Tewfik Pasha died. His son and successor, Abbas Pasha, kept Mustapha Pasha Fehmi in office till January 1893, when he was succeeded by Riaz Pasha, who, again, in April 1894, was succeeded by Nubar Pasha. In the autumn of 1895, Nubar Pasha's failing health obliged him to quit office. He was succeeded by Mustapha Pasha Fehmi.

Of Chérif Pasha little need be said. He was a Minister of the pre-occupation days rather than of the occupation. His character is almost sufficiently described in the narrative given in a previous portion of this work. To what has been already said it is only necessary to add that Chérif Pasha was the least Egyptian of any of the Moslem Prime Ministers of recent times. He was a pure Turk who, in early life, had come from Constantinople. The ordinary Turco-Egyptian is generally more Egyptian than Turk. Chérif Pasha, on the other hand, was a Turco-Egyptian in the first stage of Egyptianisation. It is true that he favoured Egyptian semi-autonomy, and that he viewed with dislike any increased interference by the Sultan in Egyptian affairs; but he was out of sympathy with the pure Egyptians, whom he regarded as a conquered race; he was, in fact, the incarnation of the policy of "Egypt for the Turco-Egyptians." Whatever was not Turkish in his character, was French. He had assimilated a good deal of the *bonhomie* which sometimes, and of the keen sense of the ridiculous which more frequently is to be found amongst the French, but he never lost the predominant characteristics of a Turkish aristocrat. He was proud, courageous, honest after his way, and, in his public life, always negligent of detail and sometimes of principle. Occasionally, he would emit flashes of true statesmanship, but he was too careless, too apathetic, and too wanting in persistence to carry out his own principles in practice. With all his faults, he was, on the whole, one of the most sympathetic figures on the political stage of Egypt during recent times.

Nubar Pasha was by far the most interesting of latter-day Egyptian politicians. Intellectually, he towered above his competitors. Bearing in mind, however, the intellectual calibre of those competitors, he deserves more than such faint praise as this. He was, indeed, a bad administrator, and this defect detracted from his political usefulness, more especially by reason of the fact that, according to his own admission,[1] Egypt stood in need of administrators rather than of statesmen. Nevertheless, even in Egypt some statesmanlike qualities are demanded from those who are at the head of affairs, and Nubar Pasha could unquestionably lay claim to the possession of qualities, which can be characterised as statesmanlike.

He was a thorough Oriental, but, unlike many Orientals, his foreign education had not resulted in his assimilating the bad and discarding the more worthy portions of European civilisation. He was far too great a man to be attracted by all the flimsy tinsel and moral obliquity which lie on the surface of European civilisation, that is to say, the civilisation of the Paris Boulevards, whose principal apostles are usually European or Levantine adventurers. He saw all these things, but unlike the Gallicised Egyptian, who is too often

[1] *Vide ante*, p. 262.

lured to his moral destruction by them, the only effect which they produced on his more elevated mind was to make him ask himself—how can I protect my country of adoption against the inroads of the quick-witted but unscrupulous European? It is clear that Egypt is to be Europeanised; how can this process best be effected?

The answer which Nubar Pasha gave to these questions was worthy of a statesman. He rightly differentiated the divergences between Eastern and Western systems of government. Personal rule, he said to himself, must give way before a reign of law. The Egyptians must learn from Europe how to protect themselves both against the arbitrary caprices of their rulers, and against the advancing and somewhat turbid tide of Europeans with whom they are destined to be associated. They can only do so by assimilating that respect for the law which forms the keystone of the arch on which European systems of government rest. It cannot be contended that this idea was very original, or that any great mental effort was required for its conception. But to Nubar Pasha belongs the credit that he was the first Egyptian statesman who conceived it, or, at all events, who endeavoured to carry it into practice. Whatever may have been the blemishes in Nubar Pasha's character, and whatever may be the defects in the judicial institutions which he created, it should never be forgotten that he first endeavoured to bring home to the Egyptian governing class and to the Egyptian people that, whereas might, whether in the person of despotic Khedives or dictatorial diplomatists, had heretofore been right in Egypt, the foundation of good government in any community pretending to call itself civilised is that the maxim should be reversed, and that might should yield to right.

Nubar Pasha had, therefore, no difficulty in grasping a European principle. Indeed, the wider the principle, the more readily he grasped it, for he dearly loved dealing in generalities. His defect was that, having once got hold of a sound principle, he would not unfrequently ride it to death. He did not sufficiently adapt it to the circumstances with which he had to deal. Or, again, he would sometimes think that, having enunciated the principle, he had done all that was required of him. He rarely endeavoured to acquaint himself thoroughly with facts, or to see that the practice was made to conform with the principle which he had adopted. Moreover, he would sometimes readily assent to some wide general principle without any serious intention of applying it at all, and he was led to do this all the more because his subtle intellect was not slow to perceive that Europeans, and especially Englishmen, are liable to be soothed by plausible, albeit often fallacious generalities.

Nubar Pasha was a brilliant conversationalist. He possessed a marvellous power of imparting a character of perfect verisimilitude to the series of half-truths, bordering on fiction, which he was wont to pour into the ears of his interested listener. The educated European was struck by his apparently wide grasp and bold generalisations, the fallacies of which could often only be detected by those who had a perfect acquaintance with the facts. The European would readily fall a victim to the fascinating manners, the graceful diction, the subtle reasoning, and deferential deportment, which distinguish the peculiar type of Oriental of whom Nubar Pasha was perhaps the most typical representative. It was only after experience and reflection that he would perceive that, the premises being incorrect, the conclusions of his teacher in Egyptian affairs were often erroneous, and that the broad enunciations of principle with which he had been charmed were intended more for academic discussion in the closet than for practical decision in the Council Chamber.

Nubar Pasha's readiness, his versatility, the audacity with which he would defend the most glaring fallacies, and his great command of language, acquired for him some reputation as a diplomatist. To a certain extent, this reputation was well deserved. On many occasions, he showed himself to be a skilful negotiator. He was especially skilful in throwing a cloud of ambiguity over his meaning and his intentions. He was a master of the French language, and one of the peculiarities of that language is that, although it is eminently precise when the writer or speaker wishes to give precision to his thoughts, on the other hand, it is full of ambiguous expressions, which afford a powerful help to a diplomatist who wishes to leave open some back door through which to retreat from the engagements which he is apparently taking, and this was not unfrequently Nubar Pasha's case. He would probably have been more successful as a diplomatist in the eighteenth than in the nineteenth century. Modern diplomacy is not mere jugglery, neither is the most successful diplomatist he who can best throw dust in the eyes of his opponent. Under the influence of publicity, and perhaps to some extent of Prince Bismarck, the whole art, if diplomacy can be dignified by such a name, has been simplified; perhaps some, including Nubar Pasha himself, would say that it has been brutalised. The affairs between nation and nation are now conducted on more business-like principles than heretofore. A plain answer is required to a plain question, and although some tricks of the trade still survive, they are, by comparison with the past, of little practical utility. It was Nubar Pasha's misfortune that, during the latter part of his career, he had to deal principally with a European nation whose members are distinguished for their straightforward mode of conducting business. In a way, he understood the English character. He once made a significant and characteristic remark. "L'Anglais," he said, "est très naïf, mais lorsqu'on pense qu'on l'a trompé, tout d'un coup il se tourne et il vous flanque un terrible coup de pied quelque part." But although he knew that intrigue was of little real use against the Englishman, he could not resist the temptation of intriguing. He could not abandon his favourite weapon of offence and defence. The natural result ensued. In spite of his real talents, his suavity, his earnest devotion to civilised principles of government, and his profuse professions of friendship and esteem, he inspired but little confidence amongst those Englishmen with whom he was brought in contact. They mistrusted him, perhaps more than he deserved to be mistrusted. He could never understand the feelings which his behaviour excited in the minds of Englishmen. He went to his grave with a hardy and unimpaired belief in the political virtues of finesse bordering on duplicity.

Nubar Pasha's political views during the early period of the British occupation of Egypt were characteristic. He was in favour of the occupation. He saw that a British garrison was necessary to maintain order. "If," he frequently said, "the British troops are withdrawn, I shall leave Egypt with the last battalion." But, on the other hand, he was opposed to what he termed the "administrative occupation." In other words, what he wanted was a military force, in whom perfect reliance could be placed, to keep him in power, whilst he was to be allowed a free hand in everything connected with the civil administration of the country. Hence his extreme civility to all British military officers, whose praises he was never weary of singing. What, indeed, for all the purposes which he had at heart, could be more perfect than the presence in Egypt of a thoroughly disciplined force, commanded by young men who took no interest in local politics, and who occupied themselves exclusively with polo and cricket? Hence, also, his constant opposition during his first period of office (1884-88) to the British civilians in the Egyptian service and to myself, as the British diplomatic representative who supported them. Our action jarred terribly with the Nubarian programme. It is strange that a really able man, such as Nubar Pasha, should have thought his programme capable of realisation, and that he should not have seen the impossibility of the British Government looking on as passive spectators whilst a British force was in Egypt, and allowing the maladministration of the Egyptian Pashas to remain practically unchecked. And this would certainly have been the result of acquiescence in Nubar Pasha's system of government.[1]

With any ordinary degree of prudence, Nubar Pasha could have remained Prime Minister for an indefinite period, and it is a pity that he did not do so, for his talents were far superior to those of his competitors. His fall in 1888 came about in this fashion. For some four years, I got on fairly well with him. On many occasions, I afforded him strong support. I shut my eyes to a good deal of intrigue, which I knew was going on around me. In an evil moment for himself, Nubar

[1] In illustration of the truth of this remark, I may refer to what happened about the Commissions of Brigandage (*vide ante*, p. 289 and *infra*, p. 405).

Pasha went to England. He had an interview with Lord Salisbury at which I was present. To my surprise, for he had not given me any warning of his intentions, he burst out into a violent tirade against the British officials in Egypt in general, and against Sir Edgar Vincent and myself in particular. All this produced very little effect on Lord Salisbury, but the ultimate result—for this was only the beginning of a breach which subsequently widened—was such as Nubar Pasha hardly anticipated. He thought he was doing a clever stroke of business. What he really did was to bring about his own downfall. He thought to pose as the defender of Egyptian rights against British aggression, and thus to mitigate the prejudices entertained against him by the Mohammedan population by reason of his race and creed. What he really did was to open the mouths of all his numerous enemies in Egypt, who had only remained silent because they thought that, strong in the support of England, his position was unassailable. Nubar Pasha failed to see that which was apparent to others possessed of none of his intellectual subtlety, namely, that the English were his natural allies, and that directly he broke up the alliance his fall was inevitable. When once it became apparent that he could no longer rely on British support, Tewfik Pasha seized on some trivial pretext for dismissing him.[1]

[1] I did nothing to hasten the downfall of Nubar Pasha. The European situation was at that time (1888) somewhat critical. Lord Salisbury, who was then in office, was, therefore, rather desirous of postponing any crisis in Egyptian affairs. On February 17, 1888, he wrote to me: "I have asked you by telegraph to try and manage to postpone any breach with Nubar to a more convenient season. . . . I believe you are right in this controversy, but if I thought you wrong, I should still think it impossible to retreat before Nubar in the face of the whole East. It is not, therefore, from any doubt about supporting you that I urge you to keep the peace for the present, but because I do not wish our administration in Egypt to be the cause to which the long European war is to be ascribed by the future historian."

I really believe that I regretted Nubar Pasha's fall more than he did himself. His Protean changes, his emotional character, and his ignorance of the rudiments of many of the administrative questions with which he had to deal, were at times exasperating. Nevertheless, I could not help liking him. It was pleasant to have to deal with a man of real ability, who could converse rationally and who, if he did not understand much which should be familiar to any politician and administrator, could at all events grasp the main lines of action which should guide the Government of a civilised community. Moreover, there was an indescribable charm about Nubar Pasha which was almost irresistible. I have never known any one more persuasive, or more skilled in the art of making the worse appear the better reason. I used often to half believe him, when I knew full well that he was trying to dupe me. I felt towards him much what Shakespeare felt towards his faithless mistress :—

When my love swears that she is made of truth,
I do believe her, though I know she lies.

I admired his talents, and I never could forget that, in spite of his defects, he possessed some unquestionably statesmanlike qualities. If he had only recognised the fact that in the government of the world mere intellectual gifts are not all-powerful, and that high character and reputation also exercise a potent influence over mankind, he would have been a really great man.

I find some difficulty in writing about Riaz Pasha, not only because, I am glad to say (1907), he is still living, but also because he is a personal friend for whom I entertain the highest regard and esteem. I may say, however, that Nubar Pasha and Riaz Pasha were the Egyptian representatives of two widely different schools of political and social thought. Nubar Pasha recognised the fact that there was only one true civilisation in the world, and that was the civilisation of Europe. Accordingly, he set to work to Europeanise the main framework of Egyptian institutions by means which were sometimes wise, and sometimes, possibly, the reverse, but he never entertained any doubt as to the nature of the object to be attained. Riaz Pasha, on the other hand, represented the apotheosis of Islamism. Why, he thought, should not the *Saturnia regna*, when Moslems were really great, return? He would barely recognise the necessity of the least European assistance in the process of Egyptian regeneration. "Seul," he said to himself, "je ferai le bonheur de mon peuple." He held that Mohammedans and Mohammedanism contain within themselves all that is needed for their own regeneration. It would be both unjust and ungenerous not to extend some sympathy to views of this sort. It would be too much to expect that a fervid Moslem and a sincere Egyptian patriot—and Riaz Pasha answers both of these descriptions—should readily accept the facts, which are almost certainly true, namely, that Islamism as a social and political system—though not as a religion—is moribund, that the judicial and administrative procedures common amongst Moslems are so closely interwoven with their religion as to be almost inseparable the one from the other, and that for many a long year to come the Egyptians will be incapable of governing themselves on civilised principles.

Riaz Pasha's political life may be divided into four different phases: first, as a Minister and as a Commissioner of Inquiry under Ismail Pasha; secondly, as Prime Minister under Tewfik Pasha during the period of the Anglo-French Control; thirdly, as Prime Minister under Tewfik Pasha during the time of the British occupation; and, fourthly, as Prime Minister under Abbas II.

He appeared to most advantage in the first phase. He was indignant at the ruin which Ismail Pasha brought on his country. He stood out boldly as a reformer at a time when a reforming Egyptian could not state his true opinions without risk to his life and property. Whatever faults Riaz Pasha may have subsequently committed, it should never be forgotten that during this phase of his career he showed a great deal of real courage and foresight.[1]

In the early portions of the second phase, that is to say, the period of the Anglo-French Control, Riaz Pasha also showed to advantage. He was placed in such a position that his dislike to European interference was of necessity tempered by the consideration that the Europeans, with whom he was principally associated, were very useful. The Controllers stood between him and the hungry creditors of the Egyptian Government, and Riaz Pasha was aware that he did not possess sufficient technical knowledge to evolve order out of the existing financial chaos without European assistance. During the later portion of the Control period, he had to deal with a question which possibly required higher qualities, and a greater degree of political insight, than any that he possessed. He was swept off his legs by the Arábi movement, of which he failed to see the importance until too late.

The third phase of Riaz Pasha's political career was when, in succession to Nubar Pasha, he was made Prime Minister by Tewfik during the period of the British occupation. At first matters went fairly well. Riaz had some advantages over Nubar Pasha. He was by far the better administrator of the two. He knew Egypt well; he was himself a

[1] *Vide ante,* vol. i. p. 45.

first-rate practical agriculturist, and could discuss all matters bearing on the condition of the agricultural classes with a thorough knowledge of his subject. He exercised great authority over the Egyptian officials. The fact that a devout Mohammedan was at the head of affairs produced a tranquillising effect on Mohammedan public opinion. On the other hand, he was too inelastic to manage so delicate a machine as the government of Egypt during the occupation period. He did not altogether appreciate the change which time and the political situation of the day had effected in the system of governing the country. He failed to see that, under a reign of law, he could not always have his own way, for Riaz Pasha, although he had a certain rough idea of justice, had but little respect for the law. He thought that when laws or regulations clashed with his ideas of what was right and wrong, they should be broken. The result of his peculiar temperament and habits of thought was that, after a while, he quarrelled with almost every one, European and Egyptian, and produced a state of administrative friction, which rendered his retirement from office inevitable.

The fourth phase of Riaz's career was when he was Minister under Abbas II.—a period with the history of which I am not attempting to deal in the present work.

To sum up, Riaz Pasha is a staunch Moslem, possessed of intellectual qualities which are certainly equal, and of moral qualities which are decidedly superior to those of the class to which he belongs. Notably, his physical and moral fearlessness deserve high commendation. It were well for the cause of Egyptian patriotism, if there were more patriots endowed with the sterling qualities which are conspicuous in Riaz Pasha's rugged, yet very sympathetic character.

The simplicity of Mustapha Pasha Fehmi's character renders it unnecessary to allude to him at any length. Loyal, thoroughly honest, truthful, and courteous, he possesses all the qualities which Englishmen usually associate with the word gentleman. He has been statesmanlike enough to see that the interests of his country would best be served by working loyally with the British officials, instead of opposing them. During his tenure of office, Egypt has made greater progress, both moral and material, than at any previous period.

Having now described the machinery of the Government, and the principal individuals who were entrusted with its working, it would appear logical to deal with the work which the machine produced. Before, however, describing what the English did in Egypt, it will be as well to say something of what they wished to do. The next chapters will, therefore, be devoted to describing that strange phantom which, under the name of British Policy in Egypt, was constantly eluding the grasp both of those to whom it owed its being and of others who endeavoured, from time to time, to understand its true significance. It was not until 1904 that this phantom disappeared, and that a more substantial political creation was substituted in its place.

PART V

BRITISH POLICY IN EGYPT

We trust it may be granted to us to labour for maintaining the interests of the Empire, for promoting the welfare of the Egyptian people, and for doing honest work towards the establishment of the peace and order of the world.

Speech of Mr. Gladstone *in the House of Commons, July* 27, 1882.

CHAPTER XLIV

THE STRUGGLE FOR A POLICY

1882–1883

Intentions of the British Government—Proposal to reduce the garrison—Sir Edward Malet's opinion—Difficulty of combining reform and evacuation—I recommend reduction and concentration at Alexandria—The Government approve of this recommendation—The reduction is countermanded.

It is probable that, if any one had told Lord Granville on the morrow of the battle of Tel-el-Kebir that twenty-five years later a British force would still be garrisoned in Egypt, and that for twenty-two out of those twenty-five years the Egyptian question, in its political aspects, would remain unsettled, he would have ridiculed the idea. For, in truth, in 1882 the British Government had a tolerably clear policy. Its execution was very difficult, but at the time the difficulties did not appear absolutely insurmountable. Their policy was to restore order, to introduce some elementary reforms, and then to withdraw the British troops. The sound of the guns at Tel-el-Kebir had scarcely died away, when Lord Granville requested Sir Edward Malet to send "as soon as possible, suggestions as to the army, finances, and the administration for the future." At that time, "Her Majesty's Government contemplated shortly commencing the withdrawal of the British troops from Egypt."

During the summer of 1883, the British force

numbered about 7000 men. On August 25, 1883, Chérif Pasha addressed a Memorandum to Sir Edward Malet urging, on grounds of economy, that the force should be reduced to 2000 men. Sir Edward Malet agreed that there could be no doubt as to the necessity of economy. "The question," he added, "which unfortunately presents itself, and to which there can be no decisive answer, is whether the existing tranquillity is not mainly due to the presence of the troops." He was unable to recommend so large a reduction as that proposed by Chérif Pasha. "An immediate reduction of 2000 men was," he thought, "the most that should be effected."

On September 6, Lord Granville wrote me a despatch, which reached Cairo simultaneously with my arrival from India. In this despatch, after alluding to Sir Edward Malet's communication, which is quoted above, he went on to say :—

"Her Majesty's Government entirely concur in the desire to reduce the force as far as is consistent with the preservation of public order, but they have been unwilling to take any fresh step for the purpose until they could have the advantage of your opinion. Sir Evelyn Wood has expressed to me personally his belief that the British garrison might be entirely withdrawn from Cairo without disadvantage. The number of troops to be retained elsewhere and their disposition, would be matter for careful consideration. I have to request that you will consult the military authorities, and report fully to me on the subject."

From recollection, and from a perusal of contemporaneous despatches and private letters, I am able to give an accurate account of my frame of mind at this time. I was deeply penetrated with the importance of the step taken by the British Government in sending a military force to Egypt, and I doubted whether the Ministers themselves fully realised its gravity. They saw, indeed, the obvious objections to a permanent occupation of Egypt; they held to the broad lines of Lord Palmerston's policy;[1] but they underrated the difficulties of getting out of the country. Nevertheless, all history was there to prove that when once a civilised Power lays its hand on a weak State in a barbarous or semi-civilised condition, it rarely relaxes its grasp. I was in favour of the policy of evacuation, and I saw that, if the British troops were to be withdrawn, no long delay should be allowed to ensue; otherwise, the occupation might drift insensibly into a condition of permanency. Total and immediate evacuation was, indeed, impossible for the reason given by Sir Edward Malet, that is to say, that by the adoption of such a measure, public tranquillity would be endangered. But although the maintenance of public tranquillity stood first in the order of importance, the question of the withdrawal of the garrison could not be decided with reference to a consideration of this point alone. The question had to be considered in another aspect. What would be the effect of the withdrawal on the future of the country? What prospect was there of Lord Dufferin's programme being carried out if the British troops were withdrawn? I did not see so clearly as at a later period that the alternative policies of reform and evacuation were absolutely irreconcilable, but I had some fairly clear perception of the fact. I saw that the system of government in Egypt had been shaken to its base, and that, if once the British troops were withdrawn, it would be necessary to leave to the Khedive a tolerably free hand in the government of the country. I saw more especially that the Egyptian Government should be allowed full

[1] *Vide ante*, vol. i. p. 92.

freedom in the direction of suppressing any attempt to disturb public tranquillity. What at the time I most feared was that the British Government, under the influence of public opinion in England, would first withdraw their troops and then cry out if the use of the courbash increased, and, generally, if the rough-and-ready means dear to the hearts of Oriental rulers were employed for the maintenance of public order. I wished to warn the Government that if they decided on a policy of evacuation, they must be prepared to turn a deaf ear to the cries, which would, without doubt, be raised both in Parliament and in the press, when the Egyptian Government proceeded to govern according to their own lights.

It was with these feelings uppermost in my mind that on October 9, that is to say, about a month after my arrival in Cairo, I answered the question which Lord Granville had addressed to me on September 6. I began by stating that, after consultation with Sir Frederick Stephenson, I had come to the conclusion that the British garrison could safely be withdrawn from Cairo, and that the total force in Egypt might be reduced to about 3000 men, who should be concentrated at Alexandria. I did not express any opinion on the question of when it would be possible to withdraw the whole of the garrison, but in a private telegram to Lord Granville, dated October 8, I told him that "for the present there could be no question of total withdrawal from Egypt." I dwelt at some length on the state of the country, and, writing with a view to ultimate publication, I indicated in a manner which was sufficiently clear that, if the Egyptian Government were to be left to themselves, they must be allowed to maintain order in their own way.

When my despatch reached London, it created a considerable stir in official circles. It became apparent that, although perhaps the Ministers were themselves aware that they could not attain two irreconcilable objects, they thought it undesirable to place this view of the case before the public. Lord Granville telegraphed to me asking that my despatch should be divided into two, and that the portion which spoke of non-interference with vigorous measures after the withdrawal of the British garrison should be treated separately and confidentially.

I accordingly wrote two despatches. The first, which was very short, dealt with the proposed reduction of the garrison and the withdrawal of the troops from Cairo. This was published.[1] The second, which was longer, dealt with the probable consequences of withdrawal. This was not published. It is, from a historical point of view, a document of some interest. It is reproduced in an Appendix to this chapter.

On November 1, Lord Granville wrote to me that the British Government approved of my recommendation that the British force in Egypt should be reduced to 3000 men, who were to be concentrated at Alexandria. "The British garrison being thus withdrawn from Cairo," it was added, "the main responsibility for preserving order throughout Egypt will, as you point out, devolve upon the Government of the Khedive, and in the execution of that task they may rely upon the full moral support of Her Majesty's Government."

Three weeks later, and before any practical steps had been taken to withdraw the garrison from Cairo, news arrived of the annihilation of General Hicks's army. Lord Granville telegraphed on November 22 directing me, after consultation with Sir Frederick Stephenson and Sir Evelyn Wood, to state my opinion as to whether the existing

[1] See *Egypt*, No. 1 of 1884, pp. 50 51

state of affairs in the Soudan was a cause of danger to Egypt. In that case, I was requested to state my views as to what measures were desirable. In my reply, dated November 24, I said that Sir Frederick Stephenson, Sir Evelyn Wood, and myself were of opinion that "the recent success of the Mahdi was a source of danger to Egypt," that the withdrawal of the garrison from Cairo should be postponed, and that for the time being no reduction should be made in the strength of the British force. On November 25, Lord Granville telegraphed that "the preliminary steps for the withdrawal of the British troops were to be postponed." The postponement has lasted until the day on which I am writing.

It will be observed that during all this time there was no question of total and immediate evacuation. Every responsible authority on the spot was opposed to any such measure, and the Government, although anxious to withdraw entirely, saw that it was impossible to carry the policy of total withdrawal into execution at once. The only question under discussion was whether the garrison should be reduced and the British force concentrated at Alexandria with a view to eventual withdrawal at no remote period. It may be doubted whether, even if the Hicks disaster had not occurred, it would have been possible within a short while to have withdrawn the whole of the British troops. This, however, is mere conjecture. What is more certain is that, when the military power of Egypt in the Soudan was crushed, the last chance of immediate, or nearly immediate, evacuation disappeared. Moreover, it is historically interesting to note that the deathblow to the policy of speedy evacuation was dealt by a statesman who was earnestly desirous to withdraw the British troops. If Lord Granville had not been so fearful of incurring any responsibility in respect to the Soudan on the ground that, in doing so, he might prolong the British occupation of Egypt, and if he had placed a veto on the Hicks expedition, it is conceivable that the British garrison might have been withdrawn after a short time. As it was, Lord Granville, in his desire to shorten the occupation, contributed by his action to its prolongation.

Before leaving this branch of my subject, I should mention that on October 28, that is, between the time when I recommended the concentration at Alexandria, and the arrival of the news of the Hicks disaster, I again urged on Lord Granville, in a private letter, the impossibility of reconciling the two policies of speedy evacuation and reform. I reproduce the whole of this letter. It was as follows :—

"I have now been here long enough to take stock of the main elements of the situation. There is an immense deal to be done, and there are many difficult questions to be solved. Looking at these questions from the point of view of their intrinsic merits, there is no reason why most of them, at all events, should not be solved within a reasonable period. But there is one obstacle which stands in the way of almost every move forward, and that is the necessity of consulting every Power in Europe before any important steps can be taken.

"To take a single instance, the Blue Book on the appointment of the Indemnity Commission last year is a positive curiosity in its way. This question was so simple that three or four people sitting round a table ought to have been able to settle it in half an hour. Yet a voluminous correspondence ensued, and endless delays occurred before Stockholm, Brussels, etc., could be got to agree.

"As matters stand, it will be scarcely possible

to carry out the whole of our programme. On the one hand, we are bound before we go to start Egypt on the high road to good government. We ought not to leave the Egyptian Government in such a position as that they may plead as an excuse for future bad government that their hands are so tied as to render them powerless to execute reforms. On the other hand, we must not, for European, Egyptian, and purely English reasons, stay too long.

"Under present conditions, it is scarcely conceivable that both of these objects should be attained. In fact, the one is almost a contradiction in terms to the other. If we are to wait until all the essential reforms have been carried out by the slow process of consulting each Power separately on every question of detail, we shall wait a very long time, and there will be danger of drifting into a policy of annexation, or something tantamount to it.

"If we cut the knot by withdrawing without having done our work, and leaving Egypt to stew in its own juice of administrative, financial, and economic anarchy, there will be a very considerable risk that something will occur before our backs have long been turned, which will raise up the whole Egyptian question again. I confess I do not see my way out of this dilemma.

"We may, indeed, before long retire without any absolute danger to public order and tranquillity in the immediate future. But surely more than this is, under all the circumstances, expected of us both by Europe and by English public opinion. If we leave a crop of unsettled burning questions behind us, we can never feel any confidence that our hands will not be forced, that is to say, that we may again find ourselves in the position of being obliged to interfere or stand aside whilst others, probably the French, take up the work which we, as it would then appear, had failed to accomplish.

"Getting out of Egypt is a very different problem from getting out of Afghanistan. In the latter case, we had to deal with a country in whose internal administration no one but the Afghans was, to any very considerable extent, concerned. There was no very great difficulty in leaving this quasi-barbarous people to be governed after their own fashion by their quasi-barbarous Governors. Here the foundations of the edifice, which are to be found in the moral and material condition of the people, are scarcely less barbarous than in Afghanistan. But, on these foundations is built a top-heavy and exotic superstructure, such as an enormous external debt, Western law-courts, complete liberty of contract, and, in fact, all the paraphernalia of European civilisation with some of its worst and not many of its best features. I do not suppose that Europe will stand by and let this superstructure fall to pieces.

"We are making very fair progress in all matters which fall within the competence of the Egyptian Government, such as prison reform, local tribunals, etc.

"But as regards international subjects—and all the most important subjects are international—we are almost at an absolute standstill.

"In spite of every effort, we have not yet succeeded in getting the house tax through. After the house tax, comes the professional tax and the stamp duty, each with its own peculiar difficulties.

"The reforms in the Mixed Tribunals and the abolition of the Consular jurisdiction in criminal cases, will probably involve interminable negotiations.

"Then there is the great question of the Law of Liquidation, with all its attendant political difficulties. There is not, I fear, the least chance of our being able to regulate the financial situation without modifying that law. I thought at one time we might manage to arrange matters by getting the consent of the Commissioners of the Debt, but the political objections to the adoption of this course are scarcely less great than if we tried to get the Powers to consent to alter the law itself.

"The question of the debts of the fellaheen cannot be settled without going to the Powers, for whatever is done will almost certainly involve some changes in the code administered by the Mixed Tribunals.[1]

"There are several questions connected with the Daira Sanieh and the Domains which ought to be settled, but here again the international difficulty bars the way.

"Even some subjects which have no direct international character, depend indirectly upon the concord of the Powers. Thus, a considerable capital expenditure on irrigation is almost a necessity; so also is the Soudan Railway. But for both of these money is wanted, and it will be very difficult to find any money until the financial situation is placed on a sound footing.

"You may well ask me why I say all this, which you already know. My reason is to ask you to consider whether it is not possible to apply some remedy to this state of things. Would it not be possible to issue a Circular to the Powers explaining our difficulties, and saying that we did not propose to consult them any more on each detail, but that, when we had put matters straight, we should ask them to accept the settlement *en bloc*, and that we should then at once withdraw our troops?

[1] This question was, many years subsequently, settled without reference to the Powers. An Agricultural Bank was established (see p. 452). In 1883, it would have been scarcely possible to have called such an institution into existence.

"Give me 2000 men and power to settle matters between the English and Egyptian Governments, and I will guarantee that in twelve months there shall not be a British soldier in Egypt, and that the country is put in such a position as to render it very improbable that any Egyptian question will be raised again for many years to come at all events.[1] But if we adhere to our present procedure, I really despair of doing much within any reasonable time—I mean, of course, as regards international questions. As regards purely Egyptian questions, there are plenty of difficulties, but they are not insurmountable.

"I put forward this suggestion with much hesitation. I am aware that the matter cannot be regarded wholly from the point of view of Egyptian internal reform. The general political situation has to be considered, and from this point of view there may be insuperable obstacles to the adoption of any course such as that which I suggest. Anyhow, I think it right to submit to you the aspect of the case which I have set forth in this letter. Your wider knowledge and experience may possibly be able to hit upon some other plan superior to my—possibly crude—suggestion.

"I may add that I am confident that I could, by developing the arguments I have briefly stated here, make out a very strong case for taking a new point of departure, but it would, of course, be useless for me to write a public despatch in this sense, unless I thought that some practical good might come out of it."

In other words, what I proposed amounted to the temporary assumption on the part of England of the task of governing Egypt. On November 9,

[1] This forecast of what was possible was unquestionably much too sanguine.

Lord Granville acknowledged the receipt of this letter. "It would require," he said, "some time to consider and answer your powerful but gloomy view of the situation in Egypt. I am afraid the remedy you suggest is too drastic, but I will reflect over what you say, and let you know my impressions, and those of others. I have escaped the Lord Mayor's dinner. Gladstone will speak shortly, and will only deal with generalities on Egyptian questions."

On November 14, Lord Granville again wrote to me as follows: "I go to Stratton[1] on Saturday, when I hope to talk over with Gladstone and Northbrook your very important letter of, I think, the 24th October. I hope you will think what Gladstone said in concert with me about Egypt at the Mansion House was harmless."

Finally, on November 30, Lord Granville wrote: "I have talked over your views on the Liquidation Law with Gladstone and with Northbrook. We do not see our way to acting *en bloc*, but it might be possible, particularly after recent events, for you to perfect a scheme on any of the most important subjects, with a view to our getting the consent of the Powers."

This was, of course, tantamount to a rejection of my proposal. I did not for many years make any other having for its object a radical change in the political status of Great Britain in Egypt. Henceforward, I devoted myself entirely to the task of evolving order out of chaos, under such political and administrative conditions as existed at the time when the occupation took place. It was not for some years that I felt at all sanguine of success.

From the time when the orders for concentration at Alexandria were countermanded, all idea of speedy evacuation was abandoned. The

[1] Lord Northbrook's country seat in Hampshire.

attention of the British and Egyptian Governments was for the next two years almost wholly directed to the affairs of the Soudan. During this period, the British officials in Cairo were slowly and laboriously taking some tentative steps in the direction of reducing the Egyptian administrative chaos into order. By the time the Soudan question had passed out of an acute stage, Egypt had been fairly launched on the path of reform. The policy, which as a *pis aller* I had suggested as possible in 1883, of allowing the Khedive and the Turco-Egyptians to govern after their own fashion, had become more than ever difficult of execution, for the country had advanced, whilst the intelligence and governing capacity of the ruling classes had almost stood still. The Turco-Egyptians, who might perhaps have been able to govern the country after a rude fashion in 1883, were incapable of doing so when once the full tide of civilisation had set strongly in. Before long, we had drifted into a position which necessitated the presence of a British garrison, not in order to admit of reforms being initiated and carried out, but in order to prevent a relapse into the confusion which existed in the pre-reforming days. That is the present stage of the Egyptian question.

Two efforts were made subsequent to 1883, one by Mr. Gladstone's Government, and the other by the Government of Lord Salisbury, to deal with the larger aspects of the Egyptian question. To these reference will now be made.

APPENDIX

Despatch from Sir Evelyn Baring to Earl Granville

Cairo, *October* 9, 1883.

My Lord—It may be advisable that in a separate despatch I should offer some further observations on the question of the withdrawal of the British troops from Egypt beyond those which are contained in my separate despatch of this day's date.[1]

I propose, in the first instance, to make some remarks upon the question of the total withdrawal of the Army of Occupation. The frequent declarations which have been made by Her Majesty's Ministers on this subject, have weakened, but have not altogether eradicated the belief entertained by some sections of the community in Egypt that the country will be permanently occupied by British troops. I have lost no opportunity of stating that there is no intention whatever of departing from the policy in pursuance of which the whole of the British troops will eventually be withdrawn from Egypt. In spite, however, of the very cordial sympathy with which I regard that policy, I regret that I am at present unable to recommend the total withdrawal of the Army of Occupation. I consider that it would be at present premature to discuss the question. Under these circumstances, the only practical questions to be considered are those which are discussed in my separate despatch. In making the proposals contained in that despatch, it may be desirable that I should add some observations of a general nature on the political situation of the moment.

It would be difficult to conceive of the existence of a worse Government than that of the late Khedive, Ismail Pasha. But that Government possessed one single merit—it preserved order. The methods by which it preserved order were cruel and oppressive in the highest degree, but the general

[1] This was the despatch to which allusion is made on pp. 352-353, and in which it was recommended that the British garrison should be reduced and the troops concentrated at Alexandria.

result was that life and property were secure from all attacks save those dictated by the action of the Government themselves. Recent events have completely shattered the system of government which prevailed under Ismail Pasha and his predecessors. The use of the "courbash" has been nearly, if not completely, abolished. Measures are being taken under which it may be reasonably hoped that arbitrary arrest and imprisonment will no longer be possible. Properly constituted tribunals are about to be established, under whose jurisdiction it may be hoped that but few persons will suffer for crimes of which they are innocent, although possibly in the first instance some guilty persons may escape punishment. In a word, a reign of law is being introduced.

The period of transition from the old to the new order of things would, under any circumstances, have been somewhat critical. It is rendered more so from the fact that recent events must have imbued the people with the idea, heretofore unfamiliar to them, that properly constituted authority may, for a time at least, be successfully resisted.

The present position of the country is that the old order of things has either passed or is rapidly passing away.

On the other hand, the new systems of administration or of judicial procedure are either in process of organisation, or have not yet acquired the stability which time alone can give to them.

I believe His Highness the Khedive and his Ministers to be sincerely desirous of introducing the reforms, whose main features were set forth in Lord Dufferin's report, and of which the country stands so much in need. But the introduction of those reforms must necessarily occupy some time. During the period of their introduction it may be anticipated that many persons, imperfectly appreciating the difficulties of the situation, may be impatient that more rapid progress is not made. On the other hand, the turbulent and lawless portion of the community may not improbably learn to disrespect a Government which does not manifest its authority, or impose its legitimate orders, by the use of those arbitrary methods to which the country has for generations been accustomed. If the system of government in Egypt is to be reformed, it is above all things necessary that order should be preserved during the process of reformation, and that any changes, whether in the existing laws or in the form of government or in the composition of the ministry, should be effected by legal and constitutional methods. Force should be put down by force, and inasmuch as the lesson has scarcely yet been learnt in Egypt that the arm of the law is as strong as that of arbitrary and capricious power, it might, under certain circumstances, become desirable in the interests of the country that a greater degree of severity should be exercised in the suppression of disturbance than would be necessary amongst a population which had for long been accustomed to a law-abiding and orderly system of government.

The main responsibility for preserving order throughout Egypt will, as I have said in my separate despatch, devolve on the Egyptian Government. Under these circumstances, I venture to think that, within any reasonable limits, full freedom should be left to the Egyptian Government in the exercise of that power, the possession of which is a necessary condition to the assumption of responsibility.

I have no reason to suppose that, should any disturbance occur at Cairo or elsewhere, the Egyptian Government would be disposed to use excessive or unnecessary severity in its suppression. The personal character of the Khedive is, indeed, of itself almost a sufficient guarantee that no such tendency exists. At the same time, it cannot be denied that the events of the last few years have shaken the authority of the Government in Egypt, a result which is not, I believe, due to any change in the personal character of the individuals who compose the Government, but to the change of system, which, most fortunately for the country, has been in course of progress since the abdication of Ismail Pasha.

In order to reassert that authority, the existence of which is essential to the progress of orderly reform, it might be deemed necessary by the Egyptian Government to exercise a degree of severity in the suppression of disturbance which might possibly not commend itself to public opinion in England.

Under these circumstances, I venture to think that it would be desirable that both the Egyptian Government and the public in Egypt should fully understand that, whilst Her Majesty's Government would view with serious displeasure any attempt to return to the system of government which prevailed in the past, they would not, save in some very exceptional case, be inclined to interfere with the discretion of the Egyptian Government in the adoption of such measures as the latter might consider desirable for the preservation of public order and tranquillity.

I make these observations not because I have any reason to suppose that any disturbance is likely to ensue upon the partial withdrawal of the British force, but because it appears to me desirable that, before the British garrison is reduced, the responsibility and the power of the Egyptian Government should alike be somewhat clearly defined.

The considerations which I have thus ventured to lay before your Lordship will, of course, apply with even greater force when the time eventually arrives for dealing with the question of the total withdrawal of the British garrison.—I have, etc.,

E. Baring.

CHAPTER XLV

THE NORTHBROOK MISSION

SEPTEMBER–NOVEMBER 1884

It is decided to send a Special Commissioner to Cairo—The policy of reporting—Lord Northbrook arrives in Egypt—His financial proposals—His General Report—The Government reject his proposals.

THE difficulties and complications of the Egyptian question were, of course, greatly increased by the events in the Soudan. Amongst other causes for anxiety, the bankruptcy of the Egyptian Treasury appeared imminent. A Conference of the Powers assembled in London in the summer of 1884 to consider the financial situation, but separated without arriving at any practical conclusions.[1] Under the circumstances, what was a well-intentioned Government, which had drifted into a position which it very imperfectly understood, to do? Undoubtedly, the question was difficult to answer.

After a short period of hesitation, Mr. Gladstone resorted to his favourite device. He determined to send to Cairo a Special Commissioner to "report and advise Her Majesty's Government touching the counsel which it might be fitting to offer the Egyptian Government in the present situation of affairs in Egypt, and as to the measures which

[1] Subsequently, some decisions were taken as regards the matters discussed at the Conference. They were embodied in an Agreement signed in London by the representatives of all the Great Powers on March 17, 1885. See *Egypt*, No. 6 of 1885.

should be taken in connection with them." The Commissioner's special attention was to be directed to the "present exigencies of Egyptian finance."

There was really little about which to report. The main facts with which the Government had to deal were patent to all the world. Only a year previously, a Special Commissioner of great experience and ability had compiled an elaborate Report on the condition of Egypt. Since then, a detailed Report on the financial situation had been prepared by a Committee of experts sitting in London. The subject had also been thoroughly discussed at the Conference. No further collection of facts was, therefore, required. Any detailed information which might have been necessary before deciding on what policy to adopt, could easily have been furnished by the various authorities on the spot. What was required was the decision of character necessary to arrive at a definite conclusion, when once the facts had been collected.

Lord Northbrook was designated as the Special Commissioner. A better choice could not have been made. His high character, his wide administrative experience, the knowledge of the East which he had gained as Viceroy of India, his power of rapidly acquiring a mastery over complicated financial questions, and the breadth and statesmanlike nature of his views—all pointed him out as exceptionally qualified to fulfil the duties entrusted to him. To myself, the appointment was especially pleasing. The relationship between Lord Northbrook and myself, and the mutual esteem and affection which we entertained for each other, were of themselves a sufficient guarantee that we should work cordially together. It was, without doubt, the knowledge that the appointment would not be displeasing to me which to some extent led Lord Granville, with that courteous consideration for others which never failed him, to nominate Lord Northbrook.

Lord Northbrook possessed another, and very important qualification for successfully carrying out the duties assigned to him. He did not blind himself to facts. He had the courage of his opinions. When he had studied his facts and come to some definite conclusions, he was in the habit of stating them without reference to whether they harmonised with any preconceived theories.

The policy of reporting, which was so dear to Mr. Gladstone's Government, appears always to have brought about results which were in each case somewhat similar. Under the graceful diction of Lord Dufferin's Report, in spite of the apparent ease with which the skilled diplomatist glided over difficulties and eluded burning questions, it was easy to observe that the main facts of the situation did not escape the statesmanlike eye of the author, and that he in reality expected the Government to recognise them. Connected, as I was, by general political sympathy with a Liberal Government, and by ties of long-standing family friendship and relationship with some members of Mr. Gladstone's Cabinet, I came to Egypt with a hearty desire to aid to the best of my ability in the successful execution of his Egyptian policy. I thought I understood that policy, and, if I understood it rightly, I felt sure that it met with my general concurrence. I soon found, however, that I was pursuing a phantom which constantly eluded my grasp, and that, even when I understood something of the general principles which were guiding the action of the Government, the vacillation shown in the execution of the detail was simply heartbreaking. I could not blind myself to facts to please Mr. Gladstone, and directly I stated the facts and pointed out the inevitable conclusions to be drawn from them, I found that, however clear they might be, they were ignored. To cite another instance, General Gordon was sent to the Soudan, not to act, but to report. General Gordon had failed to recognise the real facts in connection with the Soudan when he undertook his mission. After his arrival at Khartoum, he recognised them, but he could not enforce their recognition on Mr. Gladstone; the latter's blindness to facts, which were patent to all the world, eventually resulted in the death of General Gordon, of Colonel Stewart, and of many other brave men. Every one knows the reluctance which many men feel about making a will. Inability to recognise that death is the common lot of all has from time immemorial formed the text alike of the divine and the satirist. Mr. Gladstone appears to have lain under a similar disability in dealing with Egyptian affairs. He ignored all unpleasant facts. Lord Northbrook's fate was to be that of his predecessors. He was asked to "report and advise." It was almost certain, before he began his work, that his report would pass unheeded and that Mr. Gladstone would turn a deaf ear to his advice, unless, which was improbable, it happened to be such as he had wished to receive at the time when, *ex hypothesi*, the Government were in partial ignorance of the facts.

Lord Northbrook arrived in Egypt on September 9, 1884. He remained in the country about six weeks, during which time he laboured strenuously to master all the complicated facts connected with the situation. Before he left Cairo he prepared the draft of his report, but, inasmuch as when he arrived in London, it appeared that his views were distasteful to Mr. Gladstone, his proposals were modified before they assumed their final shape. Eventually, he sent in two reports, both dated November 20, 1884. One of these dealt exclusively with the financial situation. The other was of a more general nature.

It is unnecessary to dwell at length on Lord Northbrook's financial proposals. It will be sufficient to say that they involved: (1) adequate provision being made for the improvement and extension of the system of irrigation; (2) a prospect of the abolition of the corvée; (3) the acquisition by the Egyptian Government of greater freedom in the matter of imposing taxes on foreigners; (4) the abolition of the dual administration of the Daira, Domains, and Railways; (5) a reduction of the land-tax, and of the taxes on the export and transit of produce; and (6) the issue of a loan for about £9,000,000, the interest of which was to be guaranteed by the British Government.

"The effect of the proposals which I have made," Lord Northbrook said in concluding his report, "will undoubtedly be to substitute the financial control of England for the international control which was proposed by the Conference; but the alteration seems to me to be an advantage both to the Egyptian and to the English Governments. Nor do I see what objections the other Powers of Europe can entertain to this control being exercised by Great Britain after the sacrifices which have been made in maintaining the peace and safety of Egypt, and the financial liability which has now to be undertaken."

In his general report, after dwelling on the reforms which had already been accomplished, Lord Northbrook added: "The progress, in order to be solid, must necessarily be gradual in a country where the people have had to be taught to comprehend the first elements of decent government. . . .

"I cannot recommend Her Majesty's Government to fix any date at which the British troops serving in Egypt shall be withdrawn. In my report, I have stated my reasons for anticipating that their strength may be reduced before long to about 4000 men, but it is my duty to express my decided opinion that it would not be safe or wise to fix any definite time for their entire withdrawal, because the safety of such a step must depend on the internal state of the country, and upon the political position of Egypt, which has been left in uncertainty in consequence of the failure of the Conference of London."

It will be seen that Lord Northbrook did not attempt to solve the Egyptian question in so far as its solution depended on the continuance of the British occupation. He expressed a strong opinion that the garrison could not be at once withdrawn from Egypt, and there he left the matter. But he made some excellent proposals in respect to the finances of the country. Had these proposals been accepted by the Cabinet and carried into execution, internationalism, which has been the bane of Egypt, would have received a heavy blow, and the paramount power of Great Britain, as the guide and protector of Egypt, would have been asserted.

Lord Northbrook's views were, however, too thoroughgoing for Mr. Gladstone, who was not prepared to guarantee the interest on an Egyptian loan. The proposals also did not receive the support which they deserved from the English press. The result was that nothing was done in the direction of carrying Lord Northbrook's policy into execution. His mission was a failure.

Mr. Gladstone's Government, which fell in June 1885, made no subsequent attempt to settle the Egyptian question in its larger aspects. It is now necessary to deal with an endeavour to arrive at a solution which was made under the auspices of Mr. Gladstone's successor, Lord Salisbury.

CHAPTER XLVI

THE WOLFF CONVENTION

August 1885–October 1887

Sir Henry Wolff appointed Special Commissioner—Convention of October 24, 1885—Moukhtar Pasha—Convention of May 22, 1887—Comparison of the two Conventions—Frontier affairs—The army—Civil reforms—Evacuation—France and Russia oppose the Convention—The Sultan refuses to ratify it—Moukhtar Pasha permanently located in Egypt—Results of the Wolff mission.

It might have been thought that a sufficient number of Special Commissioners, diplomatists, and others had already reported on the affairs of Egypt. Such, however, was not the view of the British Government. Lord Salisbury determined to take a leaf out of the book of his predecessors. It was decided to send Sir Henry Wolff, who had been a prominent member of what was then known as the Fourth Party, on a mission to Constantinople and Cairo. He was given a sort of general commission to examine into Egyptian affairs. He was to invite the co-operation of the Sultan in the settlement of the Egyptian question; more especially it was thought that it was "in His Majesty's power to contribute materially to the establishment of settled order and good government" in the Soudan.

Sir Henry Wolff arrived in Constantinople on

August 22, 1885. On October 24, he signed a Convention with the Turkish Minister for Foreign Affairs. All that this first Convention settled was the nature of the subjects which were to be discussed. It provided that the British and Turkish Governments were each to send a Special Commissioner to Egypt, where the Ottoman Commissioner was to consult with the Khedive "upon the best means of tranquillising the Soudan by pacific means." The two Commissioners, in concert with the Khedive, were to reorganise the Egyptian army, and also to "examine all the branches of the Egyptian administration, and introduce into them the modifications which they considered necessary, within the limits of the Imperial Firmans." The sixth and most important article of the Convention was couched in the following terms: "So soon as the two High Commissioners shall have established that the security of the frontiers and the good working and stability of the Egyptian Government are assured, they shall present a Report to their respective Governments, who will consult as to the conclusion of a Convention regulating the withdrawal of the British troops from Egypt in a convenient period."

In a despatch, dated October 24, Sir Henry Wolff pointed out the advantages which, he thought, had accrued, or were likely to accrue, from the signature of this Convention. "The conclusion of an arrangement," he said, "of any kind has done much to allay the irritation that has existed for some time in the minds of the Turks towards England. . . . The experience of the Sultan's Commissioner, if wisely chosen, will be useful in the elaboration of institutions which must combine both Eastern and Western elements. The same reason will hold good with respect to the regulations in the Soudan. It must, doubtless, have been very difficult for English gentlemen, however able and conciliatory, to come to terms with races who had suffered so severely at our hands. The regulations which are to be undertaken, with our assent and countenance, but between the Khalif and those who recognise his authority, are more likely to lead to a rapid and satisfactory result."

Sir Henry Wolff arrived in Cairo on October 29. The departure from Constantinople of Ghazi Moukhtar Pasha, a distinguished soldier, who was named Turkish Commissioner, was delayed; he did not arrive in Cairo till December 27.

It is unnecessary to describe the lengthy negotiations which ensued. It will be sufficient to say that, after eighteen months of discussion, a further Convention was signed at Constantinople, on May 22, 1887, between Sir Henry Wolff and two Turkish Plenipotentiaries acting on behalf of the Sultan.

The two Conventions may now be compared with a view to ascertaining how far the latter accomplished the objects proposed by the former.

As regards the tranquillisation of the Soudan, Sir Henry Wolff's efforts were foredoomed to failure from the commencement. He spoke of negotiations being undertaken "between the Khalif and those who recognised his authority." Moukhtar Pasha and other Turks were naturally slow to believe that any Mohammedans refused to recognise the authority of the Sultan as Khalif. But every one in Egypt knew that the Mahdi confounded Christians and Turks alike in one common anathema, and that the idea of conjuring with the Sultan's name in the Soudan was a delusion.

On this particular point, therefore, the negotiations conducted by Sir Henry Wolff and Moukhtar Pasha ended in failure. It was reserved for Sir

Francis Grenfell and Colonel Wodehouse to arrive at some settlement of the frontier question by methods which were efficacious because they were based on the true facts of the case, and not on the imaginary facts evolved from the brains of Turkish diplomatists. The defeats which the Dervishes sustained at Arguin and Toski in the summer of 1889, gave peace to the frontier. Powder and shot proved more effective agents than the "authority of the Khalif."

Much discussion took place about the reorganisation of the Egyptian army. At one time, a proposal was put forward to recruit troops in Turkey, an idea which did not find favour with the Sultan. At another time, the notion of importing a number of Turkish officers into Egypt was started. Eventually, however, nothing was done. The British officers were fortunately left to reorganise the Egyptian army after their own fashion. On this point also, therefore, the Convention of October 24, 1885, was unproductive of result.

Much the same may be said as regards administrative reforms. A Protocol annexed to the Convention of May 22, 1887, provided that the British and Ottoman Governments should jointly address the Powers with a view to modifying the Capitulations in the sense of bringing all residents of Egypt "under a local and uniform jurisdiction and legislation." A second Protocol provided that joint representations should be made to the Powers with a view to reforming the administrations of the Domains, Daira, and Railways, defining the powers of the Commissioners of the Debt, and enacting laws relative to the press and to quarantine. But beyond making an enumeration of the points which required the attention of the reformer, nothing was done.

There remains to be considered the sixth and most important article of the Convention of October 24, 1885, namely, that which provided that the Commissioners should discuss the question of the withdrawal of the British garrison from Egypt. It was perhaps rather a bold flight of the official imagination to indulge in the hope that any possible steps taken by the two Commissioners would assure "the good working and stability of the Egyptian Government." The good working and stability of that Government are still assured by the presence of the garrison whose speedy withdrawal from Egypt formed the main subject of the discussions which took place in 1885-87. Too much attention should not, however, be attached to the wording of the Convention of October 1885. Diplomatic instruments of this sort usually abound in euphemisms and picturesque conventionalities. In plain English, the first Convention signed by Sir Henry Wolff meant that England and Turkey were to endeavour to come to terms over the Egyptian question, and, although nothing practical came of the endeavour, some cautious and intelligent steps were taken in the direction intended.

Article V. of the Convention of May 22, 1887, laid down that "at the expiration of three years from the date of the present Convention, Her Britannic Majesty's Government will withdraw its troops from Egypt." This clause seemed explicit enough, but it was followed by another clause, under the provisions of which the British troops were *not* to withdraw at the end of three years if there was any "appearance of danger in the interior or from without." It was not specifically stated who was to judge whether the internal or external danger was sufficient to justify the retention of the British garrison in Egypt, but in the absence of any specific arrangement on this point, it was obvious that the decision rested with the British Government. One important definition was, however, given to the words "danger from without." Article VI. of the Convention laid down that, after the ratification by England and Turkey, the Powers, who were parties to the Treaty of Berlin, should be invited to adhere to it. The ultimate execution of the Convention depended, in fact, on its acceptance by the Powers. In a letter attached to the Convention, which was addressed by Sir Henry Wolff to the Turkish Plenipotentiaries, he said : "If, at the expiration of the three years stipulated in the Convention of this day for the withdrawal of the British troops from Egypt, one of the Great Mediterranean Powers shall not have accepted it, Her Britannic Majesty's Government would consider this refusal as the appearance of a danger from without, provided against by Article V. of the Convention, and the means of executing the aforesaid Convention shall be again discussed and settled between the Imperial Ottoman Government and Her Britannic Majesty's Government."

More than this, Article V. provided that if, at any time subsequent to the evacuation, "order and security in the interior were disturbed, or if the Khedivate of Egypt refused to execute its duties towards the Sovereign Court, or its international obligations," both the Ottoman and British Governments would have the right to occupy the country with troops, and, moreover, that if, "by reason of hindrances," the Sultan did not avail himself of his right of occupation, the British Government could none the less take military action on their own account, and that, in that case, the Sultan would "send a Commissioner to remain during the period of the sojourn of the British troops with their Commander."

So long as the negotiations which were preliminary to the signature of the Convention were going on, the embers of diplomatic opposition smouldered. Directly it was signed, they burst into a flame. M. de Nelidoff, the Russian Ambassador at Constantinople, at once "sent to the Palace his remonstrances, and reproached the Grand Vizier with having gratuitously sacrificed the rights of the Sultan to England." "Similar language," Sir Henry Wolff reported on May 27, "had been used to the Turkish Ambassador at St. Petersburg by M. de Giers, who said that Russia would probably refuse her adhesion, and thus act in the interests of the Sultan."

The French Government also took strong exception to the right of re-entry into Egypt, which the Convention conferred on England. On June 7, the Count de Montebello, who represented France at Constantinople, addressed a minatory letter to the Sultan in which he stated that the "French Government had definitely decided not to accept the situation which would result from the ratification of the Egyptian Convention."

The Sultan was perplexed. On July 9, the Turkish Plenipotentiaries called on Sir Henry Wolff. "They said that the recent language of the French and Russian Ambassadors, both at the Palace and the Porte, had much disturbed the Sultan. His Majesty had been told that if he ratified the Convention, France and Russia would thereby be given the right to occupy provinces of the Empire, and to leave only after a similar Convention had been concluded. France might do so in Syria, and Russia in Armenia. Religious feeling had also been excited in the same direction."

Under these circumstances, it was asked, could not Sir Henry Wolff "advise as to some formula by which these difficulties might be met?" Sir

Henry could not advise the distracted Plenipotentiaries as to any formula. He "had exhausted his powers of reference" to Lord Salisbury. What was an unfortunate ruler who was torn hither and thither by rival diplomatists to do? He could at all events fall back upon his favourite device and try to gain time. Under Article VII. of the Convention the ratifications were to be exchanged within one month of the date on which the Convention was signed. The British Government were implored to prolong this period. On June 26, that is to say four days after the prescribed period of a month had expired, the Turkish Ambassador represented to Lord Salisbury that "the Sultan was much fatigued after Bairam," and wanted time to consider the whole question. A short delay was granted, but the Sultan was still unable to make up his mind as to whether he would or would not ratify the Convention. Sir Henry Wolff then announced his intention of leaving Constantinople. He at once received a letter from the Sultan's Grand Master of the Ceremonies which was to the following effect: "His Majesty is at this moment occupied with questions of the greatest importance for his Empire. In view of these occupations, which will last all next week, he is anxious that you should remain at Constantinople until Friday, July 15." Sir Henry Wolff's departure was accordingly fixed for July 15. At 8.30 P.M. of that day he telegraphed to Lord Salisbury: "Just as I am leaving, Artin Effendi has come with a personal message from the Sultan urgently pressing me to stay. I have told him that this is quite impossible." At midnight on July 15, Sir Henry Wolff left Constantinople.

Shortly after he left, the Sultan, through his Ambassador in London, made an unsuccessful attempt to renew the negotiations with the British

Government. He was informed by Lord Salisbury "that so long as the Sultan was so much under the influence of other advisers as to repudiate an agreement which he had himself so recently sanctioned, any fresh agreement would obviously be liable to meet with the same fate as the late Convention."

It should be added that one practical consequence of an unfortunate nature resulted from the Wolff mission. Before that time, the Egyptian administrative machine was sufficiently complicated. Henceforth, an additional complication was added. A Turkish Commissioner was left in Egypt. When once the negotiations had broken down, there was no plausible excuse for the continued presence in Egypt of a high Turkish official, whose functions could not be defined, whose presence would naturally be resented by the Khedive, and who at any moment might become the centre of intrigue. Moukhtar Pasha was, however, allowed to remain. In spite of his high personal character, the presence of a Turkish Commissioner in Egypt has served no useful purpose, and has at times caused some trouble.

Although the negotiations conducted by Sir Henry Wolff failed to effect their object, the British Government were in a better diplomatic position at their close than they had been at their commencement. They could henceforth point to the fact that they had made an endeavour to come to terms with the Sultan on the Egyptian question; that they had, moreover, succeeded in their endeavour; and that it was no fault of theirs if the Sultan, under the pressure of France and Russia, had refused to ratify an arrangement to which at one time he had agreed. Strong in this argument, the British Government could feel that the Wolff negotiations, although for the time being unproductive of result, had fortified their position as against both Mohammedan and European critics.

The neutralisation of the Suez Canal, to which allusion was made in Article III. of the Convention of May 22, 1887, formed the subject of further discussion, with results which will now be described.

CHAPTER XLVII

THE NEUTRALISATION OF THE SUEZ CANAL[1]

Neutralisation of Egypt — Neutralisation of the Canal — The word neutrality—Circular of January 3, 1883—The Suez Canal Commission of 1885 — The Commission dissolved — The Wolff Convention—Signature of the Canal Convention—Its application.

At one time, politicians in search of an idea flattered themselves with the belief that the solution of the Egyptian question was to be found in neutralising Egypt. Why, it was sometimes asked, should not Egypt become an "Oriental Belgium"? A point is already gained by the advocates of any political idea when they can label their pet theory with an epigrammatic ticket of this sort. The mere appellation gives their proposal the appearance of involving some sound and statesmanlike principle. Catchpenny phrases exercise a good deal of influence in the government of the world. In the *Sturm und Drang* of public life in this busy century, large numbers of people who are engaged in politics are often too much occupied with other matters to inquire carefully whether the particular phrase in question embodies, as may at first sight appear, the elements of a sound policy based on the true facts of the situation, or whether, as is not unfrequently the case, it is a mere tinsel covering beneath which some glaring fallacy may lurk.

[1] See further remarks on this subject on p. 565.

The proposal to neutralise Egypt belongs to the latter of these two categories. Its tinsel covering consists of an argument, which may conveniently be stated in the form of a syllogism thus: The most serious aspect of the Egyptian question is that it may, under contingencies which are easily conceivable, bring about a rupture between France and England. The principal element of danger consists in the two facts that England would resent a French occupation, whilst France resents a British occupation of the country. Therefore, the danger will be removed and all risk of a rupture will disappear if both France and England agree that neither of them shall occupy Egypt.

This appears at first sight a compact and plausible chain of argument. Unfortunately, it is fallacious, for the main question to be decided is not whether both England and France shall abstain from occupying the country, but whether, inasmuch as some foreign occupation is necessary, the occupiers shall be French or British. The analogy between Belgium and Egypt breaks down on this essential point, that whereas Belgium is inhabited by a highly civilised population capable of self-government, the population of Egypt is for the present incapable of governing itself on principles which would commend themselves to the civilised world. This bald fact, namely, that a foreign occupation was, and still is necessary in order to prevent anarchy in Egypt, and, therefore, in order to obviate the resuscitation of an Egyptian question which would be a source of constant trouble to Europe, has been frequently forgotten by those who have from time to time discussed Egyptian affairs. Nevertheless, I am convinced that it is true, and, moreover, that it is of a nature to quash all ideas of neutralisation, Oriental Belgiums, and similar phantasies.

Most responsible and impartial authorities who have studied the Egyptian question appear so far to have arrived at the conclusion stated above. It is true that Article V. of the Convention of May 22, 1887, provided that the Great Powers were to be "invited to sign an Act recognising and guaranteeing the inviolability of Egyptian territory"; but this was immediately followed by a provision which enabled Turkey and England to occupy the country in case any foreign occupation should become necessary. For all practical purposes, it may, therefore, be said that the idea of neutralising Egypt, in the true sense of the word, has never got beyond the stage of academic discussion.

It has been otherwise with the question of neutralising the Suez Canal. This subject attracted the attention of the Powers of Europe in 1882, notice having been more particularly drawn to it by the fact that, during the period which preceded the battle of Tel-el-Kebir, Lord Wolseley used the Canal as his base of operations. Before proceeding to state what was done in this matter, it may be as well to describe what, in this particular instance, was meant by the word neutrality.

In the words of Lord Pauncefote, an excellent authority on this subject, the word as applied to the proposals made in connection with the Suez Canal, "had reference only to the neutrality which attaches by international law to the territorial waters of a neutral state, in which a right of innocent passage for belligerent vessels exists, but no right to commit any act of hostility."

The definition of the term is important. Lord Granville was evidently apprehensive lest the mere use of the word "neutrality" should carry him farther than he intended. With commendable prudence, therefore, he directed that, in dealing with this subject, its use should be avoided and that the words "freedom" or "free navigation" should be substituted in its place.

Some three months after the battle of Tel-el-Kebir, Lord Granville addressed a Circular to the Powers in order to give them "full information on all matters, which were immediately connected with the peace, security, and social order of Egypt, and on which, accordingly, they (*i.e.* the British Government) had thought it their duty to advise the Khedive as to the best mode of exercising his governing power."

In this Circular, a prominent place was given to the arrangements which it was proposed should for the future be adopted in connection with the free navigation of the Suez Canal.

The question was then allowed to sleep till early in 1885, when, at the instance of the French Government, it was decided to assemble a Commission in Paris composed of representatives of the Great Powers, as well as of Spain and Holland, in order to discuss the question of neutralising the Canal. The British Government would have preferred "that all the Maritime Powers who applied should be permitted to send delegates,' but to this proposal the French objected. The purpose for which the Commission was convoked was to "establish by a conventional act a definite system for guaranteeing at all times and to all Powers the free use of the Suez Canal."

The first meeting was held on March 30, 1885, the proceedings being opened by M. Jules Ferry, the French Prime Minister.

M. Billot, the Director-General of the French Foreign Office, then assumed the presidency of the Commission, but the real work was delegated to a Sub-Commission, over which M. Barrère, the second French representative, presided.

It is needless to describe the proceedings of the

Commission in detail. It will be sufficient to say that the object of the majority of the Powers was to internationalise rather than to neutralise the Canal, and that the British Government were opposed to the adoption of this course.

The British delegates were obliged to fight the ground inch by inch. Although they made some concessions, they were unable to come to terms with their adversaries. Eventually, after some ten weeks of wearisome discussion, a draft Treaty was drawn up representing the views of the majority. It is unnecessary to dwell in detail on the points at issue between France and her allies on the one side, and England, supported to a certain extent by Italy, on the other. It will be sufficient to say that they were of a nature to exclude, for the time being, the possibility of any common understanding.

On June 13, the Commission held its last sitting. A few days later, Mr. Gladstone's Ministry fell. The question of neutralising the Canal was again allowed to sleep for a while. Shortly afterwards, Sir Henry Wolff started on his mission. The question of the free navigation of the Canal formed the subject of negotiation at Constantinople, with the result that an Article (III.) on this point was inserted in the Convention of May 22, 1887. Briefly it may be said that this Article embodied the views which had been maintained by the British delegates in Paris in June 1885.

Although the Convention of May 22, 1887, was not ratified by the Sultan, the idea of neutralising the Canal was not allowed to drop. It was one to which the French attached great importance. Eventually, after some lengthy negotiations, which need not be described in detail, a Convention, the text of which is to be found in *Egypt*, No. 2 of 1889, was signed on April 29, 1888. The British

Government stipulated that the Convention was not to come into force so long as the British occupation of Egypt lasted.

Nothing further was done in this matter until 1904. Under the Anglo-French Agreement, signed on April 8 of that year, the British Government agreed to put the Suez Canal Convention, of April 29, 1888, into force, with the exception of those portions which provided that a Local International Board should be created at Cairo to watch over the execution of the Convention.

Thus, another important step was taken in the direction of settling the Egyptian question.

The actual working of the Canal Convention was put to the test during the Russo-Japanese War. On the whole, it may be said that it worked well, but, as usually happens in such cases, a number of questions of detail arose in respect to which the wording of the Convention was wanting in precision. It would be desirable that an opportunity should be taken to revise the Convention by the light of the experience which has now been gained.

CHAPTER XLVIII

THE ANGLO-FRENCH AGREEMENT OF 1904

Apparent insolubility of the Egyptian question—Gradual change in public opinion—Statement of Lord Ellenborough—The business of diplomacy—The main facts of the problem—The events of 1904—Morocco—Signature of the Anglo-French Agreement—Remarks on the Agreement.

For some years subsequent to the Wolff negotiations, no attempt was made to deal with the larger aspects of the Egyptian Question. Whenever the British Government were reproached by the French, or by British partisans of evacuation, with not having fulfilled their pledge to evacuate, the reply persistently given, by both Conservative and Liberal statesmen, was that England's work in Egypt was not yet completed. This reply, though regarded by some as a mere subterfuge, was perfectly true; yet it did not convey the whole truth. It encouraged the inference that England's work would be completed at some period, which would not be very remote, whereas not one of the British statesmen who gave the reply had any precise idea as to whether the period would be remote or proximate. The better was his acquaintance with the facts, the stronger would his conviction be that the period would be remote, even to the extent of giving a distinctly permanent character to the occupation, which was originally intended to be temporary.

For more than twenty years, therefore, politicians, whether professional or amateur, French or English, wandered aimlessly in a labyrinth to which there was no clue. They sought for the solution of a question which was in reality insoluble on any basis which had, during that period, been formulated. Eventually, Englishmen relaxed their attempts to make a pyramid stand on its apex; whilst Frenchmen gradually recognised two facts. One was that the British occupation of Egypt was beneficial rather than hurtful to the material interests of France, whilst general French political interests suffered from the prolonged estrangement of the two countries, which was caused by the Egyptian Question. The other was that, unless the evacuation of Egypt was to be made a *casus belli* with England, the British view of the facts had to be accepted.

An English politician, writing in 1844, had said: "It is impossible for any statesman who carries his views forward a few years not to see that there must be eventually a contest among European Powers for the possession of Egypt."[1]

That contest, if it ever came, could only be between England and France. It was the business of diplomacy to be on the watch for any opportunity to settle the question, and thus avoid any such calamity as that predicted by Lord Ellenborough.

The main facts connected with the Egyptian Question were in reality very simple.

It was certain that, in the early days of the occupation, the British Government stated publicly their desire to withdraw the British garrison, so soon as circumstances admitted of the adoption of such a course.

It was equally certain to all who considered the subject impartially, and with a full knowledge of

[1] Letter from Lord Ellenborough, *Sir Robert Peel*, vol. iii. p. 259.

the circumstances, that the British Government could not, with a due regard to all the interests involved, carry out their declared intention.

Gradually, the truth of this latter statement came to be generally recognised, and when once it was recognised, all that was required to set diplomatic action in movement was an opportunity for negotiating with a fair prospect of success.

Such an opportunity occurred in 1904. The visits of King Edward VII. to Paris, and of the President of the French Republic to London, prepared the public opinion of both countries for a general settlement of all outstanding differences. Moreover, at this moment the affairs of Morocco acquired some prominence.

That State had been for some while past traversing the various stages on the road to ruin, which would appear to be normal in the case of Oriental countries. The final stage had nearly been reached. The exercise of unbridled personal power by the ruler of the State led to misgovernment, culminating in revolution. European intervention had become inevitable. The only practical question at issue was to decide on the nationality of the Europeans who were to intervene.

The choice practically lay between three nations, Spain, England, and France.

Spain, still staggering under the effects of a disastrous war with America, was manifestly incapable of assuming the task of regenerator.

England was unwilling to add to her already heavy burthen of world-wide responsibilities.

The duty of dealing with Morocco devolved, therefore, naturally on France.[1] But, in order that

[1] The difficulties which subsequently occurred between France and Germany, as also the proceedings of the Algeciras Conference, lie obviously outside the scope of this work. Moreover, those difficulties did not arise until a period subsequent to the signature of the Anglo-French Agreement of April 8, 1904.

the task should be taken in hand with a fair prospect of success, the goodwill of England was necessary. What, therefore, could be more natural than to barter British support in Morocco for French support in Egypt?

Negotiations on this basis were commenced in the summer of 1903, with the result that, on April 8, 1904, three Conventions were signed by Lord Lansdowne, who then presided over the British Foreign Office, and by M. Cambon, the French Ambassador in London.

Two of these Conventions dealt with the affairs of Newfoundland, Nigeria, Siam, Madagascar, and the New Hebrides. The consideration of these questions lies outside the scope of the present work.

As regards Egypt, it has been already explained that the Egyptian Government acquired financial liberty, and also that the British Government recognised the Suez Canal Convention of 1888. Further, a "Declaration" made on April 8, 1904, contained the following very important provision:—

"His Britannic Majesty's Government declare that they have no intention of altering the political status of Egypt.

"The Government of the French Republic, for their part, declare that they will not obstruct the action of Great Britain in that country by asking that a limit of time be fixed for the British Occupation or in any other manner."

In other words, the occupation was recognised, and the British Government were left a far freer hand than formerly to deal with Egyptian affairs.

The Governments of Germany, Austria, and Italy subsequently adhered to this declaration.

Thus, the "Egyptian Question," in the sense in which that phrase had heretofore been used, was partially settled. It is rare that an arrangement of this kind is of a nature to give satisfaction to all those who are directly or indirectly concerned. Such, however, was the case as regards the Anglo-French Agreement.

As to the advantages which are likely to accrue to the residents in Egypt, both European and Egyptian, there cannot be a shadow of doubt. Apart from the fact that the financial restrictions, which by a change of circumstances had become obsolete and unnecessary, have been removed, it is to be observed that Egyptian progress will now, it may be hoped, continue to advance without being hampered by that somewhat acute stage of international rivalry which has been productive of so much harm in the past.

Both England and France gained in the removal of a difference of opinion which had for long embittered the relations of two nations whose common interest it is to strengthen the bonds of close friendship.

England gained by obtaining a practically valid sanction to a position which was previously, to some extent, irregular. I had for long been convinced that the early withdrawal of the British garrison from Egypt was quite impossible, but I never regarded lightly the non-fulfilment of the engagement to withdraw. Neither did I ever think that a good deal of provocation in local matters constituted a sufficient plea to justify the annulment of that engagement. It is a distinct advantage for a nation, which is bound to a scrupulous respect of international obligations by every consideration of public morality and self-interest, that it can no longer be accused of any apparent disregard of those obligations.

France also gained. The large French interests at stake in Egypt are secured by specific engagements, and are still more amply secured by the traditional character of British predominance, wherever it has been acquired. On the other hand, any apparent loss of French political influence in Egypt received compensation elsewhere.

Lastly, the civilised world—whose principal interest I conceive to be the maintenance of peace—gained by the re-establishment of very friendly relations between two of the most important members of the European family.

Such, therefore, is the view I venture to submit of this very important and auspicious transaction. I began my connection with Egypt twenty-eight years previous to the signature of the Anglo-French Agreement, when England and France moved hand in hand together in that country. I rejoice that my connection lasted long enough to enable me to see the friendly relations of the past re-established after an interlude of misunderstanding which was detrimental alike to British, French, and Egyptian interests.

A further Egyptian Question remains behind. It consists in gradually adapting the institutions of the country to the growing needs of the population. Possibly, time will also solve that problem, but, unless disaster is to ensue, it must be a long time.

PART VI

THE REFORMS

In the East, we are attempting to put new wine into old bottles, to pour what we can of a civilisation whose spirit is progress into the form of a civilisation whose spirit is fixity; and whether we succeed or not is perhaps the most interesting question in an age abounding almost beyond example in questions of political interest.

BAGEHOT, *Physics and Politics.*

CHAPTER XLIX

THE COURBASH

Universal use of the courbash—Lord Dufferin's Circular—It was partially inoperative—Final abolition of the courbash.

Reforms in all countries, which are in a backward state of civilisation, can be divided into two categories, namely, first, those which are manifestly possible if the reformer is provided with the money and the administrative agency necessary to their execution; secondly, those dealing with long-standing abuses or faulty habits of thought, which are ingrained to such an extent into the minds of the population as to require a social almost as much as an administrative revolution in order to ensure their eradication.

The present and the two succeeding chapters will deal with the most prominent instances of Egyptian reforms belonging to the second of these categories. These are the three C's—the Courbash, the Corvée, and Corruption.

It was formerly the custom of the governing classes in Egypt to practise many cruel forms of torture on the population. One case which came under my personal notice may be mentioned as an example of the perverse ingenuity which was occasionally exhibited in discovering recondite means for the infliction of bodily pain. A Moudir was in the habit of causing a burning rag steeped in spirits of wine to be held close to the mouth of any recalcitrant taxpayer, who then received a blow on the chest, the consequence of which was that, the air being expelled from his lungs, he was obliged to take a deep breath to refill them. The flame was thus drawn into his mouth. The official who was guilty of this particular act of barbarity was by no means a bad specimen of his class. He simply followed certain caste traditions, which led him to be callous to the pain inflicted on a fellow-creature. It was with the aid of administrative material such as this Moudir that the English had, in the first instance, to create the New Egypt.

Refined forms of torture were, however, comparatively rare. On the other hand, the use of the courbash, a strip of hippopotamus hide tapering at the end, was universal. When such a simple and effective form of torture as flogging with this implement could readily be applied, there was, indeed, no need for refinements in cruelty. The courbash was employed on every occasion when coercion or punishment was required, but notably for the collection of taxes and for extracting either the evidence of witnesses or the confession of persons accused of crime.

Confession forms an important part of the Mohammedan law of evidence. If, the Mohammedan lawgiver argued, a man confesses his crime, he must surely be guilty. What, then, added the Turco-Egyptian Pasha with mediæval logic and assurance, can be more just and natural than that when I see that he will not inculpate himself, and when I know that either he or some one else must be guilty, I should flog him to see if he will confess? It is true that he may afterwards retract his confession, but no importance can be attached to his retractation; for, if he is not guilty, why did he, in the first instance, confess his crime? Moreover, if some glimmering of doubt entered into the mind of the old-fashioned Pasha as to the soundness of this process of reasoning, he would change his tactics. He would bid avaunt to the argumentative subtleties of the Frank, and would triumphantly point out that, even supposing the confession to have been made in order to obtain relief from bodily pain, no injustice was committed, for, ere one stroke of the courbash had been administered, he, the Pasha, knew that the man was guilty, and that the flogging was, therefore, a mere formality in order to obtain the confession necessary to give legal sanction to the punishment, which the criminal had richly deserved. The Pasha, having complied with the text of the law, to which, oblivious of its spirit, he attached the utmost importance, no valid complaint could be made; nor, indeed, was it necessary to ask any useless questions as regards the method adopted to ensure compliance.[1]

When Lord Dufferin came to Cairo, one of his first resolves was of a negative nature. It was not at that time clear how Egypt was to be governed for the future, but Lord Dufferin determined that in any case the country should not, if he could prevent it, be ruled by an indiscriminate use of the whip. Under his auspices, a Circular was issued forbidding the use of the courbash. It was signed by Ismail Pasha Eyoub, who was then Minister of the Interior, and is a curious and very characteristic document. Like many Oriental state-papers, it assumed a condition of things which was wholly at variance with the reality. Any one unacquainted with the ways of the East might, on reading it, suppose that the rulers of Egypt had on frequent occasions used their utmost

[1] I wish to explain that here, and elsewhere, I am speaking of the "old-fashioned Pasha," that is to say, the Pasha who existed some twenty-five years ago. This type has now almost entirely disappeared. The modern Pasha may have his defects, but he is generally an educated and enlightened gentleman.

endeavours to suppress the use of the courbash, and that they were scandalised to learn that, in spite of all their humane efforts, that implement was still very generally employed. Any such conclusion would have been wholly erroneous. No real effort had ever been made by the Egyptian portion of the administration to abolish torture.

It is, however, proverbially unnecessary to look a gift horse in the mouth. If the thistles of Pashadom could, under pressure, be made to produce figs, the business of the British statesman was to make the most of the figs, and not to dwell on the circumstances by which the change of production had been effected. Whatever Ismail Pasha Eyoub and his coadjutors may have thought on the subject of government by torture, their sentiments, as expressed in the Circular, were unimpeachably orthodox when judged by the standard of modern civilisation. It was stated, in terms of indignant remonstrance, that, in spite of reiterated Circulars in past days, the Minister of the Interior had heard, to his unspeakable regret, that recourse was still had by some perverse officials to the "reprehensible use of the bastinado." This practice was denounced as "horrible and infamous." It "degraded humanity, and violated in the gravest manner the principles of social rights." Further, it was "absolutely useless and without justification," for the Minister, who here indulged to a certain extent in a flight of his imagination, pointed out that the Government had instituted law-courts, whose business it was to deal with all litigious affairs, both civil and criminal. As to the collection of the taxes, what need could there be of the whip when the series of Decrees issued by the Government laid down with commendable precision the nature of the measures to be taken to ensure their payment? The various officials were, therefore, solemnly warned that "the only object of their mission was to secure, as much as possible, the welfare of the people, their prosperity, and their moral and material development, by dispensing to individuals equality of justice whilst defending them against all aggression and protecting their interests and their rights." They were all, down to the lowest village Sheikh, who was sometimes courbashed and sometimes courbashed others, adjured in language which, to those acquainted with the peculiar ways of the Pashadom of the time, is almost comic in its deceptive pathos, to abstain in the future from the abominable and barbarous practice of flogging.

Ismail Pasha Eyoub probably stated the truth when he said that on previous occasions orders had been issued prohibiting the use of the courbash. It is needless to inquire into this point, for, if any such orders were issued, no adequate steps were taken to enforce obedience to them. But when the Circular of Ismail Pasha Eyoub was published, the population of Egypt, and more especially that portion of it which was in the habit of being flogged, woke up to the fact that they no longer had to deal with a few meaningless platitudes intended to throw dust in the eyes of humanitarians. It was felt that, although the signature to the Circular might be that of an official who had little real sympathy with its spirit, the contents of that document had been dictated by the British Envoy, who meant what he said, and who, moreover, possessed both the will and the power to enforce his behests. One instance will suffice to show the spirit which the new order evoked. A British officer was present, shortly after the issue of the order, when a man who was accused of some crime was brought before the Moudir of the province. The man declined to answer the questions which were put to him. The Moudir directed that he should be flogged. All the steps which were usually preliminary to the infliction of flogging were taken. The man, however, was in no way impressed. "The English are here," he said to the Moudir; "you know that you cannot flog me." And accordingly, he was not flogged. It may well have been that the unwonted audacity displayed in this case was due to the presence of an Englishman. Nevertheless, the mere fact that an Egyptian fellah should have dared to assert his right not to be flogged was a striking innovation. A reflective Pasha would have noted that a new spirit was abroad.

Lord Dufferin's Circular constitutes a landmark in the administrative history of Egypt. To him belongs the credit of having dealt the first decisive blow to the system of government by flogging. He has, however, often been criticised for his action in this matter. The people of Egypt, it has been said, had from time immemorial been governed by the whip. Was it safe to abolish this system by a stroke of the pen, without substituting anything in its place? The reign of law, which Lord Dufferin held should take the place of the courbash, would necessarily be a work of slow creation. A month after the issue of the Circular he himself wrote: "At this moment, there is no real justice in this country. What passes under that name is a mockery." Would it not have been wiser to have accepted the facts of the situation, to have aimed at the gradual abolition of the courbash, and to have postponed its total suppression until some progress had been made in the direction of establishing properly constituted law-courts?

These criticisms are perhaps, to some extent, justified. There need have been no hesitation in abolishing at once the system of flogging in so far as the collection of taxes was concerned. That system had been shaken by the reforms introduced under the auspices of the Dual Control. The burthen of taxation, though still heavy, had been alleviated, and the legal process for the recovery of taxes, being a matter in which the governing body was directly interested, was in sufficiently good order to ensure the Treasury against serious loss. It was, however, otherwise in respect to the procedure of the law-courts. The principle on which the Government had heretofore acted was to mete out punishment without entering into any fine discrimination as to whether those who incurred the punishment were guilty or innocent of the crimes laid to their charge. The confessions extracted under torture, though often false, were sometimes true. The idea that any witness would voluntarily appear to give evidence was foreign to the habits of the Egyptian people. Justice, such as it was, was almost as much a terror to the innocent witness as to the accused person against whom testimony was borne. Under these circumstances, there was, without doubt, a risk that as a result of the sudden and complete abolition of the courbash, crime and lawlessness would be inadequately checked, and that Egyptian society in general would be in danger of dissolution.

It is probable, indeed, that when Lord Dufferin decided that the use of the courbash in Egypt should suddenly cease, he did not fully realise the importance of the step which he was taking. This view is confirmed by a perusal of the despatch which he wrote to Lord Granville forwarding the Circular. It was very brief. It did not contain anything from which it can be inferred that Lord Dufferin realised that he had initiated a social and administrative revolution. "The new Minister of the Interior, Ismail Pasha Eyoub," Lord Dufferin wrote, "has signalised his entry into office by peremptorily forbidding the application of this instrument of chastisement (*i.e.* the courbash). I cannot but regard such an act as significant of the introduction of a more humane and civilised spirit into the civil administration of the country."

In other words, when Lord Dufferin came to Egypt he found that the poorer classes of the population were habitually flogged by the agents of the Government. He naturally thought that they ought not to be flogged. What, therefore, could be simpler than to issue an order that flogging should cease, and to insist on the execution of the order? There is a "scorn of consequence" and a breezy lightheartedness in the conduct of the courageous Irishman which excites alike admiration and amusement. It is probable, however, that, after all that can be said, he was quite right. The action of any one who knew Egypt well would perhaps have been more cautious, but it might not improbably have been less effective. Lord Dufferin threw the Egyptian administrator into the water and called out to him from the bank that he must learn to swim as well as he could without the help of his time-honoured support.

Did the Egyptian administrator at once learn to swim? He did not. In fact, the main reason why no dissolution of provincial society took place in consequence of the Circular was that it was partially inoperative. Lord Dufferin dealt a staggering blow to the use of the courbash; nevertheless, that implement was plentifully used for some years after the issue of his epoch-making Circular. In the early days of the British occupation, crime increased to such an extent that Nubar Pasha thought it necessary to create the Commissions of Brigandage to which allusion has been already made.[1] These Commissions virtually took the place of the ordinary Tribunals. Recourse was had to the old system of torture. To quote one out of many passages which occur in a report prepared by M. Le Grelle, the Procureur-Général of the Native Courts, dated April 6, 1889 :—

"En Septembre, 1888, un acte de brigandage se commit à Manchite Gouzour (Menoufieh). Une enquête amena l'arrestation d'une série de prévenus. Quatre firent des aveux. Sur les ordres réitérés d'un Mouavin du Ministère de l'Intérieur venu à Chibin-el-Kom, la torture fut employée pendant six jours de suite, en pleine séance de la Commission Criminelle, devant le Moudir, le Juge, et le Substitut du Parquet. Les malheureux étaient frappés jusqu'au moment où ils avouaient ou satisfaisaient par leurs réponses les enquêteurs. Parmi les torturés, figurait une femme appelée Fatmah."

Eventually, the Commissions were abolished and, at the same time, Sir John Scott was named Judicial Adviser to the Egyptian Government. Then the work, which Lord Dufferin commenced, was completed. Torture ceased.

[1] *Vide ante*, p. 289.

CHAPTER L

THE CORVÉE

Connection between the courbash and the corvée—Merits and demerits of the corvée system—The corvée law—Dredging the canals—Proposed reduction of the land-tax—Proposal to abolish the corvée instead of reducing the land-tax—The Powers object—Action of the British Government—The corvée is not called out—A Decree is issued partially abolishing the corvée—Final settlement of the question in 1892.

THE gods, we know, are just, and of our vices, pleasant or otherwise, make instruments to scourge us. The Egyptian Government, not only that of the Pashas who ruled the country in these latter days of which this history treats, but that of their predecessors from the days of the Pharaohs onwards, was vicious in this respect, that it had held that the only way to govern the Egyptians was perpetually to flog them.[1] This special form of administrative vice was suddenly arrested. A superior authority decreed that flogging was to cease. Then the scourge of the gods, whose time for avenging past misdeeds had come, was at once applied in the following practical shape. The people of Egypt could not live unless they were supplied with water to irrigate their fields. The water could not be placed on the fields unless the mud, which

[1] The employment of the corvée dates from very ancient times. See, for instance, the description of Solomon's "bond-service" in 1 Kings ix. 15-22.

It is said that 100,000 men were made to work three months in the year for eighteen years to build the great Pyramid.

the rise of the Nile leaves at the bottom of the canals, was annually removed. It was in the interests of the people themselves that the mud should be removed in due time and season. But the majority of the people were blind to their own interests. They had always been accustomed to coercion. For centuries past, the practice had been to call on them to work in order to remove the mud, and, in case of need, to flog them unless they responded to the call. They now learnt that they were not, under any circumstances, to be flogged. In that case, they said, we need not, and we will not remove the mud. "The Ministry of Public Works," Sir Colin Scott-Moncrieff wrote on January 14, 1885, "finds by certain indications that the corvée system, which was enforced by the courbash, is becoming no longer possible under a milder régime. The peasantry refuse to go to the works at the bidding of the Moudirs, and they can no longer be compelled. The result is that the clearance of the canals is imperfectly performed."

Clearly, some means other than flogging had to be found in order to get the mud removed. That was one of the first problems which had to be solved by the British administrators of Egypt, and a very difficult problem it was. How was a torpid, semi-civilised Government to get on when, being suddenly overtaken by the rush of an imperious civilisation, it was deprived of the use of the only implement by which the people had heretofore been governed? The dilemma was one which might well have puzzled more capable men than these bewildered Egyptian Ministers who, by no fault of their own, were the last inheritors of the administrative vices bequeathed to them by their political ancestors. Indeed, it may be doubted whether the British Envoy, when he dictated the order that flogging was to cease, realised the fact that it might become necessary to flog the Egyptian people in order to prevent them from starving. Yet it is a fact that humanitarian diplomacy nearly received a severe check owing to the difficulty of getting a certain quantity of mud lifted from the bottom of a number of ditches and deposited on their banks.

It is in some respects unfortunate that the word "corvée" has been incorporated into the English language. The Arabic word is somewhat euphemistic; it is "Aouna," signifying "assistance which is compulsorily rendered." The word corvée conjures up ideas based on the condition of the French peasantry, who were "corvéable, taillable et tuable à volonté" in the pre-revolutionary days. It is, indeed, difficult to get Englishmen to believe that anything can be said in favour of a system with which such pitiful tales of suffering are associated.

From a theoretical point of view, however, the system of forced labour is capable of defence as one, amongst several forms of taxation. Moreover, from a practical point of view, it admits in some cases of justification. It may be that a country is so exceptionally situated that the interests of the community oblige the governing body to force a certain number of its citizens to fulfil their duties of citizenship by giving manual labour rather than money payments to the State. The existence of Holland depends on the dykes being kept in proper order. So also, the material prosperity of Egypt may be said to depend on the clearing of the canals in due season and on adequate steps being taken to guard against inundation.[1]

[1] In the seventeenth century, the corvée existed in England. Macaulay says: "Every parish was bound to repair the highways which passed through it. The peasantry were forced to give their gratuitous labour six days in the year" (*Works*, vol. i. p. 293). A

Although, however, recourse may justifiably be had to the corvée under certain exceptional circumstances, the system of exacting taxes in the form of manual labour is a bad one in this respect, that it is singularly liable to abuse.

The abuses to which it gave rise in Egypt were very similar to those which existed in France at the close of the eighteenth century.[1] When Sir Colin Scott-Moncrieff first examined this question, he found that the annual clearing of the canals required the work of one-eighth of the population during ninety days. "This number," he wrote on January 14, 1885, "would be amply sufficient, but owing to the fact that a large proportion of the agricultural population sends not a man to the corvée, the burden falls on the remainder with extreme severity. Instead of one-eighth of the whole population working for ninety days, a much larger proportion from certain poor districts is employed for 180 days." For instance, in the province of Gharbieh, "the Wakfs, which own 19,024 acres with a population of 4000 men, and the large proprietors, who own 83,200 acres with 17,000 men, send no men to the corvée, and pay no ransom money."

A well-intentioned but unsuccessful effort was made under the auspices of the Dual Control to deal with the corvée question. A Decree was issued on January 25, 1881, under which every inhabitant of Egypt, with a few perfectly legitimate exceptions, was rendered liable to be called out for corvée work. In certain cases, a money payment was accepted in lieu of personal service. This law was evaded by the rich, and rigorously enforced on the poor.

Scotch law to a similar effect was passed in 1719 (*Social Life in Scotland*, Graham, i. 167). To this day, the corvée is used for the maintenance of rural roads in France.

[1] Arthur Young's *Travels in France*, 1787-89, p. 45.

During the first two years of the British occupation, great difficulty was encountered in getting the canals cleared out. It was, however, found that scientific knowledge could, in some degree, serve as a substitute for labour. By skilful treatment, a portion of the alluvial deposit of the Nile was floated on to the fields and prevented from settling at the bottom of the canals. "By a little manœuvring of the water during the flood," Sir Colin Scott-Moncrieff wrote on January 31, 1885, "Mr. (afterwards Sir William) Willcocks has got a depth of ·80 metres to take out of a canal this year, where last year more than two metres had to be cleared. In Major Ross's hands this year, the clearance of the Ismailieh Canal (done by dredging, not by corvée) will cost not more, I hope, than £3000. Last year, it cost about £15,000. By the use of the 'Barrage' we raise the water surface in the canals, and they will not require to be cleared so deep."

It was, however, obviously impossible to substitute free for forced labour unless money was forthcoming to pay the labourers. A sum of about £400,000 annually would, it was estimated, be required in order to ensure the total abolition of the corvée in so far as removing the deposit from the bottom of the canals was concerned. It was not until the summer of 1885, that there appeared any prospect of being able to obtain even a moiety of this sum. Lord Northbrook, in November 1884, recommended that the land-tax should be reduced by £450,000 a year. A budget framed on this basis was communicated to the Powers by the British Government on December 6, 1884. After some diplomatic wrangling, a Khedivial Decree, to which the Powers had assented, was eventually signed on July 27, 1885. This Decree indirectly involved sanction to the proposed relief from taxation.

I have already mentioned that, dealing with Egyptian affairs, appearances are often deceptive. I have now to explain a remarkable instance of financial and political mirage. Under the arrangement made with the Powers, it appeared that a relief of taxation to the extent of £450,000 a year would be afforded to the Egyptian taxpayers. When, however, the question of carrying out the provisions of the Decree of July 27, 1885, arose, it was found that the boon, which in appearance was conferred on the people of Egypt, was to a great extent illusory. The figures had been so manipulated that a large portion of the money, which the Powers appeared to give with one hand, was taken away with the other. On October 1, 1885, Sir Edgar Vincent pointed out that the deficit of the Domains had been underestimated by £100,000, that certain taxes on Europeans, to which the Powers had agreed in principle and which were calculated to yield £100,000 a year, had not yet been imposed, and that a further margin of £100,000 should be left to allow for unpaid land-tax, for which credit had been taken in the estimates, but which it would not be possible to collect. He estimated the sum available for the relief of taxation, not at £450,000, but at £150,000.

Apart from the question of the amount of money really available, another question now arose, namely, in what form should relief be afforded to the taxpayers? The Powers had contemplated a reduction of the land-tax. Nubar Pasha, supported by his British advisers, now urged that, instead of this reduction, relief should be afforded by devoting the available money to the partial abolition of the corvée. The proposal was, in fact, most reasonable.

The abolition of the corvée had become almost a practical necessity, and the only possible method of abolishing it was to throw the charge of providing free labour on the land. It would have been absurd to reduce the land-tax, and, almost in the same breath, to reimpose a fresh tax in order to enable the corvée to be abolished. The Egyptian Government, therefore, issued a Circular to the Powers in which it was requested that, instead of applying the whole of the £450,000—to the nebulous existence of which no allusion was made—to the reduction of the land-tax, a sum of £250,000 should be applied to the partial abolition of the corvée, and the balance used in reducing the land-tax. This proposal was supported by the British Government, who "could not conceive that there was any doubt as to its acceptance by the Powers." It was, however, not accepted.

The next six months were spent in international burrowings of various sorts. The Commissioners of the Debt were eventually consulted, and on July 6, 1886, a Decree was submitted to the Powers under the provisions of which permission was given to add £250,000, which was to be applied to the partial abolition of the corvée, to the limit of the recognised administrative expenditure of the Egyptian Government.

In the meanwhile, Sir Colin Scott-Moncrieff and his coadjutors had been abolishing the corvée without awaiting the decision of the Powers. In July 1886, Sir Colin Scott-Moncrieff reported that the £250,000 devoted to the reduction of the corvée had enabled the number of men called out to work for 100 days to be reduced from 234,153 (the average of the previous three years) to 102,507, a reduction of 56 per cent. It appeared, therefore, that whilst the diplomatic agents had been discussing whether the £250,000 should be spent, the practical Scotchman had to a great extent solved the question by spending the money. The result, I remarked in writing to Lord Rosebery, was "most gratifying," and an echo of satisfaction was at once wafted back from the Foreign Office.

Here, then, was a solid fact. It was felt that, if once the fellah was relieved from the obligation of scooping up mud with his fingers from the bottom of a clay drain, under penalty of being flogged if he refused to scoop, it would be difficult for the united Powers of Europe to make him resume his former task.

In the meanwhile, regardless of facts, the international mill was grinding slowly on. It might have been thought that, as the Powers had made consultation with the Commissioners of the Debt a condition of their acceptance of the corvée Decree, and as the Commissioners had agreed to the Decree, the goal was not far distant. In reality, it was as yet scarcely in sight.

A pause then ensued. At one moment, it looked as if one of two courses was unavoidable—either to call out the corvée and thus plunge Egypt back again into the slough of the old administrative processes from which the country was just beginning to emerge, or to go on employing free labour and incur a serious risk that bankruptcy would ensue. It was questionable which was the worst of these two evils. There was, however, this much to be said in favour of the adoption of the first course, that a public declaration to the effect that the corvée was to be called out might perhaps shame the opposition into agreement, and, further, that it might stimulate the British Government to afford assistance. It was, therefore, decided to call out the corvée. A public notice to that effect was issued. The result was that public opinion, both in England and Egypt, was moved. A fortnight later (February 15), the French Government intimated their acceptance of the corvée Decree on condition that a clause should be inserted which virtually placed the whole of the Public Works expenditure under the control of the Commissioners of the Debt. The British Government were consulted by telegraph, and declined to accept the French proposal.

The situation was, at this moment, very embarrassing. Besides the corvée difficulty, the British Treasury was pressing for large military payments due by the Egyptian Government. Sir Colin Scott-Moncrieff, maddened by the opposition he encountered at every turn, resigned his post, but subsequently withdrew his resignation. Little confidence could be placed in the co-operation of the Egyptians, in whose interests the British Government and the British officials in Egypt were working. Nubar Pasha saw the interest Egypt had in avoiding the appointment of an International Commission to deal with the financial situation, but the Khedive and other leading Egyptians were indifferent on the subject. Some would even have preferred a Commission in order to break the exclusive influence of England, and others, for small local reasons, would not make any serious efforts to avoid one. It would, however, have been a stain on the reputation of England if the corvée system had been re-established. A strong plea for British assistance was, therefore, telegraphed to London. In reply, I received the following communication from Lord Salisbury :—

"If you will indicate in what way Her Majesty's Government can assist in extricating the Egyptian Government from the embarrassments now caused, they are willing to consider your suggestions in the most friendly spirit.

"The suspension of the measures for the abolition of the corvée would be so disastrous to the well-being of the fellaheen and the general prosperity of the country that it must if possible be avoided, and Her Majesty's Government will give their best attention to any proposals that may be submitted to them for tiding over the present difficulties, by any temporary measure, or by other means."

After some further communications had passed, it was agreed that, in case of need, the payment of the money due to the British Government on account of interest on the Suez Canal shares should be postponed in order to provide the funds necessary for dispensing with corvée labour. The following public notification was then issued :—

"L'adhésion de certaines Puissances au projet de Décret sur la corvée ayant été subordonnée à des modifications considérées comme inadmissibles, le Gouvernement Egyptien s'est vu dans la nécessité d'abandonner ce projet. Mais le Gouvernement de Son Altesse, considérant la suppression de la corvée comme une mesure à laquelle sont attachés le bien-être et la prospérité du pays, a consulté le Gouvernement Britannique, qui partage entièrement l'opinion du Gouvernement Egyptien à ce sujet.

"À la suite de cet échange de vues, des arrangements ont été pris qui permettent l'emploi du travail rémunéré. La décision du Conseil des Ministres contenue dans 'l'Officiel' du 5 de ce mois a été, par conséquent, rapportée[1] et le Ministre des Travaux Publics a été invité à sanctionner les contrats d'entreprises qui avaient été suspendus."

There are a few important landmarks in the history of Egyptian administration, and this is one of them. As the Circular issued under Lord Dufferin's auspices gave a death-blow to the use of the courbash, so the notification quoted above

[1] This decision was the notification calling out the corvée.

sealed the doom of the corvée system. Although the battle was not yet over, there could henceforward be no doubt as to the side which would ultimately gain the victory. The fellaheen were no longer to be flogged unless they scooped up mud with their fingers from the bottom of a deep ditch. The British Government had practically pledged their word that this particular Egyptian abomination should cease. Retractation was no longer possible. Nubar Pasha understood the importance of the step, and in words suitable to the occasion expressed the feelings of the Egyptian people.

"L'abolition de la corvée, vous le savez, M. le Ministre," he wrote, "a été un but que le Gouvernement de Son Altesse a visé depuis longtemps, et vers lequel ont constamment tendu tous ses vœux ; aussi, me fais-je un devoir de vous prier de transmettre au Gouvernement Britannique l'expression de la reconnaissance de toute l'Égypte pour le concours qu'elle a trouvé auprès du Gouvernement Britannique dans la réalisation partielle d'une mesure à laquelle sont attachés le bien-être et la prospérité du pays."

Egyptian gratitude is perhaps not always very heartfelt or very long-lived, but there can be no doubt that the debt of gratitude was really due. Moreover, thanks—"Evermore thanks, the exchequer of the poor"—was all the Egyptians had to give.

Amongst the many achievements which England has accomplished in the cause of suffering humanity, not the least praiseworthy is this act, that in the teeth of strong opposition, the Anglo-Saxon race insisted that the Egyptian labourer should be paid for his work, and that he should not be flogged if he did not wish to work.

As yet, however, the victory was not complete. It has been already stated that an annual sum of about £400,000 was required to abolish the corvée system in so far as the clearing out of the canals was concerned. With infinite trouble, £250,000 a year had been obtained. This enabled the system of forced labour to be partially abolished. In 1883, the number of men called out for 100 days was 202,650. In 1886, the number fell to 95,093. In 1887, only 87,120 men were called out. The corvée system having been virtually doomed, the question naturally arose of how to dispense with the enforced services of the remaining 87,000 men. To complete the reform, a further expenditure of £150,000 a year was required. The Egyptian Government wished that this sum should be added to the amount of the administrative expenditure authorised by the Powers. This proposal was not, in the first instance, accepted.

It would serve no useful purpose to narrate in detail the history of the tedious and, at times, somewhat angry negotiations which then ensued. They may well be buried in oblivion. It will be sufficient to say that, as time went on and the financial position improved, an immediate settlement became a matter of less urgency. Eventually, the death of Tewfik Pasha, in January 1892, afforded an unexpected opportunity for settling the question. The Egyptian Government, instigated by their British advisers, wished to signalise the accession of the young Khedive by the adoption of some measures which would be of general benefit to the population. They proposed to devote a portion of the economies resulting from the recent conversion of the Preference debt from a 5 per cent to a 3½ per cent stock, to the abolition of the corvée, and at the same time to reduce the salt tax by 40 per cent. The French Government would not agree to any proposals which involved touching the economies. On the other hand, they were unwilling to stand in the way of a reduction of the salt tax. But they coupled a condition with their acceptance of the Egyptian proposal.

The London Conference of 1884 had agreed in principle that Europeans in Egypt should pay the professional tax, which had heretofore been only paid by Egyptians. After some tedious negotiations, a law applicable to all residents in Egypt, whether European or Egyptian, had been accepted by the Powers. At the time of Tewfik Pasha's death, the tax was, for the first time, about to be levied on Europeans, amongst whom it was naturally very unpopular. The French Government decided to make their assent to the Egyptian proposal relative to the reduction of the salt tax and the abolition of the corvée conditional on the abolition of the professional tax. Ultimately, it was arranged that the salt tax should be reduced; that the professional tax should be abolished both in respect to Europeans and Egyptians; and that the recognised limit of the administrative expenditure of the Egyptian Government should be increased by £150,000 a year, thus enabling money to be found to pay for the free labour which had taken the place of the corvée.

Thus, after a struggle which lasted for eight years, this great reform was eventually accomplished. Begun when Egypt was in the throes of national bankruptcy, it was continued through a long period of diplomatic bickerings, which sometimes assumed an acute form and at other times lapsed into a chronic state of acerbity, and was at last concluded by the fortuitous circumstance that it became possible to drive a bargain over the grave of the dead Khedive. To Tewfik Pasha may be accorded the posthumous merit of having by his death overcome to some slight and temporary extent the demon of international jealousy, and of having thus given a final blow to the hateful system of forced labour which had existed in the country over which he ruled since the days of his Pharaonic predecessors.

So far allusion has only been made to the forced labour which used to be employed in the work of clearing out the canals during the period of low Nile. The corvée has, however, from time immemorial been employed in Egypt to attain another object, namely, to guard the banks of the river during the period of high Nile and thus obviate any risk of inundation. It is essential to the well-being and safety of the country that this work should be performed. It has not as yet been found possible to abolish completely this description of corvée, but the number of men employed every year is small, and is steadily diminishing.

CHAPTER LI

CORRUPTION

Universality of corruption—Steps taken to arrest it—Example of British officials—Diminution of corrupt practices.

In no country probably has corruption—the canker which eats away the heart of most Eastern governments—been more universal than it was in Egypt during the reign of Ismail Pasha. Ismail had inherited from his predecessors an administrative system steeped in corruption. By his own action, he made this system doubly corrupt. He believed in bribery, if not as the only, at all events as the most effective system of government. Every man, he thought, had his price. He put into practice the principles of which Byron, in one of his cynical moods, has given us a description :—

'Tis pleasant purchasing our fellow-creatures,
And all are to be sold, if you consider
Their passions, and are dext'rous ; some by features
Are bought up, others by a warlike leader ;
Some by a place, as tend their years or natures ;
The most by ready cash—but all have prices,
From crowns to kicks, according to their vices.

Ismail Pasha's subjects followed humbly in the footsteps of their master. They took and they paid bribes. From the half-naked donkey-boy, who in shrill tones demanded "bakhshish" to the extent of a piastre or two from the winter tourist, to the highly-placed Pasha, whose assistance could only be obtained by the payment of more substantial sums, all, or nearly all, were venal. The contractor bribed the Minister to obtain a contract on terms unduly advantageous to himself, and would then bribe the Clerk of the Works in order that he should not inquire too carefully as to whether the terms of the contract had or had not been strictly executed. The subordinate official bribed his superior in order to get promotion. The landowner bribed the engineer in order that he should obtain more water for his fields than was his due. The Kadis were paid by both the plaintiff and the defendant to any suit, the decision being usually given in favour of the highest bidder. The Government surveyors were bribed to make false measurements of land. The village Sheikhs were bribed to accord exemption from the corvée and from military service. The Police were bribed by everybody who had the misfortune to be brought in contact with them. The passenger by railway found it cheaper to give "bakhshish" to the guard or to the ticket-collector than to pay for a ticket. As a preliminary to bribing a Moudir to inquire into any alleged grievance, it was necessary for the petitioner to bribe the hungry satellites, who hang about the office of the Moudirieh, before the great man could be personally informed that any petition had been presented. The ramifications of the system were, in fact, endless. Egyptian official and social life was saturated with the idea that in Egypt personal claims and interests, however just on their own merits, could never be advanced without the payment of "bakhshish."

It was from the first manifest that the adoption of more healthy ideas by an administrative service and by a society so thoroughly diseased as that described above, would be a work of time. One of the main safeguards against corruption in civilised countries is that society condemns venality. The act of offering or of taking a bribe is considered dishonourable. The offender, if discovered, is visited by a social punishment often more severe than any which the law can inflict on him. In Egypt, no restraining public opinion existed, even if it now exists, on this subject. Bribery was considered a venial offence. Habits of thought of this kind cannot be changed of a sudden. They are but little affected by the passing of laws and regulations. Nevertheless, it was possible to adopt certain administrative measures calculated to diminish the temptation to accept bribes, and thus both render it less probable that bribery would obtain the objects for which money had heretofore been paid, and also facilitate the discovery of the guilty parties. Measures of this sort were initiated in Egypt during the period of the Dual Control, and were subsequently perfected during that of the British occupation.

In the first place, the inauguration of a proper system of accounts and of audit did a good deal towards putting a check on the malversation of funds belonging to the State. Vouchers were required for all expenditure. Officials were called upon to render strict account of all monies which had passed through their hands. It was no longer possible for public money to disappear as if by enchantment.

This reform was excellent in its way. It is, however, a mistake to suppose that the accountant or the auditor can alone put a stop to the corrupt dealings of dishonest officials. A hundred ways exist for eluding their vigilance. To quote a single instance, a high Egyptian official was, on one occasion, charged with the sale of certain lands belonging to the Government. Adjoining these lands, were others, which were his private property.

He sold the two lots together to the same purchaser. They were of precisely the same quality, but the price obtained for the Government was very low, whilst that obtained by the official acting in his private capacity was very high. Thus, a considerable part of the money, which should have been paid into the Treasury, found its way into the pockets of the official who was specially charged to look after the interests of the Government. No system of audit would have succeeded in preventing a fraud of this description. It could only have been discovered by some one who happened to know that the market value of the land sold by the Government was in excess of the sum which the Government received.

In the second place, the regular payment of the salaries due to Government officials has done much to free them from the temptation to take bribes. Also, in many cases the salaries of the lowest classes have been raised. So long as the Government allowed inadequate salaries to their servants, or, as in the days of Ismail Pasha, often left them for months without paying them at all, it is obvious that the temptation of the latter to increase their incomes by illicit means must have been strong.[1]

In the third place, the system of inviting tenders for most public works and for the supply of Government stores, struck a blow in that quarter where corruption on a large scale was heretofore most prevalent.

In the fourth place, the creation of an improved judicature, the careful choice of judges, and the more vigilant control which has been exercised over their conduct, have purified the law-courts.

In the fifth place, with the abolition of the

[1] It was by raising the salaries of officials that Lord Cornwallis put a stop to the corruption which existed in India towards the close of the eighteenth century.

greater part of the corvée, and the regulation of whatever remains of the system of forced labour, the necessity for paying the village Sheikhs in order to be exempted from the obligation to labour disappeared.

In the sixth place, the organisation of a proper recruiting service swept away a whole nest of corrupt practices.

Lastly, the employment of a number of honourable and capable British officials has probably done more than anything else to check corruption. Their mere example has counted for much. The Egyptians pay an unconscious compliment to English integrity by very rarely offering bribes to British officials.[1]

It cannot be doubted that these measures have been effective in checking corruption. Broadly speaking, it may be said that most branches of the central administration of the Egyptian Government and the law-courts are now little, if at all, tainted with venality. It is not, however, on this account to be supposed that the "bakhshish" system is defunct. It is, of course, impossible to state with any degree of confidence to what extent it still exists, for the people, in spite of every encouragement given to them by the superior officials of the Government, are generally reluctant to complain of illegal exactions, whilst, on the other hand, the corrupt Egyptian official displays such a singular degree of perverted ingenuity in the perpetration of fraud as to baffle the efforts of those whose wish it is to track him down. On the whole, it may be said that although corruption is no longer practised on any large scale, it cannot be doubted that in the provincial administrations, as also, I fear, in some branches of the

[1] As a general rule, the integrity of the British officials in Egypt has been absolutely unimpeachable. There have, however, I regret to say, been a very few cases of corruption and dishonesty amongst the subordinates.

Public Works Department, there is still a good deal of bribery. It will be long before all this disappears, more especially in view of the extreme difficulty of obtaining evidence against corrupt officials.[1] In the meanwhile, it can be stated with confidence that at no previous period in Egyptian history has so little "bakhshish" been paid or received as at present.

These, therefore, were the first-fruits of British interference in the country. Torture and the use of the courbash ceased. The corvée system was practically abolished. Administrative corruption was greatly diminished.

How was it that, in these three cases, the efforts of the British officials in the service of the Egyptian Government were crowned with such signal success? It was because they were either free to act, or because, as in the matter of the corvée, they were able, after a sharp struggle, to throw off the international shackles by which they were bound. The more the history of Egyptian reform is examined, the more will it be seen that in most cases success was in direct proportion to the freedom of action of the Egyptian Government, acting under British control and advice. Where no such freedom exists, the result has usually been either failure, or, at best, a modified success.

[1] It cannot be too clearly understood that fear of each other has, in the minds of the mass of the Egyptian population, largely taken the place of the fear of the Government, which formerly existed. This is a very important feature in the administration of the country. The latter of these two sentiments tended, at all events, towards the maintenance of public tranquillity. On the other hand, the fear that vengeance will, in some form or another, be wreaked by any one of whose conduct a complaint is made, or against whom evidence is tendered in a law-court, manifestly operates in an exactly opposite direction. Mr. Machell, the present Adviser of the Interior, has, in his Annual Reports, given frequent and very striking illustrations in support of this view. As regards the jealousy often entertained amongst the fellaheen for each other, see *Egypt*, No. 1, 1905, p. 45.

CHAPTER LII

EUROPEAN PRIVILEGE

Origin of the Capitulations—Difference between Turkey and Egypt—Abuse of the Capitulations—*Raison d'être* of European privilege—Anomaly of the British position—Impossibility of arriving at any general solution—Minor changes—The right to enact by-laws—The House Tax—The Professional Tax—Proposal to create a local legislature—Internationalism.

It is unnecessary to enter into any technical discussion on the rights conferred by virtue of the Capitulations upon Europeans resident in Egypt. The subject is complicated, more especially as some of those rights rest on the text of international instruments, whilst the precise nature of others, which have been acquired by custom, is still a constant source of dispute. Historically speaking, it is, indeed, incorrect in this connection to employ the term "rights." The Capitulations were originally "letters of privilege, or, according to the Oriental expression, imperial diplomas containing sworn promises,"[1] which were delivered by the Sultans of Turkey, as also by their Byzantine predecessors, to Europeans who wished to reside and to acquire real property in their dominions. A legal fiction had to be created in order to afford a justification to strict Moslems, who were guided solely by Koranic principles, for dealing with Christians on a basis of equality. Christians were theoretically deemed perpetual enemies and, as such, unworthy of peace unless they either embraced Islam or paid

[1] Van Dyck, *Ottoman Capitulations*, p. 12.

tribute to their Moslem conquerors. With unbelievers, "treaties" were impossible, and indeed impious, but it was conceivable that the Commander of the Faithful might, of his grace, condescend to grant them "privileges." The Moslem, unaware that his inelastic faith contained within itself the seeds of his own political decadence, may well have thought that the bestowal of these "privileges" would not undermine his system of government. In this, he was mistaken. As the power of the Crescent waned before that of the Cross, the Frank was gradually transformed from being a humble receiver of "privileges" into an imperious possessor of "rights." These rights were to form a potent instrument for good and also for evil, both to their possessors and to those by whom they were originally conferred. They were notably to contribute, as they are still contributing, to shatter the political and social systems of those who hold to the faith of Islam.

The rights which have been conferred by, or which have grown out of the Capitulations are not the same in Egypt and in other parts of the Ottoman dominions. The Turkish Government have been watchful of European encroachment, and have, relatively speaking, been powerful to resist it. The Khedives of Egypt, on the other hand, being wanting in vigilance, allowed a plentiful crop of European privileges, which are not sanctioned by treaty, to be drifted on the wave of custom into the position of acquired rights, and if, as at times occurred, they tardily awoke to the consequences of their own heedlessness, they were either too weak to offer resistance, or the impecuniosity, which was the result of reckless extravagance, rendered them willing to barter a portion of their political birthright for the sake of some temporary concession. Thus it came about that the European, who is privileged in Turkey, is ultra-privileged in Egypt. Abuse of privilege follows in the train of privilege itself. It happened, therefore, that in that part of the Ottoman dominions which, more than any other, has of late years been subject to the direct control of a European Power, and in which, consequently, the concession of privilege has been least of all necessary and its abuse most of all baneful to the cause of progress, the degree of privilege granted has been greater, and its abuse more pronounced, than in any other portion of the territories of the Sultan.

Although, however, nothing can be said in favour of the abuse, many valid arguments may be advanced in defence of the use of the Capitulations. At first sight, it appears monstrous that the smuggler should carry on his illicit trade under the eyes of the Custom-house authorities because treaty engagements forbid any prompt and effective action being taken against him. Those engagements have also been turned to such base uses that they have protected the keeper of the gambling hell, the vendor of adulterated drinks, the receiver of stolen goods, and the careless apothecary who supplies his customer with poison in the place of some healing drug. But when all this, and a great deal more of the same description of argument has been stated, there still remains the unquestionable fact that the smuggler, the keeper of a gambling-hell, the receiver of stolen goods, and the retailer of adulterated spirits, represent certain principles. They, and their contemptible brethren, notably represent these principles, that so long as they have not been proved to commit an offence at law[1] they have a right to continue without hin-

[1] It is to be borne in mind that, before any European can be adequately punished, he must be proved to have committed an offence not against Egyptian law, but against the law of his country of origin.

drance in the exercise of their callings, and that before they undergo punishment or molestation of any kind, it must be shown to the satisfaction of some properly constituted and trustworthy authority that they have transgressed the law. One of the great battles in the history of English constitutional liberty was fought over the person of the disreputable Wilkes. Lord Palmerston's treatment of the Don Pacifico case is another instance in point. So likewise, paradoxical as it may appear, the cause of European civilisation in Egypt is to some extent unavoidably identified with the treatment of European ruffians. For, in fact, it is often difficult to do anything towards sweeping away the abuse of privilege without incurring a considerable risk that other equally objectionable abuses may be created in the process of reform. It is reasonable that the Egyptian custom-house official should search the ship of the smuggler for tobacco or hashish, but what guarantee is there that the same official will not, in disregard of the spirit if not of the text of the law, subject the captain of a vessel engaged in legitimate trade to endless vexations? Inviolability of domicile is one of the corner-stones of European privilege in the East. It is well that the Police should be able to penetrate into a gambling-hell and stop an infamous trade, but what guarantee is there that, under the orders of an official incapable of any fine discrimination of character or of circumstances, these same Police will not invade the house of some individual who never in the course of his life held a playing-card or a dice-box in his hand? The careless apothecary should, in the interests of the public, be prevented from poisoning his customers, but his more careful rival in trade naturally requires some valid assurance that he will not be subjected to unnecessary annoyances in the exercise of his profession. Endless illustrations of the same sort might be adduced. Whenever the question of modifying the Capitulations has been broached, the contending parties have always used the same arguments. On the one side, stood the reformer rightly clamouring against the abuse of privilege which impeded his progress. On the other side, stood the European who, if he was politically unbiassed, expressed his willingness to aid in checking the abuse and in furthering the progress of reform, but who, under the influence of profound and, to some extent, justifiable mistrust of Oriental legal and administrative processes, demanded guarantees against an abuse of power before he would agree to curtail the privileges of his countrymen. The guarantees which were demanded were often excessive, and moreover, they generally took a form which involved an extension of the international system of government. The Egyptian Government either would not or could not grant them. Hence, not unfrequently arose a deadlock.

When the British occupation took place, the question of the rights conferred on Europeans by the Capitulations entered into a new and singular phase. The English took Egyptian reform in hand. They found themselves hampered at every turn by the privileges which they, in common with other foreign nations, enjoyed. The English reformer was able to plead that, under his civilised auspices, there would be no longer any danger of an abuse of power, and that, therefore, greater freedom of action could properly be accorded to an Anglo-Egyptian than to a purely Egyptian Government. In the early days of the occupation, this argument availed him but little either with his friends or with his foes. His foes scoffed at it. It is true, they said, that you are here, but you have no right to stay. Even supposing the paramount influence of England to constitute a valid guarantee against abuse, which we doubt, what is to become of the guarantee when you leave the country, as you have promised to do? More than this, are we to abandon our rights merely to facilitate the work of our rivals, who have outwitted us? Heaven forbid. We will not even make those concessions to an Anglo-Egyptian Government which we might perhaps have made to an Egyptian Government, pure and simple.

The friends of the English reformer came to much the same conclusion as his foes, but by a different process of reasoning. If, they said, you would declare your intention to remain permanently in Egypt and to undertake the administration of the country, we should not be unwilling to concede our privileges, for we should then have some solid guarantee against an abuse of power. But as you are constantly asseverating that you are but sojourners in the land, and that your occupation is only temporary, we fail to see what guarantees against abuse will exist when you carry out your declared intentions. There could be no question as to the validity of this argument. Moreover, it was one which the British Government were themselves obliged to recognise and adopt. Hence, the British nation had characteristically placed itself in this illogical position—that whilst its official representative was obliged at times to maintain privilege in British interests for fear of eventual abuse by the Egyptians, he was also called upon by the British reformer to aid in the abolition of privilege in order to further that work of reform in which the Government and people of England were deeply interested. The creation of this singular position may be regarded as a triumph of Anglo-Saxon inconsistency. "England," Montalembert once said, "fortunately for herself, is not the pedantic slave of logic." Fully as I recognise the value of this encomium, I have sometimes, as a humble agent charged with the execution of British policy, wished that that policy was a little more logical.

Under all these circumstances, only one solution was for many years possible. It was that, in so far as the main issues were concerned, there should be no solution at all. Unless the British Government were prepared to assume permanently the responsibility of governing Egypt, it was neither possible nor desirable to assimilate the legal status of all the inhabitants of the country. It was, indeed, painful enough to see the parasitic and ignoble growths which clung round European civilisation, but as Egypt was to be civilised on a European model without being formally placed under a European Government, it was inevitable that, together with many blessings, some of the curses of civilisation should devolve on the country. Apart from the practical and political difficulties which stood in the way of radical reform, it was to be observed that, looking at the matter broadly, the blessings greatly predominated over the curses. The material prosperity of Egypt depended in no small degree on the presence of a numerous European colony, and on the attractions for the investment of European capital. The European would not reside in Egypt unless he could make money by doing so, and he could not make money unless his life and property were guaranteed against the arbitrary proceedings of a Government which but recently was very bad, and which, as he rightly thought, would probably relapse into its former condition if the controlling hand of England were withdrawn.

Broadly speaking, therefore, the question of

European privilege stood, up to 1904, in much the same position as it did in 1882. Nevertheless, if we descend from general principles to detail, it will be found that a few minor reforms were undertaken of a nature to mitigate some of the worst abuses of the system which the English found in existence when they took Egyptian affairs seriously in hand.

The main blot in the system under which Egypt was, and, unfortunately, still is governed, is the absence of any legislative machinery capable of passing laws binding on all the inhabitants of the country. As the absence of any properly constituted Tribunals created, to use Nubar Pasha's expressive phrase, a "judicial Babel," so the absence of any supreme legislature creates a "legislative Babel." History affords abundant examples of countries whose systems of legislation have been bad. Egypt affords a unique example of a country well advanced on the road to civilisation which, for all practical purposes, may be said to possess no general legislative system whatsoever.

Although, however, the system of legislation by diplomacy, in so far as its main features are concerned, still holds the field, and although it is true that the continuance of this system involves an almost complete legislative deadlock, nevertheless, after vast travail, the diplomatic mountain did at last bring forth a small but not altogether ridiculous mouse, which in some degree mitigated the evils necessarily attendant on legislative impotence. Nubar Pasha, to whom must be attributed the merit of the innovation about to be described, pointed out that, apart from questions of the first importance, such as criminal jurisdiction and the right of taxing Europeans, there remained a considerable field of petty but not unimportant legislation on matters relating to what he termed "la vie journalière de la population." Questions were frequently arising as to the extent to which Europeans were subject to regulations edicted by the Egyptian Government on such matters as the maintenance of dykes and canals, the establishment of drinking-shops and places of amusement, the right to carry arms, and a host of other minor subjects, which in Europe are often treated by by-laws framed by some subordinate legislative authority, to whom power has been delegated by the supreme legislature. After some discussion, the Powers agreed to confer legislative rights on the Egyptian Government in respect to these matters, subject to the condition that the Egyptian proposals, before acquiring the force of law, should receive the approval of the General Assembly of the Mixed Tribunals. It was provided that no greater punishment than a fine of £1 or seven days' imprisonment could be incurred for infringing these by-laws.[1] The Decree introducing these changes, which is dated January 31, 1889, is a document of some importance in so far as it represents the first faltering steps taken in the direction of a real Egyptian legislative autonomy.

The arrangement is obviously open to some objections in principle. It is unusual that judges should frame the laws, which they have to administer. But the necessities of the case were such as to render it impossible to attach much weight to objections based on the undesirability of amalgamating legislative and judicial functions. In Egypt, legislators have to be caught wherever they can be found. As a legislative machinery composed of judges was ready to hand, that

[1] In very numerous cases, the penalty for infringing the law is altogether insufficient to ensure general respect being paid to its provisions. Moreover, the procedure of the law-courts is often complicated and unduly slow in action. These defects have become notably apparent in dealing with the illicit sale of Hashish, the use of which is a fertile source of lunacy in Egypt. See *Egypt*, No. 1 of 1906, p. 64.

machinery had to be utilised in default of anything better.

The fundamental idea of the Decree of January 31, 1889, was, therefore, to transfer a certain portion of the legislative functions, heretofore exercised collectively by the Powers, to the judges of the Mixed Tribunals. Some beneficent measures have been enacted under its provisions. To quote a single instance, the Egyptian Government have been enabled to control the sale of liquor in the agricultural districts, and have thus placed some sort of check on the demoralisation which the foreign purveyor of alcoholic and often adulterated drinks spreads around him.[1]

Passing to another reform, it is to be observed that when the British occupation took place, certain direct taxes were paid by Egyptians, but not by Europeans. These were the house tax and the professional tax. No valid arguments could be adduced in favour of exempting Europeans from the payment of these taxes. The reason why they did not pay them was because they did not like paying them. Secure in the support of their diplomatic representatives, they had succeeded in maintaining their fiscal privileges intact. The injustice was so glaring that the Powers were forced into applying a remedy. On March 17, 1885, they went so far, at the instance of the British Government, as to sign a Declaration stating that they "recognised the justice of making their subjects in Egypt liable to the same taxes as the natives." They agreed in principle to a Decree under the terms of which Europeans were rendered liable to the payment of the house tax; they "equally declared that they accepted the application to their subjects, in the same manner as to

[1] For further remarks on this very important subject, see, *inter alia*, *Egypt*, No. 1 of 1907, pp. 73-76.

the natives, of the stamp tax and licence tax ; and they engaged to undertake immediately, in concert with the Egyptian Government, the study of the draft laws establishing these two taxes."

Both before and after the signing of this Declaration, the usual unedifying and wearisome wrangling took place. It was not till April 15, 1886, that a Decree was at last issued which rendered Europeans liable to the payment of the house tax.

Although the Powers undertook, on March 17, 1885, to study "immediately" the draft laws necessary for the imposition of the licence or professional tax on Europeans, it is to be borne in mind that the word "immediate" is, in diplomatic phraseology, a relative term. Six years elapsed before, on March 8, 1891, a Decree was issued, under which Europeans were rendered liable to the payment of the professional tax. The law had not, however, been put in operation when, in connection with the corvée negotiations,[1] the French Government pressed for its repeal. There was a good deal to be said in favour of abolishing the tax. In spite of the prolonged study which preceded the issue of the Decree, many of its details were faulty. Moreover, in an Oriental country, a direct tax is always liable to abuse by reason of the untrustworthy nature of the agency employed in its assessment and collection. The Egyptian Government and their British advisers, therefore, decided to rest content with the victory which had been already gained. By dint of strenuous perseverance, they had remedied an injustice ; they had asserted the principle that in fiscal matters Europeans and Egyptians were to be treated on a footing of equality ; there could be no objection to a relief of taxation which would be applied to Europeans and Egyptians alike. The professional

[1] *Vide ante*, p. 418.

tax was, therefore, abolished by a Decree issued on January 28, 1892.

To sum up. The results of British intervention in Egypt, in so far as European privilege is concerned, have up to the present time been as follows:—

1. A slight advance has been made in the direction of Egyptian legislative autonomy.

2. Europeans and Egyptians have been placed on a basis of equality in so far as taxation is concerned.

With the signature of the Anglo-French Convention in 1904, the question of dealing with the Capitulations entered into a new phase. The prospects of reform brightened. It became possible to discuss the subject on its own merits without the introduction of irrelevant issues.

I have already stated that the main object of this work is to narrate the history of the past, rather than to discuss questions which now occupy public attention. Acting on this principle, I abstain from entering fully into a discussion of the method under which the existing régime of the Capitulations might advantageously be modified. In my Annual Report for the year 1905[1] I dwelt on this subject, and in my Report for the following year,[2] I sketched out the broad features of a plan, having for its object the creation in Egypt of a Council invested with powers to enact laws binding on all Europeans resident in Egypt. I concluded with the following remarks:—

"I am well aware of the danger of making Constitutions which may look well on paper, but which will not work in practice. It is one against which Lord Dufferin very wisely uttered a note of warning when he was framing proposals for the creation of an Egyptian Legislative Assembly. I

[1] *Egypt*, No. 1 of 1906, pp. 1-8.
[2] *Egypt*, No. 1 of 1907, pp. 10-26.

have endeavoured, to the best of my ability, to avoid this danger. My wish has been to create an institution which, albeit it will not be free from anomalies, and may possess many theoretical imperfections, will, on the whole, be suited to the present practical requirements of Egyptian political and administrative life. I have more particularly endeavoured to utilise such elements as are available, in order to guard, so far as is possible, against that danger to which, possibly, Egypt is somewhat specially exposed—I mean the danger of making what Burke once called 'a stock-jobbing Constitution.' I am far from saying that I have altogether succeeded, but I trust that what I have proposed may form the basis for further discussion, with the result that any defects which may be discovered in the scheme set forth in this Report may be remedied.

"Much will depend upon the views taken by the natural leaders of public opinion in Egypt. To the Egyptians, I would say that some plan based on the broad features of that which I have sketched out is, I am convinced, the only method by which they can, within any period which it is now possible to foresee, be relieved of those portions of the Capitulations which retard the progress of their country, and of which they so frequently, and, I should add, so legitimately, complain. To the Europeans who have made Egypt their home, I would say that, in my desire to guard against any reappearance of the arbitrary methods of government against which the Capitulations were intended to protect them, I am no less European than they; that though the rights and privileges which they very naturally prize are taken away in one form, they are simultaneously granted in another form of equal and far less objectionable efficacy; and that, in addition, the inestimable privilege will be granted to them of making their own laws, instead of being dependent on the vicissitudes of European politics and on the views taken in fifteen different capitals of the world by others, who, however much they may be animated by good intentions, must necessarily be ignorant of local requirements. It is only in the 'Land of Paradox' that the bestowal on a whole community of the right to manage its own affairs could be regarded as the destruction of a privilege.

"Before moving any further in the matter, I ask the leading Europeans resident in Egypt whether they wish to support an archaic system of government which has outlived its time, and which acts as a clog to all real progress, or whether they would not rather prefer to assist in reforming that system in order to meet the altered conditions of the country, and thus lay the foundation-stone of an Egyptian nationality in the best and only practicable sense of that much-abused term."

I have now only to express an earnest hope that this question will not be allowed to drop. By far the most important reform now required in Egypt is to devise some plan which will enable laws binding on Europeans resident in the country to be enacted. Until this is done, progress in many directions, where reform is urgently required, will be barred. I would add that the mere transfer of criminal jurisdiction over Europeans from the Consular to the Mixed Courts—a project which finds support in some quarters—altogether fails to meet the requirements of the situation. The main reform required is legislative, not judicial.[1]

The abolition of indefensible privileges is part and parcel of the work of modern progress. In

[1] Some further remarks on this subject will be found on p. 568.

the West, the work of destroying privilege is well-nigh complete, and the next generation will probably see democracy pass from the destructive, and enter upon the constructive phase of its existence, with what result we cannot now foretell. The backward East is still in the stage in which a privilege destroyed, whether it be of a Western or of an Eastern type, may be regarded as a battle won. The constructive period of Eastern political existence is as yet afar, neither can any one of the present generation hope to see what will eventually happen to the curious amalgam of fanaticism and agnosticism, of old-world despotism and latter-day republicanism, which in Egypt, as in other Oriental countries, is now laid on the anvil, and which receives blows from all quarters of such diverse strength as to render it a matter of haphazard conjecture to foretell what will be the shape which it will ultimately assume. In the meanwhile, assuming the abolition of such privileges as those enjoyed by Europeans in Egypt to be an advantage, it may be noted that the Egyptian Government, under British auspices, made one considerable step forward. They placed all the residents in Egypt, whether European or Egyptian, on a footing of fiscal equality. But they have so far been unable seriously to attack the Capitulations, which constitute the main citadel of privilege. These, as in the days prior to the British occupation, remain for the present inviolate. Why was this? It was because the international system of government barred the way to advance.

This work has been written to little purpose if it has not shown the radical defects of internationalism, considered as a machinery for administration and legislation. In making this remark, however, I must carefully guard against being misunderstood. In condemning executive action through international agency, I do not in any degree wish to deprecate the employment of officials of various nationalities in certain executive functions. The system which I wish to condemn is that under which executive officials are practically nominated by foreign Governments and become, as experience in Egypt has abundantly proved, the political agents of their countries of origin. Not only is there no objection to the Egyptian Government being free to choose their European officials from any country in Europe, but great advantage is to be derived from the adoption of this system. Some solid guarantee is thus afforded that the individuals nominated will be chosen solely by reason of their professional merits, and that they will not be moved by political considerations to overstep the limit of the functions assigned to them. The same remark applies, even to a greater extent, to the case of those in judicial employment. European judges for the Egyptian law-courts should continue, as at present, to be chosen from various nationalities.

The case of legislative internationalism is somewhat different. Egypt is essentially a cosmopolitan country. It follows, therefore, as a matter of course, that if any local legislature is created, it must, if it is to be truly representative, be cosmopolitan in character.

The internationalism which I wish to condemn is, therefore, confined to what may be termed political internationalism, that is to say, the system which admits of the employment of political agents, who, acting under whatever instructions they may receive from their several Foreign Offices, are prone to introduce into the discussion of some purely local question, considerations based on the friendliness or hostility, in other parts of the world, of their countries of origin. Political passions are—or, at any moment may become—too strong to allow of an international system of this latter type working smoothly. "The principles of true politics," Burke once said, "are those of morality enlarged, and I neither now do, nor ever will, admit of any other." An influential school of English politicians have been zealous in supporting the principle of action thus advocated by Burke. "I would not," Mr. Bright said in 1877, "dissociate what is true in morals from what is true in statesmanship." Few persons would wish to speak in disparaging terms of these noble principles. They certainly command my full assent, and, I may add, that during a long diplomatic career, I have persistently acted upon them to the best of my ability. But, whilst our principles may be elevated, our application of them must be subordinated to the facts with which we have to deal. Do not let us imagine that nations and Governments in general are prepared altogether to assimilate public and private morality. Mr. Lecky says with truth: "Nothing is more calamitous than the divorce of politics from morals, but in practical politics public and private morals will never absolutely correspond."[1] Internationalism, in spite of its fair exterior, which proclaims equality of governing power and equitable treatment towards subject races, means but too often in practice political egotism, a disregard of the rights of subject races, and, in the case now under discussion, a decadence in the authority of that European Power on the maintenance of whose paramount influence the advance of true civilisation in Egypt depends. That Power is Great Britain.

[1] *Map of Life*, p. 181.

CHAPTER LIII

FINANCE

The first bankruptcy of Egypt—Risk of a second bankruptcy—The Race against Bankruptcy—The era of reform—Fiscal relief—Reduction of taxation—Increase of revenue—Expenditure—Aggregate surplus since 1888—The indebtedness of the fellaheen—Distribution of land—Importance of the financial question.

"GREAT," says Carlyle, "is Bankruptcy. . . . Honour to Bankruptcy; ever righteous on the great scale, though in detail it is so cruel. Under all falsehoods it works unweariedly mining. No falsehood, did it rise heaven high and cover the world, but Bankruptcy, one day, will sweep it down and make us free of it."[1]

In Egypt, bankruptcy, of a truth, destroyed many false gods and pricked many bubbles. Notably, it dashed down Ismail Pasha, the great high-priest of Sham, from that false eminence which he had attained, and allowed him to be pulverised by the adventurers who were his former worshippers. More than this, bankruptcy, riding roughshod over all who would not recognise the irresistible nature of its action, brought home to the minds of a reluctant Egyptian Ministry that they must needs abandon the Soudan, at all events for a time, because they could not afford to stay there. These and many other benefits did bankruptcy, in its ruthlessness, confer on a land whose

[1] *French Revolution,* Book iii. c. i.

government had for many years been one gigantic falsehood.

When the British troops occupied Egypt in 1882, one act of bankruptcy had already been committed. In 1879, the Government of Egypt declared themselves insolvent. In 1880, a composition with their creditors was effected. Nevertheless, under the combined influences of the Arábi rebellion and the cataclysm in the Soudan, the Treasury was again on the high road to another act of bankruptcy. There was, however, this difference between the financial chaos of 1878-79 and that of 1882-83. During the earlier of these two periods, the hopes of every well-wisher to Egypt were based on a declaration of bankruptcy. It was impossible to apply a remedy until the true facts of the case were recognised. In 1882-83, on the other hand, it was in the true interest of every Egyptian, and of every sympathiser with Egypt, to stave off bankruptcy, for the remedy which would certainly have been applied, had a condition of bankruptcy been declared, was almost as bad as the disease. That remedy was international government *in excelsis*. Hence, the Egyptian Government had to enter upon what Lord Milner has aptly termed "The Race against Bankruptcy."

The struggle was long and arduous. For some while, the issue seemed doubtful. The final result was a complete triumph. It may be said that the period of doubt lasted till 1888. By that time, the race had been virtually won.

So long as the Egyptian Government and their British advisers were in constant danger of being throttled by bankruptcy, it was hopeless to think seriously of fiscal reform. More than this, any improvement in the administrative system which involved an increase of expenditure—and it may be said that practically every improvement required money—had to be set aside. Attention was concentrated on one object, and that was how to make both ends meet. But when financial equilibrium was assured, the aspect of affairs changed.

When it became known that the Egyptian Treasury was in possession of a surplus, all the various interests concerned clamoured for the redress of long-standing and often very legitimate grievances. The inhabitant of the country pleaded that his land-tax was too high, and pointed with justice to the fall in the price of agricultural produce as a reason for affording him relief. The inhabitant of the town complained of the oppressive nature of the octroi duty. The population in general urged that the price of salt was excessive. The possessor of live stock asked why he should pay a tax for every sheep or goat on his farm. The seller of produce at every market or fair dwelt on the fact that his goods had to be weighed by a Government official who charged a fee for the Treasury and another fee for himself. Why, again, it was urged, should railway, postal, and telegraph rates be higher in Egypt than elsewhere? Why should a boat passing under a bridge pay a toll, whilst a passenger going over the bridge paid nothing? These, and a hundred other arguments and proposals, were put forward by the advocates of fiscal reform.

On the other hand, each zealous official, anxious to improve the administration of his own Department, hurled in demands for money on a poverty-stricken Treasury. The soldier wanted more troops, and painted in gloomy colours the dangers to which the frontier was exposed by reason of the proximity of the Dervishes. The Police officer wanted more policemen to assist in the capture of brigands. The jurist urged that, without well-paid judges, it was impossible to establish a pure system of justice. The educationalist pointed out with great truth that, unless the sums placed at the disposal of the Department of Public Instruction were greatly increased, the execution of the policy of employing Egyptian rather than European agency in the administration of the country would have to be indefinitely postponed. The soldier, the policeman, the jurist, the director of prisons, and the schoolmaster all joined in asking for the construction of expensive buildings. The medical authorities clamoured for hospitals, and pointed out that, without improved sanitation, which was a bottomless financial abyss, there could be no guarantee against epidemic disease. The engineer showed that it was false economy not to extend the system of irrigation, to drain the fields, to make roads, and to develop railway communication. Following on the larger demands, came every species of minor proposal. Would it not be an attraction to the tourists, who spent so much money in Egypt, if a theatrical company visited Cairo in the winter? How could this be managed unless the Government gave a subvention to the theatre? Was it not a scandal, now that a civilised Power was virtually governing Egypt, that more was not done to protect the ancient monuments of the country from injury? What report would the winter visitors to Egypt make when they returned to Europe, if, in driving to the Pyramids, they were bumped over a road which had not been repaired since the Empress Eugénie drove over it some twenty years previously? These, and scores of other questions, were asked, in tones of more or less indignant remonstrance, by individuals who realised the desirability of paying attention to some one or other subject in which they were interested, but who had no clear perception of the financial situation considered as a whole.

Under all these circumstances, it behoved those who were responsible for the financial guidance of the Egyptian Government to act with great caution. It was clear that, as a wave of European civilisation was to sweep over the land, all the paraphernalia of civilisation—that is to say, its judges and law-courts, its hospitals, its schools, its reformatories for juvenile offenders, and so on—would, sooner or later, have to be introduced; but the main point to be borne in mind was this: that, in introducing all these reforms, Egypt should not be allowed to slip back into the slough of bankruptcy from which it had been so hardly and so recently rescued. The principal difficulty was to decide which were the most pressing amongst the many points requiring attention. It was thought that, before the sick man was provided with a comfortable hospital, before the criminal was lodged in a prison built on improved penological principles, before schools were provided, and even before rival litigants could be provided with an adequate number of honest and capable judges, or before the judges could be located in suitable buildings, it was essential to alleviate the burthens which weighed on the mass of the population. Fiscal relief had a prior claim to administrative reform. It was, therefore, decided that, whilst penuriously doling out grants to the spending Departments, the principal efforts of the Government should be devoted to devising means for the relief of taxation.

It is not necessary that I should give in detail the fiscal history of Egypt since the British occupation. It will be sufficient to say that direct taxation has been reduced by little less than £2,000,000 a year. In the domain of indirect taxation, the Salt Tax, the collection of which was attended with great hardship to the poorest classes of the population,[1] the octroi duties, the bridge and lock dues on the Nile,[2] and the tax both on river boats and on sea fishing-boats have been wholly abolished. The Registration dues on the sale of land have been reduced from 5 to 2 per cent. The Light dues have been greatly diminished in amount. So also has the tax on ferries. The Customs duties on coal, liquid fuel, charcoal, firewood, timber for building purposes, petroleum, live stock, and dead meat have been reduced from 8 to 4 per cent. The inland fishery industry has been relieved from the vexatious and onerous restrictions which were formerly imposed on it. The Postal, Telegraph, and Railway rates have been largely reduced. The only increase in taxation has been in the tobacco duty, which has been raised from P.T. 14 to P.T. 20 per kilogramme. There cannot be a doubt that the whole Egyptian population is now very lightly taxed. The taxation is, however, still unequally distributed. The urban population do not bear their fair share of the public burdens. In this, as in so many other matters, the Capitulations bar the way to reform.

In spite of these large reductions of taxation, the revenue has grown from £E.8,935,000 in 1883 to £E.15,337,000 in 1906—an increase of no less than £E.6,402,000.

The expenditure has, of course, increased with the growing revenue, but it has been carefully controlled. In 1883, it amounted to £E.8,554,000, and in 1906 to £E.12,393,000[3]—an increase of £E.3,839,000.

[1] See *Egypt*, No. 1 of 1905, p. 33, and No. 1 of 1906, p. 191.

[2] The development of Nile traffic has been very remarkable. I give a single instance. The number of boats passing the Atfeh lock, which connects the Mahmoudieh Canal and the Nile, in 1900—the year before the abolition of the toll—was only 4564. In 1905, nearly 22,000 passed.

[3] These figures are exclusive of £E.1,238,000 debited to Special Funds in 1883, and of £E.769,000 similarly debited in 1906.

The following three facts will perhaps bring clearly home to the mind of the reader the general nature of the results obtained by the financial administration of Egypt since the British occupation in 1882.

In the first place, I have to record that, up to 1888, either a deficit was annually incurred, or else financial equilibrium was preserved with the utmost difficulty. Then the tide turned. During the eighteen years from 1889 to 1906, both inclusive, the aggregate surplus realised by the Egyptian Treasury amounted to more than 27½ millions sterling.

The second fact which I have to record is no less striking. During the twenty years preceding December 31, 1906, extraordinary expenditure to the extent of £E.19,303,000 was incurred on railways, canals, and public buildings. Of this large sum, only £E.3,610,000 was borrowed. The remainder was provided out of revenue. Moreover, on December 30, 1906, a Reserve Fund of £E.3,050,000 stood to the credit of the Commissioners of the Debt. The Reserve Fund of the Egyptian Government amounted on the same date to £E.11,055,000, of which only £E.2,353,000 had at that date been engaged for capital expenditure. Both of these Funds, amounting in the aggregate to £E.14,105,000, were provided out of revenue.

In the third place, I wish to draw attention to the facts and figures relating to the indebtedness of Egypt. In 1883, the capital of the Debt, which was then held exclusively by the public, amounted to £96,457,000, and the charge on account of interest and sinking fund to £4,268,000. Since then, the Guaranteed Loan, which amounted to £9,424,000, has been issued; £4,882,000 has been borrowed for the execution of public works, and for the commutation of pensions and of allocations to the Khedivial family. The conversion operation of 1890 added £3,904,000 to the nominal capital of the Debt. In all, £18,210,000 has been added to the capital of the Debt. On the other hand, the Daira Loan, which in 1883 amounted to £9,009,000, has been entirely paid off. The Domains Loan, which in 1883 amounted to £8,255,000, has been reduced to £1,316,000. The Guaranteed Loan has been reduced to £7,765,000, a reduction of £1,659,000 from the original amount. On December 28, 1906, the outstanding capital of the Debt in the hands of the public amounted to £87,416,000.[1] The charge on account of interest and sinking fund borne by the taxpayers was £3,368,000. There has, therefore, in twenty-three years been a reduction of £9,041,000 in the capital of the Debt, and of £900,000 in the charge on account of interest and sinking fund.

These facts and figures speak for themselves. Considerations of space preclude me from describing in detail the beneficial results which have accrued to the population of Egypt in every direction from the substitution of a sound fiscal policy for the oppressive and ruinous system of government to which they were formerly subjected. I may, however, allude to one point of special importance.

Lord Dufferin, writing in 1883, alluded to "the encumbered condition of a considerable proportion of the fellaheen lands" as "one of the most distressing subjects connected with the present social condition of the country." There was a tendency, he added, "for the land to pass out of the hands of the present owners into those of foreign creditors."

[1] In addition to this, stock to the amount of £8,760,000 was held by the Egyptian Treasury and the Commissioners of the Debt. This stock will be gradually sold, and the proceeds of the sales expended on remunerative public works. In the meanwhile, the interest is, of course, credited to the Egyptian Government.

There can be no doubt of the very great importance of the question to which Lord Dufferin drew attention. In the first place, as Lord Dufferin very truly remarked, a transfer on a huge scale of the landed property of the country to foreign creditors "could scarcely take place without producing an agrarian crisis (Lord Dufferin might also have added, a political crisis) which would prove equally disastrous to the creditors, the debtors, and the Government." Then, again, the arguments in favour of small holdings apply with somewhat special force in Egypt. Owing to the fact that there is not generally any serious congestion of the population, competition rents have not as yet resulted in any grave strife between landlords and tenants. Nevertheless, as the population increases, and the area of cultivable but uncultivated land diminishes, there will be, to say the least, a risk that issues will eventually arise between landlords and tenants, somewhat similar to those which have caused so much trouble in other countries—notably in India and in Ireland. The best way to postpone this strife, as also to mitigate its intensity should it eventually prove to be inevitable, will be to avoid the adoption of any measures which will tend towards the disappearance of the small proprietors.

The political arguments in favour of this policy are no less strong than those of a purely economic character. I know of no measure more calculated to destroy any hopes that the Egyptians will eventually become really autonomous, and that they will exercise whatever self-governing powers they may some day acquire in the interests of the whole community, than the displacement of the small proprietors, more especially if the large landowners, who would take their places, were, to any excessive degree, of European nationality.

The policy which has been persistently pursued by the Egyptian Government of recent years has, therefore, been to endeavour, by a variety of indirect but perfectly legitimate means, to maintain the small proprietors in the possession of their holdings, and, whilst affording all reasonable facilities for the employment of European capital in land development, to do nothing which would tend towards ousting Egyptian proprietors and substituting Europeans in their places.

Of these means, the improvement in the system of irrigation has perhaps been the most important and the most productive of result. The establishment of an Agricultural Bank, which has advanced sums amounting in the aggregate to about £9,000,000 in small sums to the fellaheen, and of Agricultural and Horticultural Societies, which have been the means of spreading a knowledge of scientific agriculture and horticulture, and have also facilitated the purchase by the cultivators of good seed and of manure, have also been potent influences acting in the same direction.[1]

There can be no doubt that these efforts have been crowned with success. On January 1, 1907, only 665,226 acres were held by 6021 foreign landowners,[2] as against 4,765,546 acres held by 1,224,560 Egyptian proprietors. Of the latter, the holdings of 1,081,348 proprietors were of less than 5 acres in extent; the holdings of 132,198 varied from 5 to 50 acres, thus leaving 11,054

[1] Full descriptions of the creation and working both of the Agricultural Bank and of the Agricultural and Horticultural Societies are given in the Annual Reports which have been laid before Parliament.

[2] For further details up to December 31, 1905 see *Egypt*, No. 1 of 1907, p. 50. A great deal of the land now held by foreigners belongs to Land Companies. It will eventually be sold. One of the highest authorities on this subject in Egypt (the late M. Felix Suares) assured me that he was convinced that, before many years had passed, almost the whole of the land in Egypt would be in the hands of Egyptians.

proprietors of more than 50 acres. It may, I think, be confidently stated that the danger, which Lord Dufferin apprehended, has been averted.

Finance is often considered a repellent subject, and, because it is repellent, it has gained a reputation for being more difficult to understand than is really the case. There are, indeed, some few economic and currency questions which are abstruse, but the difficulty of understanding even these has been in no small degree increased by the cloud of words with which writers on subjects of this sort often surround issues in themselves simple. One merit of the Egyptian financial situation was this, that no semi-insoluble economic problem lurked between the leaves of the Budget. The Finance Minister had not, as in India, to deal with a congested population, of whom a large percentage were in normal times living on the verge of starvation. He never had to refer to the pages of Malthus or Mill, of Ricardo or Bastiat. The complications arising from a bewildering political situation had done a good deal to obscure the problems which he had to solve, and to hinder their solution. But, in truth, all that was required in Egypt, in order to understand the situation, was a knowledge of arithmetic, patience to unravel the cumbersome system of accounts which was the offspring of internationalism, and a sturdy recognition of the fact that neither an individual nor a State can with impunity go on living for an indefinite period above his or its income.

The main facts relating to Egyptian finance, when once the thread of the international labyrinth had[1] been found, were, in fact, very simple; when

[1] I use the past tense because, with the practical abolition of the Caisse de la Dette, the financial situation, and notably the system of accounts, has been very greatly simplified.

they were understood, they were not uninteresting. "Nothing," as Lord Milner truly says, "in this strange land is commonplace." The subject cannot surely be devoid of interest when it is remembered that the difference between the magic words surplus and deficit meant whether the Egyptian cultivator was, or was not, to be allowed to reap the fruits of his labour; whether, after supplying the wants of the State, he was to be left with barely enough to keep body and soul together, or whether he was to enjoy some degree of rustic ease; whether he was to be eternally condemned to live in a wretched mud hut, or whether he might have an opportunity given to him of improving his dwelling-house; whether he should or should not have water supplied to his fields in due season; whether his disputes with his neighbours should be settled by a judge who decided them on principles of law, or whether he should be left to the callous caprice of some individual ignorant of law and cognisant only of bakhshish; whether, if he were ill, he should be able to go to a well-kept hospital, or whether he should be unable to obtain any better medical assistance than that which could be given to his watch-dog or his donkey; whether a school, in which something useful could be learnt, should be provided for his children, or whether they should be left in the hands of teachers whose highest knowledge consisted in being able to intone a few texts, which they themselves only half understood, from the Koran; whether, if he suffered from mental aberration, he should be properly treated in a well-kept Lunatic Asylum, or whether he should be chained to a post and undergo the treatment of a wild beast; whether he could travel from one part of the country to another, or communicate with his friends by post or telegraph, at a reasonable or only at a prohibitive cost; in fact, whether he, and the ten millions of Egyptians who were like him, were or were not to have a chance afforded to them of taking a few steps upwards on the ladder of moral and material improvement.

This, and much more, is implied when it is stated that the British and Egyptian financiers arrested bankruptcy, turned a deficit into a surplus, relieved taxation, increased the revenue, controlled the expenditure, and raised Egyptian credit to a level only second to that of France and England. All the other reforms which were effected flow from this one fact, that the financial administration of Egypt has been honest, and that the country, being by nature endowed with great recuperative power, and being inhabited by an industrious population, responded to the honesty of its rulers. It may be doubted whether in any other country such a remarkable transformation has been made in so short a time.

CHAPTER LIV

IRRIGATION

Nature's bounty to Egypt—The work of the Pharaohs—Turkish neglect—Progress under British guidance—Programme of the future—Causes of the progress—Qualifications of the officers selected—Absence of international obstruction—Loan of £1,800,000—Support of the public—Importance of the work.

"If you dispute Providence and Destiny," says an ancient author, "you can find many things in human affairs and nature that you would suppose might be much better performed in this or that way; as, for instance, that Egypt should have plenty of rain of its own without being irrigated from the land of Ethiopia."[1] It may be doubted whether nowadays any one would be inclined to dispute Providence and Destiny on this ground. Indeed, the extraordinary fertility for which Egypt has from time immemorial been famous, which made Homer apply to it the epithet of ζείδωρος, and which led Juvenal to sing of the *divitis ostia Nili*, is mainly due to the fact that its fields are not irrigated by the rain which falls within its own confines, but by the vast stores of water which sweep down the Nile from the centre of Africa. In no other country in the world may the agriculturist be so surely guaranteed against the accidents and vicissitudes of the seasons. It is true that if the Nile is unusually high or low, the

[1] Strabo, Book iv. c. i.

cultivator is or, at all events, was exposed, in the one case, to the evils of inundation, and in the other case, to those of drought. But there is this notable difference between risks of this nature and those incidental to the cultivation of the fields in countries which depend for their water-supply on their own rainfall, namely, that whereas no human effort can increase or diminish the quantity of rain which falls from the clouds, it is, on the other hand, within the resources of human skill to so regulate the water of the Nile flood as to mitigate, if not altogether to obviate, any dangers arising from an insufficient or an excessive supply of water. In this highly favoured country, Nature seems to have said to Man: I grant you the most favourable conditions possible under which to till the soil,—a genial climate, an assured supply of water, and a natural fertilising element, which, with scarcely an effort of your own, will every year recuperate the productive powers of the soil; it is for you to turn to advantage the gifts which I have lavished on you.

How did Man utilise his advantages? In the early days of Egyptian civilisation, he made great and creditable efforts to turn them to account. "It is certain," says Colonel Ross, "that in old days, there must have been native engineering talent of the very highest order, and when we read of such and such a King restoring public works in a long and glorious reign, there must have existed a continuous supply of good engineering talent which had *carte blanche* from the ruler of the day."[1]

The Pharaohs, it would thus appear, used their talent according to the best of their lights. The Turks, who ultimately succeeded them, hid theirs in a napkin, with the result that Nature, indignant at the treatment accorded to her, minimised the

[1] Colonel Ross's *Introduction* to Willcocks' *Egyptian Irrigation*, p. vi.

value of her gifts and exacted penalties for the neglect of her laws. In later Mohammedan times, no serious efforts were made to avert drought or inundation. The general condition of Egyptian irrigation at the time when England took the affairs of the country in hand, was thus described by Colonel Ross:—

"There can be no manner of doubt that, up to 1882, Egyptian irrigation was going downhill. Every year, some false step was taken in spite of the engineer. Every year, the corvée lost ground in its out-turn of work, drains were abandoned or became useless, and canals became less of artificial and more of natural channels wholly influenced by the natural rise and fall of the Nile. . . . Owing to many causes, the native talent has sunk so low that, without modern scientific aid, the Egyptians could not work their own canals. They have sunk into a dead conservatism. . . . The absence of repairs, so common to all Mohammedan countries, and the existence of the corvée, or forced labour, have also largely contributed to the lowering of the standard of Egyptian engineers' design and method."

Here was a grand opportunity for the Englishman, and nobly did he avail himself of it. Considering the importance of the subject, and the pride which every Englishman must feel at the splendid results obtained by those of his countrymen whom Lord Milner rightly terms "the saviours of Egyptian irrigation," a sore temptation exists to deal with this matter in some detail. On the other hand, it is desirable to abridge this work; moreover, the subject has been already treated by a highly qualified writer. The lassitude which pervades both man and beast in Egypt during the hot months, when the land is baked by the fiery African sun and windswept by the scorching khamsin; the general relief experienced when the

Nile begins to rise; the anxiety to know whether the water will pass the level of those "low cubits" which, it is said, were designated by the Arabs "the angels of death";[1] the fear lest Nature should be too prodigal of her gifts and destroy by excess what, it was hoped, she would have bestowed by moderation; the revival of the whole country when the waters retire and the earth begins to yield forth her increase; all these things have been admirably related by Lord Milner in a chapter of his work, entitled *The Struggle for Water*. He has also described the care, the watchfulness, and the untiring energy displayed by the British engineers in their endeavours to direct and bridle the forces of Nature. At one time, water had to be economised and hydraulic skill exercised to make the most of a scanty supply. Again, at other times, constant vigilance was required to guard against inundation. During the season of low Nile, a system of rotations was adopted, under which the limited supply of water was turned to the best advantage in the interests of the entire population. The privileged classes learnt to their dismay that the rights of their humble neighbours must be respected. The Barrage—a work which owed its origin to the genius of a French engineer—was, in spite of strong opposition, repaired and rendered capable of doing excellent service.[2] New canals were

[1] "With good reason the Arabs designate the low cubits by the name of the "angels of death," for, if the river does not reach its full height, famine and destruction come upon the whole land of Egypt."—Mommsen's *Provinces of the Roman Empire*, vol. ii. p. 252.

[2] When the works at the Barrage were in course of construction, I visited them in company with Ali Pasha Moubarek. He was at that time Minister of Public Works, and had passed many years of his life in the service of that Department. He strongly opposed Sir Colin Scott-Moncrieff's plan for repairing the Barrage, and was in favour of the costly and wasteful alternative of erecting huge pumps. He remarked to me casually on his way down the river that he had not visited the Barrage for twenty-seven years. He was quite unconscious of the criticism on his own conduct which this admission involved.

dug. A variety of useful works were executed in Upper Egypt to guard against the effects of a low Nile. Drainage went hand in hand with irrigation. Before the British engineers had been at work ten years, the cotton crop was trebled, the sugar crop more than trebled, and the country was being gradually covered with a network of light railways and agricultural roads in order to enable the produce to be brought to market.

Much, however, as the British engineer has done for Egypt, his work is not yet complete. The whole of the cultivable lands in Egypt are not as yet brought under cultivation.[1] In order to attain this object, it is estimated that it will be necessary to store about four million cubic metres of water. The magnificent dam constructed at Assouan, which has already rendered invaluable service to the country,[2] is capable of storing one million cubic metres. Works are now in course of execution which will increase its storage capacity to about 2¼ millions of cubic metres. It is not as yet decided how any further supply will be obtained, but a general sketch of the projects which are worthy of consideration has been given in Sir William Garstin's masterly report of March 1904.[3] Probably, I shall not be far from the mark if I say that, in the course of the next fifteen or twenty years, some twenty millions sterling may profitably be spent in improving the Egyptian and Soudanese systems of irrigation.

[1] The question of the extent to which the area of cotton-bearing land is capable of increase was examined in some detail in my Report for the year 1906. See *Egypt*, No. 1 of 1907, pp. 45-47.

[2] To give one example, it is estimated that the conversion, which is now nearly complete, of 404,470 acres of land in Middle Egypt from a system of basin to one of perennial irrigation will increase the rental value of those lands by no less than £E.2,022,350, and the sale value by £E.28,312,900.—*Annual Report of the Irrigation Department*, 1906, p. 178.

[3] See *Egypt*, No. 2 of 1904.

When, eventually, the waters of the Nile, from the Lakes to the sea, are brought fully under control, it will be possible to boast that Man—in this case, the Englishman—has turned the gifts of Nature to the best possible advantage.

The operations of the Irrigation Department have, in fact, been singularly successful, perhaps more so than those of any other Department of the Government. To what causes may this success be attributed?

It has, in the first place, been due to the high character and marked capacity of the British engineers, who were chosen with the utmost care. The superior officials of the Irrigation Department came from India, a country which affords an excellent training for the hydraulic engineer. Armed with the previous knowledge which they had acquired, they studied the various problems which Egyptian irrigation presented for solution, and proposed nothing until they had obtained a thorough mastery of the facts with which they had to deal. So far as I know, they have never yet made a serious mistake.

But the qualifications of the individuals, high though they were, would have availed but little had not their labours been exerted in a sphere where adventitious circumstances were favourable to success.

The first of these circumstances was that, relatively to some other branches of the Egyptian service, the Public Works Department was from the first freed from the incubus of internationalism. It is not to be supposed that the actions of the British engineers were not in some degree hampered by the meshes which an obstructive diplomacy had, with perverse ingenuity, flung over the whole governmental machine of Egypt. Any such supposition would be erroneous. Ubiquitous internationalism, by imposing a fantastic financial system on the country, and by secreting for many years the economies resulting from the partial conversion of the Debt, limited the funds which it was possible to place at the disposal of the British engineers, and thus diminished their power of doing good. More than this, that duality, which was the bane of the Egyptian administrative system, existed at one time in the heart of the Public Works Department, but fortunately in a relatively innocuous form. This duality was, however, abolished at an early period of the occupation. It was felt that, in view of the importance of the Irrigation Department, it should be exclusively in British hands. "It is evident," Lord Dufferin wrote in 1883, "that the present irrigation service of Egypt is wanting in intelligent direction and honest and efficient inspection. . . . Egypt is so similar to many of the irrigated districts in India that it is only natural to turn to that country for advice."

Thus, the British engineers were left free to design and to execute their own plans for the canalisation of the country. They were spared the calamity of having to deal with an International Board. They could decide on the construction of a canal without having to consider whether the policy of Great Britain in the Pacific or Indian Oceans was viewed with favour at Berlin or Paris. This was a great negative advantage. The comparative freedom of action accorded to the British engineers contributed in no small degree to the success which attended their operations.

In one other respect, the British engineers were fortunate. However remarkable may have been their professional skill, and however sound their plans, it is obvious that they could have done nothing without money. Funds were fortunately provided for them. When the London Conference on the financial affairs of Egypt took place in 1884, it was proposed to borrow £1,000,000, to be applied to the improvement of the irrigation system of the country. The proposal met with a good deal of opposition. Doubts were at the time expressed by competent British authorities as to the wisdom of adopting this course. Those doubts were based on reasonable grounds. Excessive borrowing had brought Egypt to the verge of ruin, and it was pointed out that to increase the debt of a State which was then in a well-nigh bankrupt condition was, at best, a hazardous experiment. Others, who had more confidence in the future of Egypt and in the elasticity of its resources, were in favour of a bolder policy. They supported the view which, it must be admitted, at the time appeared somewhat paradoxical, that the best way to relieve the country from the burthen of a crushing debt resulting from loans, the proceeds of which had been to a large extent squandered, would be to contract a further loan, and to apply the money thus obtained to developing the resources of the country. After a sharp struggle, this latter view prevailed. A sum of £1,000,000 for irrigation purposes was included in the loan contracted for the payment of the Alexandria indemnities and other purposes. In 1890, an additional sum of £800,000 was placed at the disposal of the Public Works Department for irrigation and drainage works.

In my Report for 1891, after describing the extent to which the productive powers of the country had been increased by irrigation, I added:—

"The policy of increasing the debt of Egypt, which was adopted seven years ago, has been amply justified. I should be the last to wish that the facts which I have narrated above should be used as a justification for reckless borrowing, but they certainly do show that cases may arise in which a quasi-bankrupt State, if it be possessed of great natural resources, may be placed in a position of solvency by adding to its debt, provided always that the money borrowed be judiciously applied. In cases of this sort, the main difficulty generally is to ensure the execution of the proviso. So far as Egypt is concerned, I have no hesitation in saying that the expenditure of this £1,800,000 on irrigation and drainage has contributed probably more than any one cause to the comparative prosperity that the country now enjoys. It ensured the solvency of the Egyptian Treasury, and until this was done, no very serious effort was possible in the direction of moral and material progress."

Lastly, when once his value had been recognised —that is to say, in a very short space of time—the British engineer secured the support of Egyptian public opinion. The facts were, indeed, so strong as to bring conviction to the minds of the most prejudiced and sceptical. The fellah might fail to realise the utility and insignificance of some of the reforms instituted under British tutelage, but he knew the value of water to an extent which can perhaps scarcely be appreciated by inhabitants of northern countries. No amount of misrepresentation could persuade him that the man who brought to his fields, in a measure surpassing his wildest expectations, the element for which he thirsted, was not his benefactor.

> Till taught by pain,
> Men really know not what good water's worth.[1]

The British engineer, in fact, unconsciously accomplished a feat which, in the eyes of a politician, is perhaps even more remarkable than

[1] *Don Juan*, ii. 84.

that of controlling the refractory waters of the Nile. He justified Western methods to Eastern minds. He inculcated, in a manner which arrested and captivated even the blurred intellect and wayward imagination of the poor, ignorant Egyptian fellah, the lesson that the usurer and the retailer of adulterated drinks are not the sole products of European civilisation ; and, inasmuch as he achieved this object, he deserves the gratitude not only of all intelligent Asiatics, but also of all Europeans—of the rulers of Algiers and of Tunis as well as those of India.

CHAPTER LV

THE ARMY [1]

Disbandment of the army in 1882—History of the army—Mehemet Ali's Syrian campaigns—Ismail Pasha—The Abyssinian campaign—Tel-el-Kebir—It is decided to form a fellaheen army officered by Englishmen—The black battalions—Will the army fight?—Reasons why the reorganisation has been successfully conducted.

In leaving the work of the civilian for that of the soldier, we at once seem to pass from the involved and cautious language of diplomacy to the outspoken behests of the barrack-yard. One of the first points which had to be considered after the battle of Tel-el-Kebir had been fought and won was what should be done with the Egyptian army. The soldier advisers of the British and Egyptian Governments answered this question with military frankness. The Egyptian army, as then constituted, was worse than useless. It had proved itself a danger to the State. It could mutiny, but it could not, or would not fight. The logical conclusion to be drawn from this statement of facts was that the existing army should be disbanded, and another army created in its place. Accordingly, on September 19, 1882, that is to say, six days after the battle of Tel-el-Kebir had been fought, the following laconic Decree appeared in the Official Journal:—

[1] In the preparation of this chapter, I have been materially aided by Sir Reginald Wingate.

"Nous, Khédive d'Égypte, considérant la rébellion militaire,

DÉCRÉTONS

Art. 1.

L'armée Egyptienne est dissoute.

(Signé) MEHEMET TEWFIK.

Out of what material was a new army to be formed? Could the fellaheen, who had but recently shown themselves so destitute of military qualities, be made into good soldiers? It was impossible at the time to answer this latter question confidently in the affirmative. Nevertheless, the past history of Egypt was there to show that the behaviour of the troops at Tel-el-Kebir did not constitute a sufficient proof that the answer should be a decided negative. For centuries past, Egypt had been ruled by foreign conquerors, who introduced their own or mercenary troops in order to maintain their authority. The Egyptian fellah had inherited no warlike attributes; rather was he the outcome of a system of serfdom and slavery well calculated to stifle all military instincts.

It has been the custom to give Mehemet Ali the credit of having been the first to realise that Egypt had ready to hand in the fellaheen the raw material out of which a national army could be formed. The defeats which he inflicted on the Turkish armies in Syria are adduced in proof of the success of his military policy. To a certain extent, the praise bestowed on Mehemet Ali in this connection is justified. What he did was briefly this. His early campaigns against the Wahabis (1811-18), and his campaigns in Nubia and Sennar (1820-22) were conducted with mercenary troops. Subsequently, that is to say, in 1822-24, being carried away by the *regnandi dira cupido*, he required a larger army. It was not possible to obtain an adequate supply of Albanians or Circassians. An attempt made to utilise the blacks of the Soudan resulted in failure, by reason of the mortality which prevailed amongst them when they were transported from tropical Africa to the relatively cold climate of Egypt. Mehemet Ali had, therefore, to fall back on the Egyptian peasantry.

The experiment was crowned with some measure of success. The fellah is hardy and robust. He soon proved himself to be a docile soldier. In 1824, a battalion of Egyptians was sent to Arabia, another to Sennar, and four battalions were despatched to the Morea, under the celebrated Ibrahim Pasha. Then came the first Syrian war, when the veteran ranks were swelled by crowds of fellaheen raised under the most tyrannous of conscriptions.[1] Yet this force carried all before it. There can be little doubt that, had not European diplomacy intervened, Ibrahim Pasha might, after the battle of Konia, have marched to Constantinople with little or no opposition. It was this success, followed by the victory at Nezib over the Turkish troops in the second Syrian war of 1839, which had the effect of raising the Egyptian soldiery to a position of some celebrity as a force of acknowledged value.

Prior to the battle of Konia, the strength of the Egyptian army and navy, the former of which had been organised by French officers, consisted, according to Clot Bey,[2] of 277,000 men, of whom 130,000 were regular troops. Of the regular troops, the bulk of the infantry was nominally composed of

[1] "Women were hung up by the hair of the head and whipped till they disclosed their sons' hiding-places. Those that were taken were never seen again. Once a soldier always a soldier, in Ibrahim Pasha's army."—*Life and Letters of Lady Hester Stanhope*, p. 263.

[2] *Aperçu sur l'Égypte*, vol. ii. p. 235.

fellaheen, but the system under which they were recruited leaves little doubt that there was a considerable foreign element in the ranks. Not only the officers, but also a large proportion of the non-commissioned officers were Turks, Albanians, etc. It is said that, as the result of Ibrahim Pasha's experience in Arabia, it was decided never to promote an Egyptian above the rank of sergeant. As regards the composition of the other arms, it is not possible to obtain accurate statistics, but during the early years of the British occupation there were still many living who could remember that a large proportion of the rank and file of the cavalry were Turks and Circassians, whilst in the artillery the proportion of the latter was still greater. It is to be remembered that when, in 1826, Sultan Mahmoud ordered the massacre of the Janissaries, a large number of the survivors fled to Egypt, where they accepted service in the newly organised army. Again, during Ibrahim Pasha's campaign in Syria, he increased his strength by recruiting locally from the mountain tribes and Bedouins. It is clear, therefore, that the army with which Ibrahim Pasha won his victories was not, in the true sense of the term, a purely national army. A strong foreign element existed, not only amongst the officers and non-commissioned officers, but also amongst the rank and file.

Moreover, in judging of the importance to be attached to the military prowess of the Egyptian troops in the days of Mehemet Ali, account has to be taken of the state of the Turkish army. Prior to 1826, the armed forces of Turkey consisted of the Janissaries. After their destruction and disbandment, there was, in point of fact, no disciplined Turkish military force left. The disaster of Navarino, followed by the Russo-Turkish war of 1828-29, left Sultan Mahmoud in the position of having to send against Ibrahim "disaffected armies of raw recruits, badly officered and worse generalled."[1] In comparison with these raw levies, the Egyptian army represented a well-organised and well-disciplined force, trained by able foreign officers on European principles, and, moreover, leavened with a considerable proportion of veteran troops who had had experience of actual war in the Morea, Arabia, and elsewhere. More than this, they had in Ibrahim Pasha a leader possessed of undoubted military genius, whose actions bore the stamp of energy, foresight, and skill.

Ibrahim Pasha's successes in Syria afford, therefore, ample proof that a well-disciplined and well-led force will almost invariably defeat badly disciplined and untrained levies, however superior be the numbers of the latter. But to say more than this would exceed the limits of justifiable deduction. To make the result of the Syrian battles the standard by which to gauge the permanent fighting value of the Egyptians would involve a generalisation of too hasty and too sweeping a character. Mr. William Dye, an American officer formerly in the Egyptian service, after reviewing the military history of Egypt, says: "Ibrahim's successes at Konia and elsewhere were due to his generalship, certainly not to any peculiar qualities that the fellah may have possessed as a soldier." The fact that under Abbas I. the Egyptians were driven from Nejd, and that the Wahabite State regained its independence, confirms the correctness of this opinion.

Said Pasha, the successor of Abbas I., at first played with his soldiers, and then disbanded the greater part of the army. In 1863, it consisted of only 3000 men. The personnel was disorganised and the material defective.

[1] Creasy's *History of the Ottoman Turks*, vol. ii. p. 437.

On Ismail's accession, his first care was to increase the military power of the State. He believed, or, at all events, he acted as if he believed in the fighting qualities of the fellaheen. Said Pasha had been the first to employ men of fellah extraction as officers, but he did not allow them to be promoted above the rank of captain. Ismail Pasha made an important and hazardous innovation. He allowed Egyptians to be promoted to the rank of colonel.

The first opportunity of testing the value of Ismail Pasha's army occurred in 1874, when a rebellion broke out in Darfour. It was suppressed by General Gordon, who discarded his Egyptian soldiers and mainly employed troops raised on the spot. "The officers and men," he wrote, "are a cowardly set. They are good marchers, and bear privation well, but that is all I can say in their favour. . . . I have not the least confidence in my officers and men. . . . I cannot bear these Egyptian officers. They have no good quality. I like the blacks; now, these black soldiers are the only troops in the Egyptian service worth anything."[1]

Then came the disastrous Abyssinian campaign of 1876, when the Egyptians were, on several occasions, routed with heavy loss. Mr. Dye, in criticising these operations, says: "There was no unity of command, there was no cohesion among the parts of the army. This was due to the want of individual interest among the men in the campaign, a general need of good officers and a lack of discipline, and of any equitable system of rewards and punishments."

That the Egyptian army did not suffer any further reverses during Ismail Pasha's reign is probably due to the fact that it was not again seriously involved in warlike operations. Ismail

[1] *General Gordon in Central Africa*, p. 151.

was assuredly more successful, during the latter years of his reign, in disorganising, than he had been, during his earlier years, in organising an army. It has been shown in the course of this narrative how the son reaped, in the shape of overt mutiny, the whirlwind which the father had sown.

It is impossible for an army to mutiny without its value as a fighting-machine being impaired. We are, indeed, so accustomed to connect military efficiency with military subordination that it is well-nigh impossible to dissociate the two ideas. Nevertheless, the greater or less degree of harm inflicted on military efficiency by any mutiny must depend in some measure on the causes and circumstances of the mutiny itself. If, as happened in India in 1857, the rank and file rebel against their officers, the mutineers must of necessity take the field under circumstances of great disadvantage to themselves. The men are suddenly deprived of the leaders to whom they have been accustomed to yield implicit obedience. The case of Arábi's army was different. The men did not mutiny against their officers; it was the officers who mutinied against the Khedive, and who carried the rank and file with them. It may be said that practically the army rebelled *en bloc.* It is true that a few Turkish and Circassian officers disappeared, the Arábi movement having been primarily directed against them. But their numbers were not sufficient to dislocate the military machine. Moreover, their disappearance only enhanced the lesson, which was rudely inculcated by Lord Wolseley, as to the fighting value of an Egyptian army led by Egyptian officers. Arábi's soldiers had, in fact, every inducement to fight, and every opportunity of showing what they could do in the way of fighting. They represented, or, at all events, they purported to represent, the forces of indignant patriotism calling on the sons of the soil to repel a foreign foe. Their cause was that of the Moslem against the Christian, of the native Egyptian against the upholders of Turkish tyranny. They fought under local conditions of great advantage. Arábi occupied at Tel-el-Kebir an entrenched position of great strength. The attacking force, which had to advance up a "glacis-like slope," was numerically only one-half as strong as the defenders. Yet within twenty minutes of the first shot being fired, the Egyptian force was in full retreat with a loss of upwards of 2000 killed, whilst the British force, which delivered a frontal attack, only lost 459 men killed and wounded. Manifestly, Arábi's force was, in Dryden's oft-quoted words, nothing but a rude militia,

In peace a charge, in war a weak defence.

Europe was astonished, and some hostile critics, being unable to show that Arábi had in reality been a victor in the fray, found consolation in the fiction that the battle had been won by British gold.

The subsequent history of the Soudan confirmed the lesson which was to be derived from the experience of Tel-el-Kebir. Everywhere the Dervishes drove the fellaheen soldiers before them.

Such were the historical facts with which Lord Dufferin and his military advisers had to deal in 1882. They all pointed to one inevitable conclusion. It was that an Egyptian army officered by native Egyptians was worse than useless. The question of employing mercenary soldiers was discussed. Lord Dufferin wisely decided to put aside all idea of enrolling Albanians, Circassians, or other waifs and strays of the Mediterranean. He laid it down as a principle that the army "should be essentially composed of native Egyptians. . . . Egypt has had enough of Mamelukes and their congeners." The officers were to be supplied from England. An experiment was to be made with a view to ascertaining whether what Lord Dufferin termed "the metamorphic spirit of the age"—aided by a certain number of British officers and drill-sergeants—could achieve the remarkable feat of turning the fellah into an efficient soldier.

Sir Evelyn Wood—who was subsequently succeeded, first, by Lord Grenfell, and, later, by Lord Kitchener and Sir Reginald Wingate—was appointed to command the army. The cadres of battalions were formed by carefully selecting from the débris of Arábi's army the requisite number of officers and non-commissioned officers. The rank and file were taken straight from the plough.

The British officers had an arduous task to perform. Not only had every branch of the military administrative machine to be created afresh; not only had the oppressive recruiting system, which formerly existed, to be swept away and an improved system put in its place; not only had the Englishman to wage unremitting war against corruption and against the other chronic diseases of Egyptian administration and society; but, in reversing the old, and entering upon the new order of things, it was necessary to implant in the minds of the fellaheen the fact that discipline could be strict without being oppressive; that the period of service for which they had been enrolled would not be prolonged beyond that prescribed by law; that they would receive their pay and their food regularly; that the former would never be stopped except for misconduct; that they would no longer be subjected to brutal treatment at the hands of their officers; that any complaints which they might make would be impartially investigated, and that, if they committed any crime, they would be fairly tried and would only receive punishment in proportion to the gravity of the offence. All these difficulties were overcome. Professional skill was brought to bear on all administrative questions. High character and integrity gradually weaned the fellaheen soldiers from the idea that the exercise of authority was synonymous with the committal of injustice. Indeed, the moral reforms which the British officers achieved rank even higher than their administrative successes, albeit these latter were also remarkable. Looking to the past history and actual condition of Egypt in 1882, it might well have been thought that confidence in those placed in authority over him would be a plant of very slow growth in the mind of the Egyptian fellah. Yet, the British officers of the Egyptian army speedily accomplished the remarkable feat of obtaining the complete confidence of their men. Not only, moreover, does this spirit of confidence now pervade all ranks of the army, but it extends to every family in the country. The relations of the soldiers understand the altered conditions under which conscription is conducted, and the regulations of the army enforced. "The reappearance of the fellah soldier," Lord Milner says, "in his native village after an absence of a year in the barracks—not crawling back mutilated, or smitten by some foul disease, but simply walking in as a visitor, healthy, well-dressed, and with some money in his pocket—was like the vision of a man risen from the dead."[1]

Thus, the reconstituted army consisted, in the first instance, only of fellaheen. About 6000 men were raised. These were formed into two brigades, one of which was commanded by British and the other by Egyptian officers. It was intended that this force should mainly be used as an aid to

[1] *England in Egypt*, p. 176.

the constabulary in the maintenance of internal tranquillity. The soldiers were to "prevent the Bedouins from causing trouble along the desert border." They were to suppress "small local insurrections."[1] It was not contemplated at the time that they would ever be employed in the Soudan. As, however, events in the Soudan developed and the power of the Mahdi grew, it became evident that the southern frontier of Egypt would either have to be permanently defended by British troops, or that the Egyptian army would have to be increased and improved to such an extent as to render it possible to dispense with British aid. To have relied wholly on fellaheen troops would manifestly have been dangerous. The necessity of stiffening what Lord Dufferin called "the invertebrate ranks of the fellaheen soldiery" had arisen. An unsuccessful attempt was made to raise a brigade of Turks. The nucleus of a battalion of Albanians was formed. They mutinied, and were disbanded in a few weeks. It was then decided to fall back on the blacks of the Soudan. Thus, Lord Dufferin's fellaheen army was eventually converted into a combined force of fellaheen and blacks.

The blacks, who join as volunteers, belong for the most part to the tribes who are found on the Upper Nile from near Kodok to the Equatorial Province; others come from the west beyond Kordofan, and even from as far as Wadai and Bornou. Many of them are little better than savages. They are difficult to control, and are as thoughtless, capricious, and wanting in foresight as children. They are not quick at drill, nor are they fond of it, affording in this respect

[1] Some authorities went so far in 1882-83 as to hold that no Egyptian army was required. Lord Dufferin wisely rejected this extreme view.

a contrast to the fellah, who, true to his national characteristics, is an admirable automaton. The blacks are very excitable. On the other hand, their initiative, dash, and instincts of self-defence make them invaluable as fighting troops.

Before the British officers had been long at work, it was clear that they had created a small army superior in quality to anything which Egypt had heretofore possessed. That army was endowed with all those outward and visible signs of efficiency of which note can be taken in time of peace. Would it, however, fight? That was a question which for some while remained doubtful. But all doubts have now been removed. The history of the Soudan, which has been narrated in this work, enables the question to be confidently answered in the affirmative.

The reasons why the endeavours to form an efficient military force in Egypt have been crowned with success are clear. The British officer has been allowed a free hand; he has had even greater liberty of action than the British engineer. Even a devotee of cosmopolitan principles would hesitate to subject the command of an armed force to the disintegrating process of internationalism. In spite, however, of the success which has so far attended the efforts of military reformers in Egypt, it should never be forgotten that an army composed of Moslems and officered to a considerable extent by Christians is a singularly delicate machine, which requires most careful handling.

CHAPTER LVI

THE INTERIOR

Uncertainty of British policy—Difficulties of administrative reform—Lord Dufferin's Police proposals—Mr. Clifford Lloyd—Changes made in the Police organisation—Nubar Pasha's conflict with Mr. Clifford Lloyd—The latter resigns—Friction in the Interior—Appointment of an Adviser—And of Inspectors—Difficulties of the present moment.

CASES have so far been discussed in which the reformer was, to a greater or less extent, crippled by internationalism, or hampered by the anomalous nature of an official position in which he was expected to fulfil many of the functions of a Minister without possessing ministerial rank or authority. It is now necessary to deal with a case in which the evils arising from the uncertainty, which for many years hung over the future of British policy in Egypt, come into special prominence. Whether the British occupation was to be temporary or permanent, there could be no doubt as to the desirability of relieving taxation, digging canals, and creating a well-disciplined army which would be able to repel Dervish invasion. The financier, the engineer, and the soldier might, indeed, think that the edifice which each had reared would either collapse at once, should British influence cease to be paramount, or gradually decay when exposed to the dry-rot of unchecked Pashadom. But however that might be, there could be no doubt as to the kind of edifice which had to be constructed; its nature was, indeed, indicated by certain well-recognised professional canons.

The case of internal administrative reform was different. It might have been thought that the work of organising the Department of the Interior would, relatively to other Departments, have presented but little difficulty to the Englishman, with his law-abiding tendencies, his practical common sense, and his freedom from bureaucratic formalism. The main thing was to organise a Police force, to appoint a few Police Magistrates, and to lay down a few simple rules for the relations which were to exist between the judicial and executive authorities. Work of this sort could not surely present any insuperable difficulties to a nation whose dominion was world-wide, and who had shown a special genius for the government of subject races.

Conclusions drawn from general arguments of this nature are often liable to error from forgetfulness of the fact that certain combinations will not bring about certain anticipated results unless it be ascertained that no link is wanting in the chain of circumstances necessary to fulfil the conditions of the required combination. Even Euclid had to assume the truth of his postulates. There can be little doubt that if the conditions under which the work of Egyptian administrative reform was undertaken had been favourable, a success equal to that of which the British administrative reformer may boast in India and elsewhere would speedily have been achieved. But the conditions were not only less favourable than in other countries, they were unfavourable even when judged by the standard of Egyptian intricacy. It was not only that the British reformer was deprived of liberty of action to such an extent as to be unable to execute his own plans. It was not only that he had to pose as a subordinate and, at the same time, to act in a great measure as a superior. Difficulties even more formidable than these had to be encountered. He was in the position of an architect who was told to design a house without any indication as to whether the building was to be a king's palace or the cottage of a peasant. No one could tell him precisely what was required of him. Was he to allow the abominable Police system which he found in existence to remain in force with merely some slight modifications? Certainly not. He was expected to reform, and he was well aware that he could not make a silk purse out of a sow's ear. Was he to take the matter vigorously in hand, employ agents on whom he could thoroughly rely, and introduce a rational system based partly on the experience gained in other countries, and partly on the special requirements of Egypt? From many points of view this would unquestionably have been the best course to pursue, but he had to remember—and here the most important link in the chain of circumstances necessary to ensure success snapped in twain—that the British occupation was only temporary, that the authority of the native rulers must not be impaired, and that it was useless to begin the construction of a system which could not be completed in the limited time at his disposal, and which would of a surety fall to pieces directly the Englishman turned his back. For, indeed, a severe relapse could, in this instance, be predicted with absolute certainty. There might be some faint hope that, if the occupation ceased, self-interest would lead the rulers of Egypt to employ British engineers to supervise the supply and distribution of water. It was conceivable, though improbable, that the first outcome of the withdrawal of effective British control would not be the reproduction of financial chaos. But it was altogether inconceivable that the cause of internal administrative reform should prosper in the hands of the Egyptian governing classes, if they were left entirely to their own devices. For, in fact, the centre of gravity of Egyptian misgovernment lay in the Department of the Interior. That Department was the very citadel of corruption, the headquarters of nepotism, the cynosure of all that numerous class who hoped to gain an easy, if illicit, livelihood by robbing either the Treasury or the taxpayers, or, if both these courses were impossible, by obtaining some well-paid sinecure. Every vested interest in the country was sure to be against the reformer, who at each step would find that his views clashed with long-standing abuses, perverted morals, and habits of thought with which he was unfamiliar. Neither could he hope to gain that degree of support from local public opinion which was, however grudgingly, accorded to the engineer. He would be unable to produce material proofs, which could be visible to the eye or palpable to the touch, of the good work he was doing. In order to succeed, he would have to be a moral, even more than an administrative reformer. He would have to be engaged in a succession of conflicts on matters of detail, the mass of which, taken collectively, were indeed of great importance, but which, taken separately, were little calculated to arouse enthusiasm or sympathy on his behalf.

Moreover, besides these general causes, other special hindrances stood in the way of the internal reformer. It was no easy matter to sweep away the abuses of the ancient village system of government, without wrecking the system itself. Still less easy was it to establish a *modus vivendi* between

British ideas of Police duties and Franco-Egyptian ideas of judicial functions. The régime of the Capitulations also barred the way to many useful reforms.

The work of internal reform presented, therefore, difficulties of a very peculiar character. They were the result partly of the actual circumstances with which the reformer had to deal, but still more of the want of reality which attended the whole system of government by reason of the uncertainty of British policy in connection with Egypt.

The question of the organisation of the Police force naturally attracted the attention of Lord Dufferin. He dwelt on the necessity of forming "an intelligent, active, and ubiquitous provincial constabulary," which was to partake of a civil rather than of a military character. The force of provincial and urban constabulary, including two reserve battalions of 500 men each, was to consist of 6500 men. They were to be under a European Inspector-General, who was to act under the control of the Minister of the Interior. General Valentine Baker was appointed to this post; a few European officers were nominated to act as his subordinates.

When I arrived in Egypt in September 1883, I found that Mr. Clifford Lloyd was in Cairo. He had come on a vague roving commission to "superintend internal reforms." Even in Egypt, the chosen home of lax official nomenclature, it was found that this definition of Mr. Clifford Lloyd's functions was wanting in precision. In January 1884, he was, therefore, appointed Under-Secretary to the Department of the Interior.

I have rarely come across any man who, on first acquaintance, created such a favourable impression as Mr. Clifford Lloyd. His appearance and demeanour, his singularly sympathetic features and clear blue eyes, his courteous manner, and the rare mixture of decision and moderation with which he was wont to expound his opinions, all bespoke a man of strong will, who could assert his authority without bluster, and who could be firm without being unconciliatory. Neither was this first impression erroneous. Mr. Clifford Lloyd possessed many remarkable qualities. In spite of some obvious defects of character, this straightforward, honourable, courageous English gentleman was always to me a very attractive figure. In a disturbed district of India or Ireland, he would have been an ideal Government official. But he had not the versatility and tact necessary for the work he had in hand in Egypt. He was unable to adapt himself to local circumstances. Moreover, he wished not only to do the work, but to let all the world know that he was doing it. To quote a single instance of how little careful he was to avoid wounding native susceptibilities, he would not adopt the ordinary Egyptian custom of stamping his letters with a seal on which his signature in Arabic was engraved. He insisted on signing his name in English to all the letters he wrote to Egyptian officials. Moreover, he had never been behind the scenes of a central administration, with the result that he had no experience of how work at the headquarters of government is really carried on. These defects were sufficient to mar his finer qualities, and to detract from his usefulness as a Government official.

One of the first results of his appointment was the issue of a Decree, on December 31, 1883, laying down the nature of the relations which were to exist between the Police and the Moudirs. Egypt was, for Police purposes, divided into three circles, to each of which a European Inspector, who was to be the delegate of the Inspector-General, was appointed. European Inspectors were also to be employed in the principal towns. The Inspector was to be the intermediary between the Police and the Moudir. The investigation of crime was to be conducted by the Police, independently of the Parquet.

The adoption of these measures gave rise to a feud which lasted somewhat longer than the siege of Troy.

On the one side it was urged, more especially by Nubar Pasha, who succeeded to office immediately after the issue of the Decree of December 31, 1883, that whenever a European was placed under an Egyptian, the former would usurp the functions of the latter. There can, in fact, be little doubt that the European Inspectors looked more to the orders of the Inspector-General than to those of the Moudirs, although the latter were nominally their official superiors. No one, therefore, knew who was really responsible for the maintenance of public tranquillity. Nubar Pasha was never tired of complaining of what he called "la dualité dans les provinces." The authority of the Moudirs had, in fact, been impaired, and nothing sufficiently definite had been substituted in its place. They were not allowed to rule according to their own rude lights. On the other hand, they could not, or would not assist in ruling according to the new methods which found favour with their English coadjutors. Under these circumstances, although they were powerless to prevent the change of system, they were sufficiently strong to counteract any beneficial results which might have accrued from its adoption. They fell back on the arm in the use of which the Oriental excels. They adopted a system of passive obstruction.

On the other side, it was urged, with much force, that unless the Moudirs were placed under some European control, all the abuses of the past would reappear. When complaints were made that the people no longer respected the Moudirs, it was replied—in the words of Sir Benson Maxwell, who was then Procureur-Général—that the old respect "was merely the offspring of the terror felt by the helpless inhabitants in the presence of the officer who was armed with the courbash and the keys of the gaol. If the restoration of the power was not accompanied by fresh abuses, the respect would not revive, since the fear on which it rested would not."

If Nubar Pasha had been prepared to accept a certain limited amount of European co-operation and inspection, both at the Ministry of the Interior and in the provinces, a compromise might have been effected. But, although at first inclined to entertain proposals of this nature, he subsequently rejected them.

Apart, however, from the merits or demerits of the new Police system, it soon became clear that two men so dissimilar in character as Nubar Pasha and Mr. Clifford Lloyd could not work together for long. Early in April 1884, the first of a succession of petty crises arose. The points at issue were laid before Lord Granville. "The real question," Mr. Clifford Lloyd said, "is whether Her Majesty's Government will now face the inevitable and appoint an English President of the Council, or by withdrawing me deal a death-blow to reformation in this country."

Now, if there was one thing in the world which Lord Granville disliked, it was "facing the inevitable." He was constitutionally averse to any line of policy which, in Mr. Clifford Lloyd's words, was intended to "clear the way for all that had to be done, once and for all." Moreover, in this particular instance, he could give some very valid reasons for declining to act on the advice of his masterful subordinate. Mr. Clifford Lloyd had been sent to Egypt, not to initiate a new Egyptian policy, but to do the best he could under the difficult and abnormal circumstances of the situation. Of course, if an English President of the Council had been appointed—in other words, if England had assumed the direct government of Egypt—all administrative difficulties would have been solved. Any one, as has truly been said, can govern in a state of siege. But Mr. Clifford Lloyd had not been asked to govern, neither had he been commissioned to introduce such radical changes as would necessarily involve a complete change of governors. His task was, partly by persuasion, and partly by a moderate amount of diplomatic support, to introduce such partial reforms in the existing system of administration as were possible without shattering the flimsy political fabric with which he had to deal. He was constitutionally unsuited for the performance of this delicate task. He could not understand half measures. *Nil actum credens, dum quid superesset agendum*, was his motto. Never, probably, did he show his want of discernment more conspicuously than when he exhorted a Minister, who was pre-eminently opportunist, to resort to heroic measures. Lord Granville was equal to the occasion. He could elude the point of the rapier even when the hilt was held by a skilled diplomatist and dialectician; how much more, therefore, could he escape from the sledge-hammer blows and wild thrusts of this blunt, outspoken tyro in official life. Acting under Lord Granville's instructions, I patched up a truce between Nubar Pasha and Mr. Clifford Lloyd, but the feud soon broke out again. Eventually, towards the end of May 1884, Mr. Clifford Lloyd resigned his appointment and left Egypt.

It was a misfortune that his mission did not prove successful. Had he managed to acquire a commanding influence over the affairs of the Interior, not only would much good have accrued to Egypt, but a great deal of friction, which subsequently ensued, would have been avoided.

I have often asked myself whether, had I supported Mr. Clifford Lloyd more strongly, a more favourable result might have been obtained. If the circumstances of the time had been different, and if I had been able to devote myself more exclusively to the solution of this particular difficulty, it is possible that the conflict between Nubar Pasha and Mr. Clifford Lloyd might not have become so acute as was actually the case. But the circumstances of the time were abnormal. General Gordon was inundating me with violent and contradictory telegrams from Khartoum. Whatever time could be spared from Soudan affairs, had mainly to be devoted to finance, which was then the burning question of the day. The representatives of almost every Power in Europe were banded together in opposition to England, and to every proposal emanating from a British source. On the other hand, Nubar Pasha jauntily threw off all responsibility for Soudanese or financial affairs, and concentrated all the efforts of his astute mind on an endeavour to upset the Clifford Lloyd combination, and to free the Egyptian Government from all European control in so far as the affairs of the Interior were concerned. Under circumstances such as these, the result of the struggle was almost a foregone conclusion.

Even, however, without the special circumstances existing at the moment, I do not think that Mr. Clifford Lloyd could have remained for long in Egypt. Despite his high character and unquestionable ability, he was not the right man in the right place. He was not fitted for the delicate work of Egyptian administration. As well might it be expected that a brawny navvy should be able to mend a Geneva watch with a pickaxe.

It would, of course, have been possible to have appointed an English successor to Mr. Clifford Lloyd, but at that time the difficulties of the situation were so great, and the work was so heavy, that it was desirable to throw a certain amount of cargo overboard in order to lighten the ship. Mr. Clifford Lloyd's place was, therefore, filled by an Egyptian.

It is needless to describe the minor changes which the Police organisation underwent during the next ten years. It will suffice to say that the system did not work smoothly. The old cause of complaint always existed, namely, that the presence of European Police officers in the provinces diminished the authority of the Moudirs. One Egyptian Minister succeeded another, but all adopted an attitude of hostility to, or at best of surly acquiescence with the new system.

At last, as generally happens in such cases, an opportunity came of settling the question. When Nubar Pasha assumed office in the summer of 1894, he at once took up the matter. A plan, having for its object the decentralisation of the Police, which was to be left in Egyptian hands, coupled with the establishment of an efficient European control at the Ministry of the Interior, was elaborated and eventually accepted. An English "Adviser" was appointed, whose functions were to co-operate with the Minister in charge of the Department. Subsequently, a very few young Englishmen, who had been specially trained for Egyptian service, were appointed to be Inspectors.

Since the change in 1894, a great improvement has unquestionably taken place in the Administration of the Interior. Nevertheless, the old difficulty still remains. The presence of British Inspectors in the Provinces tends to weaken the authority and to diminish the sense of responsibility of the Moudirs. On the other hand, it is certain that the total withdrawal of the Inspectors from the provinces would be attended with a serious risk that many of the abuses of the past would reappear, and, generally, that great administrative confusion would arise. It is, in fact, impossible to avoid altogether the disadvantages of over-interference, without incurring the evils which would result from total non-interference. The most that can be done is to effect the best compromise of which the circumstances admit. But, in working a system where so much depends upon the characters and idiosyncrasies of the individuals concerned, it is inconceivable that complete success can be attained.

A heroic remedy, which has occasionally been suggested, would be to appoint British Moudirs. I greatly deprecate the adoption of this measure. It would be a very distinct step backwards in the direction of dissociating the Egyptians from the government of their own country. Moreover, although I do not mean to say that all the Inspectors are equally tactful and efficient, or that all the Moudirs possess every qualification which could be wished, I am convinced that the former are steadily gaining knowledge and experience of the country, and that the latter are generally far more efficient than their predecessors of a few years ago. If this be so, and if, as I hold, a policy of complete non-interference is not only open to great objections, but would also be very unpopular with the mass of the population, there is nothing for it but to continue to work on the broad lines of the present system, with all its recognised defects. All that can be done is to watch its operation, to choose the Moudirs with the utmost care, to constantly impress on the European Inspectors the necessity of dealing in a spirit of friendliness and sympathy with the Egyptian authorities, and to move—whenever this can prudently be done—in the direction of diminishing rather than of enhancing the degree of British interference in the details of the administration.[1]

[1] I must refer those who wish for more detailed information as regards the work of the Interior, in connection with village organisation and other matters, to my Annual Reports.

CHAPTER LVII

SUB-DEPARTMENTS OF THE INTERIOR

1. PRISONS—State of the prisons in 1882—Reform—2. SLAVERY—The Slave Trade and slavery—The Convention of 1877—The Slave Home—Change of opinion in Egypt—Success of the Convention—3. MEDICAL AND SANITARY ADMINISTRATION—Egyptian superstitions—Clot Bey—State of things in 1883—Improvements effected—Sanitary reform — Impediments to progress — Treatment of epidemics.

1. *Prisons.*

THOSE who have only a slight acquaintance with the ways of Eastern Governments may perhaps be astonished to learn of the existence of a Turkish Habeas Corpus Act. In reality, however, this is no cause for surprise. Contact with Europe has led to the adoption of the forms and the incorporation of much of the jargon of Western civilisation, but has been powerless to make the East imbibe its spirit. Oriental rulers have, indeed, discovered a plan, by the adoption of which, as they think, they can satisfy European reformers without incurring all the consequences which would result from the execution of a reforming policy. Broadly speaking, this plan consists in passing a law, and then acting as if the law had never been passed.[1]

[1] "No reform is clamoured for which does not already figure in the statute-book; no complaint is made which cannot be disproved by statistics. . . . Eastern peoples, not only in Turkey but in many other countries, form a solid national conspiracy against foreign and Christian influences. They know when their Government is forced to

According to Ottoman law, an accused person must be examined within twenty-four hours of his arrest by competent officials; when the charge against him is formulated, the conditions under which he may be admitted to bail are clearly laid down.

So much for the theory. The practice is different. Sir Herbert Chermside and Mr. Beaman, who were deputed by Lord Dufferin to inquire into the state of the Egyptian prisons in 1882, wrote: "It is impossible, in the face of the deluge of complaints as to no examination or trial during months and years of confinement, which has met us, to avoid concluding that the present system of arrest and sending to trial is, in practice, a flagrant injustice, and aggravated by venality, tyranny, and personal vindictiveness."

Two causes were at work during the pre-occupation days, one of which tended unduly to deplete, and the other unduly to crowd the prisons. On the one hand, a number of offences were committed for which no one was ever punished. This immunity from punishment tended to keep the prisons empty. On the other hand, when the authorities took cognisance of an offence, it was their practice to arrest not only every one who might possibly have been implicated in it, but also a number of their relations, as well as all the witnesses, whether they were on the side of the prosecution or of the defence. The result of this twofold injustice was that, whilst a number of persons were free who should have been in prison, at the same time a number of persons were in

give way against its will; they know when orders are meant to be obeyed, and answer the rein in a moment; they also know when they are not meant to be obeyed, but are what are called 'watery commands,' and then they do not obey them. . . . In the end, this national conspiracy, this 'invincible inertia,' nearly always wins the day."—*Turkey in Europe*, p. 138.

prison who should have been free;[1] and, once in prison, no distinction was made between those who had been convicted, those who were awaiting trial, and others, such as witnesses, who were detained, not for any offence, but because it was more convenient to keep them in prison, in case they were wanted, than to set them at liberty. "In the East," Sir Herbert Chermside wrote, "every man is treated as if guilty of the offence of which he is accused until he has established his innocence."

The condition of the prisons was horrible in the extreme. "No report," Mr. Beaman said, "can convey the feeblest impression of the helpless misery of the prisoners, who live for months, like wild beasts, without change of clothing, half-starved, ignorant of the fate of their families and bewailing their own. They only look forward to the day of their trial as synonymous with the day of their release, but the prospect of its advent is too uncertain to lend much hope to their wretchedness. From the moment of entering the prison, even on the most trifling charge, they consider themselves lost. It is impossible for them to guess at the time when a new official may begin to clear off the cases in his district, or when the slow march of the administration may reach them. It may be weeks, it may be months, and it may be years; many of them have long since ceased to care which."

In those days, the only hope of the Egyptian prisoner lay in the possession of money. A moderate bribe to the gaoler would insure relatively good treatment in prison. A further sum to the judge might hasten the trial. The tariff for an acquittal was naturally somewhat higher.

[1] "It is esteemed an act of Imperial clemency when the Sultan orders the release from prison of 'all persons against whom there is no charge.'"—*Turkey in Europe*, p. 140.

There is, however, nothing surprising in all this. The state of the Egyptian prisons in 1882 does not seem to have been much worse than that of the prisons in England before those reforms were undertaken which have made the name of John Howard for ever famous.

It is unnecessary to describe in detail the series of reforms in this Department which have been effected since 1882. It will suffice to say that, here as elsewhere, order and justice have taken the place of confusion and tyranny. The old prisons have been improved and placed in a sanitary condition. Large sums have been spent in the construction of new prisons. Special prisons have been constructed for women. Reformatories for juvenile offenders have been instituted. The prisoners have been provided with proper food and clothing. Many of them are taught trades. These reforms took time. Even now (1907) the prison accommodation can scarcely be said to be adequate to meet all the requirements of the country.

The only criticism now directed against the Prison Administration is—to quote the words of Coles Pasha, to whom the credit of reforming this branch of the Public Service is mainly due—that, in the eyes of many "prison life is not sufficiently deterrent, and that the swing of the pendulum has carried the Administration too far in the direction of humanity, if not of luxury." There may possibly be some truth in this criticism, but there can, of course, be no question of reverting to the brutal methods of the past in order to make punishment more deterrent. In Egypt, as elsewhere, the tendency of the best qualified penological experts is to move in the direction of reforming rather than in that of administering very severe punishment to criminals.

2. *Slavery.*

There is an obvious distinction between the Slave Trade and Slavery. Both are bad; but, whereas nothing can be said in defence of the Slave Trade, some mitigating pleas may be advanced as regards domestic slavery, which, although they in no degree justify the existence of the institution, are of a nature to temper the zeal of the reformer who aspires towards its immediate abolition.

Most Englishmen have been made familiar with the horrors of the Slave Trade. They have been told how peaceable villages in Central Africa have been invaded by parties of ruffianly Arab raiders; how the older inhabitants, male and female, have been shot down without mercy; how the girls and boys—the latter after undergoing the most cruel process of mutilation to which any man can be subjected[1]—have been marched long distances down to the coast; how numbers died of exhaustion on the way; and how eventually the survivors were sold to be the household servants of the Turkish and Egyptian Pashas.[2] Some arguments, more or less specious, can generally be found to defend most of the worst abuses which exist, or at times have existed in the world. The Slave Trade stands alone as an abomination which is incapable of any defence whatsoever, unless it be the vicious plea that Pashas require servants, and that they are unable to obtain them in sufficient numbers, or at

[1] The high price paid for these unfortunate boys is due to the fact that a large proportion of them die under the process of mutilation. The operation is performed in the most ruthless and barbarous manner by persons devoid of any surgical skill.

[2] It is a mistake to suppose that the black girls from Central Africa always become the concubines of their masters. It would be an exaggeration to say that cases of this sort never occur, but they are rare. The wives and concubines of the Pashas come almost exclusively from Circassia and Abyssinia. The blacks are almost always bought with the object of being employed as household servants.

a sufficiently low price, by any other means than those to which allusion is made above.

The case of domestic slavery, considered independently of the Slave Trade, is different. A slave in the Ottoman dominions lies under certain civil disabilities which shock the European's sense of justice; nevertheless, in practice, the disabilities in question lie lightly on the slaves themselves. Moreover, under unreformed Ottoman law, the slave is not free to carry his labour to any market which he chooses. This is unjust. On the other hand, as a general rule, slaves are well treated;[1] they lead an easy life and are not overworked. On the whole, save that the stigma of slavery is attached to them—a consideration which is all-important from the European, but relatively unimportant from the Eastern point of view[2]—it may be doubted whether in the majority of cases the lot of slaves in Egypt is, in its material aspects, harder than, or even as hard as that of many domestic servants in Europe. Indeed, from one point of view, the Eastern slave is in a better position than the Western servant. The latter can be thrown out of employment at any moment. In Egypt, on the other hand, although under the existing law, which is the outcome of contact with

[1] There are, however, exceptions. I remember a case which occurred early in 1885. It was brought to my notice that a white slave girl in the harem of a lady of high social position in Cairo was very badly treated, and that she wished to escape. With some difficulty, I obtained an interview with her at my house. She declared to me most positively that she was very well treated, and that she wished to return to the harem. I had no alternative but to comply with her request. Shortly afterwards, I went to England. On my return, the girl had disappeared. There were good reasons for believing that the statement she made to me was untrue, that she had been promised a large sum of money if she made it, that she was never paid the money, and that, on my departure from Egypt, she was beaten to death. But in cases of this sort it is, of course, impossible to obtain positive proof.

[2] Many Egyptians of the highest social classes are the sons of slave mothers, who are often married to their masters after having borne a child.

the West, the slave can, if he chooses, free himself from his master, no provision is made for the converse case of a master who wishes to get rid of a slave. Custom, based on religious law, obliges him to support his slave. Cases are frequent of masters who would be glad to get rid of their slaves, but who are unable to do so because the latter will not accept the gift of liberty. A moral obligation, which is universally recognised, rests on all masters to support aged and infirm slaves till they die; this obligation is often onerous in the case of those who have inherited slaves from their parents or other relatives.

On these grounds, therefore, some distinction must be drawn between the Slave Trade and Slavery. It is, however, none the less true that the one is intimately connected with the other. Where there is a demand, a supply will follow. If the institution of slavery did not exist, the Slave Trade would perish. In order to check the Slave Trade, if for no other reason, it is necessary to do all that is possible to discourage slavery. The object of the English reformer has, therefore, been twofold. In the first place, he has endeavoured to prevent slaves from being brought into the country, and has thus to some extent cut off the supply. In the second place, he has endeavoured to wean the slave-owning classes from their ancient habits, and has thus done much to diminish the demand.

Whether Ismail Pasha was moved by a sincere desire to abolish an infamous traffic, or whether he merely wished to throw dust in the eyes of humanitarian Europe, it is certain that to him belongs the credit of having given the first blow to the institution of slavery in Egypt. In August 1877, a Convention was signed between the Egyptian Government and Lord Vivian, acting on behalf of the British Government. Under the terms of this

Convention and the annexes attached to it, the Slave Trade was formally forbidden on Egyptian territory. Slave dealers were to be tried by court martial, and were rendered liable to severe penalties. The sale of slaves from family to family was to be tolerated until August 1884, after which time it was declared illegal. Any slave who chose to claim his or her liberty could obtain it on application to certain Bureaux of Manumission which were specially created.

It is now necessary to explain a point in connection with the institution of slavery in Egypt, the importance of which is often insufficiently recognised by those who are specially interested in this subject. On February 6, 1883, Lord Dufferin wrote :—

"Slavery might be abolished by Khedivial Decree, but a Convention is so much more formal and binding that it would seem preferable. I would, therefore, propose that a new Convention be entered into between Great Britain and Egypt, by which slavery would entirely cease in Egypt and its Dependencies seven years after the date of signature."

It may be doubted whether Lord Dufferin fully realised the obstacles which must have been encountered had any endeavour been made to give effect to his proposal. In 1883, those obstacles were practically insurmountable. Slavery in the East does not exist by virtue of any special Decree or law emanating either from the executive governments or from the legislatures under which Eastern countries are governed. It exists because its existence is authorised by the Sacred Law of Islam, which is as immutable as were the laws of the Medes and Persians. That law cannot be abrogated by any Khedivial Decree, and still less by any Convention signed with a Christian Power.

Kadis, Muftis, and Ulema would regard Decrees and Conventions, which infringed the fundamental religious law of Islam, much as devout French Catholics must have regarded the attempts of Anacharsis Clootz and other maniacs of the French revolution to effect the legal abolition of the Christian religion. They would altogether decline to recognise the validity of a law which, inasmuch as it altered the Sheriat, would in their eyes be considered as an attempt to justify sacrilege.

It is true that, some fifty years ago, the rulers of India ignored the Mohammedan religious law. In 1843, an Act was passed by the Indian legislature, which provided that the status of slavery should not be recognised by any law-court in the country, criminal or civil. But, although in the abstract, the Sheriat may be as inviolable at Calcutta as it is at Cairo, the question of the total and immediate abolition of slavery presented itself, from a practical point of view, in a very different aspect in Egypt under Lord Dufferin from that which obtained under Lord Ellenborough in India. In 1843, the English had been for half a century in India. They were the absolute rulers of the country. The law-courts, which they had established, inspired confidence. Moreover, they had to deal, not with one compact body of Mohammedans, but with a Mohammedan population which, though numerous, possessed little or no cohesion, owing to the fact that it was merged amongst the members of a more numerous and more tolerant creed. Under such circumstances, a radical reform, such as that effected in 1843, becomes possible. Under the political conditions which prevailed in Egypt in 1883, it would have been impossible, or at all events in the highest degree imprudent, to have attempted to follow the Indian precedent.

Under the Sheriat, a slave cannot marry or

inherit property without the consent of his master. When, therefore, it is said that, under the Convention of 1877, any slave was able to obtain his or her liberty on application to a Manumission Bureau, it is to be understood that the term "liberty" is used in a restricted sense. The Convention gave to the slave the right to go wherever he pleased, and to work or remain idle as he pleased. But it did not allow him to marry or to inherit property without the consent of his master. To this extent, in spite of nineteenth-century intervention, Islam of the seventh century still held the manumitted slave in its grip.

It was inevitable that the British occupation should give a fresh stimulus to the work of emancipation which was begun in 1877. One important consideration, however, tempered the zeal of the reformer. Almost all the slaves in Egypt were women. When they left the harems, having no means of support, they either starved or fell into a life of vice. Under these circumstances, those who were desirous of hastening the work of emancipation hesitated to act for fear of producing evils as bad as, if not worse than slavery. To remedy this defect, money was subscribed in England with the help of the Anti-Slavery Society, who, in this connection, did some excellent work. With the money thus obtained, which was supplemented by a grant from the Egyptian Treasury, a Home for Freed Female Slaves was established at Cairo. The manumitted slaves are now housed and fed in this Home until employment can be obtained for them.[1] This system has worked well. Respectable Mohammedans constantly apply to the Home for domestic servants.

[1] So few slaves now apply to the Manumission Bureaux that it will probably soon become a question whether the Home for Freed Slaves need be any longer maintained.

It would be probably an exaggeration to say that any public opinion adverse to slavery has been evoked in Egypt. The purchase and employment of slaves is not generally regarded with any moral reprobation, neither, under all the circumstances which exist, would it be reasonable to expect any such reprobation. In 1894, no less a person than the President of the Legislative Council, who was a Turco-Egyptian, was arraigned before a Court-martial for purchasing slaves, and only escaped imprisonment on account of his bad health and advanced years. Nevertheless, the slavery reforms instituted under British auspices have produced a notable change in the behaviour, if not in the opinions, of the slave-owning classes in Egypt. There are no longer any slave-markets. The purchase of a slave is a criminal offence attended with danger both to the buyer and to the seller. The slave routes are carefully watched. It is only with great difficulty that a few slaves are occasionally smuggled into the country. The result of these measures has been, not only that it has become year by year more difficult to obtain slaves, but that also, when any clandestine purchase is effected, a price considerably higher than that which formerly ruled has to be paid. The slave-owner is, therefore, beginning to ask himself whether slave labour is not, after all, more expensive as well as more troublesome than free labour, and whether it is worth while, besides committing a criminal act for which he may be severely punished, to pay a considerable sum for a slave girl who can, on the morrow of her purchase, walk out of the harem and obtain, not only her freedom, but also the strong support of the British representative if any attempt is made to tamper with her liberty of action.

Thousands of slaves have, during the last few

years, been granted their certificates of freedom. Those who remain in the harems know that they can obtain their liberty if they choose to ask for it. In the meanwhile, as very few fresh slaves are imported, and as the numbers born in slavery must certainly be inconsiderable in proportion to the number of those who have been manumitted, the supply of slaves is gradually falling short of the demand. Very few eunuchs are now to be found in Egypt. The objections to their employment from the Egyptian point of view are that a very high price has to be paid for them; that, on account of their bad physique, they are useless as servants; and that they are liable to die of consumption. It may safely be asserted that slavery in Egypt, although it will take a long time to die out completely, is moribund. It may be asserted with an almost equal degree of confidence that both the Slave Trade and slavery would revive if vigilance were relaxed.

From one point of view, the particular reform of the Egyptian social and administrative system now under discussion is remarkable. In view of the state of the Mohammedan law, of the fact that slavery, although discouraged by the founder of the Mohammedan religion, has, by a perverted view of his original preaching, become associated with the distinctive features of the Mohammedan faith; and of the further fact that material interests of some importance were involved in the abolition of slavery—it might well have been thought that the introduction of Western ideas in connection with this subject would have encountered opposition of a somewhat specially strong description. As a matter of fact, the opposition has been mild, and has been easily overcome. A great change has been going on insensibly. It has, indeed, been almost imperceptible to those who, it might be thought, were most interested in the maintenance of the existing abuse. No heroic measures have been adopted. Nothing has been done to clash with Mohammedan opinions and prejudices. Nevertheless, a considerable measure of success has been attained. This result is due to the fact that the Convention of 1877 was admirably adapted to achieve, in a prudent and unostentatious manner, the object for which it was intended. The late Lord Vivian's name is rarely, if ever, mentioned as one of the chief initiators of Egyptian reform. Yet it is due to the wise moderation of the Convention which he negotiated that slavery has been gradually disappearing from Egypt. At the commencement of this work, some words of Bacon were quoted as an example of the general principles which should guide the reformer in an Eastern country: "It were good that men in their innovations would follow the example of Time itself, which, indeed, innovateth greatly, but quietly and by degrees scarce to be perceived." That is the principle which has been adopted in connection with the abolition of slavery in Egypt. Lord Vivian's action in this matter was based on strictly Baconian principles.

In 1895, a fresh Slavery Convention was signed between the British and Egyptian Governments. It gave precision to the existing law, and in some respects altered the procedure. Moreover, it provided that it was a criminal offence to interfere in any way with the full liberty of action of an enfranchised slave. This change is important. It practically effects by a side wind all that was done by the Indian Act of 1843. Any one in Egypt who prevents a freed slave from marrying or from inheriting property is now liable to imprisonment.

A scholarly writer, who has paid special attention to this subject, calls slavery the "Nemesis of

Nations." "Civilisation," he says, "begins with the crack of the slave whip."[1] It may be placed to the credit of latter-day civilisation that the crack of that whip can no longer be heard in Egypt.

3. *Medical and Sanitary Administration.*

Whatever may be the case at present, it is certain that but a few years ago the lowest classes in Egypt rarely sought for medical aid until the patient was well-nigh moribund. The recipes of village barbers and of the old women, who were sometimes called in to attend the sick, as often as not aggravated the condition of the patient.[2] Great faith was entertained in the healing properties of written charms. These generally consisted of passages of the Koran for Mohammedans, or from the Psalms and Gospels for Copts, which were intermingled with numerical combinations, diagrams, and symbols. Persons of all creeds, being possessed of evil spirits, were said to be cured at certain Coptic convents, notably at the convent of St. Damianus[3] near Mansourah, and at that of St. Michael near Birket-el-Sab.

An operation which was "warranted to cure all diseases which were not fatal," could be performed if the sick person was fortunate enough to become

[1] Paterson's *Nemesis of Nations*, p. 53.

[2] The instances of superstition in this chapter are mainly taken from a pamphlet entitled *Medical Matters in Egypt*, written by Dr. F. M. Sandwith in August 1884. Dr. Sandwith's researches revealed a stage of medical knowledge amongst the poorer classes not materially in advance of that reached in Pharaonic times. M. Maspero (*Causeries d'Égypte*, p. 313) says that an ancient Egyptian medical practitioner was obliged to be "aussi expert en exorcismes qu'en formules de pharmacie."

[3] St. Damianus and his brother St. Cosmos were both doctors. They underwent martyrdom during the persecution of Diocletian, about A.D. 303. Pope Felix IV. built a Basilica in their honour at Rome.

possessed of a brass bowl, made in a peculiar fashion, and to the rim of which forty-one oblong strips of brass were attached. On each of these strips the words "In the name of the most merciful God," were inscribed. This bowl had to be filled on a Friday night with Nile water, into which some drugs and nuts were thrown. The sick person was instructed to stand in a basin of water before sunrise on the following morning, to drink out of the bowl, and to eat the nuts, throwing the shells behind his back. This operation had to be repeated on three consecutive Fridays.

It was, and perhaps still is a common practice amongst both Copts and Mohammedans to wear about their persons a bone taken from the body of a polytheist or of a Jew. This was supposed to afford immunity from all sorts of fevers. A bone taken from any ancient Egyptian mummy was often worn.

The remedy for sterility was for the woman who wished to become a mother to step over the corpse of an executed criminal, or into a basin of water which had been used to wash his corpse, or to tread on a human skull, or walk between the tombs of a cemetery, or step over some antique resemblance of a cat or other relic of old Egypt.

The cure for a stye in the eye was to eat bread obtained from seven different women, each called Fatma, the name of the Prophet's daughter.

Headache was cured by driving a nail into one of the gates of Cairo, called the Bab-el-Zueilah. For toothache, it was considered necessary to extract the tooth, and deposit it in a crevice of the same gate. The latter part of this operation was supposed to prevent other teeth from aching.

One of the most frequent antidotes for poison was to write certain texts of the Koran on slips of paper, which were then thrown into a dish of water. The water was stirred and the solution drunk.

Innumerable remedies existed, and probably still exist, to counteract the dreaded effects of the Evil Eye, belief in which has existed from time immemorial in Egypt.[1] The most efficacious is to steal a piece of the dress of the supposed envier, burn it, and fumigate the envied person with it. Another common practice is to heat some alum, and to prick one of the water bubbles, saying at the same time: "I prick the eye of the envier." Cornelian and charcoal are worn on the forehead by Moslem children for the same purpose. Parents also sometimes keep a monkey or a gazelle in the house in order to avert the Evil Eye.

I may here mention a curious case of superstition which came under my personal notice. Some years ago, my eldest son was dangerously ill with typhoid fever at Cairo. A short time before his illness, he had been given a black dog, which used to live in the house. The pattering of the dog's footsteps on the floor of the room disturbed the patient's rest. The dog was, therefore, sent out of the house. I afterwards learnt that my Egyptian servants looked on the dog as an "Afrit" (devil), that they considered the case hopeless so long as the dog remained in the house, but entertained no doubt of ultimate recovery directly the animal was removed. In this particular instance, as my son recovered, their belief in the power of "Afrits" must have been strengthened.

In the instances so far given, the fantastic remedies applied in cases of sickness have their

[1] "Abundant testimony exists in the oldest monuments in the world that among the ancient Egyptians belief in and dread of the Evil Eye were ever present; their efforts to avert or to baffle it, both as regarded the living and the dead, who they knew would live again, were perhaps the most constant and elaborate of any, of which we can now decipher the traces."—Elworthy's *The Evil Eye*, p. 6.

origin in superstition. Instances of prescribed cures based on complete ignorance of medical science and dissociated from any religious belief, however perverted, might readily be added. Thus, Dr. Sandwith tells of a Coptic bone-setter of celebrity, who was called in to attend a woman with a dislocated hip. He "gave instructions that the woman's hip should be tightly bound to a half-starved cow, and that the cow should then be fed until the rapid swelling of the animal had caused the reduction of the dislocation."[1]

The credit of having first brought true knowledge to bear on all this mass of ignorance and credulity belongs to an eminent Frenchman. Dr. Clot Bey, who was the father of Egyptian medical reform, was summoned to Egypt by Mehemet Ali. Under his auspices, a School of Medicine and Pharmacy, as well as a Maternity Hospital for the instruction of midwives, were created; a sanitary service for the interior of the country was also organised. A European doctor and apothecary, who were aided by Egyptian medical men and women, were appointed to every province in Lower Egypt. Under the intelligent stimulus thus afforded, considerable progress was made in the direction of medical and sanitary reform. All the superior officers possessed a European diploma.

At a later period, Egyptians, possessing only

[1] The state of things described above was but little, if at all, worse than that which existed in England and Scotland so late as the eighteenth century. During the first half of that century "medicines in common use contained brains of hares and foxes, snails burnt in the shell, powder of human skull and Egyptian mummy, burnt hoofs of horses, calcined cockle-shells, pigeon's blood, ashes of little frogs—like to the diabolical contents of the witches' cauldron in *Macbeth*" (Graham's *Social Life in Scotland in the Eighteenth Century*, vol. i. p. 51). *The Poor Man's Physician*, written by the "famous John Moncrieff of Tippermalloch," prescribes the following as a cure for whitlow: "Stop the finger with a cat's ear, and it will be whole in half an hour." In 1744, Mrs. Delany sent to her nephew, as an infallible cure for ague, "a spider put into a goosequill, well sealed and secured, and hung about the child's neck."—*Mrs. Delany's Memoirs*, p. 138.

certificates issued locally, were nominated to high posts. European control was relaxed. The reforms, which had begun to blossom, withered under the misrule of Ismail. The shadow of approaching bankruptcy fell upon the land. Useful expenditure was everywhere cut down with an unsparing hand in order to compensate for the financial vagaries of a spendthrift Khedive. "At the end of 1878," Dr. Sandwith says, "all sanitary, quarantine, and hospital buildings had fallen into ruin for want of funds, and the provincial hospitals naturally suffered to a greater degree than others."

By the time the British occupied the country in 1882, three-fourths of the good effects of Clot Bey's reforms had been obliterated. The School of Medicine still existed, but the instruction afforded to the students was very defective. The greater number of the medical officers serving under the Egyptian Government were ignorant and incompetent. They were also underpaid, with the natural result that they used the numerous opportunities afforded to them in the exercise of their official functions to increase their incomes by illicit means.[1] The state of the hospitals was deplorable. Nothing could be worse than the general administration of the Medical Department. Sir Guyer Hunter, who was sent to Egypt in 1883 to report on the cholera epidemic which then prevailed, wrote:

"The hospitals, as a rule, are in a more or less tumble-down, dirty condition, impregnated with

[1] "A dishonest man may occasionally threaten to cause some sweeping reform to be carried out in a village, unless a sum of money is immediately collected for him by the headman, or money may be obtained from a private individual by threatening to perform an autopsy on the dead body of his relative, on the plea that there is some suspicion of foul play. To the uneducated Musulman, who believes that the dead can feel and should be treated with a respect similar to the living, this idea is naturally repugnant."—Sandwith, *Medical Matters in Egypt*, p. 7.

foul odours, and containing beds filthy in the extreme; they are, in fact, noisome places, utterly unfit for the reception of human beings. . . . The medical administration is simply deplorable. I took the opportunity of examining the hospital registers. Here, as in everything else which met my observation under this administration, matters were as bad as bad could be."

As to the Lunatic Asylum in Cairo, an English doctor, who visited this institution in 1877, wrote:

"The whole place is so utterly beyond the ken of civilisation that it remains as hideous a blot on the earth's surface as is to be found even in the Dark Continent."

The veterinary art is of special importance in Egypt owing to the ravages which have at times been made by the cattle disease. The veterinary surgeons, however, Dr. Sandwith, speaking of the early days of the occupation, said, "may be fairly passed over with the remark that they are more ignorant, and not more honest, than their medical brethren."

It would be beyond the scope of this work, and moreover, would be of little interest to the general reader, were an attempt made to give the details connected with the work of reform accomplished as regards the subject now under discussion. The results may, however, be briefly summarised.

Modern medicine and surgery are essentially European sciences. The superiority of Western over Eastern therapeutic methods; the cosmopolitan character of the work performed by the physician and the surgeon; the dissociation which exists, or which at all events should exist between the art of healing the sick and political, racial, or religious rivalry; and the manifest benefits which the Egyptian people, whether as doctors or patients, are capable of receiving from European guidance and tuition—

are all so clear that it might well have been thought that, in this instance at all events, the beneficent co-operation of the Englishman would not only have been accepted without demur, but would even have been invited and welcomed. Such, however, was unfortunately not the case. The best, and, indeed, the only method of providing for the medical wants of Egypt without flooding the country with European doctors, was to take in hand the work of medical education. It was from the first evident that a few qualified Englishmen at the School of Medicine would, through the influence of teaching, be able in a few years to spread the light of Western science throughout the country. A cruel fate, however, ordained that, by a fortuitous and most unfortunate combination of circumstances, which are not worth relating in detail, the School of Medicine was for some while a hotbed of ultra-Mohammedan and anti-European feeling. This obstacle, though sufficient to retard, was powerless to arrest the progress of medical instruction. With characteristic Anglo-Saxon energy, the Englishman set to work to make the Egyptian "un médecin malgré lui." His perseverance was rewarded. The School of Medicine at Cairo was eventually, in spite of much opposition, put on a sound footing. A capable staff of Egyptian doctors, some of whom have European diplomas, is being gradually created.

The hospitals, the number of which has been largely increased, are now clean, properly equipped with beds, bedding, and clothing, and supplied with medicines, appliances, and instruments. The prejudice, which formerly existed, against being treated in a hospital, is gradually disappearing. About 31,000 in-patients and 118,000 out-patients were treated in the Government Hospitals during 1906. The number both of in- and out-patients is steadily increasing every year. A staff of trained English nurses has been attached to the principal hospital in Cairo, to the great benefit of the Egyptian nurses and pupils, whom they train and educate by precept and example. Dispensaries, where the poor can obtain gratuitous treatment, have been opened in several towns.

Vaccination has been carried out on a large scale amongst the Egyptian population, though the Capitulations hinder its extension amongst Europeans.[1]

A vigorous campaign, initiated in the first instance by the munificence of Sir Ernest Cassel, has been commenced against ophthalmia, which was formerly the curse of Egypt.[2]

A Foundling Hospital has been erected by private subscription in memory of a European lady who had endeared herself to the whole population.

The Lunatic Asylum at Cairo, which has been placed in charge of an English specialist, is now in perfect order. Another large Asylum is in course of construction.

Considerable progress has also been made in the Veterinary Department since 1886, when it was put under the control of an English veterinary surgeon. The butchers' shops, dairies, slaughter-

[1] "Half the cases of small-pox notified occurred among Europeans, a proportion which is extremely heavy when we consider the preponderance of the natives in Cairo, and was, no doubt, due to non-vaccination, many of the lower-class Europeans neglecting to have their children vaccinated. Though vaccination is compulsory on all persons residing in Egypt, the law is evaded by some of the Europeans from the fact that the births among this class of the population are not notified at the Public Health Office, but at the respective Consulates, and the Consuls in many cases do not send in the notifications to this Department, and the Government are unable to enforce the law on the parents."—*Report of the Public Health Department for* 1905.

[2] Not very long ago Mrs. Ross, the daughter of Lady Duff Gordon, visited Egypt. Forty years previously, she had had peculiar facilities for observing the condition of the people. I asked her what was the change which struck her most. I was pleased, and also surprised at her reply. She said, "The marked decrease in ophthalmia."

houses, cattle-sheds, etc., have been regularly inspected and controlled, their owners being induced or compelled to maintain them in a satisfactory sanitary condition. Several outbreaks of pleuro-pneumonia and other epizootic diseases have been stamped out. A Veterinary College, as also an Anti-Rabic Institute, have been established.

On the whole, although of course much remains to be done, it may be said that, in so far as medical instruction and organisation, veterinary administration, and the proper maintenance of hospitals, dispensaries, and lunatic asylums are concerned, an amount of progress has been realised which is as great as could reasonably be expected. The very capable Englishmen who have devoted their energies to the work of this Department, and who, like all other British officials in Egypt, have had great obstacles to encounter, have at all events succeeded in introducing the first commonplace elements of Western order and civilisation into the country.

Sanitary reform has, of course, progressed less rapidly than improvements in the medical service. In the former case, the conservative instincts of the people, and their indifference to sanitation, constitute an almost insuperable barrier to rapid progress. At the same time, much has already been done. The water-supply of the principal towns has been taken in hand. The Mosque latrines are no longer drained into the Nile or the canals, and in most of the towns the Mosques themselves have been put in a satisfactory sanitary condition. Authority has been obtained to remove cemeteries pronounced to be a danger to public health. A commencement has been made in filling up the highly insanitary pools which are to be found in close proximity to most Egyptian villages. As funds become available, it cannot be doubted that sanitary reform will, year by year, occupy a more prominent place in the Government programme.

Before leaving this branch of my subject, some brief allusion must be made to the eminent services rendered by the Sanitary Department in arresting the progress of the various epidemics which have visited Egypt of late years. In the cholera epidemic of 1883, 58,369 deaths from this disease were registered, and it is certain that the real number was far in excess of this figure. In 1896, another severe epidemic of cholera visited the country. The number of deaths was limited to 18,105. It cannot be doubted that the reduced mortality was, in a great measure, due to the improved efficiency of the Sanitary Department, under the auspices of Sir John Rogers and Sir Horace Pinching. This Department also dealt successfully with the cholera epidemic of 1902, and, moreover, gained well-deserved laurels in its treatment of the epidemic of plague in 1898 and subsequent years.

Some interesting statistics have been drawn up, showing the relative number of deaths in Alexandria from the plague epidemic which lasted from 1834 to 1843, as compared with those for the years 1899 to 1905. The number of deaths in the former period of ten years was 12,380. The number in the latter period of seven years was 647. The statistics of the earlier period are probably very imperfect. At the same time, they are sufficient to show the effect produced by the more stringent measures recently taken to check the disease, as compared with the results obtained by the methods adopted during the earlier of the two epidemics.

CHAPTER LVIII

JUSTICE

Sir Edward Malet's opinion—The Mixed and Consular Courts—The Kadis' Courts—The Native Tribunals—Justice prior to 1883—The French system taken as a model—The judicial machinery—Reforms instituted by Sir John Scott and Sir Malcolm McIlwraith—Opposition to these reforms—The personnel of the Courts—Result of the reforms.

WHEN Sir Edward Malet left Egypt in 1883, he declared that the first requirement of the Egyptian population was justice. In the present chapter, an endeavour will be made to state very briefly how far this requirement has been met.

It has been already explained[1] that the Mixed Tribunals deal with all civil cases, in which Europeans are concerned, and the Consular Courts with all criminal cases in which Europeans are the accused parties. The latter Courts apply their national laws. Of these institutions, no more need be said. Up to the present time (1907) the jurisdiction of the Consular Courts remains unchanged. The law administered by the Mixed Tribunals has merely undergone some minor modifications. In each of these cases, the reasons for this long immunity from change have, broadly speaking, been twofold. The first is that neither the Mixed nor the Consular Courts stood nearly so much in need of reform as the Egyptian portions of the

[1] See Chapter XLII.

judicial system. The second is that, hedged behind the almost impenetrable barrier of internationalism, both of these jurisdictions have so far been able to defy the efforts of the reformer.

Neither need much be said about the Kadis' Courts. These Courts deal with all questions affecting the personal status of Moslems. If they are ever to be improved, the movement in favour of reform must come from within. It must be initiated by the Egyptians themselves. Any serious attempt to impose reforms by pressure from without would be extremely impolitic, and, moreover, would probably result in failure. The British reformer, therefore, being partly convinced of the uselessness of attack and partly impelled by political necessity, turned aside from Mohammedan law-reform. Although he made some faltering steps in the direction of improving the Kadis' Courts, his energies were mainly applied in other directions, where better results were to be obtained.

There remain the Native Tribunals instituted in 1883. These deal with all civil cases in which both parties are Ottoman subjects, and with all criminal cases in which an Ottoman subject is the accused party. It can scarcely be said that these Courts took the place of any existing institutions. They were new creations. The judges were the instruments who gave expression to a phase of thought which had been hitherto unfamiliar to the Egyptian mind. Prior to 1883, a system of punishment existed, or it would be perhaps more correct to say that a method was in force by which occasionally somebody was punished for an offence which as often as not he had never committed, whilst not unfrequently others were punished without any offence at law having been committed at all. Moreover, the existence of some rude code of Civil Law was so far recognised as to enable the worst illegalities to be hallowed by legal sanction. For instance, when Ismail Pasha confiscated the vineyard of some Naboth among his subjects, the transfer was always effected in accordance with strictly legal forms. But any system of justice, properly so called, was unknown in the country. The divorce between law, such as it was, and justice was absolute. It has been already explained[1] how, in 1883, the Department of Justice was, to some extent, placed under British management; how, during the storm and stress of the years 1884-85, when the Anglo-Egyptian bark was being tossed hither and thither by the waves of Soudanese troubles, bankruptcy, and international rivalry, this Department, as well as that of the Interior, were confided to Egyptian hands; how the experiment, which was then tried, resulted in complete failure; and how eventually, with the nomination of Sir John Scott to the post of Judicial Adviser, an era of real reform commenced.

It is true that, prior to 1883, no system of justice existed in Egypt. It is not, however, on that account to be supposed that the English were free to introduce into the country any system which they preferred. Such was far from being the case. French law and procedure had already taken root in Egypt. The codes administered by the Mixed Tribunals were French. All the young Egyptians who had received any legal training had been educated in France. It was, therefore, inevitable that the new Tribunals should be based on a French rather than on an English model. The necessity was regrettable, for a simple code of law and procedure, somewhat similar to that which was subsequently introduced into the Soudan, would—more especially in criminal matters—have probably been more suited to the

[1] *Vide ante*, pp. 288-90.

requirements of the country than that which was actually adopted.[1]

Proposals have frequently been made to sweep away the system of criminal justice inaugurated shortly after the British occupation took place, and to substitute something else in its place. Apart from other and very valid objections to the adoption of this course, it is to be observed that those who have urged this radical treatment of the question have not, perhaps, sufficiently realised that, although the system is, indeed, by no means perfect, the main difficulties which have to be encountered in introducing any improvements are inherent in the situation, and cannot be removed by any mere change of system. They arise from the character of the people, from the impossibility of creating rapidly a competent judiciary calculated to inspire confidence and respect, and, generally, from the circumstances which are the necessary accompaniment of a transitionary period from arbitrary government to a reign of law. It was, therefore, decided to make no radical changes, but to remedy the defects which existed by gradually introducing such minor reforms as experience showed were calculated to adapt the system more fully to the requirements of the country.

It is unnecessary that I should describe in detail the nature of the changes which, from time to time, have been carried out under the auspices of

[1] The danger of making too faithful a copy of European judicial institutions is fully recognised by the best French authorities on colonial affairs. In an interesting article, written by M. de Lavigne Sainte-Suzanne, and entitled "La Justice Indigène aux Colonies," which appeared in the *Revue Diplomatique*, the following passage occurs :—

"C'est surtout dans l'organisation de la justice indigène que retrouve son application cette formule qui devrait servir de base à tout le programme du droit colonial : pas d'assimilation. S'il est absurde de transporter chez des peuples encore primitifs tous les rouages administratifs en usage dans la vieille Europe, il devient dangereux et inique d'imposer aux indigènes notre législation et notre organisation judiciaire."

successive Egyptian Ministers of Justice aided by Sir John Scott, and his successor, Sir Malcolm McIlwraith. The most important of these have been the establishment of a Committee of Surveillance who, without possessing any power to upset or revise judgments already delivered, watch over the proceedings of the Courts of First Instance; the partial decentralisation, first of Civil, and subsequently of Criminal justice; the revision of the Criminal Codes with the object of freeing them from useless formalism; and the establishment of Assize Courts whose judgments, save on points of law, are final.

These reforms followed what may be considered the normal course of all administrative change in Egypt. When any new measure is proposed, a certain amount of opposition is sure to be encountered. This opposition will sometimes be based on the conservative tendencies of the more old-fashioned class of Egyptians, who look askance at any one who aspires to *moliri res novas*; or, it may be based on the mental inelasticity of the Egyptian reformer, who, albeit somewhat prone to radical change, finds it difficult to get out of the special groove into which, by the accident of education and association, his intellectual forces have been directed. When the reform is eventually accomplished, it is discovered that the fears of the opposition were groundless, and that the measure, so far from having done harm, has done much good. This experience will in no degree act as a preventive to a repetition of similar tactics on some future occasion; but it is a point which the European reformer should bear in mind that, provided always that his proposals be reasonable, they will generally, after a certain amount of murmuring, be accepted. All Easterns carry fatalism into the practical affairs of life; they readily bow before an accomplished fact. In the particular cases described above, the somewhat fictitious opposition, which was at one time excited against Sir John Scott's and Sir Malcolm McIlwraith's proposals, died an unusually speedy death. The benefits derived from the reforms were, in fact, too manifest to admit of doubt. Experience soon pricked the theoretical bubbles of which the opponents of practical reforms in Egypt are at times prodigal.[1]

So far, the main features of the judicial system which were introduced have been described. The chief difficulty in this, as in so many other cases, has, however, been not to devise a system, but to find men capable of working it. Sir John Scott, writing in the early part of 1894, said:

"'Tant valent les juges, tant valent les lois,' is a principle which had been overlooked before 1890; and judges had been named in Appeal, as well as in First Instance, who were far from possessing the necessary qualifications."

In point of fact, when the Tribunals were first instituted in 1883, few Egyptians were to be found who were capable of exercising judicial functions. Moreover, amongst those few, the best men were frequently not selected. The appointments were jobbed. Gradually, the least capable men have been weeded out. It cannot be doubted that the standard of efficiency in the law-courts is steadily improving. I should add that the personnel of the

[1] Perhaps the most striking instance of the collapse of opposition was in the case of the Assize Courts. Few measures have been more violently or more universally condemned. Yet, very shortly after the change of system had been effected, one of the most competent of the Egyptian judicial officials was able to write: "Nothing shows more clearly the efficiency and excellency of the new system than the absence of all criticisms upon the results obtained by its adoption, especially when it is remembered that, when the project was under consideration, it gave rise to much difference of opinion, and to fears as to the consequence which would be entailed from the point of view of justice." The establishment of these Courts has, *inter alia*, rendered justice much more expeditious than formerly.

Judicial Department is almost wholly Egyptian. Out of a total staff of 1600, only 36 are Europeans.

Have the changes, whose main features have thus been briefly described, given to the population of Egypt a sound system of justice, on the necessity of which Sir Edward Malet insisted in 1883?

In a sense, this question may unhesitatingly be answered in the affirmative. The system, which I do not doubt Sir Edward Malet wished to advocate, was one under which law-courts should be placed in a position to protect the most humble individual of the community against the caprices of his ruler and of the Government agents, of whose malpractices Sir Edward Malet had been a scandalised witness. Law-courts possessing both the power and the will to attain this object have been created. Not only are the judges independent of the Government, but they are in the highest degree sensitive of any words or deeds calculated to call their independence in question. Justice is no longer bought and sold. It may be dilatory, and, as in other countries, it may occasionally err. It may perhaps be that, where racial or religious feelings are evoked, some—probably unconscious—bias may be discerned. But no more grave accusation than this can be brought against the Egyptian law courts. So early as March 9, 1893, I was able to write to Lord Rosebery: "It can now be said that justice in Egypt is administered on fixed principles and, with occasional exceptions, the decisions are just." The fact that no more than ten years after the British occupation commenced a statement of this sort could be recorded reflects great credit, not only on the Ministers and their Judicial Advisers, who have guided the work of reform in this Department, but also on the European and Egyptian judges and other officials who have co-operated with them.

The Anglo-Saxon race have broad shoulders. They may well pardon a little pedantry, as well as the Anglophobia which the Egyptian judges have at times displayed, and which is to a great extent the result of ignorance and misguidance, if, in dealing with the litigious affairs of their own countrymen, their "decisions are just."

The protection of the weak against the strong is, however, not the sole function of justice. It should also be able to protect society against evil-doers. That this protection has, of late years, been inadequate in Egypt, can scarcely be doubted. It is easy to indicate the main reason for this state of things. On the one hand, civilisation insists on the cardinal principle that no man is to be punished for any offence unless he is clearly proved to have committed it. On the other hand, the peculiar conditions of Egyptian society render it often a matter of extreme difficulty to obtain evidence of guilt sufficient to warrant a conviction. In the last report which I wrote from Egypt before tendering the resignation of my appointment, I made the following remarks, to which I have nothing to add :—

"I have no hesitation in stating that the increase of crime, to which I have frequently alluded in former Reports, is the most unsatisfactory feature in the whole Egyptian situation. The Government are frequently being pressed to examine into the causes which have led to the increase, and to look to the removal of those causes, rather than to the punishment of the offenders, as the true remedy for the existing state of affairs. As a matter of general principle, I entirely agree that when, in any country, it is found that the number of crimes is increasing, it is most necessary to inquire into the cause, but the possibility of applying any remedy other than that of punishment must obviously depend upon the nature of the cause when once it has been ascertained. It generally happens that increasing poverty is the parent of increasing crime. No one with the least knowledge of the country will think that the recent increase of crime in Egypt is due to poverty. There must be some other cause, and, in my opinion, it is not far to seek. It is, I think, to be found in the fact that the law does not inspire sufficient terror to evildoers. Only 43·5 per cent of the crimes committed last year (1906) were punished. In the remaining 56·5 per cent, it was found impossible to discover the criminals, or, if they were discovered, to prove their guilt. I was talking a short time ago to a distinguished Frenchman who was well acquainted with the affairs of Algeria. He explained to me that certain districts lying in the Algerian Hinterland, where military law used to be applied, had recently been brought under the ordinary criminal codes. The comment of one of the principal Algerian Sheikhs on this change was curious. 'Then,' he said, 'there will be no justice. Witnesses will be required.' I commend this remark to those who are in a hurry to apply Western methods in their entirety to a backward Eastern population. The Sheikh was not in the least struck with the fact that, in the absence of witnesses, an innocent man might possibly be condemned. What struck him was that, as no one could be condemned without witnesses, guilty people would generally escape punishment. This is precisely what is happening in Egypt. I have said over and over again, and I now repeat, that I strongly deprecate any resort to heroic remedies in dealing with this question. There must be no radical change of system. But there should be no delusion as to the time which will be required, or the difficulties which have still to be encountered, before a well-established reign of law can take the place of the arbitrary system under which, until recently, the Egyptians were governed. In the meanwhile, let us by all means do everything that is possible, not merely to improve the Police and the judicial systems, but also, by indirect means, such as education and the establishment of adult reformatories, to diminish crime and check criminal tendencies. But, simultaneously with all this, I trust that criminals will receive adequate punishment when their guilt has been brought home to them. I deprecate the false sentiment which expends all its sympathy on the criminal and reserves none for his victims. I at times observe symptoms which lead me to believe that this sentiment prevails to a somewhat excessive degree in Egypt."[1]

[1] *Egypt*, No. 1 of 1907, p. 85.

CHAPTER LIX

EDUCATION

Educational policy—Obstacles to progress—Want of money—The Pashas—Intellectual awakening of Egypt—The Mosque schools—Primary and Secondary education—Progress made in forming the characters of the Egyptians—Female education.

THE subjects which have so far been treated fall within the domain of material or administrative progress. What, however, has been done in the direction of moral and intellectual progress? Have the English made any endeavour to educate the Egyptians? "Egypt," a high authority on Eastern affairs has said, "has always been the servant of nations."[1] Have the English, as some critics of the baser sort aver, viewed this condition of political degradation with ill-disguised favour?[2] Have they discouraged the acquisition of knowledge, with a view to keeping the Egyptians in a position of servitude to the British nation? Or has a more noble policy been adopted? Have the English, casting aside all feelings based on a mistaken and ignoble egotism, endeavoured to educate the Egyptians and to lead them, so far as was possible, along the path which may possibly end in self-government?

[1] Muir, *The Caliphate*, p. 168.

[2] It was not only with surprise, but also with a feeling of keen disappointment, that I read in a work written by M. de Guerville a letter from Sheikh Mohammed Abdou, in which that eminent man appeared to give the weight of his name to insinuations of this sort. He must have known perfectly well that they were wholly devoid of foundation. I had hoped for better things of him.

In the present chapter an attempt will be made to answer these questions. They are of vital importance, not only to the Egyptians themselves, but also to all Europe, and more especially to England. The reason why they are so important is that if ever the Egyptians learn to govern themselves — if, in other words, the full execution of the policy of "Egypt for the Egyptians" becomes feasible—the Egyptian question will, it may be hoped and presumed, finally cease to be a cause of trouble to Europe, and the British nation will be relieved of an onerous responsibility.

Many years ago, Lord Macaulay asked a pertinent question in connection with the system under which India should be governed. "Are we," he said, "to keep the people of India ignorant in order that we may keep them submissive?" His reply was an indignant negative. "Governments, like men," he said, "may buy existence too dear. *Propter vitam vivendi perdere causas* is a despicable policy both in individuals and in States."[1]

The English in Egypt have acted on the principle advocated by Macaulay. They may repel, with equal truth and scorn, the insinuation that, for political reasons, they have fostered Egyptian ignorance and subserviency. If a race of Egyptians capable of governing the country without foreign aid has not as yet been formed, the fault does not lie with the English. It must be sought elsewhere, neither need any impartial person go far afield to find where it lies. It lies mainly in the fact that two decades are but a short time in the life of a nation. Material progress may, under certain conditions, be rapid. Moral and intellectual progress must of necessity always be a plant of slow growth. It takes more time to form the mind of a statesman, or even to train a competent administrator,

[1] Speech in the House of Commons, July 10, 1833.

than it does to dig a canal or to construct a railway. When the unpromising nature of the raw material on which the English had to work is considered, when it is remembered that for centuries prior to the British occupation the Egyptians were governed under a system eminently calculated to paralyse their intellectual and warp their moral faculties, and when it is further borne in mind that the circumstances under which reform was undertaken were of an exceptionally difficult and complicated nature, it may well be a matter for surprise, not that so little, but that so much progress in the direction of a real Egyptian autonomy has been made in so short a time.

Consider what is generally meant by Europeans when they talk of Egyptian self-government. If they meant that the Egyptians should be allowed to govern themselves according to their own rude lights, the task of educating them in the art of self-government would not merely have been easy; there would have been no necessity that it should have been undertaken. The indigenous art of self-government had already been acquired in 1882, and we know with what results; no European instruction would have been able to improve on its recognised canons. What Europeans mean when they talk of Egyptian self-government is that the Egyptians, far from being allowed to follow the bent of their own unreformed propensities, should only be permitted to govern themselves after the fashion in which Europeans think they ought to be governed.

I am not one of those who think that "any State can be saved, and any political problem solved, by enlightened administration."[1] At the

[1] This was the view held by Peregrino Rossi, who was subsequently assassinated, during the early struggles for Italian unity.—Trevelyan's *Garibaldi's Defence of the Roman Republic*, p. 74.

same time, looking to the magnitude of all the interests involved in Egypt, there is a limit to the degree of maladministration which can be tolerated in order to ensure all the advantages of self-government. It cannot be doubted that that limit would be passed, if complete autonomy were suddenly bestowed on the Egyptians.

To suppose that the characters and intellects of even a small number of Egyptians can in a few years be trained to such an extent as to admit of their undertaking the sole direction of one of the most complicated political and administrative machines which the world has ever known, and of guiding such a machine along the path of even fairly good government, is a sheer absurdity. I must apologise to those of my readers who have any real acquaintance with Egyptian affairs for indulging in platitudes of this description. If I do so, it is because it would appear that the race of those who dream dreams of real autonomy in the very near future is not yet extinct.

The main reason why it is hopeless to expect that any immediate and important political fruit can be gathered from the tree of educational progress in Egypt has been already indicated. It is now necessary to explain the further obstacles which have stood in the way of rapid progress in the work of education. They were mainly twofold.

The first and principal obstacle has been want of money. In 1877 and 1878—that is to say, during the worst periods of the financial chaos created by Ismail Pasha—the Government expenditure on education only amounted to the paltry sum of £E.29,000 a year. Under the Dual Control, the grant was raised to about £E.70,000 a year. During the early days of the British occupation, that is to say, whilst the issue of the "Race against Bankruptcy" was still doubtful, the utmost economy had to be practised; and even when the race was won, it was felt that, however necessary it might be to provide schools for Egyptian children, it was still more necessary to limit the excessive demands which the tax-gatherer had heretofore made on their parents. Fiscal relief, therefore, took precedence of everything. It was not until 1890 that the Financial Department found itself in a position to increase the sum of money spent by the State on education to £E.81,000. Since then, it has been steadily increasing in amount.[1] It would long since have been largely increased had not internationalism, by depriving the Egyptian Government of the free use of their own resources, barred the way.

Want of money, therefore, was the first obstacle in the way of rapid progress. The idiosyncrasies of Pashadom constituted the second. It was not that the Pashas did not wish to advance the cause of education in Egypt. Far from it. Many of them yearned — and very naturally and rightly yearned—for educational progress. They recognised that the acquisition of knowledge was the sole instrument by the use of which Egypt might perhaps eventually be freed from foreign control. But they were themselves too ignorant of educational administration to be able to initiate the only measures which would have satisfied their very legitimate yearnings. The execution of their own policy was perpetually leading them to conclusions which their prejudices forced them to reject. The natural result ensued. The policy of Pashadom was a mass of inconsistencies. Moreover, the

[1] £E.305,000 was expended on education in 1906. The provision made in the estimates for 1907 amounted to £E.374,000, and this amount has been increased to £E.450,450 in the estimates for 1908. These figures represent only "ordinary" expenditure. They do not include the special credits for the construction and maintenance of school buildings.

evil effects of those inconsistencies were enhanced by the fact that, at every turn of the wheel of nepotism, some fresh individual was, during the early years of the occupation, appointed to direct the affairs of the Department of Public Instruction. "The frequent changes in educational policy during past years," I wrote in 1892, "have proved a great obstacle to educational progress in Egypt. During the past twenty-nine years, the Minister (or Director-General) of Public Instruction has been changed twenty-nine times. At each change, the schools have for a time been more or less completely upset and demoralised, as it has been the prevailing tendency of the Minister to reverse the administrative methods of his predecessor."

At one moment, recourse has been had to the usual remedy of the Egyptian reformer. A servile copy was made of some foreign institution. "On s'était contenté," says Yacoub Artin Pasha, who is by far the highest Egyptian authority on educational matters in Egypt, "de copier les programmes des écoles de France, et sans se donner la peine de chercher à les modifier selon les besoins du pays et de notre culture future."[1] At the next moment, the undisciplined mind of the old-fashioned Pasha, with characteristic want of moderation, would spring at a bound to the opposite extreme of anti-European sentiment. He might own that European knowledge was good, but he refused to accept the inevitable conclusion that, at all events until a capable staff of Egyptian teachers had been trained, Europeans alone could impart it. Sciences cannot be learnt save in those languages which possess a scientific literature and vocabulary. Yet the Pasha, under the influence of prejudices which his powers of reasoning were

[1] *Considérations sur l'Instruction Publique en Égypte*, p. 116.

too feeble to stem, declared that a science which could not be taught in Arabic, should not be taught at all. There was one thing which the Pasha could do, and which, in fact, he did. He could multiply schools and scholars without any regard to the qualifications of the professors, to the value of the instruction imparted, or to the schoolroom accommodation which was available. He could thus practise his favourite art of self-deception. He could give statistical proof that he was moving rapidly forward, whilst all the time he was in reality stationary, if, indeed, his movements were not retrograde. On the whole, it may be said that one of the chief obstacles to the adoption of an enlightened educational policy in Egypt in the early days of the occupation was the presence of a few leading Pashas who, in theory at all events, favoured educational progress. There can be no doubt that, if the English had from the first had a free hand in this matter, greater progress would have been made than has actually been the case.

From one point of view, however, the English took in hand the work of educating the Egyptians at a propitious moment. Almost simultaneously with the occurrence of the British occupation, the country underwent an intellectual awakening. The people of Egypt had, in fact, slumbered since the days of Mehemet Ali. One of the most singular traits in that remarkable man's character was that, although he was himself uneducated, although he could never write, and did not learn to read till he was forty-seven years old, and then imperfectly, he placed a high value on European knowledge.[1] He established schools in the towns and large villages. Mehemet Ali was, however, in some respects, in advance of

[1] See M. de Lesseps' remarks to Mr. Senior, *Conversations, etc.*, p. 129.

his time. "Knowledge was then so unpopular that mothers blinded their children to keep them from school."[1] More than half a century later, the population generally appreciated the value of education almost as little as they did in the days of Mehemet Ali. Writing in 1894, Yacoub Artin Pasha said:—

"Il n'y a pas une dizaine d'années que le public en général, non seulement ne s'intéressait pas à l'instruction de ses enfants, main encore y était opposé, quoique dans une moindre mesure qu'il y a soixante ans."

It is not to be supposed that the Egyptians were suddenly inspired with a thirst for knowledge for its own sake, or that they awoke to a keen sense of shame at their own ignorance. The new spirit was, at all events in the first instance, rather to be attributed to the fact that, in a country where a large section of the upper and middle classes of society depends on Government employment, parents suddenly realised that, unless their children were sent to school, they would probably not be able to gain their livelihood. Contact with the West, the partial Europeanisation of the administrative services, and the emulation inspired by the presence of European, Levantine, and Syrian competitors, produced, therefore, at least one beneficial result.

But whatever be the cause, there can be no doubt of the fact. The best test of whether the Egyptians really desire to be educated is to ascertain whether they are prepared to pay for education. On this point, the evidence is conclusive. In the early days of the British occupation, nearly all the pupils who attended the Government schools were taught gratuitously. Before many years had

[1] See M. de Lesseps' remarks to Mr. Senior, *Conversations, etc.*, p. 130.

passed, by far the greater proportion paid for their instruction.[1]

In 1889, I visited many remote villages of Upper Egypt in which the face of a European is rarely seen. No request was more frequently made to me than that I should urge the Government to establish a school in the village. "De différents côtés," Yacoub Artin Pasha wrote at about this period, "on demande des écoles, et là où il en existe déjà on demande quelquefois leur dévéloppement, sans se rendre bien compte, il est vrai, de ce que l'on demande." The Egyptians have, in fact, made one great step forward in the race for a national existence. They have learnt that they are ignorant. They wish to be taught.

It is now necessary to explain what measures were adopted for teaching them.

"The chief aim and object of education in Islam," Mr. Hughes says, "is to obtain a knowledge of the religion of Mohammed, and anything beyond this is considered superfluous and even dangerous."[2] Under these circumstances, it was clear to the British reformer that the education imparted at the famous University of El-Azhar could not be utilised to raise the general standard of education in Egypt. He, therefore, left that institution alone.

The El-Azhar University stands at the summit

[1] The policy which has of late years been pursued in connection with the matter to which allusion is here made, has been vigorously attacked. The grounds on which, as it appears to me, it may be successfully defended are stated at some length in *Egypt*, No. 1 of 1906, pp. 82-89.

In this work, I have merely endeavoured to give a general sketch of the progress which has been made in the various branches of the administration. It would lead me to too great length were I to attempt to answer all the criticisms which have, from time to time, been made on the working of the various Departments. This remark applies with special force to the work of the Department of Public Instruction. It has formed the subject of a great deal of very unjust animadversion.

[2] Hughes's *Dictionary of Islam*, p. 106.

of the purely Moslem educational system of Egypt. The village schools (Kuttabs), which are attached to most of the Mosques in the country, stand at the base of that system. As regards the quality of the instruction afforded in these schools, Mr. Hughes makes the following remarks:—

"The child who attends these seminaries is first taught his alphabet, which he learns from a small board on which the letters are written by the teacher. He then becomes acquainted with the numerical value of each letter. After this, he learns to write down the ninety-nine names of God, and other simple words taken from the Koran. When he has mastered the spelling of words, he proceeds to learn the first chapter of the Koran, then the last chapter, and gradually reads through the whole Koran in Arabic, which he usually does without understanding a word of it. Having finished the Koran, which is considered an incumbent religious duty, the pupil is instructed in the elements of grammar, and perhaps a few simple rules of arithmetic. . . . The ordinary schoolmaster is generally a man of little learning."

It would be an exaggeration to say that these Mosque schools are absolutely useless. Through their instrumentality, a certain number of children are taught to read and write. Organised as they were at the time the British occupation commenced, they were, however, as nearly useless as any educational establishments could be. Want of funds at first stood in the way of any attempt to reform them, but about 1897 the matter was taken in hand. A reasonable curriculum, based on the teaching of the three R's, was adopted. The teaching of any foreign language was rigorously excluded. Since 1898, the number of village schools under Government supervision has increased year by year.

In 1906, 4554 village schools were either directly under Government control or under departmental inspection for grants-in-aid. They gave instruction to 165,000 pupils, of whom nearly 13,000 were girls.

It is on every ground of the highest importance that a sustained effort should be made to place elementary education in Egypt on a sound footing. The schoolmaster is abroad in the land. We may wish him well, but no one who is interested in the future of the country should blind himself to the fact that his successful advance carries with it certain unavoidable disadvantages. The process of manufacturing demagogues has, in fact, not only already begun, but may be said to be well advanced. The intellectual phase through which India is now passing stands before the world as a warning that it is unwise, even if it be not dangerous, to create too wide a gap between the state of education of the higher and of the lower classes in an Oriental country governed under the inspiration of a Western democracy. High education cannot and ought not to be checked or discouraged. The policy advocated by Macaulay is sound. Moreover, it is the only policy worthy of a civilised nation. But if it is to be carried out without danger to the State, the ignorance of the masses should be tempered *pari passu* with the intellectual advance of those who are destined to be their leaders. It is neither wise nor just that the people should be left intellectually defenceless in the presence of the hare-brained and empirical projects which the political charlatan, himself but half-educated, will not fail to pour into their credulous ears. In this early part of the twentieth century, there is no possible general remedy against the demagogue except that which consists in educating those who are his natural prey to such an extent that they may, at all events, have some chance of discerning the imposture which but too often lurks beneath his perfervid eloquence and political quackery.

Considerations of space render it necessary that I should abstain—albeit somewhat reluctantly—from giving a description of the progress made of late years in Egypt in the direction of Primary and Secondary education. For the same reason, I do not deal with the very important question of Technical education.[1] I must, therefore, confine myself to stating the bald fact that, in 1906, 505 educational establishments, exclusive of village schools, existed in the country. These gave employment to 4341 teachers, and instruction to about 92,000 pupils, of whom about 20,000 were girls. Under the enlightened administration of the present Minister, Saad Pasha Zagloul, and of his Adviser, Mr. Dunlop, education of every description is making rapid strides in advance.

It cannot be doubted that the quality of the instruction afforded at the Government schools has of late years been greatly improved. The skilful methods and direct personal influence of the

[1] Very full explanations have been given on all these subjects in my successive Annual Reports.

The following remarks made by Mr. Lecky (*Democracy and Liberty*, vol. ii. p. 6) apply, with great force, to the Egyptian educational system : "The great mistake in the education of the poor has in general been that it has been too largely and too ambitiously literary. Primary education should . . . teach the poor to write well and to count well ; but, for the rest, it should be much more technical and industrial than literary, and should be more concerned with the observation of facts than with any form of speculative reasoning or opinions. There is much evidence to support the conclusion that the kinds of popular education which have proved morally, as well as intellectually, the most beneficial have been those in which a very moderate amount of purely mental instruction has been combined with physical or industrial training."

In a very interesting article published in the *Edinburgh Review* for October 1907, and entitled "Signs of the Times in India," the disastrous results which have ensued from unduly encouraging a purely literary education in that country to the neglect of scientific and technical training are very clearly indicated.

new European teachers, who have been introduced into the Department of Education, have been steadily raising the general level of the schools, in spite of the numerous obstacles encountered. Whilst there has been an increasingly strict supervision of the teaching of Arabic and the Koran, the study of European languages has been placed on a new basis. Previously, pupils were allowed to waste their time and addle their brains by attempting the study of an impossible number of languages. It was a great step in advance when the time-honoured methods adopted in Egypt of loading the memory without exercising the mind were abandoned. English and French are now no longer merely treated as additional subjects of linguistic study. Either of these languages is used as the medium of instruction in certain subjects, such as history, science, etc. In course of time, as the number of highly trained Egyptian teachers increases, instruction will, without doubt, be given in Arabic to a much greater extent than heretofore.[1]

From the political point of view, the most important educational question is this: Do the educated Egyptians, whose number is now rapidly increasing, possess the qualities and characteristics of potentially self-governing Egyptians? To put the same question in another way, if we speak of education in the broadest sense of the term—that is to say, if we include the formation, not only of the intellect, but also of the character—if, in a word,

[1] That the absence of an adequate staff of trained Egyptian teachers has greatly retarded the progress of education both in Egypt and in the Soudan cannot be doubted. In my Annual Reports, I have frequently alluded to this important subject. The cause has been the same as that which has operated in other Departments of the State, viz. want of money. It is only since the Anglo-French Convention was signed that it has become possible to take seriously in hand the question of rendering the profession of teaching attractive by increasing the salaries of the teachers.

we comprise all those manifold mental and moral influences which tend towards preparing a boy or girl for a career of usefulness in after life, has any substantial progress been made?

It is obviously impossible to give more than a conjectural answer to this question. Nevertheless, although no positive proof can be adduced that such an opinion is correct, it may be stated with a fair amount of confidence that something has been done towards forming and elevating the characters of the Egyptians. The mere acquisition of the linguistic knowledge, which has enabled a certain number of young Egyptians to study the literature and sciences of Europe, must surely have tended in some degree to engender that accurate habit of thought which is the main characteristic of the Western as opposed to the Eastern mind; whilst it is difficult to believe that constant contact with a number of high-minded Europeans, the example afforded by the elevated standard of thought from which all social and administrative questions have for some years past been approached, the abolition of barbarous punishments, the suppression of forced labour and of torture, the introduction of the new ideas that the rights of property are sacred and that all men are equal in the eyes of the law, the practical abolition of slavery, the discouragement of nepotism, the stigma attached to the worst kinds of vice, and, generally, the fact that the Egyptian social and political atmosphere has for some years been heavily charged with ideas which should act as antidotes against moral degradation—have not in some degree contributed to a partial assimilation of the best European code of morals, in spite of the adverse influence exercised by the immoral or dishonest acts of individual Europeans. Whilst, however, it may reasonably be held that something has been done in the direction of imparting rectitude, virility, and moral equipoise to the Egyptian character, it must be admitted that there is still abundant room for improvement in all these directions. If the moral influences to which the Egyptians are now exposed were withdrawn, or even weakened, a relapse would inevitably ensue.

Let any one who is inclined to take a sanguine view of this subject cast, for a moment, all details aside, and consider the general nature of the problem which presents itself for solution. It is nothing less than this, that the new generation of Egyptians has to be persuaded or forced into imbibing the true spirit of Western civilisation. Although Europe was Christianised first and civilised afterwards, it may perhaps be argued with some degree of plausibility—more especially with the example of Japan before us—that the *post hoc ergo propter hoc* fallacy would be involved if it were held that Christianity is the necessary handmaid of European civilisation, and that it is impossible to assimilate the true spirit of that civilisation without adopting the Christian faith. I am insufficiently acquainted with the state of Japan to draw any precise inferences from its recent history. I confine myself, therefore, to arguments derived from facts and subjects which have come under my personal observation, merely observing that both the religion and the social system of Buddhism, and, I believe, of Shintoism, present greater possibilities for the assimilation of exotic secular ideas and forms of government than any which can be claimed for rigid Islamism. Looking then solely to the possibility of reforming those countries which have adopted the faith of Islam, it may be asked whether any one can conceive the existence of true European civilisation on the assumption that the position which women occupy in Europe is abstracted from the general plan? As well can a man blind from his birth be made to conceive the existence of colour. Change the position of women, and one of the main pillars, not only of European civilisation, but at all events of the moral code based on the Christian religion, if not of Christianity itself, falls to the ground. The position of women in Egypt, and in Mohammedan countries generally, is, therefore, a fatal obstacle to the attainment of that elevation of thought and character which should accompany the introduction of European civilisation, if that civilisation is to produce its full measure of beneficial effect.

The obvious remedy would appear to be to educate the women. The remarkable and continuous progress of female education in Egypt within the last few years marks, in fact, very clearly the changes of custom and alteration of ideas which are taking place in the country. When the first efforts to promote female education were made, they met with little sympathy from the population in general. When, many years ago, this matter was first taken in hand, Yacoub Pasha Artin was the only Egyptian who took the least interest in it. More than this, most of the upper-class Egyptians were not merely indifferent to female education; they were absolutely opposed to it. They did not want the women to be educated. Even when girls' schools were, with much difficulty, established, parents, in the first instance, sent their daughters to school reluctantly, and took them away early. In order to encourage the education of girls, it was necessary to admit a large number of free pupils. Most of these came from the poorer classes, and left early, either to be married or because it was thought unbecoming for a girl to attend school after she had passed the earliest years of childhood. All this has now been changed. The reluctance of parents to send their daughters to school has been largely overcome. Free education in the Government Primary Schools has been practically abolished. Demands are frequently made for the establishment of other schools in different parts of the country. The number of private schools for girls has also greatly increased of late years. Further, it is to be observed that the steady output of boys from the Secondary Schools and Higher Colleges has indirectly stimulated the movement in favour of female education. The younger generation are beginning to demand that their wives should possess some qualifications other than those which can be secured in the exclusion of the harem. The interaction of the two branches of education does not stop here, for not only has the growth of education among boys stimulated the desire for instruction to girls, but it has also tended to improve the quality of the education given to girls by prolonging the period of instruction. There appears good reason for supposing that, where education has made progress, the age of marriage has risen, and that, in consequence, the girls are allowed to remain longer than heretofore at school. The prospects of the future are, therefore, distinctly bright in connection with this all-important question.

It, of course, remains an open question whether, when the Egyptian women are educated, they will exercise a healthy and elevating influence over the men. The few Moslem women in Egypt who have, up to the present time, received a European education are, with some very rare exceptions, strictly secluded. It is difficult, therefore, to form any matured opinion as to the results so far obtained.

In Christian Europe, the religious faith of women is generally stronger than that of men. The woman feels and trusts, the man reasons.

The faith of Moslem women, on the other hand, is probably rather less strong than that of Moslem men. Neither need this be any matter for surprise. It is not merely due to the curious impulse which appears almost invariably to drive the East and the West in opposite directions. It is a consequence of the fundamental differences which separate Christianity from Islamism. Although it is an error to suppose that Mohammed's general plan did not involve a future life for women,[1] there can be no doubt that not only did he, by precept and example, relegate women to a position in this world inferior to that of men, but also that the religion which he founded is eminently one conceived by the genius of a man and intended for men. It is, therefore, natural that women should generally be less fervent Moslems than men.

But the Moslem woman is, after all, a woman first and a Moslem afterwards. She would belie her sex if she were not impulsive and inclined, even more than the men, to run to extremes. Although, therefore, the faith of the Moslem woman may perhaps be comparatively weak, her prejudices in respect to all the customs and habits of thought which cluster round Islamism are as strong as, if not stronger than those of the men. A Europeanised Egyptian man usually becomes an Agnostic, and often assimilates many of the least worthy portions of European civilisation. Is there any reason why European education should not produce the same effect on the Europeanised Egyptian woman? I know of none. Indeed, in so far as the Agnosticism is concerned, the woman, on the assumption that her faith is relatively lukewarm, would probably find less difficulty than the

[1] Surah III., verse 193, and Surah IV., verse 123, of the Koran are conclusive as to Mohammed's teaching on this subject. There can be no doubt that all devout Moslems believe that a future life is reserved for women.

man in shaking herself free from the ideas and associations which have surrounded her from her cradle.

It would obviously be neither safe nor just to draw any general conclusion in connection with this subject from such a limited number of facts and examples as can at present be adduced. If it be once admitted that no good moral results will accrue from female education in Egypt, then, indeed, the reformer may well despair of the cause of Egyptian education generally in the highest sense of the word. The experiment of female education should certainly be continued with vigour. Few people now living can hope to see its results. All that can at present be said is that those results must necessarily be uncertain. But whatever they may eventually be, this much is well-nigh certain—that the European reformer may instruct, he may explain, he may argue, he may devise the most ingenious methods for the moral and material development of the people, he may use his best endeavours to "cut blocks with a razor" and to graft true civilisation on a society which is but just emerging from barbarism, but unless he proves himself able, not only to educate, but to elevate the Egyptian woman, he will never succeed in affording to the Egyptian man, in any thorough degree, the only European education which is worthy of Europe.

What the Egyptian man most requires is the acquisition of all those qualities comprised in the expressive Greek term *αἰδώς*—poorly translated by the English word "self-respect"—and those qualities he can never fully acquire unless, like the Christian European, he becomes monogamous, and thus learns to honour the one woman whom he will also have sworn to love and to cherish until the hand of death parts him from his life-long helpmate.

CHAPTER LX

THE SOUDAN

The nature of the Soudan problem—Extent—Population—Results obtained by the Convention of 1899—Executive agency—Finance—Railways—Slavery.

HAVING dealt with the affairs of Egypt, I now propose to give a very brief sketch of the progress of administrative reform in the Soudan.[1]

The problems with which the Government has to deal in the Soudan are not only very different, but also, for the time being, far more simple than those which await solution in Egypt. This latter country has advanced half-way—perhaps many would think more than half-way—on the road towards Western civilisation. It has certainly passed beyond the stage in which the undivided attention of the reformer may be devoted to financial and administrative questions. It has entered on a phase where, unless I am much mistaken, it will year by year become more apparent to all but very superficial observers that the further adaptation and effective assimilation of Western ideas is quite as much a social as a political or administrative question. The really vital issues which the future has reserved for Egypt are not how exotic political institutions can be forced to take root in a soil which is uncongenial to their

[1] Most of the remarks contained in this chapter have already appeared in my Annual Reports from the year 1899 onwards.

growth, but how the relations of the sexes can be brought into conformity with modern ideas, how the moral code on which the laws of all civilised countries are based can be made to penetrate into the daily life and manners and customs of the people, and how, without shattering all that is worthy and noble in the Moslem religion, the quasi-religious institutions of the country can be reformed to such an extent as no longer to constitute an insuperable barrier to progress. The Government have sometimes been accused of moving too slowly in Egypt. Does any one who has reflected on the problems which I have briefly indicated above, and who really understands the facts connected with them, consider it possible that they can be solved with rapidity? If so, he must be imbued with an optimism which I am unable to share. Nevertheless, until they are solved, the aspirations of the irresponsible advocate of reforms must always be tinged with a certain degree of unreality, whilst some disappointment must inevitably await the well-intentioned efforts of the responsible man of action.

The case of the Soudan is, for the present, wholly different. Even the most advanced portions of that country are still in a very backward condition. For at least a generation to come, no complex question of how Western methods may best be adapted to Eastern minds will probably arise. Political issues are few in number and relatively simple in character. The most important, probably, is how slavery may be completely abolished without causing serious disorder. The rise and fall of some religious impostor may cause some temporary trouble, but the methods for dealing with cases of this sort command the assent alike of Westerns and of educated Orientals. Any danger from religious fanaticism may be mitigated, and perhaps altogether averted, by imposing some reasonable and salutary checks on the freedom of action of missionary bodies. Whatever may be the case in Egypt, there can be no question that what the Soudanese now most of all require is, not national government, but good government. Hence, Sir Reginald Wingate and his very capable staff will be able for the present to devote their entire attention to overcoming the physical difficulties with which they have to deal, and to the introduction of administrative, judicial, and financial measures suitable to the requirements of the primitive society whose interests are entrusted to their care.

The Anglo-Egyptian Soudan covers an area of 950,000 square miles. By far the greater portion of this large territory consists of what the late Lord Salisbury once termed "light sandy soil." The area under cultivation has been steadily increasing of late years. Nevertheless, at the close of 1906, only about 1576 square miles were cultivated. The remainder consisted of desert, swamp, and primæval forest.

The researches made by Sir Reginald Wingate into the past and present population of the Soudan, bring into strong relief the terrible results which ensued from Dervish misrule. It is estimated that, prior to the establishment of the Mahdi's power, the population of the Soudan was about 8½ millions, that of these about 3½ millions were swept away by famine[1] and by disease, notably by small-pox, and that 3¼ millions were killed either in the engagements with the British and Egyptian troops, or in inter-tribal wars. The latter of these two causes accounted for by far the greater portion of the terrible mortality in warfare. Several tribes opposed to the Baggara, who constituted the

[1] The Dervish soldiery used to rob the inhabitants of their grain reserves, with the result that large numbers died of starvation.

mainstay of the Dervish power, were well-nigh obliterated. These figures, Sir Reginald Wingate remarked, "seem almost incredible." Nevertheless, he considered them substantially correct. He cited a fact, which came under his personal observation, in support of their correctness. Prior to 1882, the district lying along the banks of the rivers Rahad and Dinder contained upwards of 800 villages. When Sir Reginald Wingate visited this district in 1902, "not a village remained." In an official report prepared on the Berber district towards the close of 1903, it was stated that "villages, which used to produce 500 fighting men, have now only fifty to sixty adults, and in some cases even less." My personal experience is of a nature to confirm this testimony. Shortly after the battle of Omdurman, I visited Metemmeh, a town formerly inhabited by the Jaalin, and situated on the Nile between Berber and Khartoum. It was clear from the buildings which remained that it had formerly contained a large population. At the time of my visit, the inhabitants numbered about 1300, of whom all but 150 were women and children. The men had almost all been killed by the Dervishes.

During the last few years, the population has been increasing, but it is probable that it does not now exceed two millions.

The Convention between the British and Egyptian Governments, signed on January 19, 1899, of which a general description has already been given,[1] may be termed the Constitutional Charter of the Soudan. In spite of many anomalies, which were inevitable under all the circumstances of the case, it has conferred an immense boon, both on the people of the Soudan, and on the Egyptians, who, whatever some of them may at

[1] *Vide ante*, Chapter XXXIII.

present think, are, and must always be deeply interested in the development and good government of that country. The Convention freed the Soudan from the incubus of the Capitulations, and it also obviated the very serious risks which would certainly have been incurred had the adoption of a highly civilised system of government been forced prematurely on the country. I do not suppose that the most ardent advocate, whether of internationalism or of equality of treatment to all creeds and races, would seriously contend that it would have been possible in practice to have worked a system under which Kwat Wad Awaibung, a Shillouk who murdered Ajak Wad Deng because the latter bewitched his son, and caused him to be eaten by a crocodile,[1] would have been tried by a procedure closely resembling that followed at Paris or Berlin, which would have necessitated a civil action brought by some chance European, resident on the upper waters of the Blue Nile, being tried by a body of Judges sitting at Cairo or Alexandria, and which would not have allowed the executive Government to close a liquor shop belonging to a Greek subject at El-Obeid or Mongalla without the presence of a Consular janissary.

I need not describe in detail the executive agency through which effect has been given to the

[1] A Shillouk named Kwat Wad Awaibung was tried on the charge of murdering Ajak Wad Deng. He pleaded guilty, and made the following statement: "The murdered Ajak Wad Deng owed me a sheep, but would not pay me. He said he would show me his work, and next day my son was eaten by a crocodile, which was, of course, the work of Ajak Wad Deng, and for that reason I killed him. We had had a feud for years, as I was a more successful hippopotamus-hunter than he was, and for that reason he was practising witchery over me and my family." Mr. Bonham Carter, the Legal Secretary of the Soudan Government, in reporting on this case, said: "The accused's belief that the crocodile was acting as agent of the murdered man in killing the accused's son was supported by several other witnesses, and represents a common local belief."

principles embodied in the Convention of 1899. I content myself with saying that the country was, in the first instance, divided into districts, each of which was placed under the control of a military officer. It would, however, be an entire mistake to suppose that the country is under a military government in the ordinary acceptation of that term. The Government, in all its more important features, is essentially civil, although the Governor-General and many of his principal subordinates are military officers. I have frequently rendered testimony to the very valuable services performed by these military officers. I need here only add that the system of education adopted at our Public Schools and Military Colleges is of a nature to turn out a number of young men who are admirable agents in the execution of an Imperial policy. The German, the Frenchman, and others may be, and sometimes are better educated, but any defects on the score of technical knowledge are amply compensated by the governing powers, the willingness to assume responsibility, and the versatility under strange circumstances in which the Anglo-Saxon, trained in the free atmosphere which develops individualism, excels beyond all other nations.

I know of only one disadvantage in employing military officers, and that is, that they are liable to be removed for service elsewhere, more especially in times of national emergency. A Civil service is, therefore, being formed, composed of young men taken from the British Universities. These will gradually take the place of the military officers now employed.

I do not propose to dwell on the progress made in education, the establishment of a judicial system, the preservation of forests, and other administrative matters. Full details on these subjects will be found in my Annual Reports.

I confine my remarks to one or two points of special importance.

Finance is, of course, the keystone of the situation. It was felt from the first that in the Soudan, as in Egypt, a sound financial position was the source from which all other reforms and improvements would have to flow. In the first instance, the situation certainly did not look promising. Those who had had most experience of the country had declared that the Soudan was, and was likely always to remain, a "useless possession." The ravages committed by the Dervishes deepened the sense of its inutility. The population had, as I have already shown, been more than decimated. Flocks and herds had been destroyed. Date-trees, which constitute one of the principal products of the country, had been hewn down in large numbers. Neither life nor property had, for many years, been secure. Under these discouraging auspices, the Soudan revenue for 1898 was estimated at the very modest figure of £E.8000. As a matter of fact, a revenue of £E.35,000 was collected. The expenditure was £E.235,000, thus leaving a deficit of £E.200,000, which had to be made good by the Egyptian Treasury. Eight years later, in 1906, the revenue was £E.804,000, and the net charge on the Egyptian Treasury, exclusive of interest on 3½ millions advanced for capital expenditure, amounted to only about £E.30,000. Inclusive of interest at the rate of 3 per cent on the capital advanced, the charge which had to be borne by the Egyptian Treasury, in 1906, was only £E.130,000.[1] The amount is trifling in comparison to the unquestionable advantages derived by Egypt from the maintenance of a settled government in the Soudan, and

[1] From January 1, 1908, the Soudan Government will commence to pay interest on a portion of the capital advanced.

from the assured possession of the Nile Valley. I should add that, at the close of the year 1906, a Reserve Fund, amounting to over £E.315,000, had accumulated in the hands of the Soudan Government.

Thus, a very great and rapid improvement has taken place. Moreover, it has been effected without increasing the burden of taxation. The fiscal legislation of the Soudan has been based on the unquestionably sound principle that, in the assessment and collection of the taxes, no innovation, based on Western ideas, should be introduced unless its introduction is altogether unavoidable. The main fault of Oriental fiscal administration has generally been, not so much that the principles on which the taxation is based are unsound, as that the method of applying them has been very defective. On going through the list of the taxes which were collected under the Khalifa's rule, it was found that, although the manner in which they had been levied had been cruel and extortionate to the last degree, they were based on principles which are generally recognised in all Moslem countries. No radical change of system was, therefore, necessary. Broadly speaking, all that was required was that the rates of taxation should in each case be fixed by law; that the taxes should be moderate in amount, and that every care should be taken that no demands were made on the taxpayers save those which the law allowed.

With every desire, however, to avoid the premature introduction of Western methods of administration into the Soudan, it was found practically impossible to devise any proper system for the recovery of taxes without having recourse to some of the principles on which European procedure in such matters is based. The Dervish system consisted in practice in taking as much as the taxpayers could pay. On the other hand, if the land yielded no crop, the tax collector recognised the futility of making any demands on the cultivator.[1] The experience of other Eastern countries has shown that the elasticity thus obtained goes a long way to mitigate the rigour even of the worst fiscal systems.

The European administrator, who has to look to financial equilibrium, naturally desires to introduce a system which will enable him to know, with tolerable accuracy, the amount of revenue on which he can count, not only for a single year, but for a series of years. It is comparatively easy for him to rectify the main defect of the Oriental system. He can substitute a fixed and moderate demand for one which was capricious and generally exorbitant. It is far less easy to obviate the rigidity which is, in some degree, an almost unavoidable accompaniment of the change of system. Notably, it is impossible to dispense altogether with the system of legal expropriation in cases of default, albeit this practice is wholly foreign to the ideas of a backward Oriental population. Something, however, may be done to temper the comparative rigidity of European modes of procedure. Thus, in Egypt, although for many years past expropriation has been legalised, the best part of the Oriental fiscal system has been preserved. It has never been the practice, after imposing a fixed rate on land, to exact the amount of the taxes in good and bad years alike. Liberal concessions have been made to the holders

[1] The execution of a system under which the tax is made proportionate to the crop of the year is, of course, in some degree facilitated by the practice, common in all Moslem countries, of taking payment in kind. It has been found necessary to continue this practice in some parts of the Soudan. But it is one which leads to numerous abuses, and it will be desirable to abolish it as soon as possible. It was abolished in Egypt some twenty years ago.

of Sharaki, or unirrigated land. In the Soudan, an attempt has been made to carry this principle somewhat further. It has been laid down that, when a summons is taken out against any man for non-payment of the land tax, the Magistrate, "if he is satisfied that the crop upon the land has failed through no fault of the owner or cultivator, and that the tax cannot be paid without depriving the owner of the means of earning his living as an agriculturist," may adjourn the summons, and report the case to the Governor-General. The latter can then, if he thinks fit, remit the tax.

The clothing of the owner and that of his wife and children, the tools of an artisan or the implements of a cultivator, as well as cattle ordinarily employed in agriculture, are exempted from seizure. Further, the process for the recovery of taxes, though it may perhaps be criticised on the ground of being somewhat too elaborate, is manifestly devised with the express object of obviating a resort to expropriation, save in cases of absolute necessity.

I make these remarks because the points here discussed are, in my opinion, of vital importance in the administration of all Eastern countries.

I explained in a former part of this narrative[1] that, at a moment when reckless borrowing had brought Egypt to the verge of ruin, resort was had to what at that time appeared the bold expedient of contracting a fresh loan. The causes which had led to the creation of a situation in the Soudan which, at one time, seemed almost desperate, were different from those which had operated in Egypt, but the remedy adopted was, in principle, the same. The country was practically isolated. It was cut off from the world by a waste of burning and almost waterless desert.

[1] *Vide ante*, pp. 462-64.

Manifestly, the first thing to do was to establish the link through whose agency civilisation could gradually be introduced into the country. Scarcely had the sound of the guns of the battle of Omdurman died away, when works were commenced with a view to extending the Nile railway, which then extended only to the Atbara, to Halfaya, opposite Khartoum. It was, however, obvious that some port on the Red Sea coast constituted the natural outlet for the trade of the Soudan. After a full examination of the various alternatives which were available, it was decided to create such a port at a spot, now named Port Soudan, a short distance north of Suakin, and to connect it by railway with the Nile Valley. By January 1906, the railway works were completed. The harbour works are still in course of progress. Thus, the connection between the Soudan and the rest of the world was established.

There is only one further point of special importance to which I need allude in connection with the administration of the Soudan. What has been done to remove the plague-spot of slavery?

The Soudan, of course, no longer constitutes the happy hunting-ground of the Arab slave-hunter. Nevertheless, in spite of every effort, the Slave Trade has not, as yet, been wholly suppressed. Slave raids are still, at times, made, more especially along the Abyssinian frontier. A recent report from Captain McMurdo, the head of the Department for the Suppression of Slavery, contains the following passage: "Speaking generally of the repression of slavery in the Soudan, I venture to state that progress is steadily being made, and that slavery has turned the corner into the high road of abolition, but it is a very long road, and it will take years to get to the end of it. It is not in nature that customs which have existed for centuries can be at once put aside. It is only by bringing to bear a steady pressure on slave-traffickers that abolition will be obtained."

Domestic slavery in the Soudan itself is gradually dying a natural death. On this subject Sir Reginald Wingate wrote some two years ago: "By carefully protecting the interests of those who were previously slaves, and at the same time gradually employing them on remunerative work in other capacities—should they be unwilling to return to their masters as ordinary servants—we shall eventually, with the concurrence and assistance of the inhabitants themselves, gradually transform the status of slavery, and substitute for it a system of paid labour, which will probably be acceptable to master and servant alike."

Thus, the Soudan has been launched on the path which leads to moral and material progress. With reasonable prudence in the management of its affairs, it should continue, year by year, to advance in prosperity.

CHAPTER LXI

CONCLUSION

Summary of this work—Changes since the time of Ismail—The British reformers—Their Egyptian allies—Stability of the reforms

A SHORT account has thus been given of the reforms which, during the last few years, have been carried out in all the more important branches of the Egyptian and Soudanese State administrations. The description given of those reforms is, indeed, defective. Several important subjects have not been even mentioned. No allusion has been made to the services of many officials who have done excellent work in their special spheres of action.[1] All that has been attempted is to give a general sketch of the progress of Egyptian reform. Even this imperfect sketch may, however, suffice to indicate the main features of the work which has been accomplished. It has been shown how the extravagance and maladministration of Ismail Pasha led to his own downfall, and to the imposition of a qualified European tutelage on the Egyptian Government; how, at the moment when that tutelage was beginning to produce some

[1] I take this opportunity ot testifying to the excellent services rendered by the first Secretaries in the Diplomatic Service who acted for me during my temporary absences from Egypt. These were Sir Gerald Portal, whose premature death was a great loss to his country, Sir Arthur Hardinge, Sir Rennell Rodd, and Mr. Findlay. I cannot speak too highly of the invaluable assistance I received from all of these gentlemen.

beneficial results, the country was thrown back into disorder by a military mutiny, the offspring of Ismail's reckless conduct, and by the growth of national aspirations in a form which rendered them incapable of realisation; and how England finally intervened and bade disorder and administrative chaos cease. The readers of this book have been conducted, subject by subject, through the complicated mazes of the Egyptian administrative system. The degree of progress which has been made in the direction of introducing Western civilisation into the country has been described in some detail.

No one can fully realise the extent of the change which has come over Egypt since the British occupation took place unless he is in some degree familiar with the system under which the country was governed in the days of Ismail Pasha. The contrast between now and then is, indeed, remarkable. A new spirit has been instilled into the population of Egypt. Even the peasant has learnt to scan his rights. Even the Pasha has learnt that others besides himself have rights which must be respected. The courbash may hang on the walls of the Moudirieh, but the Moudir no longer dares to employ it on the backs of the fellaheen. For all practical purposes, it may be said that the hateful corvée system has disappeared. Slavery has virtually ceased to exist. The halcyon days of the adventurer and the usurer are past. Fiscal burthens have been greatly relieved. Everywhere law reigns supreme. Justice is no longer bought and sold. Nature, instead of being spurned and neglected, has been wooed to bestow her gifts on mankind. She has responded to the appeal. The waters of the Nile are now utilised in an intelligent manner. Means of locomotion have been improved and extended. The soldier has acquired some pride in the uniform which he wears. He has fought as he never fought before. The sick man can be nursed in a well-managed hospital. The lunatic is no longer treated like a wild beast. The punishment awarded to the worst criminal is no longer barbarous. Lastly, the schoolmaster is abroad, with results which are as yet uncertain, but which cannot fail to be important.

All these things have been accomplished by the small body of Englishmen who, in various capacities, and with but little direct support or assistance from their Government or its representative, have of late years devoted their energies to the work of Egyptian regeneration. They have had many obstacles to encounter. Internationalism and Pashadom have stood in the path at every turn. But these forces, though they could retard, have failed to arrest the progress of the British reformer. The opposition which he has had to encounter, albeit very embarrassing, merely acted on his system as a healthy tonic. An eminent French literary critic[1] has said that the end of a book should recall its commencement to the mind of the reader. Acting on this principle, I may remind those who have perused these pages that I began this work by stating that, although possibly counterparts to all the abuses which existed, and which to some extent still exist in Egypt, may be found in other countries, the conditions under which the work of Egyptian reform has been undertaken were very peculiar.[2] The special difficulties which have resulted from those conditions have but served to bring out in strong relief one of the main characteristics of the Anglo-Saxon race. Other nations might have equally well conceived the reforms which were necessary. It required the singular political adaptability of Englishmen to execute them. A country and a nation have

1. Joubert.

2 *Vide ante*, vol. i. p. 5.

been partially regenerated, in spite of a perverse system of government which might well have seemed to render regeneration almost impossible.

Yet, when it is said that all these things were accomplished by the Englishmen who have served the Egyptian Government, one qualifying remark should in justice be made. It should never be forgotten that many Egyptians have themselves borne a very honourable and useful part in the work of Egyptian regeneration.

Is the skilled labour, the energy, the perseverance, and the patient toil of the English reformers and their Egyptian allies to be thrown away? Is Egypt again to relapse into a semi-barbarous condition? Will posterity declare that this noble effort to elevate a whole nation ended in ultimate failure?

I cannot say what will be the future of Egypt, but I hope and believe that these questions may be answered in the negative.

According to the Eastern adage, the grass never grows again where once the hoof of the Sultan's horse has trod. In the sorely tried country of which this history treats, the hoof of the Turkish horse, whether the rider were Sultan or Khedive, has, indeed, left a deep imprint. Nevertheless, I would fain hope it is not indelible. We are justified in substituting a sanguine in the place of a despondent metaphor. Where once the seeds of true Western civilisation have taken root so deeply as is now the case in Egypt, no retrograde forces, however malignant they may be, will in the end be able to check germination and ultimate growth. The seeds which Ismail Pasha and his predecessors planted produced little but rank weeds. The seeds which have now been planted are those of true civilisation. They will assuredly bring forth fruit in due season. Interested antagonism, ignorance, religious prejudice, and all the forces which cluster round an archaic and corrupt social system, may do their worst. They will not succeed. We have dealt a blow to the forces of reaction in Egypt from which they can never recover, and from which, if England does her duty towards herself, towards the Egyptian people, and towards the civilised world, they will never have a chance of recovering.

PART VII

THE FUTURE OF EGYPT

Nullum numen abest, si sit prudentia ; nos te,
Nos facimus, Fortuna, Deam coeloque locamus.

JUVENAL, *Sat.* x. 365.

The essential qualities of national greatness are moral, not material.

LECKY'S *History of England*, vol. i. p. 490.

CHAPTER LXII

THE FUTURE OF EGYPT

Quo Vadis?—The question of the occupation—Its duration—Egyptian autonomy—The Capitulations—Desirability of training the Egyptians—Importance of finance—Display of sympathy—Conclusion.

It is probable that few Englishmen ever ask themselves seriously the question of *Quo Vadis* in connection with either Indian or Egyptian affairs. Even fewer are tempted to hazard any confident answer to this crucial question.

The practical instincts of our race lead us to deal with whatever affairs we have in hand for the moment, and to discard any attempt to peer too curiously into the remote future. That instinct seems to me to be eminently wise. Whether, however, it be wise or unwise, it certainly exercises so powerful an influence over my mind as to preclude me from endeavouring to forecast what will be the ultimate solution of the Egyptian Question. That solution, moreover, depends, in no small degree, on a factor which is at present both unknown and uncertain, viz., the conduct of the Egyptians themselves. We cannot as yet predict with any degree of assurance the moral, intellectual, and political results likely to be obtained by the transformation which is at present taking place in the Egyptian national character.

Although, however, I will not venture to predict the goal which will eventually be reached, I have no hesitation in expressing an opinion as to that which we should seek to attain. So far as can at present be judged, only two alternative courses are possible. Egypt must eventually either become autonomous, or it must be incorporated into the British Empire. Personally, I am decidedly in favour of moving in the direction of the former of these alternatives.

As a mere academic question, I never have been, neither am I now in favour of the British occupation of Egypt. Looking at the matter from a purely British point of view, I believe that the opinion enunciated by Lord Palmerston in 1857[1] still holds good. More than this, however much I should regret to see the noble work of Egyptian reform checked, I am quite prepared to admit that, if it be in the interests of England to evacuate Egypt, we need not be deterred from doing so by the consideration that it is in the moral and material interests of the Egyptians, however little some few of them may recognise the fact, that we should continue our occupation of the country. It does not appear to me that we need stay in Egypt merely to carry out certain administrative reforms, however desirable they may be, unless those reforms are so essential that their non-execution would contribute to produce serious political or financial complications after the British garrison is withdrawn. All that we have to do is to leave behind us a fairly good, strong, and—above all things—stable Government, which will obviate anarchy and bankruptcy, and will thus prevent the Egyptian Question from again becoming a serious cause of trouble to Europe. We need not inquire too minutely into the acts of such a Government. In order to ensure its stability, it should possess a certain liberty of action, even although it may use that liberty in a

[1] *Vide ante*, vol. i. p. 83.

manner which would not always be in accordance with our views. But it is essential that, subsequent to the evacuation, the Government should, broadly speaking, act on principles which will be in conformity with the commonplace requirements of Western civilisation. The idea, which at one time found favour with a section of the British public, that Egypt may be left to "stew in its own juice," and that, however great may be the confusion and internal disorder which is created, no necessity for European interference will arise, may at once be set aside as wholly impracticable. It is absurd to suppose that Europe will look on as a passive spectator whilst a retrograde government, based on purely Mohammedan principles and obsolete Oriental ideas, is established in Egypt. The material interests at stake are too important, and the degree of civilisation to which Egypt has attained is too advanced, to admit of such a line of conduct being adopted. Public opinion would force the most sluggish Government into action. If England did not interfere, some other Power would do so. Of the many delusions which at one time existed about Egypt, the greatest of all is the idea that England can shake herself free of the Egyptian Question merely by withdrawing the British garrison, and then declaring to the world that the Egyptians must get on as well as they can by themselves. Lord Granville pursued a policy of this sort in dealing with the affairs of the Soudan, and we know with what result.

It has sometimes been argued that, even if misgovernment were again allowed to reign supreme in Egypt, British interests would be sufficiently secured if all danger of occupation by any other foreign Power were averted. I have already[1] alluded to this aspect of the question, but the point

[1] *Vide ante*, p. 383.

is one of so much importance that I need make no apology for reverting to it.

It cannot be too clearly understood that neutralisation, under whatsoever conditions, wholly fails to solve the Egyptian Question. The solution of that question would be little, if at all, advanced by merely obtaining guarantees against foreign interference in Egypt. The main difficulty would remain untouched. That difficulty is to decide who is to interfere, on the assumption that some foreign interference is indispensable. If it were thought desirable to prevent competition and rivalry amongst the different offices of the Metropolitan Fire Brigade, the object might readily be obtained by forbidding any one of them to aid in extinguishing a fire. The practical result would hardly be considered satisfactory. This, however, is the political system which would be involved in the neutralisation of Egypt. Each member of the European Fire Brigade would be under an obligation not to turn his hose on to an Egyptian conflagration, in order to avoid wounding the susceptibilities of his neighbours. In the meanwhile, the whole edifice of Egyptian civilisation might, and probably would be destroyed, to the infinite detriment not only of the indigenous inhabitants of Egypt, but also of the large number of Europeans who would be ruined if the country were allowed to relapse into anarchy and barbarism. The failure of international action to deal effectively with misgovernment in other parts of the Ottoman dominions serves as a warning in dealing with Egypt.

Is it, however, possible to ensure the existence of a fairly good and stable government in Egypt if the British garrison were withdrawn? That is the main question which has to be answered.

I make no pretension to the gift of political prophecy. I can only state my deliberate opinion, formed after many years of Egyptian experience and in the face of a decided predisposition to favour the policy of evacuation, that at present, and for a long time to come, the results of executing such a policy would be disastrous. Looking to the special intricacies of the Egyptian system of government, to the licence of the local press, to the ignorance and credulity of the mass of the Egyptian population, to the absence of Egyptian statesmen capable of controlling Egyptian society and of guiding the very complicated machine of government, to the diminution of the influence exercised by the British officials and by the diplomatic Representative of England in Egypt which would inevitably result from the evacuation, and to the proved impotence of international action in administrative matters —it appears to me impossible to blind oneself to the fact that, if the British garrison were now withdrawn, a complete upset would most probably ensue. It has to be borne in mind that the Egypt of to-day is very different from the Egypt of the pre-occupation days. A return to personal rule of the Oriental type—and it is in this direction that events would probably trend—would create a revolution. A transfer of power to the present race of Europeanised Egyptians would, to say the least, be an extremely hazardous experiment, so hazardous, indeed, that I am very decidedly of opinion that it would be wholly unjustifiable to attempt it.

It may be that at some future period the Egyptians may be rendered capable of governing themselves without the presence of a foreign army in their midst, and without foreign guidance in civil and military affairs; but that period is far distant. One or more generations must, in my opinion, pass away before the question can be even usefully discussed.

The fact, however, that the occupation must last for a period which cannot now be defined, need not stand in the way of a gradual movement in the direction of autonomy in the sense in which I understand that term as applied to the special case of Egypt. The mere withdrawal of the British garrison would not render Egypt autonomous; on the contrary, it would diminish the prospect of eventual autonomy. It is a contradiction in terms to describe a country as self governing when all its most important laws are passed, not by any of its inhabitants or by any institutions existing within its own confines, but by the Governments and legislative institutions of sixteen foreign Powers.[1] Such, however, will be the condition of Egypt until the existing régime of the Capitulations is altered. There are, so far as I know, only two methods for effecting a radical alteration of that régime. One is that Egypt should cease to form part of the Ottoman dominions and should be annexed by some foreign Power—a solution which I discard. The other is that means should be devised for establishing a local legislature competent to deal with all local matters. The only real Egyptian autonomy, therefore, which I am able to conceive as either practicable or capable of realisation without serious injury to all the various interests involved, is one which will enable all the dwellers in cosmopolitan Egypt, be they Moslem or Christian, European, Asiatic, or African, to be fused into one self-governing body. That it may take years—possibly generations—to

[1] It has also to be borne in mind that unanimity amongst all the foreign Powers is necessary before any law can come into force. Prior to 1867, the German Zollverein was constituted on a somewhat similar basis. Every state of the union had an absolute right of veto on any proposal submitted for its consideration. The system, Mr. Percy Ashley says (*Modern Tariff History*, p. 49), caused "innumerable difficulties and delays." It has, of course, long since ceased to exist.

achieve this object is more than probable, but unless it can be achieved, any idea of autonomy, in the true sense of the term, will, in my opinion, have to be abandoned. I stated in the last Report I wrote from Egypt that it is well for every individual and every nation to have an ideal. The ideal of the Moslem patriot is, in my opinion, incapable of realisation. The ideal which I substitute in its place is extremely difficult of attainment, but if the Egyptians of the rising generation will have the wisdom and foresight to work cordially and patiently, in co-operation with European sympathisers, to attain it, it may possibly in time be found capable of realisation.

In the meanwhile, no effort should be spared to render the native Egyptians capable of eventually taking their share in the government of a really autonomous community. Much has already been done in this direction, and it may be confidently anticipated, now that the finances of the country are established on a sound footing and the most pressing demands necessary to ensure material prosperity have been met, that intellectual, and perhaps moral progress will proceed more rapidly during the next quarter of a century than during that which has now terminated. Only, it should never be forgotten that the rapidity of the progress must be made contingent on the means available for ensuring it. "Sound finance," as has been most truly said, "is the foundation of the independence of States."[1] Nothing can compensate the Egyptians for a financial relapse.

Lastly, it should never be forgotten that, in default of community of race, religion, language, and habits of thought, which ordinarily constitute the main bonds of union between the rulers and the ruled, we must endeavour to forge such artificial

[1] Oliver's *Alexander Hamilton*, p. 304.

bonds between the Englishman and the Egyptian as the circumstances of the case render available.

One of the most important of these bonds must always be the exhibition of reasonable and disciplined sympathy for the Egyptians, not merely by the British Government, but by every individual Englishman engaged in the work of Egyptian administration. This sympathy is a quality, the possession or absence of which is displayed by Englishmen in very various degrees when they are brought in contact with Asiatic or African races. Some go to the extreme of almost brutal antipathy, whilst others display their ill-regulated sympathy in forms which are exaggerated and even mischievous. The Egyptians rightly resent the conduct of the one class, and ridicule that of the other. A middle course, based on accurate information and on a careful study of Egyptian facts and of the Egyptian character, will be found more productive of result than either extreme.

Another bond may, to some extent, be forged by appealing to the person or the pocket. A proper system of justice and of police can protect the former. Material interests can be served by various means, the most effective of which is to keep taxation low. Do not let us, however, imagine that, under any circumstances, we can ever create a feeling of loyalty in the breasts of the Egyptians akin to that felt by a self-governing people for indigenous rulers if, besides being indigenous, they are also beneficent. Neither by the display of sympathy, nor by good government, can we forge bonds which will be other than brittle. Sir Herbert Edwards, writing to Lord Lawrence a few years after the annexation of the Punjab, said: "We are not *liked* anywhere. . . . The people hailed us as deliverers from Sikh maladministration, and we were popular so long as we were plaistering wounds. But the patient is well now, and he finds the doctor a bore. There is no getting over the fact that we are not Mahommedans, that we neither eat, drink, nor intermarry with them."[1]

The present situation in Egypt is very similar to that which existed in the Punjab when Sir Herbert Edwards wrote these lines. The want of gratitude displayed by a nation to its alien benefactors is almost as old as history itself.[2] In whatever degree ingratitude may exist, it would be unjust to blame the Egyptians for following the dictates of human nature. In any case, whatever be the moral harvest we may reap, we must continue to do our duty, and our duty has been indicated to us by the Apostle St. Paul. We must not be "weary in well-doing."

I take leave of a country with which I have been so long associated with the expression of an earnest hope that, in the future, as in the recent past, Egypt will continue to be governed in the interests of the Egyptians, and I commend to my own countrymen the advice which was given to Rome by one of the later Latin poets:[3]

Quod regnas minus est quam quod regnare mereris.

[1] *Life of Lord Lawrence*, vol. ii. p. 20.

[2] Gregorovius (*Rome in the Middle Ages*, i. 323) says, speaking of the rule of Theodosius in Italy: "The unhappy King now learnt by experience that not even the wisest and most humane of princes, if he be an alien in race, in customs, and religion, can ever win the hearts of the people."

[3] Rutilius.

APPENDIX

KHEDIVES OF EGYPT

Name.	Born.	Died.	Reigned.
Mehemet Ali . .	1769	1849	1811–1848
Ibrahim . . .	1789	1848	1848 (June-Nov.)
Abbas I. . . .	1813	1854	1848–1854
Said	1822	1863	1854–1863
Ismail	1830	1895	1863–1879
Tewfik . . .	1852	1892	1879–1892
Abbas II. . . .	1874	...	1892–

BRITISH SECRETARIES OF STATE FOR FOREIGN AFFAIRS

Name.	From	To
Earl of Derby . .	February 21, 1874	April 2, 1878
Marquess of Salisbury .	April 2, 1878 .	April 28, 1880
Earl Granville . .	April 28, 1880 .	June 24, 1885
Marquess of Salisbury .	June 24, 1885 .	February 6, 1886
Earl of Rosebery . .	February 6, 1886 .	August 3, 1886
Earl of Iddesleigh .	August 3, 1886 .	January 14, 1887
Marquess of Salisbury .	January 14, 1887 .	August 18, 1892
Earl of Rosebery . .	August 18, 1892 .	March 11, 1894
Earl of Kimberley .	March 11, 1894 .	June 29, 1895
Marquess of Salisbury .	June 29, 1895 .	November 12, 1900
Marquess of Lansdowne	November 12, 1900	December 11, 1905
Sir Edward Grey . .	December 11, 1905	...

BRITISH AGENTS AND CONSULS-GENERAL IN EGYPT

Name.	From	To
Lord Vivian . .	May 10, 1876 .	March 20, 1879
Sir Frank Lascelles .	March 20, 1879 .	October 10, 1879
Sir Edward Malet .	October 10, 1879 .	September 11, 1883
Earl of Cromer . .	September 11, 1883	May 6, 1907
Sir Eldon Gorst .	May 6, 1907 . .	...

CHRONOLOGICAL TABLE OF EVENTS

1875

Adhesion of the British Government to the International Law Courts	July 31.

1876

Mr. Cave reports on the Finances of Egypt	March 23.
The Khedive suspends payment of his Treasury Bills	April 8.
Creation of the Commission of the Public Debt	May 2.
Issue of the Goschen-Joubert Decree	November 18.
Appointment of English and French Controllers (Mr. Romaine and Baron de Malaret)	December 25.

1877

An English Commissioner (Sir Evelyn Baring) appointed to the Commission of the Debt	March 2.
Signature of the Anti-Slavery Convention between the British and Egyptian Governments	August 4.

1878

The Khedive consents to a full inquiry into the financial position of Egypt	April 4.
Treaty of Berlin	August 3.
First Report of the Commission of Inquiry	August 19.
The principle of Ministerial responsibility is recognised. Nubar Pasha charged with the formation of a Ministry. Suspension of the Dual Control. Sir Rivers Wilson and M. de Blignières appointed Ministers of Finance and Public Works respectively	August 28.
Issue of the Domains Loan of £8,500,000	October 29.

1879

Nubar Pasha and Sir Rivers Wilson assaulted by a crowd of Egyptian officers	February 18.
Resignation of Nubar Pasha	February 19.
Prince Tewfik appointed Prime Minister . .	March 10.
Dismissal of the European Ministers. Chérif Pasha appointed Prime Minister . .	April 7.
Second Report of the Commission of Inquiry, and resignation of the Commissioners .	April 10.
The Sultan deposes the Khedive . . .	June 26.
Ismail Pasha leaves Egypt	June 30.
Chérif Pasha resigns office	August 18.
The Dual Control revived. M. de Blignières and Sir Evelyn Baring appointed Controllers	September 4.
Riaz Pasha forms a Ministry	September 22.

1880

Repeal of the Law of the Moukábala . .	January 6.
Appointment of a Commission of Liquidation .	April 2.
Sir Auckland Colvin appointed Controller in succession to Sir Evelyn Baring . .	June 23.
Promulgation of the Law of Liquidation . .	July 17.

1881

Mutiny of the Egyptian Army. The Minister of War is dismissed	February 1.
The Egyptian Army again mutinies. Fall of the Riaz Ministry. Chérif Pasha becomes Prime Minister	September 9.
The Sultan sends two Commissioners to Egypt	October 6.
At the instance of the French and British Governments, the Turkish Commissioners leave Egypt	October 19.
M. Gambetta assumes office	November 12.

1882

The British and French Governments address a Joint Note to the Khedive	January 8.
M. Gambetta resigns office. He is succeeded by M. de Freycinet	January 31.
Chérif Pasha is dismissed from office. Mahmoud Pasha Sami appointed Prime Minister, with Arábi as Minister of War	February 5.

M. de Blignières resigns his appointment of Controller-General	March.
The Arábist Ministers resign, but are reinstated in office	May 23.
The British and French Consuls-General demand that Arábi should leave the country. The Arábist Ministry again resigns	May 27.
The Arábist Ministry is again reinstated	May 28.
The Sultan sends Dervish Pasha as Special Commissioner to Egypt	June 4.
A serious riot, attended with loss of life, occurs at Alexandria	June 11.
Ragheb Pasha is named Prime Minister, with Arábi as Minister of War	June 17.
A Conference, in which Turkey refuses to take part, meets at Constantinople	June 23.
Bombardment of Alexandria. The Arábists set fire to the town	July 11.
On the motion of M. Clemenceau, the French Chamber passes a vote adverse to the Ministry. M. de Freycinet resigns. M. Duclerc forms a Ministry	August 1.
Battle of Tel-el-Kebir	September 13.
Cairo occupied by British troops. Arábi is arrested	September 15.
The Egyptian Army is disbanded	September 19.
Lord Dufferin instructed to go to Egypt	October 29.
Arábi condemned to exile	December 3.
It is decided not to re-establish the Dual Control	December.
Death of M. Gambetta	December 31.

1883

Issue of a Circular prohibiting the use of the courbash	January 16.
Capitulation of El-Obeid	January 19.
Sir Auckland Colvin appointed Financial Adviser	February 4.
Promulgation of the Organic Law	May 1.
General Hicks's army leaves Duem	September 8.
Massacre of Egyptian reinforcements sent from Suakin to Sinkat	October 16.
Sir Evelyn Baring appointed Agent and Consul-General	September 11.
The British Government agree to the reduction of the garrison and the concentration of British troops at Alexandria	November 1.
Sir Edgar Vincent appointed Financial Adviser	November 4.

Total defeat of the Egyptian troops sent to the relief of Tokar. Death of Captain Moncrieff, R.N.	November 4.
News of the annihilation of General Hicks's army arrives at Cairo	November 18.
Sir Evelyn Baring recommends the abandonment of the Soudan	November 19.
The British Government agree to the policy of abandoning the Soudan	November 20.
The reduction of the British garrison in Egypt countermanded	November 25.
Defeat of the Egyptians at Tamanieb . . .	December 2.
Fall of Dara. Slatin Bey is taken prisoner. The Province of Darfour falls into the power of the Mahdi	December 23.

1884

Chérif Pasha resigns office. Nubar Pasha forms a Ministry	January 8.
General Gordon and Colonel Stewart leave Cairo for Khartoum	January 26.
Defeat of General Baker's force at El Teb .	February 4.
Annihilation of the Sinkat garrison . . .	February 8.
General Gordon arrives at Berber . .	February 11
General Gordon arrives at Khartoum . .	February 18.
Sir Gerald Graham defeats the Dervishes at El Teb	February 29.
The British Government finally refuse to employ Zobeir Pasha in the Soudan	March 5.
Sir Gerald Graham defeats the Dervishes at Tamai	March 13.
The British Government refuse to send troops from Suakin to Berber	March 25.
Fall of the Bahr-el-Ghazal Province . . .	April 9.
All communication with Khartoum is cut off .	April 19.
Fall of Berber	May 19.
First Meeting of the London Conference on Egyptian Finance	June 28.
Last Meeting of the London Conference .	August 2.
The British Government obtain a vote of credit in the House of Commons on account of the Soudan Expedition	August 8.
Zeyla occupied by British troops	August 24.
Lord Wolseley appointed to the command of the Soudan Expedition	August 26.
Murder of Colonel Stewart and Mr. Power .	September 18.

Berbera occupied by British troops	September 24.
Lord Northbrook reports on the Egyptian situation	November 20.

1885

Battle of Abu Klea	January 17.
Sir Herbert Stewart is mortally wounded. The Desert Column arrives at Gubat . .	January 19.
Sir Charles Wilson leaves Gubat for Khartoum .	January 24.
Fall of Khartoum and death of General Gordon	January 26.
The Italians occupy Massowah	February 5.
Action of Kirbekan. Death of General Earle .	February 10.
An Egyptian loan of £9,000,000 is guaranteed by the Powers	March 18.
Action at Hashin (Eastern Soudan)	March 20.
Action of Tofrik (Eastern Soudan)	March 22.
Sir Francis Grenfell appointed to command the Egyptian Army	April 19.
Evacuation of Harrar	April 26.
The British troops retire from Dongola . .	June 13.
Death of the Mahdi	June 22.
Capitulation of Sennar	August 19.
Capitulation of Kassala	September 30.
Convention signed at Constantinople under which Sir Henry Wolff and Moukhtar Pasha proceed as Joint-Commissioners to Egypt .	October 24.
Battle of Ginniss	December 30.

1886

The last of the British troops leave Suakin .	January 26.
Europeans resident in Egypt are rendered liable to the payment of the House Tax . .	April 15.

1887

Signature of the Wolff Convention	May 28.
The Sultan having refused to ratify the Wolff Convention, Sir Henry Wolff leaves Constantinople	July 15.
Sir Gerald Portal's mission to Abyssinia . .	October 12.

1888

Issue of a Decree partially abolishing the corvée	April 2.
The Suez Canal Convention is signed, but not made operative	April 29.

Fall of Nubar Pasha. Riaz Pasha forms a Ministry	June 9.
Decree issued constituting a Reserve Fund of £2,000,000	July 12.
Action of Gemaizeh. The Dervishes are driven from the neighbourhood of Suakin . .	December 20.

1889

The power of making by-laws applicable to Europeans is conferred on the Egyptian Government	January 31.
Stanley and Emin Pasha meet at Kavalli . .	February 17.
Sir Evelyn Baring reports that the "Race against Bankruptcy" is practically won .	February 18.
Battle between the Abyssinians and the Dervishes. Death of King John . . .	March 9.
Abolition of the Commissions of Brigandage .	July.
Colonel Wodehouse defeats the Dervishes at Arguin	July 2.
Sir Francis Grenfell defeats the Dervishes at Toski. Death of Wad-el-Nejumi . .	August 3.
Sir Elwin Palmer is appointed Financial Adviser in succession to Sir Edgar Vincent . .	October 23.

1890

The repairs to the Barrage are completed .	June.
Issue of a Decree converting the Preference Stock	June 7.
Issue of a Decree converting the Daira Stock .	July 5.

1891

Appointment of Sir John Scott to be Judicial Adviser	February 15.
The Dervishes are defeated, and the Province of Tokar is reoccupied	February 19.
Fall of Riaz Pasha. Mustapha Pasha Fehmi forms a Ministry	May 14.

1892

Death of the Khedive Tewfik	January 7.
Total abolition of the corvée for dredging purposes. Reduction of the Salt Tax. Abolition of the Professional Tax . . .	January 28.

Sir Herbert Kitchener succeeds Sir Francis Grenfell in command of the Egyptian Army	April 9.

1893

Dismissal of Mustapha Pasha Fehmi . .	January 15.
Riaz Pasha forms a Ministry	January 18.
The Dervishes are defeated by the Italians at Agordat	December 4.

1894

Resignation of Riaz Pasha. Nubar Pasha forms a Ministry	April 14.
Kassala captured by the Italians . . .	July 17.
Appointment of Sir Eldon Gorst to be Adviser to the Department of the Interior . .	November 2.

1895

Nubar Pasha resigns. Mustapha Pasha Fehmi is appointed Prime Minister . . .	November 11.

1896

Defeat of the Italian Army at Adua . . .	March 1.
The British Government decide to recapture Dongola	March 12.
The Caisse de la Dette advances £500,000 to the Egyptian Government . . .	March 26.
Battle of Firket	June 7.
Dongola occupied	September 23.
The Court of Appeal order the Egyptian Government to refund the money advanced by the Caisse de la Dette	December 2.
The money is repaid	December 6.

1897

Capture of Rejaf by the Belgians . . .	February 7.
British mission despatched to Abyssinia . .	March 10.
Abu Hamed captured	August 7.
Berber occupied	August 31.
Suakin-Berber road opened	October 18.
Railway from Wadi Halfa to Abu Hamed completed	October 31.
Kassala reoccupied by Egyptian troops . .	December 26.

1898

National Bank created with authority to issue promissory notes	June 25.
Signature of the contract for the construction of the Nile Reservoirs	February 20.
Battle of the Atbara	April 8.
Signature of the contract for selling the Daira property	June 21.
The French arrive at Fashoda	July 10.
Battle of Omdurman	September 2.
Sir Malcolm McIlwraith appointed Judicial Adviser	October 20.
Sir Eldon Gorst appointed Financial Adviser, and Mr. Machell appointed Adviser to the Interior	October 20.
The French evacuate Fashoda	December 11.

1899

Lord Cromer's speech at Omdurman . . .	January 4.
Death of Nubar Pasha	January 14.
Signature of the Soudan Convention . . .	January 19.
Destruction of the Khalifa's army. Death of the Khalifa and his leading Emirs. The Soudan declared open to trade	November 24.
Lord Kitchener leaves Egypt. Sir Reginald Wingate assumes command of the Egyptian army	December 21.
Soudan railway opened to Halfaya	December 30.

1900

Post-Office Savings Banks established . .	January 1.
Navigation dues on the Nile abolished . .	November 29.

1902

Creation of an Agricultural Bank	June 1.
Commercial Convention signed with France .	November 26.
Inauguration of the Nile Reservoirs	December 10.

1903

Octroi duties abolished	January 1.

1904

Sir William Garstin's report on the Nile . .	March 12.
Signature of the Anglo-French Agreement .	April 8.
Sir Vincent Corbett appointed Financial Adviser	April 12.
Issue of a Decree giving effect to the Anglo-French Agreement	November 28.

1905

Daira debt paid off	October 15.

1906

The Salt Monopoly abolished	January 1.
The Nile-Red Sea Railway opened . . .	January 27.
Mr. Dunlop named Adviser to the Department of Public Instruction	March 24.
Sir Nicholas O'Conor addresses a note to the Porte which terminates the "Sinai Peninsula" incident	May 15.
Liquidation of the affairs of the Daira . .	October.
Appointment of Saad Pasha Zagloul to be Minister of Education	October 29.

1907

Lord Cromer leaves Egypt. He is succeeded by Sir Eldon Gorst	May 6.
Mr. Harvey appointed Financial Adviser . .	October 9.

INDEX

THE END

Printed by R. & R. CLARK, LIMITED *Edinburgh.*

For Product Safety Concerns and Information please contact our EU
representative GPSR@taylorandfrancis.com
Taylor & Francis Verlag GmbH, Kaufingerstraße 24, 80331 München, Germany

www.ingramcontent.com/pod-product-compliance
Lightning Source LLC
Chambersburg PA
CBHW071711300426
44115CB00010B/1385

* 9 7 8 1 1 3 8 0 0 7 3 6 9 *